CONTINENTAL SHIFT

Also by Kevin Bloom from Portobello Books

Ways of Staying

CONTINENTAL SHIFT

A Journey into Africa's Changing Fortunes

KEVIN BLOOM & RICHARD POPLAK

Portobello
BOOKS

Published in Great Britain by Portobello Books in 2016

Portobello Books
12 Addison Avenue
London
W11 4QR

First published in South Africa in 2016 by Jonathan Ball Publishers (Pty) Ltd

A CIP catalogue record for this book is available from the British Library.

1 3 5 7 9 10 8 6 4 2

ISBN 978 1 84627 374 2 (trade paperback)
ISBN 978 1 84627 496 1 (ebook)

Design and typesetting by Triple M Design, Johannesburg
Typeset in 11/15pt Rotis Serif Std

Offset by Avon DataSet Ltd, Bidford on Avon, B50 4JH

Printed and bound by CPI Group (UK) Ltd, Croydon, CR0 4YY

www.portobellobooks.com

For Manny

AUTHORS' NOTE

Sixteen African countries were visited during the book's reporting phase: Angola, Botswana, Cameroon, the Central African Republic, the Democratic Republic of the Congo, Ethiopia, Kenya, Mozambique, Namibia, Nigeria, South Africa, South Sudan, Tanzania, Uganda, Zambia and Zimbabwe. Supplementary trips were made to the People's Republic of China and to India. Over 600 interviews were conducted – no names have been changed, and there are no character constructions.

To limit confusion on matters of currency exchange, all monetary values are displayed in US dollars (unless otherwise noted). Naming conventions reference as far as possible local norms.

CONTENTS

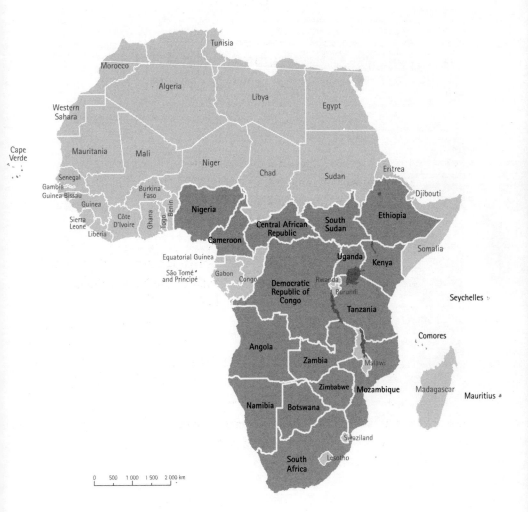

Juba, South Sudan, November 2012

We think: there is no peace for those caught in the process of becoming.
– Njabulo Ndebele, *Fine Lines from the Box*

I was born into a landscape that became unfamiliar as I grew to know it.
– Guy Tillim, notes from *Avenue Patrice Lumumba* exhibition

The future is already here – it's just not evenly distributed.
– William Gibson, interview in *The Economist*

CENTRAL AFRICAN REPUBLIC

SOUTH SUDAN

CAMEROON

CONGO

GABON

Congo River

Lake Albert

Goma

Lake Kivu
Bukavu

RWANDA

UGANDA

BURUNDI

DEMOCRATIC REPUBLIC
OF THE CONGO

*Lake
Tanganyika*

TANZANIA

KINSHASA

Cabinda

LUANDA

*ATLANTIC
OCEAN*

ANGOLA

ZAMBIA

Kalay

Kavango River

NAMIBIA

BOTSWANA

ZIMBABWE

0   150   300Lm

ONE

OUTSIDE, IN

'Crossroads possess a certain dangerous potency. Anyone born there must wrestle with their multiheaded spirits and return to his or her people with the boon of prophetic vision, or accept, as I have, life's interminable mysteries.'

— Chinua Achebe, *There Was a Country: A Personal History of Biafra*

A story from the road.

Or, for now, from *a* road: a 150-kilometre ribbon of grit that wound its way along the banks of an exploding lake. The byway, we'd been told by the man partly responsible for building it, would change the fortunes of his country. It would connect Bukavu and Goma, the principal cities in the eastern Democratic Republic of the Congo, Africa's second largest state. It was a road that traversed a region still thought to be amongst the most turbulent on earth, which, in the context of this story, is a detail both unimportant and supremely important. It's that sort of story, and that sort of road.

The road, as it turned out, was a riddle. It existed, we could see it – it was the rich amber shade of autumn in Johannesburg. But it could not be travelled, at least not by us. Our Virgil on this impossible quest was the security advisor to the governor of South Kivu, who had been pressed into service by the renowned Kimbembe Mazunga, whom we had met in State House in Kinshasa the week before. The people of South Kivu, of which Bukavu is the capital, get a distant look in the eye when hearing of Kinshasa, a place so far away it might inhabit

1

the realm of myth. Yet Mazunga, whose function as the president's consigliere made him a credible source, had sworn that the 3 000 kilometres separating State House from the eastern border were a mere technicality. The road was proof that the Congo was knitting together; that it was maturing, reformulating, *becoming.*

'You will go there and drive it,' he'd said, 'and you will see for yourself.'

Dutifully, we had boarded a plane. We'd come in for landing above the boundless tented city of MONUSCO, the United Nations mission in the DR Congo, a 17 000-strong force tasked with keeping Kabila's army and the various rebel groups from perpetuating the sorts of atrocities for which the region had become a stereotype.

En route from the airport into Bukavu, our driver had pointed to the road. It was flat and fresh and promising. We had wanted nothing more than to ride on it into Goma, and thus bear personal testimony to Mazunga's remarkable claims. That sighting from the taxi was as close as we would come.

Back at State House, Mazunga had said that the road was secure, that we'd be able to negotiate it in a hatchback. The security advisor to the governor of South Kivu believed otherwise. He recommended a sturdy four-by-four, and insisted that we hire several armed guards to ensure our safety. A trip that was supposed to cost us $80 each for car and driver was now budgeted at $800 each, given that we would have to rent a small militia in Bukavu and garrison it in Goma. This was weeks into our DRC leg, our dollars were dwindling, and the local Western Union was more often than not shut. The road we had travelled so far to travel was, in a word, un-travellable.

It was March 2012, just past the midpoint of our on-the-ground research. In the DRC, our tenth country since setting out, we had stumbled into a situation that seemed to perfectly embody our themes. In almost every sense that counted, our story had become one of paradoxes, of binaries, of confounding dualities. If Africa was indeed deserving of its enhanced reputation, why were we finding it so difficult to get simple things done? If Africa was *not* deserving of its enhanced reputation, why did so much of our reporting appear to support the fact that momentous things – transformative things – were getting done across the continent every day?

The paradox wasn't only in our notebooks. At the time of our catch-22 in Bukavu, sub-Saharan Africa could claim six of the world's 10 fastest-growing economies and almost four out of 10 of its refugees.[1] It could claim income per capita that had risen by nearly two-thirds since 1998, with one in every four people malnourished.[2] It could say that it offered some of the best returns on foreign direct investment while close on half its people lived on less than $1.25 a day.[3] And then there were the big numbers, the numbers that mattered *beyond* Africa's vast reaches: the continent had 60 per cent of the world's unused arable land[4] and its fastest rates of desertification;[5] its most celebrated wildlife and some of its fastest rates of extinction;[6] and its fastest-growing population compounding each of these problems at once.

Current forecasts put that population at two billion by 2050; by the end of the century, more than half as many people as were alive in 2012 would live in Africa.[7] And yet in many of its regions, the continent was empty. Neighbours Namibia and Botswana encompassed a landmass the size of France, Germany and Italy combined, but were home to barely four million.

The binaries extended further and deeper: into governance, education, technology. While men like Robert Mugabe in Zimbabwe and Teodoro Obiang Nguema in Equatorial Guinea were clinging jealously to power after decades of misrule, one in three of the 120 executive elections held in Africa since 2000 had brought a transfer of leadership.[8] While Nigerian writers had announced a new golden age with the likes of Teju Cole, Sefi Atta, Chimamanda Ngozi Adichie and Helon Habila, 11 million of that country's children would never see the inside of a schoolhouse. And while 68 per cent of the continent's Twitter subscribers used the service as their primary source of news, only a quarter of the population of sub-Saharan Africa had any access to electricity.[9]

As we languished in Bukavu, willing but unable to drive to the Promised Land in Goma, we were overcome by a familiar sensation.

Africa was at a crossroads, and the world – more than at any point in history – was depending on her sense of direction.

◆

When we first set out on the road in December 2006, we were, like most of the world, fast asleep on Africa.

It was the age of the Global War on Terror, and a time of unmatched prosperity in the West. Money and fundamentalism were the memes, and while it would be a vast oversimplification to say that the United States and Europe were blind to African affairs, it was no secret that the continent was near the bottom of their list of priorities. As South African journalists, the stories that we submitted to international newspapers encompassed the panoply of Western editorial obsessions: Aids, aid programmes, conflict, corruption, conservation. There were, of course, exceptions, but even in our Johannesburg home base the focus was narrow. Our local media was fixated on the looming succession battle within the ruling African National Congress, and thus on the parochial squabbles that defined daily life. Our careers were a feedback loop, and the press we consumed was the press that we wrote.

So, if we were to pick one moment when our curiosity as African journalists was piqued – when the loop frayed and allowed for another narrative to take shape – it would be an early summer morning exactly a week before Christmas 2006, when we pushed off from the banks of the Kavango River, one of the chance divisions between Namibia and Angola. On joint assignment for a pair of publications that needed travel stories, we encountered an anomaly that would first reveal itself as a trope and eventually as a cliché: change so whiplash rapid it snapped our heads back.

It was no small coincidence that this moment should have occurred on an African border, for in time African borders – their historical arbitrariness, their increasing irrelevance – would serve as one of our primary lodestars. As we set out in a cast-iron riverboat, we saw Angolans crossing from the far side in wooden dugouts called *vatos*. These vessels plied a single trade route, crossing back and forth from

4

the Angolan town of Kalay to the Namibian town of Rundu, where we had installed ourselves in a fetid bungalow. As we tracked their passage, the *vatos* simultaneously erased and reified the border; by paying off the somnambulant customs officers, their skippers made what wasn't there manifest and made unmanifest what was there.

Kavango River, Angola, December 2006

It was also no coincidence that the epiphany should have struck in Angola, which, when we were growing up in the 1980s, was the Cold War battleground that dominated our television sets. This was South Africa's Vietnam, where our crack troops fought alongside American-backed rebels to defeat the Soviet-funded People's Movement for the Liberation of Angola (MPLA), the much-reviled communists who would later come to run their country as jacked-up capitalists. In our pre-teen years, in primary school speeches and sleep-away camps, we were told that the Angolan front was our destiny. The Cold War ended in 1990, conscription fell away with the demise of apartheid, but Angola's civil conflict would drag on until 2002. Our presumptions, through all of this, had remained the same: the country was a war zone, a rite of passage, a graveyard.

Our guide on that first voyage was a young Angolan who had fought

5

on the side of the MPLA. His name was Francesco, and he wore an early-Castro beard and an advertising executive's smile. He told us that his ferry business had so far proved an effective dodge of Kalay's endemic unemployment, and that the rare South African holidaymakers who made it this far north, for whom Angola still represented an extreme adventure, were his main clientele. Then, proving his mettle as a moonlighting tour guide, he apologised for the weather.

'The villagers will stay inside today,' he said as we disembarked. 'They say the rain brings malaria.'

Instead of citizens, what we saw when we entered the town was concrete and mudbrick scar tissue undergoing a complex process of healing. Bombed out, bullet riddled, machete hacked – the ruins were being swallowed by new structures, filaments of skinny rebar swaying in the tropical shower. In 2002, said Francesco, the year the Angolan civil war had tapered out, there was nothing in Kalay – no school, no running water, no work. Four years later, we were told, the town's population had exploded from 7 000 to 35 000, and while jobs were still scarce, 'there is all this life, man!' At the Centro Commercial do Kalay, the first shop opened when the AKs were laid down, the shelves were stocked with cooking oil, pilchards, bread, washing powder, methylated spirits, toothpaste; on a wooden rack, three cotton dresses. None of it a big deal for two Johannesburg boys accustomed to the finest malls in the world, but the presence of these scant items made Francesco glow. This, finally, was progress, the arrival of a state-of-being that linked his town with the outside world, for which washing powder was not a luxury but an afterthought.

And to welcome the outside world, when finally it arrived expecting amenities in abundance, was the Kalay Hotel. Francesco marched us into a reception area with freshly whitewashed walls, a spotless stone floor, and lime green finishes on the doors and window frames. The hotel had yet to install an operational kitchen, but there were a dozen tables in the dining room, waiting for the day when plates would be set on checked tablecloths. Appending the dining room was a pinewood bar, six stools on terracotta tiles.

'No beer yet,' said Francesco, 'maybe they will serve it soon.'

Breathing in concrete and dust, smelling fresh paint, we felt the grip of a mantic revelation: the Kalay Hotel was a metaphor for the city, the city a metaphor for the region, the region a metaphor for the country, the country a metaphor for all of Africa south of the Sahara. In 2002, we knew, Angola had registered a GDP of $11.4 billion; towards the end of 2005, that had risen almost fourfold, to $42 billion.[10] There was no real mystery as to what drove this – Angola was an oil economy. But was Kalay the result of simple trickle-down economics, we wanted to know, or some other, more significant phenomenon?

Throughout sub-Saharan Africa, countries were growing at rates that had not been seen since the heady days of liberation.[11] While there was certainly evidence of *growth* all around us, was this *development* in the proper sense of the term? Would the rebar one day hold up roofs, would roofs be linked by lengths of electrical wire, would houses be connected by roads, would roads eventually connect to highways? Would something other than a few branded products come to join Kalay with Luanda, or with Johannesburg, or with other African centres of economic and political power? Would the emaciated kids in second-hand football T-shirts, kicking a ball between heaps of rubbish and pig shit, magically blossom into college graduates? Kalay's boom felt at once miraculous and unsustainable, corporeal and spectral – a theatre set constructed long before the play had been written.

Nonetheless, *four years*: the speed of the town's rebound was incredible. As South Africans, we were used to the vertiginous seesaw between the first and third worlds, between the twenty-first century and the Stone Age that defined life in developing nations. Kalay, though, was a different order of magnitude entirely. From a base of zero, suddenly the town was a contender. Yet its trajectory appeared to us decoupled from history, unattached to any continuum we could identify. The town was the first among many signs we would encounter of Africa's ... *what*? We were at a loss for the perfect descriptive noun, or was it a verb? Later, over tea-warm beers on the south bank of the Kavango, we would make a decision to devote a chunk of our lives to go out in search of the word. We were young and bullish, and hoped even for an adverb or two.

7

'Friends!' beamed Francesco, as the tour was nearing an end. 'Come to see this!'

He was pointing at several dirt tracks heading out into the bush, which he swore would sweep us to Lubango, a city 1 000 or so kilometres to the northwest. It proved an early lesson.

Just because there was a road did not mean it could be travelled.

◆

This, then, is a book of many voyages, distilled into ten essays.

It took us a long time to warm up to writing them. First, we both wrote books about our experiences as South Africans during different moments in our homeland's tumultuous history. Then, when we began travelling north, we considered a book about Africa's white communities – how they had morphed, faded, fled, and resurfaced elsewhere on the continent. And although we hoped to draw links between these communities and the retreat of the West – our working title was *Whiteout* – the focus, we came to realise, was too inward, too narrow.

As our research progressed, we were inevitably drawn into the orbit of the Chinese engagement with Africa. The papers and academic studies accumulated, and it seemed to us that China-in-Africa was the defining phenomenon of the time, with the Asian giant's thirst for raw materials acting as the catalyst for sub-Saharan Africa's ecstatic GDP graphs. The inaugural Forum on China-Africa Cooperation, or FOCAC, held in Beijing in 2000, presaged one of the more fundamental shifts in the global status quo since the Cold War. Four African leaders arrived in the Chinese capital to an effusive welcome, the first step in the evolution of a 'south-south kinship'; when the third FOCAC was again held in Beijing, only two months before our arrival in Angola in December 2006, on this occasion 44 African heads of state showed up – the pomp was such that the forum was used as a dry run for the 2008 Olympic Games. And yet, while there is a lot of China in this book, it too turned out to be the wrong lens for the job.

In the latter stages of our fumbling towards a focal point, we had grand literary designs – a travelogue-cum-mystical text that would render the picture in metaphor and allegory. But sure enough, as soon as we started to harvest the symbols, our problem became the opposite: the lens was now taking in too much; we couldn't tell the structure from the form. And so we refocused again, which is to say we read more, wrote more, travelled more, *listened* more. Our aim in the final analysis was to choose a limited set of snapshots and carefully develop them, nothing more and nothing less.

Each of the ten essays in this book, apart perhaps from this introductory chapter, proposes an answer to the question of Africa's *what?* Each deals largely with a single country and a single theme. In a series of interstitials, running between them, is a procedural – a murder mystery – that complicates the question of victim and perpetrator in a universe defined by change. Although we have travelled and worked widely across Africa since 2006, ultimately visiting a third of her countries, the bulk of the text represents investigations that took place between the years 2011 and 2015, and concentrates on around half of the countries we have come to know.

The so-called emergence of the new middle class; the interrogation of an accepted African 'success story'; the interrogation of an accepted African 'failed state'; the commercial explosion of the continent's cultural product; the supremely controversial and yet supremely important matter of Africa's mines; the supremely controversial and yet supremely important matter of Africa's farms; the use of the lessons of history to create a state from scratch; the perpetual battle not to have history imposed on Africa from the outside.

The countries included in this text do not represent a hierarchy, but rather happenstance levelled by a measure of journalistic science: if we felt we could cover a story without undue interference, we packed our bags and travelled forth. Exclusion does not mean irrelevance; inclusion does not necessarily represent importance – and while the 54 countries of Africa find themselves at radically different points in their historical and political arcs, and while a country like Angola may have more in common developmentally with Venezuela than it does with neighbouring DRC, there are deep links between the countries south of the Sahara, links we have endeavoured to explore.

◆

Regarding the Bukavu–Goma road, we had reached an impasse even before setting out. We were without options, it seemed, until the security advisor let slip an infinitely better option: why not travel *across* Lake Kivu? Hailing from landlocked Johannesburg, it hadn't occurred to us to enquire about a boat. But boats there were in abundance, waiting in the harbour to slice their way through the water. Such a trip, the security advisor told us, would cost $25 for a one-way ticket, which represented a saving of $775 each.

'I take it your silence means everything is okay?' the SMS read, while we waited to board. The message was from Mr Mazunga, and we had no option but to call him and confess. 'You should have made arrangements in South Africa!' the consigliere shouted down the line. 'You should have done your research! What kind of idiots don't bring enough dollars to the Congo?' We felt bad. We shouldn't have let him down. But then Mazunga had proved a compromised travel agent, and short of printing dollars, what were we supposed to do?

Lake Kivu was beautiful. The boat was deep hulled with a low ceiling to keep it from capsizing in the storms that swept in from Rwanda without warning. It was better than driving by any measure. We bought sweet, small bananas at a stop at a rotting pier, and marvelled at the fact that beneath us burbled methane in such quantities that, should the right seismic conditions present themselves, the lake would explode and release enough CO_2 to choke the entire region to death. The paradox seemed almost too perfect, until it was unravelled by another of Africa's binaries.

In a technologically dazzling undertaking, an outfit called Project KivuWatt planned to spend $91.5 million building a facility on the Rwandan side of the lake that would extract the methane and transform it into electricity via a 25-megawatt power plant. Instead of dispensing death, the lake would soon turn the lights on.

We would see it only in hindsight: between the bustle of Bukavu and the grime of Goma, between abjection and innovation, atop nature's equivalent of a thermonuclear bomb, lay a continental shift.

The circle of black earth could mean anything. A film of dark dust, no bigger in circumference than a barbecue grill, a spit for roasting goats, two or three overturned rubbish bins. Around the edges lie crushed cans and torn shopping bags, bottle caps and discarded milk cartons. Then, beyond the barbed wire fence to the north, a mobile home reclining on bricks; beyond that, a taxi rank. The new Cashbuild that rises immediately to the south is already the tallest structure in the village, its steel girders a testament to all the money swirling around town. And it's here, in this recent prosperity, that the key to the mystery resides. In a few weeks, the dark earth will be gone – the garbage will be cleared, another shop will replace the shop that has burnt down.

We have come to Ganyesa, a rural municipality on the fringes of the Kalahari, to investigate the death by fire of four Chinese nationals in their place of work. The sole report in our possession, a few column inches buried deep inside The Star *newspaper of 14 November 2011, tells us that the deceased 'were in contact with their relatives and friends until their last breath'. One such friend, a so-called 'Pakistani businessman', felt compelled to inform the newspaper that the Chinese were running a successful wholesaler, that 'they were very peaceful and would not have made enemies'. Another interviewee, Mi Zheng, a brother of one of the dead men, has said through his tears, 'It was impossible that the fire could have been caused by a stove, cigarette or electricity connections.'*

And so we have driven from Johannesburg to South Africa's North West Province, to a settlement 70 kilometres outside the town of Vryburg, to explore an insinuation of murder. The names of the dead, as provided by the report, are Chen Chun He, 35, Yun Cai Yu, 19, and Chen and his wife Xu Guang, both 25. They are names that will change repeatedly in the days ahead – not because the people of Ganyesa are unsure exactly of who has died, but because they are names that are foreign, because the four who were burnt alive each endeavoured, in their attempts at integration, to offer the locals a set of syllables that were easier on the tongue.

TWO

NAMIBIA

Tending the Shoots of a New Middle Class

'The Namib was born of God's forgetting. He'd always meant to come back and put something here, but alas, he didn't. So it goes with this country.'

— Peter Orner, *The Second Coming of Mavala Shikongo*

THE PLACE WHERE WE MIGHT WANT TO BE

Rain at last had come to the kiln-dry city of Windhoek. It descended from the sky in chutes, inundating the koppies and uprooting the aloes that were botanically undesigned for such cloud-borne bounty. Further afield, the red dunes of Sossusvlei had sprouted an emerald carpet, and the Kavango River had sprung its banks. A landscape with which we were familiar had suddenly been rendered strange, as if a sepia film set had been colourised and submerged undersea.

Four years earlier, in 2006, we had travelled the length of Namibia in a rental econo-car; we were now thankful for the pick-up that kept us above the floodwaters surging down the Katutura road. 'Turn there to your left,' said Simeon Bernardino, who'd just the previous day explained how he'd never in his 20 years seen weather quite like it. 'Ja, maybe Windhoek is jealous of Swakopmund,' he'd said, in an allusion to the storm-lashed resort on the country's Atlantic coast.

The township of Katutura, as it had been doing since 1961, was spreading itself across the granitic hills that formed Windhoek's north-western flank. It was in every way a typical southern African township,

13

built to house a black population forbidden from living in the white suburbs they serviced. Katutura has meant many things to its residents over the years, but in Otjiherero it means 'the place where we do not want to be'. Like its archetype, Soweto in Johannesburg, it was still a world unto itself – one where BMWs with spinning rims were parked in front of lean-tos, where chickens pecked in the yards of brand-new five-bedroom houses, where soccer fans poured into the stadium while ad hoc games were played on the streets outside. Namibia's entire class strata, from newly arrived subsistence farmers to long-established professionals, were living here alongside each other as communities in flux.

Simeon guided us into his section of the township by way of an incline, the truck's wheels spinning raggedly for purchase. The Bernardino family home, standing apart from a nearby cluster of shacks, consisted of two brick structures and an outhouse perched on what – thanks to the flooding – had lately become a bluff. The previous year, during a rare official tour, President Hifikepunye Pohamba had apparently wept over the abjectness of living conditions for the poorest of Katutura's residents. He'd promised to connect the entire township to Windhoek's electricity grid, a vow that at the time of our visit remained largely unfulfilled. When Simeon wanted to read at night, he said, he had to do so by flashlight: the family had not bought a generator because they owned no appliances that required one.

The single appliance they did own, a battery-powered device Simeon referred to as 'the machine', was kept inside a hatbox beneath the dining table. As he bent down to retrieve it, a dog sniffed at our knees. 'His name is Tjikuzu,' said Simeon. 'We called him this because of a famous Namibian soccer player, who's now playing in the Chinese leagues.'

A detail, we would learn, that simply wasn't true. Razundara 'Razzie' Tjikuzu had spent his most productive years as a defending midfielder in the German leagues, bequeathing his talents to his country's first colonial masters, and had ended his international career in Turkey. Still, if this was the story doing the rounds in Katutura, its veracity was clearly less important than its message. In order to qualify as properly of the moment, Tjikuzu *had* to kick a ball under the glare of Shanghai's skyscrapers – for most of the residents of these parts, that city was the centre of the world.

As it happened, Simeon had spoken to us at length of the Chinese. Not as a people, a culture, or even as a rising superpower, but of the role they had played in his young life as a game changer, as catalysts for shunting him and his family up the economic ladder. While Simeon's home would barely qualify as a shelter in the West, its store-bought furniture and satchels of schoolbooks identified the Bernardinos as lower middle class in the context of Katutura. Simeon wanted to show us how the arrival of the Chinese, one amongst a series of factors, had influenced his high-tension toggle between the formal and informal sectors, between mere subsistence and upward mobility. And this was exactly why we had returned to Namibia – to examine how one African country was struggling, sometimes successfully, more often less so, to establish a class of Bernardinos across its heat-baked vastness.

Simeon placed the hatbox in the centre of the dining table. 'Please sit,' he said. Carefully, as his family gathered around, he lifted the lid.

◆

Branded the Aculife by its makers, 'the machine' was a silver contraption that ran a current from its battery, through a simple cord, to a stylus. It worked, Simeon explained, according to the ancient Chinese principles of acupuncture and palmistry, and its function was to administer slight shocks to parts of the hand that corresponded with maladies elsewhere in the body – pain at the top of the thumb, for instance, indicated a bronchial infection.

The Aculife, which cost Simeon roughly $350, an enormous sum by Namibian standards, had completely changed his circumstances. He was now a 'five-star' member of the Tiens Group, a multinational conglomerate that extended into 110 countries from its production plants in Tianjin, a northern Chinese city not far from Beijing.[1] The company had been founded in 1995 by Li Jinyuan, a suspiciously fresh-faced

15

septuagenarian from Cangzhou, based on his business philosophy of 'Serving Society by Restoring Health to Mankind'. Like Amway in the United States, which called itself a 'direct-selling company', Tiens made it clear in its literature that it was not involved in pyramid selling. And like Amway, Tiens rewarded its members according to the number of new salespeople they brought in.

This sort of work suited Simeon. There was a fleetness about him, a lightness of step that made him seem irrepressible. Nothing beat him down, the green Rasta beads around his neck implying weed-infused good cheer, although he was unlikely to have ever held a joint, much less smoked one. He was a product of the random borders that had come to define Africa – his home village was in northern Namibia, his heritage firmly Owambo, yet he carried the Portuguese surname that was an accident of his father having been born on the far side of the Kunene River, in Angola.

After graduating from high school in Khomasdal, Simeon had gone on to complete a tertiary course in information technology, and was now studying business administration at the local polytechnic. 'I want to know how to manage a business more,' he told us, 'which is one of the reasons I tried this Tiens, to learn.' He was learning fast: for the 18 months he'd been at it, Simeon had done well. His five-star status was two levels off the bottom, and he'd used the money he'd saved to fund his education, contribute to living expenses in Katutura, and effect repairs and renovations to the family homestead in the village up north. 'It's hard work,' he said, 'but you get rewarded.'

Rarely is hard work in Africa attended by reward. Consider Namibia's particulars: 2.25 million people rattling around in a landmass 20 per cent larger than Texas, barely generating the GDP of St Louis,[2] and distributing that wealth less evenly than either Haiti or Afghanistan.[3] In this, it was hardly a surprise that Simeon's education hadn't shunted him forward vocationally – IT was barely an industry in Namibia. He instead held a Man Friday position at a local nursery, a gig that mirrored the types of jobs black Namibians had been doing for white Namibians for five generations. Although the job plugged him into the country's scant but growing tax base, and while it ensured he wasn't contributing to the woeful unemployment statistics – President Pohamba, during his State of the Union address in 2013, would mention with apparent satisfaction that unemployment had *dropped* to 37 per cent[4] – Simeon's upward mobility came from his informal activities, powered by an entrepreneurialism often described as urban Africa's Last Great Hope.[5] Barely out of boyhood, and in less than two years, Simeon had hoisted his family out of what counted as 'lower income' in Africa.

It went without saying that he'd been amongst multitudes attempting the climb. In 2008, an International Labour Office report had elucidated one of the key structural challenges facing Africa as a whole: as in much of the rest of the continent, around 70 per cent of economically active Namibians above the age of 15 worked in the informal sector, out of the taxman's reach, hired and fired at whim, high-wiring it through life without social protections or safety nets.[6]

According to Simeon, the vast majority of Katutura's residents woke up to this reality each morning, and so had adjusted their aspirations to fit. 'You know, there's a lot of multi-level marketing businesses going down here,' he said, using the preferred Tiens parlance for recruitment-based direct selling. Being badgered to join one pressure-selling scheme or another was part of Katutura's social fabric, and Tiens was no exception. 'Every day, this woman was saying to me, "Join, join!" I thought it would be the same as the others, that it would last a year and I'd waste my time.' But the woman wouldn't let up, and when Simeon had finally relented it had been with his in-built brand of optimism. While he would have to pay $15 for a life membership, as well as purchase the full range of Tiens healthcare products, he would focus on the upside. Buy in, he'd said to himself, and don't look back.

The machine had by now buzzed fully to life, and Tjikuzu was mimicking his namesake by performing end runs around the dining table. Simeon opened the palmistry chart, and spread it flat in preparation for a consultation.

'So, you joined knowing this was a pressure-selling scheme?' one of us asked.

'Well, *direct* marketing,' he said, with some emphasis. 'But ja, of course.'

'So what happens if the scheme collapses? What happens to you?'

Simeon smiled. 'If the business collapses? I have nothing to lose.' With no equity in the game, Simeon explained, he carried a stock that was hardly a tough sell in Katutura – the genius of the Tiens wellness model was that it was designed for countries in which healthcare was either non-existent, unpleasant, or unaffordable, a detail articulated on the one hand by the foreboding Katutura State Hospital lurking nearby, and on the other by the fact that the group would shut down its North American operations by the end of 2011.[7] And while health-care seemed to be the most profitable sector for this business, Amway's cleaning products weren't doing much worse. In sub-Saharan Africa, where infrastructure and distribution remained major obstacles to the pursuit of commerce, selling peer-to-peer – or more specifically, neighbour-to-neighbour – had become one of the surest routes to the creation of supplementary wealth.[8]

Every weekend, Simeon and a friend would pack crumpled news-paper as extra padding into the hatbox, and tout the machine in the streets and alleyways of Katutura. The aim was twofold: to recruit and to consult. At $2.50 a consultation they were often making $300 on a Saturday, on their best days even more. 'And since I've been using these Tiens products myself,' said Simeon, 'I don't know where my hospital card is any more.'

Our consultation fee paid and our palms placed on the table, Simeon got to work. The stylus emitted an astonishing amount of energy, send-ing spasmodic bursts into our hands; to listen to the machine, we were dying in catastrophic increments. The most significant jabs of pain afflicted the tender muscle over the metacarpus below our thumbs, which, we soon learned, represented the journalist's *bête noire* – the liver. Simeon recommended Tiens Nutrient High Calcium Powder, to be taken with Beneficial Capsules. He warned us of the perils of excessive alcohol consumption, and sent us on our way.

◆

We took the long route back to central Windhoek, through Katutura's outlying neighbourhoods, where the shacks were so new that the zinc roofs sloughed off the rain as if oiled. In late 2006, when around 150 000 people lived in the township, these areas had been open hills and valleys; now, in January 2011, reflective of a population that was growing by 600 migrants per month, they were the site of one of Africa's most inexorable twenty-first century tropes. As in Katutura, urbanisation everywhere on the continent was being driven by the age-old human impulse to rise up, to do better, to get ahead,[9] but here the impulse had recently found a name – many residents, Simeon had told us, had taken to calling it *Matutura*: the place where we *do* want to be.

What, aside from the newly urbanised's almost obligatory reliance on hope, had brought about this change in outlook? In macro terms, we thought we knew at least part of the answer. Although sub-Saharan Africa had dodged the direct effects of the global recession that had followed the collapse of the American economy in 2008, it had *not* escaped the after-shocks. African economies had dipped precipitously in 2009, ending what had been the region's second great period of growth since liberation. But then the extraordinary had happened – in 2010, those economies bounced back. Trillions of dollars' worth of capital had been erased from Western markets, and the result was nothing less than a rewrite of the global script: America was suddenly conceived of as an unregulated casino economy run by Wall Street hucksters; European nations were defaulting on their debts like drunks after last call; and China was propping up the planet by purchasing commodities to service its own unhindered expansion. The resource-rich continent of Africa had shifted even further to the east, with several of its leaders grabbing the opportunity to display a touch of *schadenfreude*,[10] and people like Simeon Bernardino praising China for keeping their dreams alive. Of course, our job was to parse what this turning away, or this turning *toward*, meant for the majority of Namibia's people; to test whether it was really creating new social orders. We had bumped into Simeon and his story mostly by accident, and we weren't yet certain where he stood in relation to a competing narrative.

When we'd arrived in Windhoek the week before, we'd done so in the shadow of a profoundly altered skyline. Since our last visit, Namibia's capital had been overrun by government construction projects, none of them more visible than the presidential palace, erected to house Hifikepunye Pohamba and his court. As we entered the city from the east, navigating our way along Robert Mugabe Avenue, New State House had revealed itself on an aloe-covered ridge to our left. The thick steel fence complete with gilded motif, tiled guard turrets with one-way mirrored glass, and half-dome over the main building had all evoked for us the Tripoli compound of Muammar Gaddafi, bombed by the Americans in 1986.

The comparison, we knew, was strange – and yet the truth was palpably stranger. It had been easy enough to discover that a North Korean company called Mansudae Overseas Projects had built the palace, and that Kim Yong-nam, president of the presidium of the Supreme People's Assembly of North Korea, had been present at the inauguration in March 2008. The project's cost, over US\$70 million according to the country's leading newspaper (official figures placed it closer to \$50 million[11]), had not included the president's residence itself, which had been completed with a grant from the Chinese government. Covering an area of 25 hectares, the compound boasted offices for cabinet ministers and 200 members of the presidential staff, a guesthouse and luxury apartments for visiting dignitaries, on-site accommodation for police force and security personnel, and two helipads.

On our second evening in the city, intent on getting a closer look, we'd provoked the wrath of a minivan-full of these security personnel. Within minutes of leaving our truck, which we'd parked on a residential side street, they'd pulled up to confront us on the sidewalk. From their features, accents and nametags the two most hostile members of the group had revealed themselves as North African – it was they who yelled the loudest, insisted on searching our vehicle, accused us of being spies. 'Would you take photographs of the president's house in your own country?' the larger of the two had asked.

New State House, Windhoek, January 2011

Days later, their warning that we would be 'watched' still ringing in our ears, we were no closer to decoding the incident's meaning. Why did Namibia, with no avowed enemies and the world's second-lowest population density, have to import rent-a-thugs from the Maghreb? When had this country, amongst the most peaceful and sedate of African states, become so wary of foreign journalists? The rumours abounded. We'd been told that somewhere deep in the Namib Desert the government had established an enclave, an entire *city*, for newly arrived Chinese migrants. Hundreds were said to pour from charter flights every day, already dressed in their coveralls and ready to perform jobs that would otherwise have gone to Namibians. And these were no regular labourers, the stories went, but prisoners dumped into Africa in order to empty Chinese jails. At a camping store, the proprietor painted for us the picture of a shadowy overlord, a mastermind who was guiding the Asian hand in southern Africa. 'A Mister Lee, or a Mister Lin,' said the gentleman, pulling at his walrus moustache. 'All the Chinese run through him. He built Oshikango's Chinatown, built

Windhoek's Chinatown, built the northern industrial zone Chinatown. Nobody has seen him, nobody knows what he looks like. But he's the man.'

This latter story ran parallel with news reports of a certain Sam Pa and his 88 Queensway Group, properly known as the China International Fund (CIF), a Hong Kong-registered outfit with uncomfortably close ties to several African strongmen, most notably José Eduardo dos Santos of Angola.[12] Beijing had repeatedly disavowed any knowledge of Pa, his associates, his organisation, and his multiple real estate and energy interests across the continent. As indisputably opaque as the CIF may have been, it was reported that the organisation owned JPMorgan Chase's 23 Wall Street skyscraper and an enormous high-rise complex on Hong Kong's Queensway – hundreds of millions of dollars of premium first world real estate. Pa was the ultimate post-crash global player, at once real and mythological, moving money around the planet with one click of his Bat-phone while his identity remained concealed behind firewalls of mystery.

We'd hear these stories time and again throughout our journey. Like images on a television monitor, they degraded into fuzz as we leaned in for closer examination. The occasional editorial welcomed the spectral newcomers. A lot more did not. 'We don't want to have a situation in which the one moment a child is sitting in class listening to a history lesson,' read a *Windhoek Observer* op-ed piece, 'and the next moment the roof flies off! Yes, we all know what the response to that is going to be: China, vely cheap! No galentie!' As African newspapers pumped out the bilge water of local anxieties, African governments were building relationships that to many citizens seemed sinister, inscrutable, unmanageable.

So where, we wondered, did Simeon Bernardino fit into all of this? Did he represent something larger, or were his circumstances too unique to be of symbolic use? We carried along with us, like a talisman, an enthusiastic McKinsey Global Institute report published in June 2010 entitled 'Lions on the move: The progress and potential of African economies'. At this point, it was impossible to know whether the roaring we heard was an assertion of dominance or an anguished expression of bewilderment. In Namibia's case, the stability, the *dignity* that had been fought for through two decades of war against apartheid Pretoria seemed suddenly under threat. And nowhere, in the opinion of McKinsey and others, was there a more effective counter to that threat than in the rise of a class of middle earners – an empowered caste who would drive Africa into the future on wave after wave of consumption.

MIDDLE ON THE MARCH

What *is* a middle class?

'Arguably no class in human history has received so much comment, but so little systematic study,' the academic Robert D Johnston once wrote.[13] While Johnston was in this case referring to America, we can safely multiply that statement by orders of magnitude when it comes to the developing world. If the nation that consecrated the middle class as a cultural and political force couldn't properly decide on who, or most importantly *what*, the cohort represented, could there be any hope for the rest of us?

Not really, it turns out, at least as far as ironclad definitions are concerned. Studies that have reached at global or more specifically African notions of a middle class are difficult to find, and those theories that do exist are scrambled by the distorting influence of colonialism – there's no way to chart a continental middle without first interposing colonial iterations, and then working gingerly outward to try and build a unifying, post-liberation version of who these people may be, where they may live, and what they might want.

One thing most commentators tend to agree on is that the conditions required for the establishment of a middle class, such as inclusive economic institutions, rule of law and the availability of credit, remain the hallmarks of a stable state. And that's as far as consensus goes: free market adherents believe that developing societies naturally trend towards a caste of peacefully voracious consumers, while statists consider the middle class to be a phenomenon that requires nurturing should a society hope to come into its own. Only relatively recently have African policy makers waded into this debate in order to influence the outcome one way or another.

That said, data supporting the emergence of an African middle class began appearing in the Western media around 2010. Starting with a *Newsweek* encomium entitled 'Africa is Becoming the New China and India',[14] and followed by *The Economist*'s famous 'Africa Rising' cover in December 2011,[15] impressions regarding Africa's status as a locus of middle class consumerism strode into the mainstream. Although to some this seemed to be yet another Western-generated invention divorced from the continent's reality, it was backed up by a market brief compiled by the African Development Bank (AfDB) under the header 'The Middle of the Pyramid: Dynamics of the Middle Class in Africa'. Published in April 2011, the AfDB report became the pillar of the canon, ushering in an Africa rebranded as an investment destination.

The AfDB was unambiguous on what an entrenched middle class might mean for the continent:

> Empirical evidence shows that growth of the middle class is associated with better governance, economic growth and poverty reduction. It appears that as people gain middle class status, they are likely to use their greater economic clout to demand more accountable governments. This includes pressing for the rule of law, property rights and a higher quantity and quality of public services.[16]

Empirical evidence shows no such thing[17] – as members of apartheid-era South Africa's white middle class, the above sounded to us like little more than wishful thinking. Nevertheless, presenting 'evidence based on research and studies of 45 African countries,' the AfDB report stated that in 2010, Africa's middle class represented 34 per cent of the continent's population, or over 350 million people. Since 1980, this group had increased at a rate of 3.1 per cent, handily outpacing population growth. Middle class-driven consumer spending reached $680 billion in 2008, or nearly a quarter of Africa's total GDP for that year, and was set to reach $2.2 trillion by 2030. Were Africa to stay on its current growth trajectory, noted the report, the majority of the continent would enjoy lower middle class status by the onset of the century's fourth decade.

These numbers found stardom on the front pages of consulting company brochures and Power Point presentations. But the AfDB's middle class was a somewhat amorphous designation. The group included anyone earning an annual income above $3 900, or those spending between $2 and $20 a day. The bank further divided this cohort into three tiers: a 'floating class' with per-capita consumption levels of $2 to $4 a day, a lower middle class spending between $4 and $10 a day, and an upper middle class spending between $10 and $20 a day.[18]

The report acknowledged that income inequality remained appallingly high: some 100 000 individuals controlled about 80 per cent of sub-Saharan Africa's wealth, while 61 per cent fell below the $2 a day poverty line, and 44 per cent struggled under the barely life-sustaining $1.25 threshold.[19] Those in the lowest strata of the middle class teetered on the edge of poverty's cliff, subject to 'exogenous shocks' – outside factors such as Europe sliding into a Mediterranean Sea of penury. That no mention was made of endogenous shocks, inside factors like coups and wars and botched politicking that have for decades hobbled Africa's economic growth, struck us as a telling omission. This was Africa reconceived as an investor's playground, with 54 disparate political and economic systems tempered by this new and growing middle class, all set to arrive at some inchoate but stable mean at a point in the near future.

Regardless of how the data was received, and by no means was every economist buying it,[20] the AfDB brief introduced a select Western audience to facts that Chinese or Indian players would have found almost too obvious to mention: Africa wasn't a basket case in need of aid and development initiatives, but rather a massive and growing market in need of servicing. And while this began to change perceptions *outside* of Africa, the matter of what Africans thought, or of how these categories applied to any human being's lived experience, went largely without comment.

◆

That would change in October 2013, when the AfDB's findings were revealed in photonegative by an ambitious non-partisan research project called Afrobarometer. Setting out in late 2011, a team of researchers began compiling surveys in 34 African countries, asking respondents what it felt like to be an inhabitant of a continent in which everything and everyone was hurtling along at Mach 10.

The resulting twin policy briefs proved a bracing corrective.[21] Despite the middle class numbers promulgated by the AfDB, the Afrobarometer surveys' major finding was that since 2002, lived poverty on the continent had remained largely unchanged. 'This,' noted the briefs' compilers, 'suggests either that growth is occurring, but that its effects are not trickling down to the poorest citizens ... or alternatively, that actual growth rates may not match up to those being reported.'[22]

There was no doubt that African economies were growing, but precisely how fast was the subject of enormous dispute. A Canadian-based academic named Morten Jerven, who wrote a book called *Poor Numbers: How We are Misled by African Development Statistics and What to Do About It*, would effectively be banned from a symposium on national statistics at the United Nations Economic Commission for Africa, held in Addis Ababa in September 2013, for daring to suggest that the math didn't compute.[23] Two months later, the Mo Ibrahim Foundation would release its annual summary, reminding readers that most African countries – with the exception of Seychelles, Mauritius, Cape Verde and Egypt – lacked the statistical capacity to compile data that would allow for informed policy-making decisions.[24] In other words, vaunted GDP figures were often best guesses, which meant that Africa's growth was not being accounted for in a systematic, scientific manner, and could not be interpreted without a *caveat emptor* clause or three.

The doubt was only bolstered by the fact that Afrobarometer's Lived

Poverty Index, the measure of Africans' perception of their economic reality,[25] had not moved so much as a percentage point in over a decade. Levels of felt 'moderate poverty', a designation corresponding to the AfDB's vast floating middle class, had flatlined since 2002, a contradiction of the growing middle class story at least as it pertained to those on the ground. Indeed, Africans in almost all of the 34 nations surveyed accorded governments a failing grade for job creation, economic management and improved living conditions for the poor. The report was blunt: 'The overall finding is that levels of poverty have been stagnant, rather than declining as some official statistics – and high growth rates – might suggest.'

A tale, then, of warring briefs. One set of data fed into the new, generally embraced story of Africa Rising, another hacked that narrative down to its stump. And in the centre of it all was Africa's contested middle class, men and women like Simeon Bernardino, who were trying to get ahead. The AfDB concluded that in order for the middle class to sustain itself, the bank's member nations needed to ensure 'stable, secure well-paid jobs with good benefits', along with 'higher tertiary education'.[26] But which jobs, exactly? The South African economist Duncan Clarke would later observe that sub-Saharan Africa in 2011 resembled Europe at the cusp of the Industrial Revolution, with a mass of rural poor moving to the cities for work – work that in Africa's case did not yet exist.[27] While populations across the continent may have been rapidly urbanising, economies were not industrialising at rates that could accommodate them. A super-class of hundreds of millions of 'entrepreneurs' – a polite word for the strivers slugging it out in the brutal cage fight of the informal sector – could not of its own accord provide stability, benefits and university degrees. Nor, the AfDB's critics argued, was it going to offer sub-Saharan Africa the steady uptick in growth that the middle class had provided other markets and regions at different points in time.

In all of this, the critical question that the duelling reports left unanswered was whether the numbers reflected the emergence of an *actual* socioeconomic class, one that would be a deciding factor in Africa's future development, or merely a middle ground measured in local terms, subject to the smallest fluctuations in economies at home or abroad. Asked another way, did the future of 350 million Simeons have a precedent in recent socioeconomic history, or were Africa's emerging middle earners a new phenomenon, wandering groves of development that remained, for the most part, unmapped?

MY ENEMY'S ENEMY

On the morning of 20 January 2011, we found ourselves in a baking prefabricated office on the outskirts of Katutura. We had come to interview Bernard Milinga, a committed protector of the working class, a former freedom fighter who had joined forces with his old white overlords in battle against his own black government and their friends from afar, the Chinese.

Milinga, shaved head, sad eyes, sat in a beat-up desk chair. At just thirty-seven years of age, he served as general secretary of the Metal and Allied Namibian Workers Union (MANWU), presiding over a steadily dwindling membership of 17 000.[28] The union compound, which stood at the opposite end of Katutura to Simeon's home, was an amalgam of rusting huts and low-slung concrete. The walls in Milinga's office, shedding hospital green paint, bore revolutionary placards covered in Post-it notes, as if the revolution itself had been consumed by banalities.

'A memory that stands out for me from the war?' said Milinga, in response to our request for a defining image. 'It is that of my father, strapped to the belly of a helicopter.'

The technique was not unfamiliar to us, although we had always believed it was a canard, a *Full Metal Jacket*-like elaboration. But no, the South African Air Force appeared indeed to have maintained it in their repertoire during the border war, dusting it off to deal with 'terrorists' of an especially intransigent stripe – SWAPO, or the South West Africa People's Organisation, had been waging a guerrilla campaign against Pretoria since the mid-1960s, and as the attacks had intensified so had the reprisals.

It was the early 1980s, said Milinga, and he watched as the helicopter flew low over the Kavango floodplain, his father's body 'bounced' through the river and the reeds. As he knew even then, this extravagant form of waterboarding had not been devised to garner intelligence; its intention was rather to subjugate and subdue, to shock SWAPO operatives and their families into submission. In many cases, of course, it had the opposite effect, radicalising a new generation of Namibians, sweeping them towards freedom.

Liberation was not a distant historical milestone for Milinga. Like his comrades, he could trace colonialism in his country back to the moment the British had first occupied Walvis Bay, in 1797. He could recite by rote the lowlights of Otto von Bismarck's claiming of South West Africa as a possession in 1884 – the mass slaying of the Herero as an early act of industrial ethnic cleansing; the merciless slaughter of the Namaqua. Following Germany's defeat at the hands of the Allies in World War I,[29] Milinga could imagine the sense of betrayal after his country was handed over to South Africa by the League of Nations; worse yet, how South Africa had illegally retained its prize after World War II, a fact met with shrugs of indifference by the international community. He could recall the brutality of the apartheid regime with blunt matter-of-factness. But he could more clearly still remember the joys of that March day in 1990 when independence was declared – the uncoiling of a century of subjugation, as if a python had been forced to relinquish its prey.

If anyone had told the young Bernard Milinga that 20 years after independence he'd be compelled to wage war against SWAPO, the movement for which he and his father had once been prepared to die, he would have found the idea ludicrous. But here he was, at loggerheads with the ruling party over what he felt was the only issue that counted – the rights of Namibia's workers, those who had functioned as the expendable engines of growth for successive colonial regimes, and those whose interests were now being overlooked by the very party they had helped to install in power.

◆

'So,' said Milinga, nodding his head in the direction of Katutura, 'we are busy increasing the poverty in this country.'

Milinga may not have known Simeon Bernardino, but he did know that old definitions of 'work' were no longer working. Indeed, as 2010 bled into 2011, the sector powering the country's growth was not mining, as had almost always been the case, but construction.[30] And yet Milinga's role was complicated by the same phenomenon that had infused Simeon with hope – the arrival of the Chinese as competitors to the German and South African firms whose roots dated back to colonialism.

'The Chinese, they are here trying to finish the unions,' he said. Although Milinga acknowledged that labour movements were under fire across the world – as we were speaking, Governor Scott Walker of Wisconsin was preparing his unprecedented full-frontal assault on the collective bargaining rights of his state's public sector workers, which would usher in massive protests and spur on the nascent Occupy Wall Street movement[31] – he reminded us that Namibia was not America. In southern Africa, he insisted, unions were as central, *more* central, to liberation than the AK-47. In his view, apartheid had been a handmaiden of brute capitalism, and after its dissolution the economic gap had been filled by the exigencies of globalisation. Namibians were getting poorer, said Milinga, because political transition had not resulted in economic transition, which meant that the mechanics of exploitation remained virtually unchanged. And as difficult as organising had always been, it had decomposed into a nightmare in which formalised labour – those who paid dues, powered the unions, and helped drive southern Africa's political agenda – had become a minute slice of those who *really* needed protection: the millions upon millions of informal workers who were adrift in the economic ether.

Milinga, echoing the sentiment of his fellow unionists across the region, felt that his organisation had made a major strategic blunder in so completely throwing in its lot with government. By powering down its resistance machinery, MANWU and its sister organisations had handed SWAPO the political equivalent of a blank cheque. This had resulted in a dangerous apathy among union members. Although

30

it was then almost three years before the published Afrobarometer report would offer a measurable counter-narrative to the rampant Afro-optimism, the survey was well underway when we were conducting our own Namibian investigations. When finally collated, the data would allow that the country was but one of three exceptions wherein a majority of respondents, in this case 62 per cent, said that the economy was doing either fairly or very well.[32] These findings, we would later learn, squared with the AfDB's data, which placed Namibia seventh on the African middle-class sliding scale, with 47.4 per cent of the population in the 'floating' category, and 9.1 per cent firmly ensconced as middle income earners.[33] Nonetheless, an astonishing 43.75 per cent of Namibians were living on less than $1.25 per day,[34] right in line with the continental average, a radically uneven socio-economic structure that was as explosive as it was unsustainable.

'You will obey Swapo', Windhoek, January 2011

The construction industry, which had the ability to generate stable, well-paying jobs, had been identified as the antidote. But the sector, according to Milinga, was being disembowelled by an influx of construction companies from the People's Republic of China.

'The majority of workers on Chinese construction sites are not registered in terms of the Labour Act,' he said. 'If they are injured, they do not get protected. They are paid less than minimum wage.'[35] Under Milinga, MANWU had grown increasingly aggressive in trying to ensure Chinese compliance with Namibia's labour laws, legislation that he felt was both progressive and comprehensive in its response to the legacy of the past.[36] In August 2010, MANWU had brought the unions, a group of locally registered construction companies, and the ad hoc Chinese Construction Business Association (CCBA) to the table. The tacit agreement had been to have all labour regulations properly upheld by the end of the year. At the time of our investigation that deadline had come and gone, and when MANWU had insisted on a follow-up meeting with the CCBA, they'd been told, via email, that February was Chinese New Year, 'so no one is in charge of this thing now'.

The deeper Milinga delved into the details, the more his bile seemed to rise. The 17 000 workers he represented were, he insisted, Namibian citizens, entitled to their rights under the law. 'No minimum wage, no paid overtime, no public holidays, unfair dismissals,' he said, counting off the Chinese infractions. 'It is not right.'

For MANWU and a number of other Namibian trade unions, the showdown had developed into something of an existential farce. According to a recent study we'd come across, unions were now fully haemorrhaging members. As one retail employee had told the researchers: 'The Chinese have an attitude of treating us the way whites treated our fathers during the colonial era. The Chinese refuse to recognise the union. They solve their problems with the labour commissioner's office [instead].'[37]

A commissioner's office, it transpired, that was ignoring the labour movements with which it was mandated to engage. At any moment, said Milinga, the cord that tied the ruling party to the unions that filled its ranks could snap. The last available allies, he told us, had become the old guard. Milinga, who as a boy saw his father tortured beneath an SAAF Puma Heavy Assault chopper, was teaming up with a former enemy in battle against an estranged comrade.

'We are desperate,' he shrugged. 'They are desperate. The rules of the country are not being respected. What must we do?'

◆

And so Bernard Milinga and a man named Karl-Heinz Schulz were joined in expedient matrimony. Neither Schulz's German ancestry nor his family's long history in the construction sector necessarily made him a supporter of the colonial regime, but he was without doubt a beneficiary. Schulz was a member of Namibia's *entrenched* middle class, one of the well-heeled professionals who'd come of age in a system built and maintained for his gain. At independence, he could not have been faulted for suspecting that he was about to lose a chunk of his lucrative government contracts to a politically connected black elite. In the event, the spoils of liberation were distributed in a way he could never have anticipated.

'What we are looking for is a level playing field,' he told us, in the inimitably clipped tones of the German Namibian. 'But then you have guys like our Chinese friends, who just don't give a damn.'

An imposing two metres in height, Schulz was seemingly made from the same steel girders and concrete with which he'd helped to shape the country. As co-owner of Namibia Construction, a leading local firm, and acting president of the influential Construction Industries Federation (another CIF, not to be confused with Sam Pa's China International Fund), he was an unlikely celebrity. Famously, at least as far as the local press was concerned, Schulz was suing the Namibian government over a botched tender he believed his company should have won. The winning bid had gone to a Chinese firm, which had undercut the local, mostly white-owned companies by more than 20 per cent. 'I don't care about the fact that the winning bidder wasn't Namibian,' he told us, 'but I *do* care that they could come in so low because they don't pay attention to the country's laws.'

Almost every year since 1990, said Schulz, when Namibia won its independence from Pretoria, the flow of work in the construction sector had been on the increase. By rights, he declared, local construction companies should have been doing very well. But, as the presiding head of the CIF, Schulz was also aware that over 80 per cent of the capital projects from government were being awarded to foreign concerns, almost all of them Chinese. For Schulz, this could be explained by one fact alone. 'It's a very clear sign,' he said, 'that there are questions to ask about people on high level in government getting big, big kickbacks.'

He had, we knew, a compelling reason for making such a claim. In a recent case that had drawn international attention due to a series of articles in the *New York Times*, the name of Hu Haifeng, the son of China's then-president Hu Jintao, had emerged in a kickback scheme involving the sale of Chinese-made X-ray scanners to the Namibian government.[38] But when we asked Schulz whether it wasn't simply a matter of SWAPO wanting to give business to its old friends in China ahead of colonial-era firms like Namibia Construction, his gut response was to reach for the tabloid newspaper on his desk.

'This is one of Namibia's most successful businesspeople,' he said of the man on the front page, stabbing a stout forefinger into the photograph. 'Frans Aupa Indongo. I tell you, that man was successful prior to independence. I've got enormous respect for that man.'

The headline, laid out in crude English, was a statement of blatant and borderline racist intent: 'Chinese the worst capitalist'.[39] By having so near to hand the opinion of a black Namibian who'd thrived during – and despite – the white regime, the CIF president could effectively argue that *everybody* was now suspicious of the government's relationship with Beijing. Which, of course, didn't make it any less of a convenient tactic for sidestepping the historical facts.

SWAPO, whether Schulz was prepared to admit it or not, had a tradition of political friendship with the Chinese Communist Party that dated back to the earliest days of the liberation effort – a history that repeated itself, in slightly different guise, in more than a dozen African countries. 'We will always be grateful to China for the support extended to our struggle,' President Pohamba once said.[40] In 2006, Sam Nujoma, Namibia's liberation hero, made his thirteenth visit to the People's Republic, and two years later Hu Jintao touched down in Windhoek for the first time, a 130-person entourage in tow.[41]

Allegations that Hu's son was linked to a $56 million airport security equipment scandal – linked, in turn, to the X-ray scanners mentioned above, and strenuously denied by the Chinese – had done nothing to dampen SWAPO's starry-eyed Sinophilia.[42]

The numbers did a lot to explain why. In 2003, Sino-Namibian trade amounted to $74.57 million;[43] by 2009, that figure had grown to $600 million.[44] Between 1990 and 2009, China awarded Namibia two grants worth roughly US$10 million, an interest-free loan of almost US$4 million, a concessional loan of $130 million, and a low-interest credit line of over $100 million[45] – not insignificant sums in a country with a 2011 GDP of $11.03 billion,[46] even if people like Schulz believed that Beijing had done more harm to the national economy than good.

'By law, we have certain rules and regulations, and things we have to hand in with our tender bids,' he said, repeating the lament of his new friend and ally, Bernard Milinga. 'You must prove that you pay minimum wages, you must prove that you're affirmative action compliant. Nowadays, all these Chinese are suddenly compliant. Last year none of them handed in any documentation, and now suddenly they're all compliant?'

For their part, despite our repeated attempts, the officials at the Chinese embassy in Windhoek would not make themselves available to counter the allegation. If Chinese construction firms were really exempt from this most basic of post-independence laws – the law that attempted to redress a century of exploitation by mandating an incremental transfer of wealth – we would have no way of proving it. We were intrigued, nonetheless, by what the economic and commercial councillor at the embassy, Liu Kaungyuan, had once said in an interview with regard to minimum wages. 'The labour cost is too high,' he'd explained to a researcher in April 2008, some years before MANWU and the CIF would take on the embassy's effective proxy, the CCBA. 'Namibia does not have production. In China, if you have [$120] you are rich but in Namibia you cannot buy anything with it because you import everything. If you sacrifice on labour costs now for future generations, then Namibia will develop. Let people be paid lower wages now and attract more FDI and set up manufacturing so that the future generation will reap the benefits of the sacrifices.'[47]

Indeed, the minimum wage increases that would soon be negotiated between MANWU and the CIF – although not, unsurprisingly, with the involvement of the CCBA – would read as absurdly rich to Asian observers. By the end of 2011, pay packets would rise 7.5 per cent, with a further 8 per cent pending in 2012.[48] With inflation hovering at around 6.5 per cent,[49] those would represent real increases; in combination with 12 paid statutory holidays and 144 hours of so-called 'service allowance' tacked onto December vacation remuneration packages,[50] the cost to the economy would add up. To its critics, the arrangement would apply more to twenty-first century industrialised Germany than to a tiny African nation navigating the rapids of development.

Needless to say, Schulz and Milinga would have ripped such an argument apart. According to them, local labour had powered SWAPO into the swank presidential digs, and if the idea was to sacrifice the current generation of Namibian workers as a gift to the gods of growth, then that should have been made explicit in the 1992 Labour Act.

Schulz and Milinga were alleging that members of government were conspiring with Beijing-backed construction firms, thereby undercutting an industry that should have been a wellspring of employment and an igniting spark for a new middle class. Did a population of black, formerly marginalised Namibians stand any chance in such an environment, we wanted to know?

HARD WORK ACTION NO. 2

Through wind and rain, we followed the directions on the hand-drawn map into the far north. The flooded flatlands were mottled with black circles, as if shadows were swallowing the earth from below. The B1 highway took us straight into Oshakati's featureless grime, past drinking hole after drinking hole – Booze Booze Bar; Hard Work Action No 2; Chance Never Return. We were 70 kilometres from Oshikango and the Angolan border, where a Chinese business community had first arrived in 2003, expecting the end of the civil war to bring roads and an eruption in cross-border trade. Oshakati, we'd heard, was supposed to provide the perfect service base.

But the roads, and the attendant opportunities, had yet to materialise. Along with the usual retail stores, the Chinese traders had built warehouses, which remained largely unused, and while the town felt busy and moneyed, the wealth was Namibian in character – patches of development abutted thatched huts, and glinting Landcruisers roared past donkey carts driven by boys in rags.

Taliban Bar, Oshakati outskirts, January 2011

By late afternoon the rain had stopped and the heat had come up, and the sun was baking hard cakes of mud onto the asphalt. We slept in a hotel near the highway, disturbed all night by the throaty rumble of passing trucks. After breakfast, referring to the hand-drawn map, we took the short drive to the worksite, situated roughly in the centre of town. Behind us was a PEP clothing store, a Pupkewitz MegaBuild, and a Pupkewitz Toyota dealership, all owned by the country's wealthiest man, the 95-year-old Harold Pupkewitz.[51] In front of us was a dirt lane lined with rubbish and rank with spilled kerosene. A woman with a baby strapped to her back scrabbled through a garbage bin.

We hopped out of the pick-up and walked alongside a barbed wire fence on which laundry had been hung out to dry, stopping to bear witness to a large clearing marked by mountains of gravel and hundreds of prone steel girders. The site was dominated by the framing of a structure that would, according to the blueprints we had studied a few days before, become a clock tower.

Through the fence and across the clearing, the first Labour Act infraction revealed itself. Two local teenagers fiddled with a girder frame, dressed in nothing more than T-shirts, shorts and sandals – 'Section 96', we knew, stipulated the wearing at all times of boots, safety helmets and overalls.[52]

We entered the site via an open gateway guarded by an uninterested watchman with a shotgun across his lap. The teenagers were supervised by three Chinese workers, who sat on their haunches in the shade of a half-built retaining wall. They wore camo field hats, sandals, button-up shirts. We exchanged tentative greetings, making botched use of our few words of Mandarin, and were alerted to the approaching figure of a man in a golf shirt.

His name was Tony, he said, and he was employed as the translator of Jiangsu Zhengtai Construction Group. The boots on his feet, Timberland knock-offs, were the closest thing to work equipment we'd yet seen on the site. Tony had a gap in his teeth that made him look boyish, and an air of inherent melancholy no doubt exacerbated by the fact that he found himself in Oshakati.

'Today is Sunday,' he said, after we asked him why the site was so quiet. 'Today, the Namibians go drinking.'

He had been in Oshakati for four months, he continued, and his tenure would last three years. He would go home after two years, for a month.

'I miss my parents, my girlfriend,' he said. 'I message, I Internet, but it is not the same. My pay here is very low.' He pointed to the local workers.

'The Namibians, even their pay is higher.'

A flock of cormorants passed low above us, their caws echoing over the empty site.

'It is not a good place,' said Tony.

◆

Kerry McNamara, the man who had sent us to the Oskakati site, had patience for very little, and even less for newfangled definitions of the middle class. 'I *made* the middle class in this country,' he had spat, in the sun-dappled front room of Kerry McNamara Architects Inc, which overlooked the aloes at the edge of Robert Mugabe Avenue. 'And then they killed it.'

Moments later, during a relative lull in a near unbroken disquisition, McNamara would inform us that, 'in the bad old days', his firm had become one of the rare few in the country committed to designing low-income housing for black Namibians. 'There were two laws that defined life here,' he'd reminded us. 'The Population Registration Act, which defined colour, and the Influx Control Act, which controlled property ownership. It was illegal for a black person to have a freehold title to land. And he could not migrate.' By building houses for people who weren't allowed to live in them, McNamara, by his own reckoning, had waged his own war against apartheid.

In the regime's fading years, when Administrator-General Gerrit Viljoen[53] had asked for recommendations on how best to jumpstart a modest black middle class, McNamara – who at this point in his oration was resembling a Latin master from a Dickens novel – had known exactly what to do. 'They made me a one man building society,' he'd said, referring to the co-operative mortgage lending institutions South Africa had copied from the British. 'They gave me about 20 million dollars, and I could lend.' McNamara and Viljoen had then gone blow for blow as the regime, in an attempt to choke off the initiative before it became anything more than good optics, tried to impose usurious interest rates. 'I *knew* that would happen,' he'd explained. 'They got terrified because black guys were streaming in from the north to buy properties. And they said, "No, but you don't understand the black man. He doesn't want to live in Windhoek. He wants to live in his homeland." And I said, "Are we in the seventeenth century? Because *you* don't understand. That's what cities are all about. It's got nothing to do with colour or race. It's got to do with *commerce*."'

Now seventy and winding down, McNamara found that his dream of a Namibian middle class was being hijacked by Tiens and similar schemes, which to his thinking stood for the 'illusion' of wealth creation rather than the real thing.

If there was an abiding question that seemed to drive him, one that fuelled the hundreds of missives he'd lately been sending out to magazines and newspapers and public officials, it must have been the one he was asking now. 'Why would the government of a country, which sacrificed thousands of their people's lives to get rid of one foreign oppressor, hand their poor people over to another foreigner? We can only speculate.'

Like Schulz, whose alliance with Milinga he firmly supported, McNamara had recently backed such talk with action. He was campaigning to throw a Chinese construction company off a site in Oshakati, an event unheard of since the day the People's Republic had first landed on liberated Namibian soil. The Oshakati Open Market, tendered in 2010 by the town's municipality and won by a company called Jiangsu Zhengtai Construction Group, appeared to be the hill on which McNamara was willing to die. In addition to his architectural work, he had told us, he sat on the government tender board as an advisor to its two independent judges – which meant that he knew better than anybody how a tender application needed to abide by the Labour Act, meet employment equity requirements, and uphold the standards negotiated between MANWU and the CIF.

'So the Jiangsu Zhengtai tender comes in,' he'd said, 'and I say, "the Chinese do not adhere to the CIF agreement. I cannot recommend them." This is my assessment. And the government *still* chose the Chinese.'

McNamara shook his head as if he'd just absorbed a blow. 'The Namibian government allows its people to work for less than one third of minimum wage! And then no pensions? They'll die poor! Why are they doing that? *Why?*'

For McNamara, as for Schulz, the answer was obvious.

So the Oshakati Open Market would be the first time a concerned Namibian would attempt to stop work at a site, and McNamara, who doubled as the project's architect, was in theory able to do so because of an addendum he had forced Jiangsu Zhengtai to sign. While the Chinese company had tendered around $1.65 million lower than the lowest Namibian bidder, an offer the Oshakati municipality had no choice but to grab, McNamara wanted guarantees.

'I said, "you will agree to give us every month your pay slips, and show *every* month what you've paid. You will join the pension fund, and you'll show us the slips. Any breach of this is a breach of contract, and you'll be thrown off the site." Has any of this happened? Not bloody likely!'

A mere four months later, the Namibian government would make an announcement that would restore at least some of McNamara's faith. At its grand unveiling in April 2011, the Targeted Intervention Programme for Employment and Economic Growth would promise to address Namibia's persistent unemployment problem by creating 100 000 formal jobs over a three-year period. TIPEEG, by its very nature, would be forced to focus closely on the construction sector, where informal workers could easily be brought into the tax-paying fold. But at the time of our interview the debate about the programme's ultimate success was years in the future,[54] and the government's *bona fides* had yet to be proved.

'Go to the site and see for yourself,' McNamara had suggested. If we wanted to gauge the ultimate health of the Namibian middle class, he'd said, the Oshakati project offered an unambiguous diagnosis.

◆

On our second morning in Oshakati, we returned to the site for a follow-up visit. Slightly suspicious but appreciative of the fact that we'd been sent by the project's architect, Tony walked us through the site, brick by concrete brick. It seemed to us that not a single element of the Namibian Labour Act was in effect, but if this was apparent to our guide, he was playing it cool.

We watched as a worker in cheap wraparound shades took an angle-grinder to a girder, sparks flying like pellets around his eyes.

'Are they given the proper training for this kind of thing?' one of us asked.

'It must not go wrong,' said Tony, 'so they learn how to do it. These girders are very expensive.'

Contrary to what we'd been expecting, only a small portion of the material here was of Chinese provenance. If Jiangsu Zhengtai were to purchase and ship all their material from mainland China – something companies from the People's Republic were routinely accused of doing – they would have to haul it overland from the port city of Walvis Bay, about 800 kilometres to the southwest. Instead, the company bought its steel and wood from around the corner.

'We get it from Pupkewitz,' said Tony.

Shortly, we made our way to the Chinese workers' quarters. It was a compound roughly the size of a tennis court, ringed with an electrified fence. The barracks were bare concrete, and there were two metal-framed beds per cramped room, each draped with mosquito netting. Laptops blinked on wobbly desks that had been repaired many times with duct tape. Adjacent to the sleeping quarters was a larger work-room, with plans spread out over an executive desk. A muted television was hooked up to DStv, the South African pay-TV provider.

'Here is where we watch some films,' said Tony. 'Action films. And some Chinese programmes.'

In a small coop, chickens pecked at a bowl of rice mulch. Behind the birds, in a well-tended garden, sharp red chillies and cherry tomatoes grew alongside bok choy and other Chinese greens.

'This,' said Tony drily, 'is how we live.'

Clearly, Jiangsu Zhengtai Construction Group was not denying Namibian workers the perks it lavished on its Chinese employees; there were simply no perks to go around. Allegations of bribery aside, it became obvious to us on this second visit how Jiangsu Zhengtai was able to undercut the local competition on price – wages, benefits and safety equipment were simply slashed off capital costs. As per the greater logic, the logic of the Chinese embassy, the site's grimness, its emphasis on cheerless toil, was accepted as a down-payment on the future.

But McNamara, for one, didn't believe in a future without a present. Later that day over the phone, he would say, 'I sympathise with these little Chinamen, who don't know what's happening here. They're just farmed out, they work harder than any Namibians. Saturday, Sunday, they work like slaves. And they do some bloody good work. But why work this way? Why underpay?'

The most straightforward response, had McNamara been inclined to hear it, was written in the post-2008 global script: because this was how the People's Republic had transformed itself into the world's second largest economy; it was how Namibia was supposed to advance. In China, 300 million had recently moved up from absolute poverty, 200 million from farms to industry, 100 million into the middle class, while half a million had became millionaires. For his part, Tony counted as one of the 100 million arrivistes. By his own telling, his life didn't accord with notions of the bourgeoisie that were once standard in Western literature and sociological studies. His was an existence of loneliness, of long days, of cultural disorientation, his only tether to home and those he loved the digital strings that stretched, however tentatively, to his family in Sichuan. Tony was somebody who, as the commercial councillor at the Chinese embassy had put it, was making a sacrifice for the benefit of coming generations.

And the electric fence surrounding his makeshift compound stood for the contested nature of that sacrifice. Indeed, MANWU and its allies were fighting for a different conceit of the middle class, one that embodied the dignity and privilege of the old regime's protected professionals. They wanted work with guaranteed payoffs – stability, a pension, time off, benefits. But the world had changed and the ground had shifted, and the old classifications no longer held. MANWU, Schulz and McNamara were chasing an ideal that flew in the face of this worksite's dust-blown reality; this was a place defined by the new global money chain, by new cultural constructs of class.

Tony had now trailed us for almost an hour, and was growing agitated by our presence. Our questions had become too probing; he wanted us gone. There was, however, one last thing he wanted to explain.

'Sometimes, I cook for all of them,' he said, pointing to a group of Namibian labourers gathered around a girder. 'I make rice, some meat, Chinese vegetables. But they don't like to eat it. They think it is poison.'

STOP LOOKING FOR A FRIEND

The Tiens depot was installed in a shady office building on the corner of Windhoek's Newton Street and Robert Mugabe Avenue, and we drove there with Simeon before the start of his morning shift at the nursery. Along the way, he talked us through what to expect. 'Inside, we have all the machines, and people come in and get tested. We have health supplements, immune boosters, calcium, you name it.' The depot, which functioned as the nerve centre of the Tiens Group in Namibia, had become Simeon's spiritual home.

If the air in the offices belonging to Milinga, Schulz and McNamara was stagnant with pronouncements of decay, the Tiens depot buzzed with promise. A row of plastic chairs seated those waiting to be tested by the in-house Aculife. Nearby, a flatscreen television was bolted to the wall above a unit displaying boxes of Intelligent Rejuvenating Mask Low Frequency Face Treatment Apparatus. Inspirational strings blared forth from the speakers, and we strolled over to take a closer look at the images.

'*Stop looking for a friend,*' intoned a voice-over, '*and be one yourself.*' We saw a great hall jammed with ululating Africans, and a Chinese woman wearing a Tiens blazer handing out laptops and other big-ticket hardware. Simeon explained that this was the annual southern African awards ceremony, an event he had recently attended in Durban, South Africa. We watched a Mozambican win a holiday, a Zimbabwean win a car, and an ecstatic Batswana accept the keys to a yacht. Later, when we

44

pointed out the absurdity of someone in a landlocked country owning an ocean going vessel, Simeon responded with an edge of impatience. 'There are others who have come to Namibia and started a tourism business in Swakopmund,' he said. 'Or she can just *sell* it.'

On screen, the ululating increased in pitch, and a ticker scrolled in an endless loop:

> *Tiens gives you the OPPORTUNITY!!!*
> *Opportunity to change your daily routine!*
> *Opportunity to live your dreams!!!*

A woman named Busi sidled up to offer her opinion. 'At first,' she said, 'no one wanted to join, because this is a Chinese thing. But they promised us, "this is not poison, it's a hundred per cent herbs, it is good".' Like Simeon, Busi had done her research, which bore out the ease and harmlessness of giving the business a try. 'You don't need your CV or your what-what, you just need $15 to join. And if you do well, you can become a millionaire.' A stout woman wearing mom jeans and a pullover, Busi walked the floors of the depot with comfortable confidence. She wanted us to know that for her, Tiens was a means to any number of ends – ends that most certainly coincided with the creature comforts being handed out onscreen. 'I will not lie,' she said. 'I have done well.'

Despite the cult-like atmosphere, despite the snake oil nature of some of the products, despite our ingrained scepticism of anything that smacked of a pyramid, there was no denying the sheer *energy* in the depot, or the fact that Tiens provided a genuine option for those who wanted to make money of their own volition. And if we were still circumspect regarding the utility of Simeon's machine, the Namibian government apparently harboured no such reservations. 'Tiens was officially launched by the Honourable Petrina N Haingura, Deputy Minister of Health and Social Services, on 28 July 2010,' read a plaque within sight of the roaring television.

We got the impression that these bustling, efficient, laughing, chatting, vitamin water-drinking strivers carrying boxes of Tiens product out the door didn't want government programmes, didn't want unions. They merely wanted the country to build the infrastructural capacity to allow their micro-businesses the chance to grow – when President Pohamba had said he would connect Katutura to the power grid, Simeon had expected him to make good on that promise. Much later, the words of Jay Naidoo, former general secretary of South Africa's powerful federated union, COSATU, would end up resonating with our Tiens experience. 'African governments can't provide the jobs, not anywhere near the rate we're growing population-wise,' he would tell us. 'What we need is to formalise the informal sector, to be like America, where bankruptcy for a small entrepreneur isn't a death sentence, but a point on a learning curve.' For Naidoo, as for others, it came down to creating a society in which strivers could strive if they had the impulse, and those that ended up working for them could be protected from exploitation by the rule of law.

But what of the laws we saw flouted in Oshakati, those regulations that were being ignored on dozens, perhaps hundreds, of construction sites across the country? In late 2013, we would follow up with both Karl-Heinz Schulz and Bernard Milinga's successor, Justina Jonas, in order to determine what they had achieved in the intervening years. For his part, while nothing had come of the court case, Schulz would tell us that he had helped to pressure the Chinese embassy into negotiations with the Namibian government. SWAPO was beginning to understand, he would claim, that the construction industry couldn't absorb informal labour if there was no such thing as minimum wage. According to what Schulz would say, TIPEEG had successfully met at least some of its goals, as per President Pohamba's recent boast of unemployment dipping to 37 per cent.

Justina Jonas would prove even more effusive. 'For the last year, we have been happy,' she would say. 'We met with the national president Mr Pohamba, and we told him that the Chinese were not compliant. He agreed. He said, "the Chinese must not benefit unfairly from national tenders".' Pointedly, she would observe that the meeting between the president and MANWU had taken place a week after May Day, and that the union now felt it was being heard on matters of national policy. The Oshakati project, meanwhile, which was a municipal rather than a national tender, would barely move forward, and by the end of 2012 it would look much as it had when we'd visited almost two years before. Namibia's GDP would rocket up from $11.03 billion in 2011 to $13.07 billion in 2012.[55] The country's brutal income disparities would not be bridged at all.

Still, a government that had once paid North Korean and Chinese construction companies the obscene sum of $49 million to build its presidential palace was resetting its development model: the turning, we would learn, was by no means a constant; *nothing* in this climate was a constant.

Afrikaans, the tongue of South Africa's former oppressor, and Setswana, the tongue of her formerly oppressed, are the languages of choice in Vryburg. But 17 years after the inauguration of the country's first black president, Afrikaans is still the language of money. For Vryburg's economy is run by Boers, by the men in their kortbroek *and* velskoen *who oversee the country's largest beef producing district, by the ranchers who take pride in the fact that this place is sometimes called 'the Texas of South Africa'.*

As we drive through Texas backcountry, then, we too are uitlanders, *foreigners. Our car, a weathered Mercedes from the early 1990s, distinguishes us immediately from the white landowners in their pristine pick-ups – Hilux Raiders and Nissan Hardbodies and Ford Rangers that bear the roll bars and bull bars of the upmarket rural workhorse. The Mercedes, significantly, belongs to one of our grandfathers, a 93-year-old man who bombed Rommel's forces in North Africa during World War II. Recently, he's been deemed too old to drive; the car is on loan until we find a replacement for our former vehicle – stolen months earlier outside a Johannesburg mall – and it's in what the Mercedes symbolises, in how it connects us to our own immigrant heritage, that we recognise its value.*

Like the Chinese in Ganyesa's stores and wholesale outlets, the first sizeable generation of Jews in South Africa had been overcome by the ancient impulse to leave. After fleeing the pogroms of Tsarist Russia, many trekked far into the new country's hinterland, learning Afrikaans and setting up shop to sell goods at prices that local traders could not hope to match. Termed smouse, *a pejorative for 'Jewish hawkers', the immigrants coalesced into a stereotype: cunning and exploitative, a blight on the land, a people that tricked the real inhabitants out of an honest, God-fearing living.*

As Jews, connected by our car to a living ancestor who witnessed the worst of such prejudice, our sympathies have already been tied to the victims of the fire out there in the village. Was it murder in Ganyesa? We can't know yet, but history and context suggest a precedent.

We park the Mercedes in the lot of a chain restaurant, a branch of the same franchise outside of which our old vehicle was stolen, and escape the heat. At the table next to us, as we wait for our meals to arrive, we overhear a woman conversing in the de facto first language of the town.

'That Chinese man spoke a beautiful Afrikaans, I swear to you, auntie. I couldn't believe it, he spoke just like you and me.'

Detail, image of Cantonese migrants arriving in Cape Town, early twentieth century,
Overseas Chinese Museum, Xiamen, September 2012

THREE

BOTSWANA

How the Builders of the Three Gorges Dam
Tested an African Anomaly

*'That night, the Lord appeared to him in a dream and asked him,
"What would you like me to give you?"*
*'Solomon answered: "Oh Lord God, you have let me succeed my
father as king, even though I am very young and don't know how to
rule. So give me the wisdom I need to rule your people with justice,
and to know the difference between good and evil."'*

— Seretse Khama Ian Khama, quoting from 1 Kings
at his presidential inauguration, April 2008

THE KENNEDYS OF THE KALAHARI

Allow us to share with you the story of three African chiefs, three Tswana
elders who in 1895 travelled from their homes in Bechuanaland all the
way to the United Kingdom in order to change the future. Their names
were Khama, Sebele and Bathoen, and they arrived with the backing of
the non-conformist missionary movement, which was advocating for
'Little Englandism', a Britain shorn of empire. The calamity that was
about to befall them involved their ancestral lands assuming the status
of a railroad yard, a transport corridor for minerals. The mastermind
behind this caper was one Cecil John Rhodes, and the chiefs had come
thousands of miles to execute a masterstroke of their own: through a
series of speeches and appearances, they hoped to make it politically
untenable for Joseph Chamberlain, the all-powerful colonial secretary,
to underwrite Rhodes's plan.

51

The British press, who knew the value of an underdog when they saw one, dubbed the Africans the 'Three Kings', but the public relations drive had been set in motion by the chiefs themselves. Intuiting that the history of their country would hinge on the outcome of their endeavours, they commissioned a press cuttings agency in London to scan the newspapers for all references to their trip. The resulting narrative, as with everything Africans did in those days, would otherwise have been told in footnotes – instead, it became the founding-cum-liberation story of a unique African nation, a riff on colonial themes played in an extraordinary key.[1]

After all, when the Three Kings were trying to win the sympathies of Secretary Chamberlain, Rhodes was in the process of turning the bulk of southern Africa into a personal fiefdom.[2] In the last years of the nineteenth century he was strong-arming the British government into granting him a royal charter for the British South Africa Company, a front for a federated colony he hoped would stretch from the Indian Ocean to the Atlantic. With the Zambezi River as an initial border in the north, Rhodes's company proposed to annex the swathes of land the Three Kings called home.

'All that Red, that's my dream.' In six syllables, Rhodes had conjured up an Africa united under the British flag, a proto-African Union that served first his own interests and second, as an unavoidable condition, his queen's. With an ambition to match his ego, and the facility and cruelty to match both, Rhodes admitted he would 'annex the planets' if he could. The region belonging to the Tswana was critical to his project. 'I look upon the Bechuanaland territory as the Suez Canal of trade of this country,' said Rhodes[3] – by 'country' implying open space, of course, not the sovereign terrain of local chiefs.

For us, heading into Botswana in early 2011, it was a story that suggested a continuum, a clear line from the country's beginnings to its contemporary status as an African anomaly. Throughout the previous decade, we knew, Botswana had posted GDP per capita figures that were often richer than those of Mauritius and almost always ahead of South Africa's.[4] With a currency, the pula, stronger than the South African rand, 'economic freedom' scores well above the sub-Saharan

African average, an independent judiciary that unfailingly protected property rights, and Africa's highest sovereign debt rating, it had become, in the decades since independence, a bastion of effective African governance.

But hiding under all that good news was *our* story – beneath a new dam on Botswana's eastern border, a dam that promised to address the country's near-catastrophic water shortages, lay the latest existential threat. We had come to see whether the current president, Ian Khama, would be as effective at outwitting the future as his great-grandfather had once been.

◆

Many things made Botswana worth saving from Rhodes, but there is one thing that history has deemed the most important. The Three Kings presided over a centralised, relatively pluralist political system that balanced royal power against the will of the people.[5] Anthropologists have spilled much ink analysing the Tswana *kgotla,* a tribal council where anyone could speak and where chiefs were often overruled by reasoned argument, but superstar economists Daron Acemoglu and James A Robinson would, in their bestselling *Why Nations Fail: The Origins of Power, Prosperity and Poverty*, be the first to decode the significance of this for a global audience.

From as early as 2001, the US-based economists had been trying to unravel the Botswana conundrum: why, they asked, in a paper published by the Massachusetts Institute of Technology in July of that year, did the nation post the highest rate of per-capita growth of *any country in the world* over the previous 35-year period? While Acemoglu and Robinson were preparing the groundwork for this paper, *The Economist* magazine had just published its infamous 'The Hopeless Continent' cover story, and the pair's Afro-pessimism was as statistically defensible as it was mainstream. Despite some success stories in the 1960s and early 1970s, they wrote, Africa was poor and getting poorer, with an average growth rate that had been negative since 1965, and a 35-fold difference between the typical sub-Saharan country and the per-capita income of the United States.[6] Botswana, in other words, was an outlier.

Eleven years later, shortly after *The Economist* had released its equally consensus-defining 'Africa Rising' cover, not only had the continent's average rates of growth broken through the negative, they'd surged to amongst the highest on earth. Acemoglu and Robinson now found themselves in an Afro-pessimist camp that had been separated from its most convincing data. In *Why Nations Fail*, they would nonetheless insist that the Industrial Revolution had *still* not spread to Africa, and that countries like Zimbabwe and Sierra Leone had remained stuck in 'a long vicious circle ... of extractive political and economic institutions.'[7] Botswana, in other words, had endured as the African exception.

Kgosi ke kgosi ka marafe, the Tswana once said: the king is king by the grace of the people – for Acemoglu and Robinson, this pre-colonial proverb would lay the foundations for Botswana's postcolonial success. In their view, inclusive political institutions like the *kgotla* had always bred inclusive economic institutions, and while slavery and colonialism had mostly destroyed such institutions in the rest of Africa, the Tswana had managed to retain the imprint of traditional governance into independence and beyond. Other African societies may once have had similar philosophies, the economists would note, but none had ever demonstrated the guile – or boasted the luck – of the Three Kings.

As Khama, Bathoen and Sebele trail-blazed across the English provinces, the guile was on full display. The Three Kings addressed audiences from Southampton to Yorkshire, speaking at everything from church services to cake sales. At first, since the trade was associated with the British South Africa Company, they spoke about the evils of liquor, and thus won the sympathies of England's temperance groups. Then they appealed to British paternalism, stressing Queen Victoria's benevolence over the rapacious character of Rhodes. Most astutely, they brought their oratorical skills to the Midlands, Joseph Chamberlain's political base.

But their luck, in the end, came gift-wrapped courtesy of the enemy himself. While the Three Kings were in Britain winning the support of the public, Rhodes was in Africa lending his support to Dr

Leander Starr Jameson, the administrator of Rhodesia, and the muse for Rudyard Kipling's ode to imperial manliness, *If.* On 29 December 1895, Dr Jameson led 500 troops from Pitsane in Bechuanaland deep into the Transvaal, and met a blaze of Boer rifle fire. The raid, which went ahead without Chamberlain's blessing, would prove a disaster for Queen Victoria and a historical hinge for the wider world – it would swing southern Africa toward the Second Boer War, and Europe toward the horrors of 1914.

In effect, the Chamberlain Settlement, signed between the Crown and the Three Kings in 1896, guaranteed the Tswana their land, insofar as a colonial agreement could be said to guarantee anything. Should Rhodes never have endorsed the Jameson Raid, there's no telling what he would have accomplished in the north. Might he have built that great railroad from Cape Town to Cairo? Might the British South Africa Company have been able to acquire assets deeper into the central interior? The questions are moot, because the raid kicked off the company's 30-year slide into obsolescence,[8] the railway was never to be, and the British protectorate of Bechuanaland was fiddled with as gently as any Batswana could have hoped.

The Three Kings and their successors were spared the worst ravages of colonialism. With the arrival of independence in 1966, the Republic of Botswana may have been one of the poorest countries in the world, but it had in place a system of governance that made development both a possibility and an imperative.

◆

To achieve *real* development, of course – which is to say, to raise the living standards of not just the elite but of the majority of Botswana's people – the situation now called for a lot more guile than luck. And perhaps the new country created all the luck it needed when it chose Seretse Khama, a man whose leadership philosophy was the very essence of economic inclusiveness, as its first prime minister.

Born in Serowe in 1921, this grandson of the fabled King Khama became *kgosi* of the Bamangwato at four years old, having kept the

title thanks to the collective authority of the *kgotla*. In 1949, the council had saved him when he'd returned from a term at the University
of Oxford with a white British wife. The young Seretse's uncle,
Tshekedi Khama, had demanded that he either divorce Ruth Williams
or renounce his chieftainship, but 'the grace of the people' had prevailed. Later in 1949, however, the British government, under pressure from a scandalised apartheid South Africa, would ban Seretse
and Ruth Khama from the Bechuanaland protectorate; a sympathetic
British cabinet minister would only lift the ban in 1956.[9] In 1961, as an
African nationalist politician and qualified English barrister,[10] Seretse
Khama was considering how best to apply the principles of the *kgotla*
to the modern world.[11]

After his Bechuanaland Democratic Party – later the Botswana
Democratic Party, or BDP – won legislative elections in 1965, Prime
Minister Khama ratified the Chieftaincy Act, which diminished the
power of the chiefs in favour of the authority of the central state. As
president, a title he assumed after independence in 1966, he further
unified the country with legislation that made English the sole official language, and the only one to be taught alongside Setswana in
schools.[12] Clearly, with a given name that meant 'the clay that binds
together', Seretse Khama was not always going to bow to the *kgotla*
tradition of pluralism. In this, his task was to balance the old customs
against a responsive and clear-eyed pragmatism.

The wider BDP made this something of a mantra, and its effects were
felt most keenly by the industries that would serve as the drivers of
Botswana's growth. While land was communally held in Bechuanaland,
cattle were considered both private property and individual units of
wealth. With the establishment of the Botswana Meat Commission in
1967, the government created a central agency for the slaughtering
and marketing of beef – acting in the primary interest of the country's citizens, many of whom were cattle owners, the commission set
prices, controlled bovine diseases like foot-and-mouth, and developed
a genuine export economy.

But diamonds were the real test. Western economists have long the-
orised that its abundant natural resources have served as Africa's most

intractable curse; if this theory were universally applicable, the prospecting of the Orapa diamond fields in 1967 should have spelt the end of Botswana's flirtation with inclusive development. Instead, in one of African liberation's almighty ironies, the discovery signalled a new phase. The BDP government partnered with the diamond monopoly that Rhodes had founded in Kimberley, and rather than pummel the country back into the Stone Age, the venture would secure it a place on the World Bank list of middle-income states.

How this had come to be was, again, a function of the character of President Khama. During the colonial era the Tswana chiefs had used every means at their disposal to block mineral prospecting.[13] Events in South Africa and Rhodesia had made it plain to them that, for their own people at least, a 'big find' in Bechuanaland could not end well. No doubt, had Rhodes known that one of the world's largest diamond deposits lay beneath the Bamangwato's ancestral lands, he would have pushed a lot harder to bring the protectorate under the control of the British South Africa Company – and Joseph Chamberlain, armed with the same knowledge, might just have given it to him. As it turned out, mere months before two massive kimberlite pipes were found at Orapa, President Khama had initiated a change in the law that removed all subsoil mineral rights from the tribe and vested them in the nation. While Blood Diamonds became synonymous with countries like Zimbabwe and Sierra Leone, where the political elites would mimic the rent-seeking policies of the colonisers, in Botswana the traditional institutions had remained inclusive, intact and inviolable.[14] Meaning, when geologists confirmed the existence of unimaginable stores of wealth beneath his tribe's home soil, that it would have been borderline treasonous for Khama to reinstate the original law.

To nationalise or not to nationalise? This was Khama's *only* question following the discovery. For the dozens of liberation movements that were handed the keys to colonial mineshafts and oil fields, the question implied an ideological conflict as stark as it was oversimplified – privatised extraction in a liberalised economy versus state-controlled extraction in a closed economy. The BDP, true to its outlier nature, dealt with the issue via the execution of a deft sidestep: it entered into a 50-50 joint venture with De Beers, calling the company Debswana. By the 1980s, when Quett Masire had taken over the presidential reins, the diamond, copper and manganese mines operated by Debswana were accounting for half of Botswana's GDP.[15] Although a steadily diversifying economy had since dropped that percentage closer to a third, it was in large part thanks to the joint venture that an income of $80 per capita at independence had reached almost $7 000 by 2008.[16]

◆

Then came 2009. In that fateful year, Botswana posted the sharpest GDP decline of any nation in Africa,[17] a painful reminder to the government that it hadn't diversified the economy nearly as fast as it should have – the Western financial crisis arrived to show the ruling party that, for all its efforts, it was still relying too heavily on a single luxury export. And so the new national development plan, when it was unveiled before parliament in July of 2009, reflected a panic where previously there'd been calm.

Not that NDP 10, as it was termed, veered that much in substance from NDP 9 or NDP 8, or any of the earlier national development plans stretching back to the Seretse Khama era. The party, after all, had been channelling its diamond revenues into public services for more than four decades already. Aside from education and healthcare, infrastructure spend – with its innate ability to boost employment and stimulate growth – had always been at the core of the strategy. As party officials liked to boast, a paved road network of 12 kilometres at independence had been extended to almost 8 000 kilometres by 2008.

No, if NDP 10 *was* different, it wasn't in substance but in emphasis. Due to the unforeseen reduction in the amount of available capital, the government felt compelled to announce at the plan's launch that while some of the minor projects had been shelved, the major ones were going ahead. 'We are ... not going to abandon poverty alleviation projects and public works which are labour-intensive,' promised Dr Taufila Nyamadzabo, the acting permanent secretary at the Ministry of Finance.[18] When the good doctor then proceeded to outline the projects that had been kept on the books, it would have been apparent to most of those listening that the contractors were almost all Chinese – how, some might have asked themselves, did that count as *labour intensive*?

And yet behind the cultural tensions brought on by the Sino-African encounter there was a challenge way more symbolic and sweeping: if, as claimed by the Afro-pessimists, the continent's rampant period of modern growth had simply been mirroring the upward curve in commodity prices, what would happen when the wave crested and started to fall? Could the region implement the sorts of economic changes needed to sustain the growth when the downturn arrived?[19]

On this score, there could be no better benchmark than Botswana. Because, although it was impossible in early 2011 to predict when global commodity prices would peak, in Botswana the end of the boom times had been dated, documented and confirmed. Following a brief spike in output that was expected off a new plant at Jwaneng, Debswana and the IMF had forecast total depletion of the country's diamond reserves by 2029.[20]

In the interim, the BDP would be taking a large dose of its inspiration from China. Growth through infrastructure was a major focus of NDP 10.[21] Lieutenant General Seretse Khama Ian Khama – great-grandson of King Khama, son of Sir Seretse Khama, paramount chief of the Bamangwato – had made this much clear in his introduction to the plan. As president of the Republic of Botswana, an office he'd assumed in 2008, this latest scion of the 'Botswana Kennedys' had implemented what he'd called *Vision 2016: Towards Prosperity for All.*[22] Where the first Khama had run the almost impossible gauntlet of colonialism, where the second Khama had jumped the hurdles of independence and the resource curse, this third Khama would attempt to reach the promised land of a self-sustaining middle class. Like Franklin Delano Roosevelt had done with the New Deal and the Hoover Dam, like Deng Xiaoping, Jiang Zemin and Hu Jintao had done with the Three Gorges Dam, Ian Khama would be looking to large public projects to fuel his economic quest.

Except for one thing – Botswana's skills deficit had meant that the know-how would need to be imported. How could President Khama apply Vision 2016 in a globalised world? How could he keep his political inheritance 'inclusive' when he'd invited in the dragons of Beijing?

Model of the Three Gorges Dam, Chongqing, PRC

DAMMING UTOPIA

The site lay 55 kilometres northeast of the mining town of Selebi Phikwe, through the village of Mmadinare, along a graded ochre track that bumped up and over a series of koppies. Following a right turn at a deserted T-junction, it announced itself with a billboard. The illustration, framed against the empty bush and wide-open sky, depicted a hybrid dam, launch pad and dry dock, all laid out to accommodate

60

vehicles from some ecstatic future. We were, we believed, looking at a Utopianist's rendition of Sinohydro's signature development, the Three Gorges Dam on the Yangtze.

'Keep truthful and faithful,' read the text. 'Create the best.'

The Chinese compound was boomed and gated, three corporate flags raised high above the billboard and an elevated wall. As we were taking notes the gate slid open; a security officer saluted, a Landcruiser tore off west. We continued east, towards a second compound, where the project's engineering consultants had made their base. Here, although the unguarded entrance spoke of a company more at home on the continent, the relaxed atmosphere only went so far.

'I can be quoted,' said our contact, 'but I cannot be quoted by name.'

The son of a British policeman who'd operated in Kenya during the Mau Mau rebellion, this man, with his moustache and his ruddy knees, considered himself a Zimbabwean. He was born in England, he said, and left after school for Swaziland, where he received training as a technician. Now a senior engineer in his mid-fifties, he'd worked on dam construction projects across southern Africa, and had a residence permit from the government of Botswana for the duration of this particular job.

'Difficult,' he said, in answer to our question about his working relationship with the Chinese. 'Difficult insofar as they have not sent their most capable people as foremen.'

Hence his reluctance to allow us to use his name – although the name of his employer, he conceded, was no secret. Headquartered in Gaborone, the engineering firm of Bergstan Africa was incorporated in Cape Town in 1954. Its principals, we would learn, made the decision to venture north in the mid-1990s, when white South African companies were no longer treated as vassals of a pariah state. Aside from Botswana and South Africa, Bergstan Africa had since claimed the completion of major contracts in Angola, Namibia, Nigeria, Malawi, Mauritius, Mozambique, Seychelles, Tanzania and Uganda.

'Well, I can get on this computer and do a beautiful drawing,' said the engineer, 'but if I want to put it into position on the ground, I'll need a third party to come in and help me. This would be an artisan type, under the direction of a foreman.'

Sinohydro, he told us, had a policy of sending its most junior recruits to Africa. The continent was treated as a training ground, he added, where mistakes were cheap and skills could be gained on site.

That may or may not have been the case. Either way the claim did not augur well for one of the key allegations we had come here to test – the assumption, widespread and vehemently argued, that China's infrastructure projects in Africa were built for quick profit at the expense of lasting quality. While our Namibian trip had already given us some insight into the reasons Chinese construction firms were able to tender below competitors on price,[23] it was beyond reckless to assume that the practices of those companies were representative of Beijing's policy in Africa at large. The Sinohydro Corporation, on the other hand, the world's largest hydropower firm and one-time employer of then-president Hu Jintao, was about as representative as it was possible to get.

As of 31 December 2010, according to *China Daily*, Sinohydro was working on 261 projects in 55 countries across the globe;[24] in October of that year, China Radio International had pegged the sub-total of African countries at 21.[25] In revenue terms, of the $4 billion the corporation had generated off overseas projects in 2010, Africa was said to account for over 40 per cent.[26] But what was of equal importance to us was that Sinohydro, as a leading state-owned enterprise, was subject to the rules and regulations of the assets supervision commission of the State Council, the chief administrative authority of the People's Republic – its actions could be seen as an embodiment of the attitude to Africa of the Chinese Communist Party itself.

◆

In late January 2011, the Dikgatlhong Dam was the single largest civil engineering project under construction in Botswana. The $153 million development would take 47 months to complete, and all was on schedule at the time of our arrival in month 35. When operational, Dikgatlhong would be Botswana's primary dam, with a capacity of 400 million cubic metres and a 74-kilometre pipeline feeding into the country's north-south carrier scheme. Environmental and archaeological consultants had delivered detailed impact assessments, and the Botswana government had paid the villagers of Polometsi and Matopi a total of $96 000 for relocation, plus a further $179 000 for exhumation and reburial of their dead.

These last facts, along with the engineer's statement before we left for a tour of the site that hard-hats were mandatory – 'we've got strict safety standards,' he said – led us to believe that we were in a very different world from the one we'd encountered in Namibia. And yet, as soon as we were inside his four-by-four, he was lamenting the effect of the Chinese work ethic on local labour.

'I mean, 20 years ago, you had a lot of Portuguese and Italian artisans in all of these countries. Particularly in Zimbabwe, we did. Those guys, they *lived* for their work. And those people working underneath them? They actually emulated that level of work. Whereas now ...'

We caught each other's eyes in the rear-view mirror, and duly rolled them. This was the sort of room-temperature racism that we were accustomed to hearing in Johannesburg's leafy enclaves. The engineer veered naturally from nostalgia to outrage. 'Those cattle are not supposed to be there!' he shouted, as the four-by-four rounded a corner. We honked our way through the herd, reminded that in rural Botswana the proliferation of these beasts presented a more endemic environmental problem – one that not even the government seemed willing to solve.[27] We then came to a stop on the dam wall.

The edifice rose in a concave half-moon from the valley floor, its highway-wide rim offering a panorama across rolling expanses of veld. At 4.6 kilometres in length and 42 metres high, it was a structure that could not fail to impress. We made no attempt to hide our awe, and asked for five minutes to walk up a bit further and look. 'That's Zimbabwe you were looking at,' said the engineer when we returned. The dam was located at the confluence of the Shashe and Tati rivers, he explained, trapping the flow before it spilled over the border.

More figures for us to scratch in our notebooks: the dam wall weighed 8 million tons; from the time of impounding, the basin would take four years to fill. But then it was back to his bugbear. 'Roughly 140 locals and a 140 Chinese have worked until now on construction. The

Chinese have been trying to cut costs, and they're not really employing. For instance, the locals will operate the graders and stuff unless it's a paid weekend, in which case the Chinese will drive the graders.'

So when a young Chinese man came over, his hand extended in greeting and a smile on his face, we were fully prepared for the show. In fluent English, a discussion about the coating of the dam wall ensued; the atmosphere was haltingly collegial, the dialogue peppered with signifiers of faux respect.

'This is Mr Chung,' said the engineer, turning to introduce us, 'he is one of the translators on the site.' We had already been told that it was men such as Mr Chung who acted as the 'narrow gate of communication' between Bergstan Africa, Sinohydro and the local labourers – a piece of knowledge that, like a playbook, served to enliven the drama.

'I work from seven in the morning to five-thirty every day,' said Mr Chung, taking his cue from the engineer that it was safe to talk. 'On Christmas I have the day off. I go to the rhino sanctuary.'

The echoes of Tony from the market project in Oshakati continued to resonate – in his spare time, Mr Chung watched TV, perfected his English, played table tennis. As a junior, he was allowed three weeks of leave every 14 months.

'What are you doing tomorrow?' one of us asked.

'Same as I did yesterday,' he said. 'Same as I do every day.'

◆

Later, as we were standing above an enormous quarry, watching earthmoving trucks emblazoned with Mandarin characters redistributing Botswana's boulders, three Sinohydro employees approached our Zimbabwean engineer. Through Mr Chung, who had joined us on the tour, they asked his opinion on the viscosity of a concrete mix. 'We'll work it out,' said the engineer. 'Tonight I'll stay awake thinking about it.'

The sarcasm didn't translate. 'See, they don't do humour,' the engineer explained as the men were walking away. Back in the four-by-four, he expanded on his *weltschmerz*. We were told that five weeks prior to our visit, in mid-December 2010, a spontaneous demonstration by local workers had erupted outside the Chinese compound. A brick had been thrown over the wall, injuring a Chinese worker. 'They put him on the next flight home. We haven't seen him since.'

It was an incident about which Bergstan Africa's principal engineer on the project, Boikanyo Mpho, preferred not to comment. And while we had already gleaned from the Zimbabwean that the demonstration had been the result of a labour dispute – a consequence of a rift in expectations involving work hours and pay – at least now we were speaking to a citizen of Botswana, a man more interested in the context than the conflict.

'I think what my observation has been is that, you know, you're dealing with contractors who are bringing work ethics from their own country,' Mpho said. 'What we have realised is that the Chinese have an inability to adapt readily to local situations.'

Mpho occupied a chair at the head of a boardroom table strewn with blueprints, his stout frame and creased brow an apt correlative for the weight of his task. Dikgatlhong, he explained, was part of a large-scale initiative by the Botswana government to secure potable water for a country where the resource had always been scarce. The water strategy, as he termed it, fell within the broader infrastructure objectives of NDP 10. 'What use is a new airport and a big highway if you've got no water to drink?' is how he put it.[28] Mpho acknowledged that for the government to capitalise on its finite diamond revenues and meet the twenty-first century head-on, Dikgatlhong was a cornerstone, the most ambitious project in a sector that had contributed a full percentage point to GDP growth during NDP 9. In the period under review, he believed, the sector would contribute a lot more.[29]

As for the tender process, Mpho was adamant that Sinohydro were chosen according to the strictest of evaluation criteria. He went on to outline a system that sounded like the stuff of Kerry McNamara's Namibian dreams. In Botswana, he said, it was customary to re-tender at every stage of an infrastructure project, a rule that applied as much to Bergstan Africa as to the Chinese. He pointed out too that all Dikgatlhong contracts were bound by the terms of Fédération

Internationale des Ingénieurs-Conseils, a global association of consulting engineers set up to safeguard quality of service.

Mpho then paused, leaned forward on his elbows, and spoke of 'the thing that is not written'.

By way of clarification, he said: 'You have to develop it, nurture it, until you get to a point where you can trust one another. That happens anywhere. Now, I think initially we didn't trust them, they didn't trust us. But through intense interaction...'

For the first time, Mpho smiled. Progress had been made, he suggested. The project was moving towards – not away from – common understanding.

◆

Access to the Sinohydro compound was provided courtesy of Mpho's say-so, which in turn was an expression of his rank. The guard waved us through the gate into a scene that was not quite as ecstatic as the illustration on the billboard, but nodded to the future nonetheless: air-conditioned aluminium containers laid out in rows upon the African hillside; corporate logos and Mandarin insignia exhorting the faithful to create the best; the afternoon sun whipping the cicadas into an unending shriek.

Once inside the management offices, we saw that Sinohydro had further stamped its presence on calendars, posters and hard-hats. We were directed to the workspace of the commercial manager, a man who did not offer a business card and introduced himself only as 'Mr Xu'. Xu requested that we pack away our voice recorder, and we took it as a minor victory that he consented to our use of the notebooks.

In his mid-thirties, compact and well presented, Xu was born in the province of Henan, on the south bank of the Yellow River. He had a master's degree from a university in Jiangsu, and had been with Sinohydro almost 10 years. When he landed in Botswana, he said, he was afraid to shake hands with the locals. He knew that there was no possibility of contracting HIV by touch alone, but in his heart, he admitted, he had 'discrimination'.

It was a statement to which we would return – for the moment, Xu was more comfortable outlining for us his employer's commissions on the continent.

As of January 2011, he said, Sinohydro was active on five projects in Botswana, and had deployed to the country a total of 600 staff. The corporation's largest project in the country was the Dikgatlhong Dam, next was the new terminal at the Sir Seretse Khama International Airport in Gaborone, third the reboot of the 80-kilometre road from Francistown to the Zimbabwean border, fourth the rehabilitation of the 115-kilometre Kang-Hukuntsi road in the west, and last the Lotsane Dam in the east. Outside of Botswana, he mentioned projects in Ethiopia, Kenya and Sudan, the latter a dam 'two to three times the size' of Dikgatlhong.[30] 'To use the wrong word,' said Xu, 'we are *flooding* Africa.'[31]

Throughout the interview, Xu would stop at regular intervals to consult the electronic translator on his laptop. When we returned to his fear of HIV, a fear compounded by his awareness of the fact that Botswana had the second highest prevalence of the virus on the continent,[32] he first searched for and located the word 'epidemic', then 'intimacy'. He had come to accept, he said, that you are safe if you don't touch *those ladies*.

'We are coming from Asia,' Xu told us, 'here is Africa. It's the very beginning.' Next, his translator supplied him with the word 'heartbreak', which functioned as his assessment of the damage wrought by the cultural gap.

And yet while Xu agreed with Mpho's opinion that the project was moving in the direction of common understanding, his optimism dissolved when applied to the question of local labour.

'All the Africans are the same problem,' he said. 'They are lazy! They are not diligent like the Chinese. They don't want to work, but they want a better life. That is the conflict!'

We exchanged a quick look between us, a replica of the look we'd exchanged earlier, through the rear-view mirror of the Zimbabwean's truck. What the white engineer had made of Chinese work habits was being repeated in what this Chinese manager made of the work habits of the Africans. The way Sinohydro dealt with the issue, said Xu, was by granting bonuses for high work attendance. The African foremen were encouraged to manage the African workers, and if there was trouble, the Chinese blamed it on the foremen. But that didn't mean there was no give on the Chinese side, Xu said. The company had retained the services of a subcontractor to take care of 'entertainment'; the belief was that the provision of football tournaments would lessen the inclination of the locals to abuse drink and drugs.

Before we left his office, Xu told us with genuine feeling that he had recognised and overcome his prejudices. He compared the mainstream Chinese view of Africans with the mainstream American view of the Chinese. He looked up one last word on his translator, and struggled to enunciate it, until we realised that the word he had found was 'bias'.

'Yes, *bias*,' he said. 'That's what the Americans get off the Internet about the Chinese.'

KHAMA INC AND THE CHINESE STRAW MAN

Beneath the shade of a flamboyant tree outside the Selebi Phikwe district labour office, hundreds of men were playing trumps. Cards slapped onto overturned crates and boxes, the sound mingling with the players' low mutter. The sound, we were about to learn, of those waiting for what they knew would not come.

Our task that morning had been to track down the mayor of a town that had once promised an alternative to Botswana's reliance on diamonds, hear what His Worship Lekang Mokukumani thought about the dam that was being built to slake the region's thirst, and ascertain what plans he may have had to stem the municipality's decline. Our instincts had led us here, down streets where women walked the beat in the fitted blue skirts of the Botswana Police Service, trailing their hands through planters of daisies and hibiscus. For a town that was supposed to be on life support – the Selebi Phikwe Economic Diversification Unit, or SPEDU, had been launched as a last-gasp initiative in 2008[33] –

it hadn't at first *looked* to us like the place was breathing its last. On this payday in January, there were queues at all the banks, business was brisk at the formal and informal stores, and it could even be said that the public spaces were pretty. But then we'd rounded a corner, and Selebi Phikwe had revealed a different truth.

The town's double-barrelled name was an amalgam of the two tiny villages that had existed in the area before nickel and copper were discovered in 1963. Its main driver of growth had for decades been Bamangwato Concessions Limited, formed by Tshekedi Khama and the British when Seretse Khama was still in exile in the mid-1950s. In the early years, with nickel and copper prices stable, BCL built amenities, offered generous pensions, did everything it could to create a virtuous circle of development. Then, in the late 1970s, the international market for these commodities crashed, showing the BDP government what the universe beyond diamonds – where prices were controlled by its partner De Beers – could do to the most inclusive of its plans. As global demand fluctuated so too did the town's fortunes, until one day BCL learnt that it had something in common with Debswana after all: its product was not literally 'forever'. The landscape-dominating smelter, in operation since 1973, had by the new millennium become Selebi Phikwe's sole reason for existence – once the opencast pit had been mothballed and it had dawned on geologists that the underground shafts weren't going to yield limitless supplies of ore, the company had been forced to change tack. Ore was railed in by steam-train from elsewhere, and the services of the Australian mining giant Xstrata were contracted, in order to increase the efficiency and output of the plant. According to BCL, which had remained 94 per cent owned by the BDP government, 4 200 people would be kept on the payroll come 2011, making it 'the largest employer in Botswana based in one town'.[34]

A PR line, it would later occur to us, written by a master of political spin. Because, although Selebi Phikwe's population had stayed constant at around 50 000 since 2001, the town had never been where BCL's responsibilities had ended. Since inception, the company's employment footprint had encompassed the broader region, which included the dust-blown towns of Bobirwa and Mmadinare, a district that made up 153 353 people as per the 2001 census, or 8 per cent of Botswana's total population.[35]

As the most immediate reflection of the government's failure to service this population, the jobless had taken to gathering every weekday at the labour office, where they would settle beneath the trees for eight straight hours of cards. And it was under one such tree, a group of men having suspended their game at our first question, that we found ourselves talking about Dikgatlhong.

'They said when they come to build this dam, that there will be jobs and jobs,' said a young man named Gosego. 'Now we can see that there are 1 000 Chinese working there, and no one from *this* place.'

'Well,' we responded, 'we've been to the dam, and the managers told us that there are as many Batswana working as Chinese. They can prove this.'

The men all shook their heads. 'It is not like that,' said Gosego. He informed us that he'd been born in Mmadinare, and that at age 21 he came here every morning, waiting to pick up an employment slip from a box.[36] Once, his father had also travelled to Selebi Phikwe every morning, he said, but *he* had come to work the mines; when Gosego was a boy, he believed he'd do the same. Now all he could think about was moving to Johannesburg. Despite the heat, we noticed that Gosego was wearing blue coveralls over a knitted sweater. 'You can see here that I'm ready for work,' he explained. 'But where is the work?'

An older man named Tshepo chimed in. 'The treatment there is not good. It is as if the blacks are not human. There are sleeping too many in a room. This is why there is trouble.'

We were reminded of something Mr Xu had told us, that 'the blacks want single rooms', but that such demands could not be made by ordinary labourers, that only senior staff got single rooms.

'The unions?' continued Tshepo. 'Where are they? All we do is piecework here. The mine is dead. The smelter is dead. What is there for us here? And now with these Chinese. They take the work and they do nothing for us.'

◆

Some of this wasn't properly true, and we suspected Tshepo knew it. Employment at the smelter had remained steady, even if jobs weren't that easy to come by. And while the recent closure of a string of local textile firms could have been *indirectly* linked to cheap imports from China,[37] it wasn't fair to heap Selebi Phikwe's woes on Beijing. That morning, before leaving our lodge, we'd scrolled through an authoritative report by the South African Institute of International Affairs, entitled *China's Role in Infrastructure Development in Botswana.* Among the sentences we'd highlighted was one that stated, 'the overall benefits of Chinese engagement ... have been to substantially lower the costs of infrastructure projects and create new employment opportunities for the local people'.[38]

As the report also observed, Chinese involvement in Botswana's infrastructure sector dated back to 1985, when the China Civil Engineering Construction Company had arrived with aid money in hand, all set to rehabilitate the country's railroad. The project, eventually completed in 2001, had been locally interpreted as the Chinese buying their way into the sector with a high-profile freebie. As a raft of Chinese companies had followed CCECC into Botswana, so had their collective reputation among ordinary citizens worsened, until the unemployment problem – averaged out at about 18 per cent from 1991 to 2010[39] – had come to be seen as partly their fault. Addressing this misperception, Counsellor Gong of the Chinese embassy had provided SAIIA researchers with documentation to the effect that 5 270 locals were on the payroll of Chinese-owned firms in 2009, against a total of 900 expat Chinese.[40]

According to the embassy, 16 state-owned enterprises had been at work in Botswana in 2009, 13 of which were big construction companies like Sinohydro, along with another 10 to 20 firms 'run by overseas Chinese'. Many had benefited by borrowing cheaply from Chinese policy banks – they were essentially *subsidised* to enter the southern African infrastructure market. But in Botswana's highly regulated environment, where (unlike Namibia) regulations were for the most part enforced, bids had to be detailed and comprehensive, as per the rules of the Public Procurement and Asset Disposal Board, an independent authority that had been set up in 2002 to deal with the increasingly complex nature of tenders.

Further, the SAIIA report confirmed that Chinese SOEs, irrespective of their status as wards of Beijing, had *not* been operating in a Shangri-La of mutual back-slapping – they'd been locked in a state of brutal rivalry. After concessional loans had been successfully negotiated between China and the host country, the Chinese ministry of commerce would hold its own tender process, in which SOEs would be invited to submit competing bids.[41] In the context of road building in rural Botswana, where logistical headaches were practically guaranteed by the vast distances, Chinese firms could have been forgiven for thinking they were damned if they did and damned if they didn't. They needed to win bids in order to justify their existence, but the competition had been shaving margins down to the bone.

Most of these SOEs had structured their budgets for a 10-15 per cent profit margin, whereas South African and European companies wouldn't tolerate anything less than 30 per cent. Mr Xu at Dikgatlhong had been earning in the region of $700 a month; an American in his position would take home closer to $10 000.[42] As our engineering contact at the Dikgatlhong Dam had noted, this tended to result in work that was 'just scraping through' – a state of affairs that, if anything, he'd *under*emphasised when it came to the Chinese in Africa. In such a context, cheap would almost always outweigh qualitative considerations.

Yet working out of Botswana had proved so successful, at least in terms Chinese SOEs had been defining as success, that the Gaborone offices of companies like CSCEC had morphed into launching pads for projects in North and South America, where the construction megalith had won bids worth hundreds of millions of dollars.[43] This, as we were now witnessing in eastern Botswana, was globalisation in its latest guise: Selebi Phikwe was merely a thread in an intricate tapestry of infrastructure financing and development that stretched from the borderlands of the Kalahari to the Ecuadorian Amazon, from the Sudanese Nile to the banks of the Yangtze. Needless to say, there could be little comfort in such tales for Gosego and Tshepo, who were still firmly attached to the notion that the Chinese were at the root of their misfortunes.

'Put on your paper there,' said Tshepo, nodding at our notebooks, 'that the Chinese must go. The government must take the control, and kick them. Or we will kick the government.'

Kgosi ke kgosi ka marafe, the king is king by the grace of the people. Indeed, the Sandhurst-educated President Khama, who'd taken office by automatic succession in April 2008 and had earned a popular mandate a year later, appeared keenly aware of the anger of the unemployed – if anything, addressing it had been the crux of *Vision 2016: Towards Prosperity for All*. Still, on assuming the presidency, Khama had been accused of not only enhancing the power of the central state, but of consolidating power around his old army cronies, his family, and ultimately himself. Khama's cousin, the former brigadier-general Ramadeluka Seretse, had temporarily resigned after a $100 million corruption charge had been brought against him in 2010, only to take back the reins at the all-important Ministry of Defence, Justice and Security in 2011.[44] There was also Sheila Khama, the president's aunt, a former chief executive of De Beers Botswana, who had remained a non-executive director on a range of mining group boards; Dale ter Haar, the president's nephew, who was general manager of CIC Energy, a company involved in the planning of a giant coal-mining operation north of Gaborone; and Johan ter Haar, the president's ex-brother-in-law, who chaired the Business and Economic Advisory Council, the government outfit in charge of economic diversification.[45]

'Yes,' said Gosego, 'everywhere there is a big soldier to run this, and a cousin to run that.'

Like the rest of the Botswana electorate, Gosego and Tshepo had grasped the significance of the fact that in March 2010 the BDP had experienced its first-ever leadership split. This, they claimed, was a direct result of the party's transformation into what disgruntled members were calling 'Khama Inc'.[46] But would they, as part of the vast jobless class, bring such knowledge to the ballot? Come the 2014 elections, would Gosego and Tshepo exercise their rights and vote for this new breakaway faction, the Botswana Movement for Democracy? The answer, they told us, wasn't yet clear.

An hour later, over cups of tea in the mayoral office, His Worship Lekang Mokukumani stared at us vacantly. For the most part, Botswana's bureaucrats seemed to cultivate a studied rudeness; His Worship used a secondary tactic: devastating blandness.

'What is to say about the dam?' offered the mayor. 'Soon it will be built.'

'But how will this influence the employment picture here?'

The mayor shrugged. If he understood the threat that those hundreds of card players outside the labour office posed to his own political skin, he wasn't letting on. Neither was he saying anything about the recent violence at the Dikgatlhong Dam, which may or may not have been an admission that all of this Sinophobia was – for a local BDP man – strangely convenient. We drank our tea in uncomfortable silence.

FROM AN AFRICAN BUSH LODGE TO THE GLORY OF CHONGQING

The eventual closure of the BCL mine and smelter, long accepted by the BDP government as a *fait accompli*, had since the mid-2000s inflected the plans for the survival of the Selebi Phikwe district with a distinct sense of urgency. After the formation of the Selebi Phikwe Economic Diversification Unit in 2008, a number of feasibility studies had been commissioned: the industries earmarked as potential saviours had run the gamut from agriculture and heavy engineering to tourism and leisure. The Letsibogo Tourism Study, for one, had announced that there was a 'prima facie case' for the town becoming a stopover point on a well-travelled route to the wildlife parks in the north, with the Letsibogo Dam and soon-to-be-built Dikgatlhong Dam serving as major attractions. Given that the mayor had refused to provide us with an update on any of these identified opportunities, we thought we would ask some locals who could.

'No, man,' said Darren. 'They told us that when they put in the

Letsibogo Dam, there would be some recreational facilities, so we could dock boats, and *braai* and *kak*. But of course, nothing happened.'

There were four of us sitting around a table in the lush gardens of the Phokoje Bush Lodge, peacock and guinea fowl screeching through some unfathomable avian war. Darren, a pilot and private *bureau de change* bagman, had been invited to join us by Savvas, the 30-year-old proprietor of the lodge.

The whites of Selebi Phikwe, once 5 000 strong, now numbered 600 or so. When the opencast mine had been at full production, 'SP', as it was known, was in its heyday. The country club had boasted squash and bowling and cricket and any number of sporting activities meant to fill out the long lazy afternoons. BCL and its government shareholders had needed the skills brought by these expat South Africans and Europeans, and so the community had been left alone to soak up the sun, to swim in their pools. But in midsummer 2011 it was mostly the less demanding Chinese who'd been contracted to address the region's skills deficit, while the town's remaining whites were forced to eke out an existence on the margins.

Darren had arrived with a stack of dollars, all of which we would need in a newly 'dollarised' Zimbabwe, our next stop. He seldom flew any more, he told us, and what he really liked to do was put his feet up on a piece of land he owned about an hour north. Savvas, a second-generation Cypriot, had inherited the Phokoje property from his father, who'd arrived in 1973 and had promptly secured a 50-year lease. As the new proprietor, Savvas now lived here with his wife and young son, and ran what was widely regarded as the finest restaurant in the district.

'Hell, you're getting fat, boy,' said Darren, poking a roll of his friend's flab with the butt of his beer bottle.

'Fuggof, man,' said Savvas, squirming.

The Letsibogo Dam, completed in 1998 under the supervision of the London-headquartered firm Arup – which had won global fame off its structural design for the Sydney Opera House – had been the government's first major initiative to supply potable water to the region, yet had clearly proved a disappointment to Darren and his coterie. '*Ag*, so another big fukken swimming pool we can't even swim in,' was his considered view of the new one. 'Just spending money, lining their pockets.'

'You don't think,' we responded, 'that without drinking water, things might get a little tense in Botswana?'

'*Ja*, maybe. Maybe. It's hard to say what they're doing.'

But it wasn't as though Gaborone had done all that much to explain the government's infrastructure strategy – *pace* Selebi Phikwe's mayor, this was not a country of communicators. And what had been true for Letsibogo was true for Dikgatlhong. Hardly any of the locals seemed aware that Botswana's 2004 Millennium Development Goals had identified water scarcity as one of the key issues likely to constrain economic growth,[47] or that aside from potable water, the new dam was meant to address the unprecedented industrial demand coming from the mines around Francistown. Neither was there much appreciation for the fact that the mooted Mmamabula coal-fired power station, which was being driven by the president's nephew at CIC Energy, would effectively be 'dead in the water' without the cooling resources provided by Dikgatlhong. Granted, the wording of NDP 10 was dull to the point of turgid, but if the sons of Selebi Phikwe had bothered to read the document they would have noted that Botswana's coal reserves were estimated at a staggering 212 billion tons, and that Mmamabula was being developed with the export of energy to South Africa in mind.[48]

Of course, in light of the death throes at BCL, Selebi Phikwe's residents had begun to understand that Botswana, to survive the end of its resource boom, needed to transform itself into something else entirely. Thanks to a media narrative that was by then firmly mainstream, it wasn't news to the likes of Darren or Savvas or Gosego that Chinese firms were actually *building things* in Africa, and that African governments, whatever the benefits to the individual pockets of the elite, needed things built.

In early 2013, during a trip to China that would take us to the Three Gorges Dam, we would witness the thinking behind this hunger for infrastructure up close.

◆

The Municipality of Chongqing, population 32 million, had been known for a time as the 'Invisible City', less for the fog that enveloped it than for its reputation as a bumpkin stronghold. But the backcountry anonymity had disappeared in 2011, when Bo Xilai, the princeling assigned the task of dragging the city into the twenty-first century, had fallen foul of the Politburo due to his radical Mao revivalism and the wealth he'd accumulated over the course of a controversial career. When it appeared that Bo's wife had poisoned a British national named Neil Heywood because of a business deal gone sour, the debacle had exploded on front pages and web pages and, more troublingly, on the Chinese micro-blogging site Weibo.

Yet long before the famous scion had arrived on the banks of the Yangtze, Chongqing's destiny had been etched out on a drawing board in Beijing. The municipality, it was determined, would function as an intake system for a development programme of colossal proportions. The Three Gorges Dam was set to flush 1.3 million people from their homes over a 14-year period – a plan that dovetailed with a national urbanisation policy that would move the equivalent of the population of the United States from fields into cities.

To environmentally conscious outsiders, and certainly to many of the peasant farmers who were forced off their lands, the Three Gorges Dam came to represent everything that was inhuman about the CCP's relentless focus on growth: lives as widgets; GDP as godhead; concrete above all. The party faithful, for whom the project represented a glorious future, came to see things differently: for them, the dam was the ultimate expression of Chairman Mao's dictum that 'man must conquer nature'. Although Western technology had been employed in the early years, with companies like ABB, Siemens and General Electric manufacturing the turbines and generators in cooperation with local partners, the Chinese had proved excellent students, and by 2003 were exporting their own hydropower technology – at much cheaper prices – to dam projects around the world.[49] Sinohydro, the major local contractor, was by all accounts the principal beneficiary of this on-the-job training. According to the NGO International Rivers, come 2012 the corporation would control 50 per cent of the global

Wall frieze detail, Three Gorges Dam Museum, Chongqing, PRC

hydropower market, with dam-building projects on the go in South-East Asia, South Asia, Latin America, Eastern Europe and, of course, Africa.[50]

As a showpiece for its talents, Sinohydro could hardly have done better than its signature achievement, the largest renewable source of electric power anywhere on earth. Government delegations were flown into Chongqing from Ethiopia, Nepal, Pakistan, the DRC, South Africa and dozens of other developing world nations where infrastructure was critical if economies were to grow. The delegates were shuttled 660 kilometres downstream, to the dam wall at Sandouping, where they were informed that the distance they'd just travelled was the length of the reservoir. With an initial 26 generators belting out 18 200 megawatts of power, they were told that the energy produced was equivalent to 10 nuclear plants, a capacity that substituted for the burning of 30 million tons of coal per year. They were told that flood control and navigability of the Yangtze were key benefits of the project, and that the former had extended the river's natural flood cycle from once in a decade to once in a century. They were *not* told, unless they really pushed the issue, that the dam had necessitated the destruction of 13 cities, 140 towns and 1 350 villages. Neither were they apprised of the ecological consequences, a list that to Western eyes was looking more catastrophic by the month.[51]

Instead, the government delegations were shuttled back to Chongqing, where the Three Gorges Museum had been inaugurated in 2005. The African delegate, like the ordinary tourist – or, for that matter, the foreign journalist who'd spent time on a Sinohydro construction site in Botswana – would be treated to the trove of cultural artefacts that teams of archeologists had saved from the dam's impounding. Paintings, calligraphy, currency from various periods in the river valley's 100-generation history; all would serve as evidence for the fact that Dam-as-Concept had traversed ideologies and epochs. The African delegate would learn that in the long-distant year of 1919, back when nationalism on his own continent had seemed an impossible dream, a Chinese nationalist named Sun Yat-sen had drafted a plan to tame the Yangtze and harness its energy. In the 1950s, he would note, Mao had written of 'holding back the clouds and the rain 'til a smooth lake rises in the narrow gorges'. He would discover that Deng Xiaoping had set the timeline, and that Jiang Zemin had cut the ribbon on 14 December 1994.

On a didactic panel entitled 'Preface', the African delegate might read the following:

> The long evolution, the magnificent scenery, the lofty spirit, the brilliant culture, the Three Gorges Project, the resettlement of a million migrants and the emergent protection of historical relics in

the Three Gorges area – all the miracles of nature and creations of mankind are displayed as a splendid scroll painting which is being stretched out gently...

In such a conception, the delegate would see, the Three Gorges Project was an exalted moment in a timeless narrative. The reservoir had not drowned a vital part of China's cultural heritage and destroyed a beautiful and essential ecosystem; it had merely inscribed the next chapter in an inexorable chain of events. The dam was as 'natural' as a pile of million-year-old fish bones – the displaced became 'migrants', and their story was one of 'personal sacrifice for the public interest', a 'steady trip to getting rich'.

A point of view that, for many delegates, must have seemed as intoxicating as it was tough to resist. For the African cabinet minister tasked with diversifying the pillars of his economy, this angle might have provided the ideological antidote to the investment dogma of the West. Had the minister arrived in Chongqing during the years that the great reservoir was being impounded, he would have known that China Exim Bank was already funding environmentally sensitive dam projects in countries like Ghana, Zambia and Sudan, and that these were the same projects that Western investors had refused to touch.[52] He would have understood that securing funds from the World Bank or IMF meant jumping through a lot of hoops, whereas Beijing, with very few conditions, was offering a one-stop solution for his brand new – and urgently required – national power grid. The best thing about it, he might have told himself, was that he didn't even have to consult his budget. All he had to do was sign away a few mineral rights as a guarantee against Exim Bank's concessional loan, which he would then use as a down payment on Sinohydro's construction of his very own Three Gorges.

And if this, as Western commentators were saying, was a short-term fix that would perpetuate the African resource curse, it could also be said that Western commentators had been wrong about Africa before.

THE SUEZ CANAL OF TRADE

'The landscape,' JM Coetzee once wrote, 'remains alien, impenetrable, until a language is found in which to win it, speak it, represent it.'[53] The author was pondering South African writing at the birth of colonialism, and the question of 'finding a language to fit Africa, a language that will be authentically African'. Which is to say, 'White African'. So an empty, unpeopled landscape was conjured, a blank space that could be simultaneously civilised and owned by the written word. So-called spare land as manifested by spare prose – a loop that fed back to us as we gazed at the expanse outside our truck.

Mohembo Border Post, facing Botswana, February 2011

It was a sparseness Coetzee had long subverted with his own flayed sentences. As for us, we had been filling the world beyond the windscreen with Botswana's numbers. Those cattle we dodged as they loped across the tarmac? There were five million head in the country, 2.7 per citizen, and they were grazing the delta into desert. In data such as this, culled from the cold facts that pronounced on a country's economic present and prognosticated upon its future, emptiness became something more than a literary condition.

How, we wondered, would Botswana overcome the curse of its borders? A question that applied equally to Rwanda, Burkina Faso, Mali, and other landlocked African states. We thought of Rhodes's stillborn dream of a railroad linking Cape to Cairo. We imagined a Botswana bullet train ripping through the Okavango, past row homes and tenements and Singaporean skyscrapers. Most of all, we pictured the famous satellite image of Earth from above the Greenwich Meridian, the one we'd seen in countless conference halls, the one in which the lights were ablaze throughout Europe and South Africa's major metropoles, and in which the rest of the African continent floated in a sea of darkness. In the white writing that Coetzee had so neatly eviscerated, remoteness was a stepping stone on a path to salvation. In filling its blank spaces, Africa would become Europeanised, civilised, monetised, vitalised. Once, this had been a corrupt religious and cultural concern. Now, it was a problem to be solved by African technocrats.

In February 2011, as we were driving northwest across this sculpted emptiness from Selebi Phikwe to Maun, *The Economist* magazine's commodity price index peaked. Of course nobody knew this at the time, least of all the magazine's editors. But looking back from September 2013, when the editors decided to analyse whether China's slowing demand for resources would wipe out Africa's GDP gains, the date was a milestone. That year, in an article entitled 'Little to fear but fear itself', it was noted that the index had been falling by as much as 14 per cent year-on-year, and that since around half of sub-Saharan Africa's 45 countries were heavily dependent on resource exports, the continent would be 'lucky' if it got out unscathed. Then, fulfilling the promise of its headline, *The Economist* said there was nothing to fear.

For starters, the magazine declared, the direct effect on mining output was likely to be small, as prices hadn't yet fallen below variable costs. At the same time, it appeared *un*likely that public expenditure would be vastly curtailed, as low debt and improved fiscal management had given many African governments access to private credit. For Africa's major oil exporting countries, it was seen as a good thing that China was shifting its economy towards consumer spending, as this would boost the demand for crude. For the others, the good news was to be found in the 'fast-growing consumer class', in the fact that the continent was becoming 'a place to do business other than digging stuff out of the ground'. Africa, according to *The Economist*, was diversifying.[54]

Which may have been true. Then again, we thought, maybe the editors had too big a stake in their own 'Africa Rising' trope, a catchphrase that had recently gone viral.[55] What if the magazine's arguments, solid as they seemed, were unwittingly serving a sentiment? To get at whether there was truth in the sentiment, we reasoned, the place to look was the so-called exception. Of all the African countries that could point to a future beyond resources – and by close association, beyond the quick fixes offered by China Exim Bank and Sinohydro – Botswana still had to be it. Gaborone, largely because of the Debswana effect, had never been the ideal target for Beijing's classic infrastructure-for-resources swap;[56] and because the country had remained liquid enough to finance its own public tenders, it had also remained free enough to dictate its own terms. But if Africa's shining light wasn't meeting the diversification objectives of its own national development plan, if its tradition of political inclusiveness was suddenly under threat, and if it hadn't gotten the most out of its relationship with Beijing, wasn't there in fact *more* to fear than fear itself?

In March 2012, the Gaborone-based *Mmegi* had reported that five unfinished projects, poor performance and a heavy workload had cost Sinohydro the $175 million North-South Water Carrier II tender. The newspaper had gleaned this sensitive information from the files of a court case, in which it transpired that Sinohydro had challenged the Public Procurement and Asset Disposal Board for its award of the tender to competing firms. Apparently, Sinohydro had taken the board's decision to the Independent Complaints Review Committee of the Ministry of Finance and Development Planning, and when this appeal had been dismissed, they'd taken the matter on second appeal to the

High Court. In order to defend its position, noted *Mmegi*, the PPADB, in conjunction with various government departments, had compiled a dossier on the world's largest hydropower firm – among other things, the dossier had concluded that *all* of Sinohydro's projects in Botswana were either over schedule or unsatisfactory.[57]

What, we'd wondered, would Mr Xu have said? After all, the five projects listed in the dossier had been the same five projects that the young commercial manager had enumerated for us in January 2011. These had included: the new terminal at the Sir Seretse Khama International Airport in Gaborone; the 80-kilometre road from Francistown to the Zimbabwean border; the 115-kilometre Kang-Hukuntsi road in the west; the Lotsane Dam in the east; and, of course, the Dikgatlhong Dam.

But Mr Xu hadn't furnished us with a business card, and all our attempts to reach Sinohydro in Botswana had failed. The *Mmegi* reporters hadn't been any more successful at getting comment, and we had followed their thin trail of stories until July 2013, when a piece had appeared under the header 'Sinohydro relocates from Botswana'. The lead for this article had come from an item in the *Botswana Advertiser*, in which it was announced that the Chinese conglomerate was selling off its local assets, including cranes, scaffolding, construction tools, vehicles and office furniture.[58]

Boikanyo Mpho, on the other hand, had been more forthcoming with the Botswana press. Almost two years to the day after he'd told us about his balancing act at Dikgatlhong, the engineer had been compelled to tell the nation that the dam wall was *not* about to crack. There had recently been reports in the Zimbabwean media that cracks had started to appear, and Mpho had addressed the source of these 'rumours' – in so doing, he had distanced the dam from Sinohydro's other work in Botswana. 'Remember,' he'd said, 'that most of the construction projects they were given were surrounded by controversies, like ... the Sir Seretse Khama International Airport project, which they failed to complete, leading to government dumping them.' And according to Mpho, the 'uneasiness' hadn't only been the fault of Sinohydro; in his estimation, the majority of projects run by Chinese companies were 'either collapsing or not safe'. In finishing, Mpho had disclosed that the Dikgatlhong Dam would soon be handed over to Botswana's Water Utilities Corporation, under which it would presumably do the job it had been commissioned to do.[59]

For us, this series of events said a lot about what remained of Botswana's lauded system of governance. Under severe pressure from the world's largest hydropower firm, a conglomerate that had the backing of the State Council in Beijing, its institutions had not buckled. On the contrary, Sinohydro's processes had been subjected by the PPADB to severe scrutiny, and the company had eventually left Botswana under a cloud. What's more, the president himself had come out fighting – in an interview with South Africa's *Business Day* in early 2013, Ian Khama had openly blamed China for the embarrassing power cuts his country had been experiencing, attributing the problem to a Chinese contractor that had 'let down' the government on the $1.6 billion expansion of the coal-fired plant at Morupule. 'The best way I can put it is that we are very, very particular now,' Khama had said. 'We are going to be looking very carefully at any company that originates from China in providing construction services of any nature.'[60]

No doubt, had Gosego and Tshepo from the Selebi Phikwe district labour office read these words, they would've been comforted. Although not exactly for the reasons they'd hoped, the BDP had undeniably 'kicked' the Chinese, so maybe they wouldn't have to 'kick' the BDP. Indeed, since the 2010 split in the ruling party, when many believed that the son's iron-fisted methods had finally destroyed the legacy of the father, the Khama name had only gained in strength. By mid-2013, the Open Society was reporting that the Botswana Movement for Democracy was a failed initiative: its leadership in disarray and re-defecting back to the BDP; its plans for spearheading an unbeatable coalition of opposition parties unravelling; its dreams of taking the 2014 general elections in tatters. At the same time that Botswana's labour unions had been throwing their weight behind the joint opposition effort – and for good measure, sanctioning a months-long public service strike where anti-Khama slogans were *de rigueur* – the president had been marshalling a counterattack on the flanks. Mimicking the United States electoral system, fundraising dinners were held at which the BDP promised continued support for the country's business community; mimicking the populist politics of pro-poor leaders like Venezuela's Hugo Chavez, the poverty alleviation programmes were re-energised, and free meals for short-term workers on large-scale development projects were dished out every day.[61] In October 2013, when Afrobarometer's groundbreaking survey of 34 countries revealed widespread dissatisfaction despite a decade of strong African growth, Botswana posted a continental first place that reflected the success of the BDP's manoeuvres. Asked how they felt their government was doing in its management of the economy, 67 per cent of Batswana respondents opted for the box that said 'very-to-fairly well'.[62]

◆

And yet, Khama had failed to wring the desired results from Sinohydro, a company that had once embodied the friendship between Beijing and Gaborone. As per the italicised plea in his foreword to NDP 10, the people of Botswana had been asked to deliver on the proposed programmes 'within the stated time frame and within [their] means'.[63] The biggest of those programmes, the one that was supposed to facilitate the growth of the private sector and grease the wheels of the economy, was the infrastructure plan – by his own standards, Khama had fallen short on both counts. Yes, a careful approach to the management of his diamond revenues had allowed him to enter into an agreement with the Chinese giant that was in no way based on 'conditional aid'. And yes, he'd been sold by Sinohydro's unbeatable price and its pedigree on the Three Gorges. But if he had assumed that his governance structures would save him should things go awry, the president had assumed wrong. On its cancellation of the airport terminal contract, which had run irredeemably over budget and late, the BDP government had already paid around $70 million to Sinohydro;[64] its subsequent suspension of payment on the Kang-Hukuntsi road – due to a dispute over the 'unlawful' use of a quarry – had only resulted in the contractor downing tools.[65]

Still, as noted by *The African Aviation Tribune*, which had been hoping that the new terminal would establish the Gaborone airport as a regional hub, there'd been a real and long-term benefit to Chinese engagement in the African infrastructure space: if companies from Europe or America wanted to compete, they'd need to cut down on their profit margins.[66] And if that didn't suit contractors from the developed world, if the old risk premiums for operating in Africa remained sky-high, there were other players desperate for the work. In September 2012, when India's Jindal Steel and Power acquired the Canadian-owned CIC Energy for $115 million, it was a sure sign that the scales had tipped. Once again, an emerging market multinational had opted to do a job in Africa that the West had considered its private preserve. Within a few weeks of the acquisition, the Delhi-based conglomerate had demonstrated its sensitivity to local conditions by adding a Botswana page to the Jindal Africa website, acknowledging in the very first line Vision 2016 and its priority to 'align with the country's national goals'. Only in the third paragraph did the company come to the three surface mines it intended to operate in the coalfields of Mmamabula, adding that the coal would feed a planned 600 megawatt power station, which in turn would service the region's export markets and employ around 2 000 people.[67]

◆

Selebi Phikwe, it so happened, was to collect on the cheque signed by Mr Naveen Jindal. In February 2013, a local councillor, Mompati Seleka, appeared alongside the SPEDU marketing and communications manager, Kenneth Boikhutswane, to announce that a coal wash plant would be built in town – this plant, they said, would process the product from Mmamabula and Morupule. The two gentlemen were at pains to point out that the plant wouldn't be the half of it. The bigger story was the railway line, which would link Botswana and Mozambique, via Zimbabwe, to markets in the Far East. Selebi Phikwe was to be a major hub on the line; it was envisaged that investment would flood into the region as the transport network grew.[68] A conception of the territory not entirely different from the one Cecil John Rhodes had all those years ago. Where King Khama of the Bamangwato – grandfather of Sir Seretse Khama, great-grandfather of Ian Khama – had deftly resisted the vision of the British imperialist in 1895, modern Botswana would embrace the ideal of the 'Suez Canal of Trade'.

But something would have to be sacrificed.

The *kgotla*, the in-built checks and balances on the power of the king, the tradition of political inclusiveness – none of these things would thrive under the binge mentality of the infrastructure-building state. In one of the more unsettling episodes in Botswana's political history, Gomolemo Motswaledi, the secretary general of the opposition coalition running against the BDP in the 2014 elections, was killed in a car crash. His colleagues were convinced that there was foul play, and given what happened next, few observers in the region would disagree: a second opposition leader was dumped in a ditch and left for dead, later claiming from his hospital bed that he had been kidnapped and tortured by agents of the intelligence services. As the date of the elections approached, and as the complaints of intimidation from journalists and activists increased, Botswana's formerly sterling reputation was badly besmirched.[69]

Why had all this happened? Was there something inherently corrupting in dealing with the Chinese, something that other African nations would need to take into account? Was there something missing in Acemoglu and Robinson's Botswana research, some element of the *kgotla* they had failed to properly consider? Or was it simply impossible to be politically democratic and economically inclusive when your country's borders were closing in, when mines were drying up almost as fast as dams, when diversification was proving to be more and more of a desert chimera? Park Chung-hee had cracked down on the freedoms of the South Korean people in the 1970s, Lee Kuan Yew had done the same in Singapore – Asian Tigers leading African Lions

88

through groves of development. In the process of *becoming*, Botswana was becoming something else.

And so the sacrifices were all but complete. The BDP would win at the polls, albeit with a decreased majority against 2009. In this light, the empty landscape would look decidedly full, somewhat scarred, and remarkably unlike an anomaly.

We are having trouble with the cops. The officer-in-charge of the Ganyesa Police Station cannot, or will not, help. We must approach the provincial headquarters in Potchefstroom, he says, only they have the authority to comment. His deputy is even less solicitous. 'You are talking like you're still going to write this thing,' the deputy says. 'We have told you the matter is off limits.'

One of us coughs, a speech at the ready for just such a détente.

'Officers, with respect, we need to say again that we are accustomed to police and journalists working together. In Johannesburg' – and the deputy bristles at mention of the big city, as if we are mocking him with the remoteness, the nothingness, of his beat – 'in Johannesburg, we have excellent relationships with your colleagues. Doors are open to us. And obviously you know that in South Africa we have a constitution. If you look under section sixteen, you will see that freedom of speech is protected. So yes, we are going to write this thing.'

The officer-in-charge leans back, smiles, while the deputy looks down at his boots. To police a village like Ganyesa, we know, is not really to police at all. Rather, it is a delicate act of social management, a means of keeping behaviour in check without overstepping the lines of consent. These policemen live in the community, their children go to school in the community, they might own a small business in the community. Anything that enters the ecosystem, any small event, can disturb the balance – and our presence, we understand, is disturbing.

We leave the building and walk out into the sunlight, past the hastily built jail; two prisoners stare at us through the bars. Our next port of call is a gas station, where we ask an attendant if he knows of anyone in the village who is from Pakistan. Their stores are across the highway and by the Shoprite, he says, down the gravel track and to the left. We find them without difficulty, but the clerk in the electronics retailer does not recognise the name from the newspaper report. 'Josim Uddin Miridha?' he asks. 'No, he is not one of us.' Nor have the salesmen in the adjacent shop heard this name. Nor in the shop after that.

Yet all remember the fire. Here, fire is an event, an occasion. There is no wood used in construction in Ganyesa, because there is no decent wood in North West. Just bricks and steel and concrete and tin. As for electrical fires, the current, should it be running, is weak. Nobody in the village worries about electrical boxes exploding – the thought itself elicits smirks.

So the deaths of the Chinese merchants are readily recalled. But not a single shop assistant can point us to the relatives of the deceased, or to the Pakistani businessman who spoke so movingly to a Johannesburg reporter a few short weeks ago.

The words that saw us out of the police station have begun to taste like a promise.

'Go then,' said the deputy. 'You will learn nothing in this place.'

South African Police Service (SAPS) on patrol, rural village, May 2014

ZAMBIA

Zambezi River

Lake Cahora Bassa

MOZAMBIQUE

*Lake
Kariba*

ZIMBABWE

HARARE

Marondera

Mutare

Gweru

Marange
Diamond Fields

Bulawayo

Chisumbanje

BOTSWANA

Chiredzi

Sove River

0   60   120km

Beitbridge

MOZAMBIQUE

SOUTH AFRICA

FOUR

ZIMBABWE

Hall of Mirrors

'Mugabe, if it's not too late, must learn from his Chinese benefactors how Deng Xiaoping did it.'

— *Zimbabwean Independent*, 2013

GUERRILLA IN THE CLASSROOM

Fay Chung was very young when she learnt that white people were greedy because they wouldn't allow others to own land. At four years old, she remembered, she would stand by her grandfather's chair, in the little bakery he ran near the Salisbury railway station, and listen to him debate politics with his best friend, the Somali. Sun Yat-sen would always fare better in these discussions than Mao Zedong, as her grandfather was an educated nationalist, a man deeply suspicious of the communist leader. But white Rhodesians would fare even worse than Mao. Fay Chung's grandfather, you see, had come to Africa in search of land, and the laws of the colonists had ensured that he could never have the farm of his dreams.

In this distinctive story, told to us in the quiet of a garden in Harare's upmarket suburb of Avondale, we were reminded that racial exclusion had long been the southern African default. As Chung spoke, Zimbabwe's history took on nuances that only served to highlight the lessons we'd learnt in Botswana. Avondale, about 15 minutes by car to the bakery where Chung's grandfather held court, had until 1980 been a restricted domain for the city's whites – now this house was a backpackers' lodge that belonged to George, a political adept with ties to Robert Mugabe's ZANU-PF ruling party, and by chance a friend of the woman for whom we were pouring a second cup of tea.

We were in Zimbabwe to learn what constituted a failed state, or what commentators *said* was a failed state, or what commentators wanted – or *needed* – to be a failed state. This was, of course, the country where the British broadsheets, the *New York Times* and *The Economist* had reported as fact the causal link between the violent, government-endorsed appropriations of white-owned farms and total economic collapse. We were both familiar with the Zimbabwean refugee crisis as it had manifested in our own country.[1] In our wallets, we were each carrying a 100-trillion Zimbabwean dollar note, useless as legal tender now that the treasury had adopted the despised Yankee dollar in an attempt to stabilise the economy.

That said, while we thought we had found the smoking gun that could serve as a more plausible explanation for what was happening in the country, we were having trouble locating the bodies. And if anyone knew where the bodies were buried, we reckoned, it had to be Fay Chung.

'I'm not sure what I can tell you here,' said Chung. 'I think everything I've wanted to say is in my book. Above all, I'm just someone from insulated, isolated Zimbabwe. I don't know how much I know about the new Chinese.'

It was apparent, however, that she'd been keeping up. She mentioned the academic Chris Alden, who, despite his Sino-African expertise, was not exactly a household name, and was read in the main by scholars, policymakers and specialists.[2] She cited studies from the South African Institute of International Affairs, whose work on Botswana we had used as a source. But then there was our smoking gun – the money trail that reportedly led from companies associated with China's military-industrial complex, via the blood diamonds of Marange, into the coffers of the Mugabe regime. Of this, Chung refused to say a word. It wasn't in her book, and we wouldn't get it from her directly. What we *would* get was a unique and extraordinary account of the state's birth, an account that would render her self-effacing statement largely moot: the 'new Chinese', it turned out, were not that new.

Chung's memoir, published in 2006, opens with the same anecdote that we had just heard first-hand – a four-year-old girl in the shop of her grandfather, taking in through her ears the indelible lessons of race. The old man, Chung writes in *Reliving the Second Chimurenga: Memories from the Liberation Struggle in Zimbabwe*,[3] was the fifth son of a large peasant family; he wasn't in line to inherit a plot from his father, and so had come to Rhodesia in 1904, at the age of 17. As a student of the precepts of Chinese nationalism, Yee Wo Lee quickly grasped the mechanics of subjugation in his adopted homeland. His education was likewise the reason he forbade his children and grand-children from growing up as 'mountain dogs', illiterates who leave China and know nothing about Chinese values and culture. Even so, while he would become one of the first people in colonial Rhodesia to provide financial support to black nationalists, the wisdom of Yee Wo Lee was no match for the system. Whatever he did, he could not avoid the personal tragedies that were all too often that system's fruits. Writes Chung:

> Up until the 1950s, there was no secondary school for Coloureds and Asians. I first became aware of this problem when I was about seven years old. My mother's youngest sister, Yu Kong Lee, who had been baptised Caroline Lee, had completed primary school at the age of eleven. A brilliant scholar, she was unable to enroll in a secondary school because she was Chinese. My grandfather went to every secondary school in the city to try to get her enrolled, but these schools were for whites only. She was forced to repeat the last grade of primary school for five years until she left school at the age of sixteen. Perhaps the lack of possibilities for profes-sional independence contributed to her premature death at the age of twenty-one.[4]

Perhaps, too, the death of her aunt played a part in Fay Chung's life-long dedication to the cause of educating her country's dispossessed. For, after joining the banned liberation movement then known as the Zimbabwe African National Union (ZANU), after schooling the country's freedom fighters while she herself was in exile in Zambia, Tanzania and Mozambique, after surviving various attempts on her life, she would be named, in 1988, Minister of Education and Culture in the cabinet of the only president Zimbabwe had ever known – Robert Gabriel Mugabe.

◆

As she appeared in the chair opposite us, a woman in her seventieth year, there was little to distinguish Fay Chung from the photographs of her earlier self. She wore a simple navy cardigan, off-the-rack slacks of the same colour, and the round spectacles that had once been the uniform accessory of her caste. Small of stature, her hair shaped in a short bowl, she regarded us through the permanent rictus of a smile. If there was anything that betrayed her age it was her hands, veined and stiffening.

'You see,' she said, 'for us, education really was more important than anything else. It was not a small number of us, pushing that agenda. But that's how ZANU felt. Education vented Zimbabwean frustration. It would allow us to join the world.'

We were aware that her personal commitment to the ideal had sustained a number of attacks over the years, theoretical as well as literal. On her first day as a professional teacher, after she'd beaten the racial odds to graduate from a Rhodesian university, the riot squad had stormed her school. The problem was again the quota system, which decreed that only 2 per cent of black pupils could get a secondary education, a policy that tended to provoke desperate if isolated counter-reactions. From a barricaded classroom at Ascot Secondary, Chung had looked on as the teargas and Alsatians did their work.[5] The year was 1963, and by 1964 she'd be transferred to Harare Secondary, where the violence that had marked her introduction to black education would endure. Over the next half-decade, she would confront every challenge associated with a township posting: pupils abused by hostel dwellers who were not permitted to live with their wives; boys beaten as scabs for coming to school when boycotts were called; one after another her brightest students dropping out – the only way for them to break the cycle, they'd tell their teacher, was to join the armed struggle.

So by 1968, when she arrived at the University of Leeds to further her own studies, this last option had been lying as a latent possibility in even the diminutive, 'non-black' Chung. Coinciding as it did with the students' revolution, which affected universities across Europe, her first year away from Africa would enable her to reflect with new clarity on the continent she called home. She became secretary of the African Society, an organisation that represented the interests of over 100 African students, and editor of its magazine *Uhuru*. She wondered what liberation would mean for Africa, and began to read Lenin and Marx. And as 1968 was also the third year of the Cultural Revolution in China, she considered deeply the teachings of the man her grandfather had loathed. 'Mao's concept of the just war based on peasant support was the most practical model for Africa,' she would recall of that time, 'a continent that was yet to be industrialised and where the peasants formed the majority.'[6]

Chung, although she had come to Leeds believing in the liberating power of education, was not immediately put off by Mao's purges of Chinese intellectuals. On the contrary, there was a period when she asked herself whether the war against the intellectual was 'essential for change'; whether the intellectual was the enemy and the peasant the hero.[7] She'd been radicalised by her environment into seeing that her non-black status didn't exempt her from moral responsibilities at home, and her memories of Harare Secondary – where her best students had swapped their textbooks for AKs – were still fresh in her mind. But if Chung's anti-intellectualism was a transient phase that would soon be dropped, her rebellion, when it properly began in 1973, would embody entire passages from Chairman Mao's *Little Red Book*.

The Zimbabwe African National Liberation Army (ZANLA), the armed wing of ZANU, had been formed in response to Prime Minister Ian Smith's Unilateral Declaration of Independence in 1965. A devout white supremacist, Smith had been supported in his secessionist endeavour by 90 per cent of the Rhodesian electorate, even though it was clear that the British government would dub the declaration an 'act of treason'.[8] By 1973, ZANLA was racking up decisive victories against the Rhodesian forces. A big reason for this was the army's new grounding in guerrilla warfare, particularly the strategy of merging with the peasantry, a technique ZANLA's officers had learnt from the Chinese. After the losses of the 1960s, when the locals had simply betrayed the freedom fighters to Rhodesian authorities, the ZANLA high command had decided to take up Mao on his offer of military training in the People's Republic. The essence of such training was its focus on political indoctrination, and the Zimbabwean officers had returned with the know-how to create their own cadre of political commissars, whose job it would be to win over the peasant population. So integral would these commissars become to the liberation effort, so sacred their ideal of politicising every peasant, that the second of ZANLA's 'three main rules of discipline' would borrow directly from the Maoist playbook: 'Do not take a single needle or piece of thread from the masses.'[9]

Chung, who had left England for Zambia, had discovered in ZANU a movement that viewed education through the prism of her earliest values. ZANLA may have inherited a lot from Maoist China, most notably a philosophy that led to welcome victories on the battlefield, but it did not inherit the Great Helmsman's disdain for the intelligentsia. At the University of Zambia, where she'd taken up a lecturing post in 1971, Chung had reached the conclusion that her educated countrymen would need to play the 'dirty game' of politics if Zimbabwe was to stand a chance when *its* independence came. From the streets of Lusaka, then the headquarters for many of Africa's liberation movements,[10] she'd taken note as Kenneth Kaunda – Zambia's 'morally motivated' leader – had outsourced his development vision to foreign advisors. These Westerners, she'd seen, would fly in on short-term contracts, remove their pre-packaged models from their briefcases, and dispense their wisdom as if there was no real difference between New York and Ndola. The result was a national development programme totally divorced from Zambia's climate, social structures and peasant communities. Chung had learnt from this a lesson that would stick:

Africa's future depended on its local educated elites, men and women who understood the grassroots. In 1973, as a fresh ZANU recruit, she worked with Zimbabwean lecturers and students at the University of Zambia to map the problems her country would face after independence. In 1974, she drew up a plan to use these same staff and students to run an education programme for ZANLA guerrillas.

It was a plan whose implementation would be indefinitely delayed. With local socialists taking the reins from the Portuguese colonists in Mozambique and Angola, the map of southern Africa, in the eyes of one Henry Kissinger, was looking alarmingly Red. The US secretary of state, backed up by Prime Minister John Vorster of South Africa, hatched a plan in 1974 to engineer a Rhodesian *détente*. Although the plan didn't succeed in its primary aim of declawing ZANLA and establishing a pro-West black government in Zimbabwe, it succeeded beautifully on a secondary front – through the release of old-style nationalists, including Robert Mugabe, from Rhodesian jails, it exacerbated a leadership crisis that had long been brewing in ZANU.[11] While the Maoist Josiah Tongogara retained his command of ZANLA, ZANU itself gave way to the ascendancy of the rightwing. As a member of the leftist 'university group' and a non-black to boot, Chung found herself on the wrong side of the divide. One day in early 1978, when she was teaching at the headquarters of the ZANU education department in Gondola, Mozambique, she was bundled into a Landcruiser and taken by force to a military camp. On her lap was her six-month-old daughter Chipo, and soon enough, to prevent any contact with the outside world, mother and infant were moved again – at Pungwe III, amongst the largest of the ZANLA military bases in Mozambique, from where 'it was possible to walk for weeks without meeting anyone,' Chung and Chipo survived on a single daily meal of boiled maize.

This wasn't the first time Chung had suspected that factions within ZANU wanted her removed,[12] but the dangers were still less than the threat posed by the common enemy. On a July morning in 1978, shortly after she had resumed her teaching duties, thanks to the intervention of Tongogara, the Rhodesian Air Force bombed the school at which she was stationed. While the planes swooped, Chung strapped Chipo to

her back and ran for the tall grass. Around her were children screaming and falling, three-year-olds and five-year-olds tearing off their
clothes in fright. She got separated from the others and spent a night
with Chipo in the bush. Later, she discovered that her school had been
destroyed, that a number of other schools had been bombed that same
day. In *Reliving the Second Chimurenga*, she would write, 'Throughout
the war, the Rhodesians were either unwilling or unable to attack military camps, but consistently bombed schools and refugee camps.'

In May 1980, following the signing of the Lancaster House agreement, which had established both the terms of ceasefire and the legal
framework for Zimbabwean independence,[13] Chung was flown home
on a plane chartered for the ZANU elite. Despite her ideological way-
wardness, her reputation as an educator had prevailed. She had been
away from home for 12 years. Her family, who'd heard stories of conditions in the rear Mozambican camps, had assumed she was dead.

◆

'I don't know whether I can consider myself Chinese any longer,'
said Chung, 'but I can and do admire the entrepreneurial spirit of the
Chinese. I can't help hoping that it will infect the worker culture here.
Zimbabweans are naturally entrepreneurial.'

These words, although reminiscent of sentiments we'd come across
time and again in Namibia and Botswana, held an added poignancy
in the mouth of Chung. As a freedom fighter of Asian origin in a
country where the war was fundamentally between white and black,
as a self-avowed anti-racist who for almost 40 years had endured the
insults of race – first from white Rhodesians before going into exile,
and then from a small yet vocal group of black cadres while *in* exile –
there was for us no-one better suited to complicate the Zimbabwean
conversation. And her opinions on the 'natural' inclinations of one
group or another were only part of it, subsumed as they were by the
ideological positions she'd taken post-independence. Because towards
the end of *Reliving the Second Chimurenga*, in passages written long
after ZANU's 'farm invasions' had become a Western media meme, she

Hawkers sell goods on the streets of Zimbabwe's capital Harare,
17 September 2015. REUTERS/Philimon Bulawayo

espoused a form of governance that was far from democratic.[14]

How did Chung, whose life story signified nothing if not the triumph of the individual over mind-boggling injustice, come to believe that Zimbabwe would be better off as a one-party state? Regardless of our suspicions, she would not allow us the possibility that China served as the example. She stuck to the line in her book, arguing that the emergence of populist politics in the country after 1980, which ensured that candidates would henceforth need to pander to the whims of an ethnically divided electorate, as well as what she termed the ruling party's swift decline 'from a liberation movement into a business conglomerate',[15] had meant the death of the revolutionary ideals of social transformation. The country's opposition parties, she felt, had protested the corruption and criminality only insofar as it benefited their own selfish ends. For her, only a 'strong state' could overcome the inertia, and only ZANU-PF had the legitimacy to govern in such a state. In *Reliving the Second Chimurenga*, Chung called for a renewed programme of national development: one that would place nation-building before democracy; one that would be as internally 'self-correcting' as ZANU had apparently been during the war (she clearly didn't begrudge the movement its various attempts at correcting *her*); one that would recognise the ravages of Western neoliberalism in a local context. Which was why we weren't quite ready to let the obvious parallels with the Chinese Communist Party go.

'The kinship with China was not invented,' said Chung, the smile still affixed to her face, 'although at times it's been over-emphasised.'

But Chung, we knew, was hedging. How did we know this? We still had our smoking gun.

A DIFFERENT CAMOUFLAGE

Fists of granite lined the road, occasionally cumulating in large boulders. This was a country that changed around every corner – the sort of landscape that induced frenzy, that when you said you were of a place, that place was highly specific, and different from that of your neighbour. The tollgates outside the city of Bulawayo were kept by sour people in labour union T-shirts; in the distance a granary loomed, its concrete crumbling into the veld. As we came into the industrial exurbs, we saw factories rotting into each other, their pipes like diseased intestines, their smoke towers teetering.

On our first night in the city, we broke bread with the South African *Mail & Guardian*'s major asset in Zimbabwe, Ray Ndlovu.[16] One of only 50 or so journalists in the country not under the ruling party's thumb, Ray, we thought, could be called fearless if the term wasn't so inadequate in describing just how few concessions he had made to his own safety over the years.

In a bustling chicken franchise, Ray – startlingly young, lean, and sensitive on a molecular level to the minute shifts in his surroundings –

began by outlining for us the inner workings of a political party that, for him, was less a party than a going concern. There was almost no sector of the economy, said Ray, where ZANU hadn't tapped a vein, funnelling blood from across the land into its engorged heart in Harare. But there was one sector in particular that we needed his advice on, and it hardly took a journalist of Ray's calibre to guess which.

'Diamonds,' he said.

While it had been our intention to travel to the Marange diamond fields in the country's east to investigate for ourselves what was transpiring, Ray wasn't encouraging. 'It's run by the army,' he said, 'and what are you going to find out there? No one will talk to you. It's probably best to stay away.'

Still, we were holding what we felt was a trump card, a mobile number provided by a Zimbabwean academic at a South African university. The number belonged to Jonathan Moyo, ZANU's long-serving politburo member and attack-dog public relations guru – or 'Zimbabwe's Goebbels', as the official opposition referred to him. As the academic had noted, Moyo was considered something of a political genius, which perhaps was why he'd been bouncing in and out of favour for so long. In 2004, his failed bid to install parliamentary speaker Emmerson Mnangagwa as vice president, ahead of Mugabe's preferred candidate Joice Mujuru, had appeared to be his death knell. But like a kid at a video-game console, he'd cheerfully popped in a handful of coins and kept playing. We were hoping therefore that Moyo could get us into Marange and secure our protection while there, even if it was a scenario Ray thought unlikely on both counts.

'You never know, though,' he shrugged, 'it's worth a try.'

Two days later, on our way back to Harare, we dialled the number. Moyo answered on the first ring. Halfway into a summary of our credentials, he cut the call short.

'Ah, yes, yes,' he said, the double affirmative suggesting he'd already heard from our contact in South Africa. 'Not a problem meeting with you. Currently, I'm out of Harare. Call me Tuesday.'

But well before Tuesday our surprise at his accessibility had curdled into paranoia. Calling Moyo for a second time had proved unnecessary, because he'd been calling *our* number. Constantly. Every few hours, his name would flash across our phone. We took turns answering. 'Um, hello, Mr Moyo?'

'Ah, yes, yes,' he offered, as if this game of phone pong were the most natural thing in the world. 'Tomorrow, call tomorrow.'

We never would make the meeting with the propaganda chief, and the gurgling on our line, which had been consistent since a few hours after that first call, would leave us in no doubt that we were being watched. It was a sobering reality check, one that increased our admiration for every Zimbabwean willing to go on record.

Thomas Deve, for instance. A prim, forthright man in a heavily starched shirt, Deve, head of a think-tank called the Southern and Eastern African Trade Information and Negotiations Institute, connected a few threads for us. He told us that he saw nothing remarkable in the allegations, which had been doing the rounds for more than six years now, that the Chinese military remained deeply involved with Zimbabwe's ruling party. 'Who was training the army during the *Gukurahundi* of the 1980s?' he asked, referring to the so-called 'Matabeleland massacres', when Mugabe's notorious Fifth Brigade, ministered to by the North Koreans, had killed between 6 000 and 10 000 Ndebele in an attempt to quell an uprising abetted by South Africa's apartheid regime.[17] 'The Russians and the Chinese armed us during the war. The other side? The Americans, the British, the South Africans. We've *always* bought weapons from the Chinese. Why is this a surprise?'

Deve, echoing Fay Chung, felt it was worth acknowledging that, had Zimbabwe not so offended the West over the course of the land reform saga, Mugabe would be remembered as a less charismatic, more pedantic Nelson Mandela; his inauguration speech was still considered one of the more beautiful in the continent's history.[18] But despite the initial optimism at independence, said Deve, Zimbabwe never stood a chance. The state entered the world carrying $700 million of Ian Smith's war debt. It suffered from the apartheid regime's violent meddling, got hit by the worst drought of the century in 1991, accepted a punitive structural adjustment package that bled the economy of

60 000 jobs, and lost to emigration the brains of two million educated citizens. The political crisis that followed saw Morgan Tsvangirai's union-backed Movement for Democratic Change (MDC) become a countrywide force,[19] while the war veterans' movement agitated for the land they were promised at independence. Then land reform, at first aggressively opposed by ZANU-PF, and later adopted as policy to ensure Robert Mugabe's survival.

And yet, unlike Chung, Deve was no advocate of one-party rule – his deep understanding of Zimbabwe's troubled history did not prevent him from critiquing the autocratic bent of his president. He wanted us to know, in the event we mistook him for a loyal ZANU cadre, that much of what the party had perpetrated over the years was unconscionable, and had set the precedent for a military operation that stained the regime's soul far more than Fast Track Land Reform ever had.

Hakudzokwi, four syllables as dissonant as gunfire, a Shona term meaning 'you will not return'. In the early summer of 2008, the Zimbabwean military had swept into the Marange diamond fields, their intention to drive out the civilians they found there. The ruling party did their best to keep their actions hidden, but it shortly became known that more than 30 000 artisanal panners working the alluvial beds had been chased into the bush by infantry and helicopter gunships.[20] Newspapers across the world reported that *Hakudzokwi* had left behind scores of dead, with thousands more beaten, raped or tortured.[21] As far as most – but amazingly not *all* – industry watchdogs were concerned, this would drench the stones of Marange in blood.

Meanwhile, reports surfaced of a not-so-mysterious Chinese presence appearing in the tale.[22] At the time of our visit, Ray Ndlovu was on the story. He told us of an entity called 'Anjin', which he believed was active in Marange and funded by China's Exim Bank. Exactly one year later the link would be proved beyond doubt, when Marange would be revealed as the most important organ in ZANU-PF's anatomy.

◆

Wars in Zimbabwe, as the next day's visit would remind us, didn't end when the ceasefires were signed. Over the phone a woman named Kerry Kay had provided us with an address straight out of a Le Carré novel: a beauty salon not far from our backpackers' lodge in Avondale. Kay's office lay at the end of a passage that smelled of nail varnish and hair product. She had warned us to ensure that in driving over we weren't followed, but it was advice she needn't have offered.

Kay's memories were Chung's in photonegative – in February 2011, more than 30 years since the agreement at Lancaster House, both women were having trouble reconciling past and present. From the age of 19 to 26, before she got married, Kay had served in Ian Smith's police forces: first in the crime prevention unit, then on the communism desk of the Special Branch hunting down the likes of Fay Chung, then as a regional court orderly in the charge office at Fort Vic. A stint in Chiredzi, doing rural patrols and some urban work, had been followed by an investigative assignment in Marondera. Towards the end of the war, back in Chiredzi, she had been tasked with deploying police reservists into various positions on the front. In the interim, under legendary spook Ken Flower, Special Branch headquarters had been incorporated into the Central Intelligence Organisation.[23] Mugabe would keep both Flower and the CIO after 1980, and the brutality of the intelligence agency would eventually drive Kay to set up operations as a 'human rights activist' behind the ruse of a beauty salon.

Kay had joined the MDC, ZANU's mortal political enemy, in the month of its formation in 1999. Longevity had earned her a place on the national executive committee, and after serving as the party's deputy secretary for health, she had been promoted, in 2006, to secretary for welfare. Her husband, Iain Kay, was at the time of our visit the MDC's legislative representative for Marondera, the family's home base.

'For 12 years now, we've been recording the government's abuses in documents and photographs,' said Kay. 'As you know, our farm was the first to be invaded.'

There was, it seemed to us, an ontological problem here – although the BBC and various big name media brands had endorsed Kay's version of events, they had all read history selectively. Farm invasions had long been endemic in this country. There were the systematic appropriations following World War II, when returning white veterans had been granted land on which black farmers had lawful claims, a Whitehall-sanctioned programme that would effectively double the number of white farms by the 1950s. Before that, during the First Chimurenga of 1896, white settlers had been encouraged by Cecil John Rhodes to take up arms against Shona and Ndebele factions who wanted their land *back*. Before *that*, Ndebele moving north from South Africa had driven the Shona from their pastures in the country's verdant west.

But as far as the dominant narrative was concerned, the Kays were the first. Convinced that the occupation of their farm was a cheap political ploy, they had filmed the attack as it unfolded. The footage had been smuggled out of the country over a period of several months, and the resulting documentary, *Zimbabwe – Hounded Out*, had jolted the BBC's viewership into outrage when it aired in 2003.[24]

'And that was the end of that,' said Kay. 'That was the end of the farm and everything.'

It was, however, the start of a new life in Harare – a life in which Kay could put her previous experience as a Rhodesian policewoman to good use. Three years after the loss of her farm, in mid-2005, Kay would witness a showdown on the streets of the capital that would reflect her past back at her. And at the heart of it, she told us, were the Chinese. Where Fay Chung saw the new Chinese as a benevolent force, a phenomenon that could teach Zimbabweans how to be better entrepreneurs, Kay saw them as a case to be solved, one that would require all of her investigative skills.

◆

At the time of its implementation, in May 2005, Operation *Murambatsvina* – Shona slang for 'drive out the rubbish' – was described by the Zimbabwean government as an 'urban renewal campaign', an effort to deal with the illegal housing and attendant diseases in the country's various slums. But according to the MDC, *Murambatsvina* was Mugabe's way of delivering retribution to the homeless and unemployed, many of whom had expressed their dissatisfaction with ZANU-PF at the polls. Seeing as the clearances had come in the wake of the March parliamentary elections, when the MDC had made significant gains in the cities, the opposition may have had a point. Aware of these conflicting narratives, the United Nations decided to focus instead on the numbers. In a report released in July 2005, the global body stated that 'Operation Restore Order', the government's official nomenclature for the programme, had resulted in 700 000 people across the country losing their homes, their livelihoods, or both. Where the UN report did comment, it was therefore with remarkable force:

> Even if motivated by a desire to ensure a semblance of order in the chaotic manifestations of rapid urbanisation and rising poverty characteristic of African cities, nonetheless Operation Restore Order turned out to be a disastrous venture based on a set of colonial-era laws and policies that were used as a tool of segregation and social exclusion.[25]

Kerry Kay was there with her camera. She was in Mbare, she told us, the Harare township that suffered the worst of the devastation.

'I personally witnessed them bulldozing brick houses,' she said. 'Legitimately built brick houses. Shocking. Burning stuff. That night, I took photographs of Mbare market... I saw a lorry that had military people in it, a military lorry with Chinese or... I don't know, Korean or Chinese. But I presume from the features, in *their* military uniform, not our military uniform ...'

'Do you have picture evidence of that?' one of us interjected, in an effort to get at something more concrete.

'No, I don't. I don't.'

'Can you describe the uniforms?'

'Well, it's a completely different camouflage to ours. It's like, how can I say ... I suppose it's like an autumn garden in England when all the leaves have fallen and all the different types of browns.'

Not exactly conclusive evidence. Still, this wasn't the first we'd heard of a Chinese military link to *Murambatsvina*.

Back in South Africa, during our preparations, we'd established contact with an activist colleague of Kay's, a woman who'd sent us reams of material on the subject, including an eyewitness account of Chinese 'advisors' patrolling the streets in green Peugeots. Although much of her material was similarly vague, this woman had helped to write a report sponsored by the NGO Africa Fighting Malaria – her name, she'd informed us in an email, could not appear on the list of authors 'for security reasons' – in which China's role was dealt with more directly. Attributed amongst others to Archbishop Pius Ncube, of the Catholic Archdiocese of Bulawayo, and to Dr Roger Bate, of the American Enterprise Institute in Washington DC, the paper alluded to an economic objective at the core of the operation.

It stated: 'Speculation over the motives behind Operation *Murambatsvina* has pointed to the removal of local competition threatening newly arrived Chinese businessmen, whose stores sell cheap and often poor quality goods. It is estimated that, as a result of the government's aggressive "Look East" policy, up to ten thousand Chinese citizens have moved into the country, and some have moved onto farms taken from highly skilled commercial farmers, notably to grow tobacco for China's 300 million smokers.'[26]

There was a clear pattern in these accusations, mimicking much of what we had heard and were subsequently unable to prove in Namibia and Botswana: change happened quickly, brutally – whether at the hand of the state or due to some other, unnamed phenomenon – and strands of Beijing's DNA, however spectral, clung to the wreckage. Kay recalled for us how, during *Murambatsvina*, she'd observed the destruction of an informal marketplace in the Harare city centre; how the riot police had smashed the stands of the traders and confiscated their wares. 'All of a sudden,' she said, 'after Operation *Murambatsvina*, all these little Chinese shops with all this Chinese stuff just inundated the country. So it's like, hello, why are you destroying the informal sector and the next minute the Chinese are in here with all their rubbish to sell?'

To our reckoning, there was a simple answer: *Murambatsvina* had coincided with one of globalisation's more transformative moments, the suspension of the infamous Multi-Fibre Arrangement in 2004. During the course of 2005, Chinese textile and clothing imports to the West *alone* would increase by over 100 per cent. At the same time, Tony Blair was fighting the 'Bra Wars' with Beijing, as 75 million pieces of Chinese clothing languished in European ports. All across Africa, Chinese manufactured goods were streaming into local markets, through border posts that were porous with corruption and inefficiency. And by late 2013, if any suspicions lingered that *Murambatsvina* had been ordered partially for the benefit of the Chinese, they would be undercut by the fact that Mugabe's newly re-elected government, in a revived and highly publicised indigenisation drive, would force all small traders in the country to hand over their businesses to Zimbabweans or face arrest. The Chinese and Nigerian trading communities would be all but wiped out, a purge that acted as a sop to ZANU nationalists, and functioned as a muted corollary to the land invasions 13 years earlier.[27]

Nonetheless, Kay had been marked by what she saw during *Murambatsvina* – and she remembered those Asians in uniform. The year after the operation, she told us, in September 2006, she was arrested at a trade union protest; a riot policeman had struck her across the back with a baton, and had seized her camera and mobile phone. En route to the Harare Central police station, she and another prisoner – 'the MDC lady, black lady, Grace Kwinjeh' – were transferred from a Land Rover belonging to the riot police into a second Land Rover, occupied by members of the CIO. Before the vehicle left, said Kay, the driver got out to consult with two Asian men, who were wearing smart suits and carrying long-lensed cameras.

'And I said to the CIO guys, I said, "Those Chinese there, I bet you they are organising all of this like Tiananmen Square, they are teaching you guys what to do when we demonstrate." And they just chuckled.'

This time, Kay's allegations could be substantiated. She referred us to an article written by Kwinjeh, which we would retrieve and read later that day. Published in *The Zimbabwean*, a newspaper founded for Zimbabweans in exile, it confirmed Kay's version and more besides.[28] This account would be further bolstered by a news report in South Africa's *Mail & Guardian*, which linked the civil unrest to the deteriorating economic situation, adding that Chinese military advisors were training Zimbabwean forces in methods for dealing with popular revolt.[29]

Our question, of course, was *why?* Kerry Kay, for all of her interest in the subject, did not have an answer. The foreign faces peeking out of military trucks, the Asian men with cameras, the products in the stalls that Zimbabweans referred to as *zhingzong* – aside from some deeply felt intuition about this new invasion, she had not managed to assemble her observations into a coherent case docket.

And yet all of this, all of Kerry Kay's diffuse testimony, everything she'd told us about *Murambatsvina,* was already in the process of exploding out into its proper global context. On 4 February 2011, a week before our meeting, a *Bloomberg* headline had seeped its way into the Zimbabwean ether. 'China wants Marange gems, Zimbabwe platinum', it read. It quoted from a *Zimbabwe Independent* exposé, which in turn cited government documents. 'Export-Import Bank of China has proposed lending Zimbabwe $3 billion in exchange for control over the revenue of gems from the Marange diamond fields ...'[30]

Which brought us back to our smoking gun. Operation *Hakudzokwi.* You will not return.

MANY-HEADED HYDRA

But should we drive east to Marange and see it for ourselves, or should we listen to Ray Ndlovu, our instincts, and the gurgling on our phone, and sit this one out? The decision was made for us over lunch at an Avondale restaurant, by a ZANU-affiliated ex-Reuters stringer. She explained that the CIO kept tabs on foreign journalists, and it was her opinion that we had 'zero lives' left. 'They've known about you since you came in,' she said. 'What's saved you so far is that you've taken the trouble to talk to people in ZANU. If you try to get into Marange, they will connect the dots. Then good luck, my friends.'

We would have to content ourselves, then, with further research, and where better to start than with the following ecstatic declaration:

'Chiadzwa is the eighth wonder of the world.' So said Obert Mpofu, Zimbabwe's one-time diamond czar, regarding the ward in the Mutare District in which the 60 000-hectare fields of Marange lay spread out.[31] Chiadzwa's star had risen in 2006, when Mugabe's government received from the De Beers conglomerate some astonishingly good news: one of the world's richest diamond deposits, worth perhaps $800 billion, existed beneath this patch of the province's soil. Prospectors agreed that the deposit was freakishly enormous, and could ameliorate, if not solve, most of Zimbabwe's financial problems 'at a stroke'.[32]

De Beers, it turned out, had 'locked' the concession – an age-old means of controlling supply to the international market in order to keep prices inflated – and when their exploration contract expired, an irritated ZANU-PF, which had been desperate for the revenue, deigned not to let them back in. Instead of looking west to Botswana and copying the mostly successful Orapa joint venture, the party elite claimed control of the fields for itself, through the state-owned Zimbabwe Mining Development Corporation.

After De Beers was nudged out in December 2006, panners flooded in, living an existence medieval in its viciousness. The newcomers – to say nothing of the villagers who'd been in the region for generations – were subject to constant raids by the military, culminating in 2008 with the massacre known as *Hakudzokwi*. Despite the fact that the newly formed Government of National Unity was supposed to be an equal part ZANU and MDC affair, the army was firmly in the ZANU ambit – when the fields became a military stronghold, they became a ZANU bank machine. But, as Ray Ndlovu had reminded us, diamonds don't sell themselves. Enter the two joint venture companies that functioned as Marange's money suck: an ingenious construction called Anjin Investments, working in consort with the nubilous Mbada Diamonds.

Anjin was set up as one of globalisation's many-headed hydras, an entity almost impossible to destroy because its power derived from its diffuseness. According to a devastating Global Witness report that would do the rounds in early 2012, Anjin was a joint venture between a vast Chinese construction company called Anhui Foreign Economic Construction Group (AFEC(G)) and a Zimbabwean outfit inventively christened Matt Bronze. In a letter from the Zimbabwe Ministry of Mines addressed to Anjin, the government made it clear that Matt Bronze would function as AFEC's funnel into Marange, although AFEC's management hardly needed their hands held in Africa.[33] At the time, amongst other projects on the continent, they were under contract to build the $124 million John Akii-Bua Olympic Stadium in Uganda, had won the tender for the renovation of the Maputo International Airport in Mozambique, and – most significantly – were starting work on the $98 million National Defence College outside Harare.[34]

AFEC was obviously linked to the top brass in Beijing, because two of the above projects had secured the cooperation of the Chinese policy bank Exim – the Chinese government's means for funding foreign policy initiatives abroad. In fact, repayment for the Defence College loan would, according to the Global Witness report, come directly from the diamonds mined by Anjin. And in a series of revelations that came as a surprise to absolutely no one, Anjin's Zimbabwean board members were found to be ZANU-PF stalwarts, military men, and members of the Zimbabwe Republic Police. It was also said, amidst denials, that Jonathan Moyo's one-time vice-presidential pick – Defence Minister Emmerson Mnangagwa – had granted Anjin the Marange concession when he'd served, ever so briefly, as the acting minister of mines.[35]

Regarding Mbada Diamonds, it would have taken us a week and a half to make a lick of sense out of their chain of ownership. Suffice to say, the company was another global hydra, this time of no known provenance, belonging to no one, benefiting no one knows whom. It was co-owned by Hong Kong, Mauritian, South African and Zimbabwean nationals, with chunks registered in tax havens such as the Bahamas and the British Virgin Islands.[36] And while the Chinese Communist Party was certainly implicated in Marange's abuses, when we widened the aperture, the frame crowded with a host of collaborators, all of whom functioned within an international financial system designed to support exactly the kind of opacity that allowed the likes of Anjin and Mbada to flourish.

Take, for instance, the Kimberley Process Certification Scheme,[37] initiated in 2002 to keep the stones mined in killing fields from reaching the international market. Global Witness, which had long expressed reservations about the scheme's methods, resigned from the Kimberley Process in disgust when Marange stones were deemed fit for placement in the world's engagement rings – according to the scheme's criteria, these stones were *not* blood diamonds because they did not fit the definition of 'rough diamonds used by rebel movements or their allies to finance conflict aimed at undermining legitimate governments'.[38] By 2013, while Zimbabwean diamonds would remain illegal in the United States due to the economic sanctions imposed against ZANU-PF and its institutions, most other markets would lift restrictions. Anjin and Mbada could legitimately tender their product in Antwerp, Tel Aviv, Mumbai and other global trading centres.

In the not so distant past, Africans at least knew who and what to blame when their resources were being exploited. They slapped the names of big corporations onto placards, they waved those placards in the air, while their supporters in foreign countries chanted: *Anglo American Out! Shell Must Go!* Half a decade on from the exit of De Beers from Zimbabwe, in its stead would exist wisps, incorporated noth-ings, registered in havens where they enjoyed permanent tax holidays while spiriting away the country's wealth under the cover of darkness. Even our old friend Sam Pa and his CIF were said to have their claws in Marange – his Bahamas-registered Airbus 319CJ flew into Harare once a month in order to ferry stones out for Mugabe's government, which was in turn connected to his interests in Angola, which was in turn con-nected to an Israeli billionaire diamond dealer in Namibia.[39]

Aperture properly widened, a panorama of the 'failed state' came sharply into view – its only worthy citizens were the untouchable cor-porations tied in some measure to the ruling party, all of whom were working in consort to strip Zimbabwe of essential tax revenue.

In this, all roads led to one of Harare's tallest and most famous buildings, a modernist structure on the edges of the CBD with the silhouette of a rooster, the mascot of the liberation movement, gazing out from the roof to the four cardinal points.

◆

On the day of our appointment any number of things could have kept Comrade Rugare Gumbo from returning to ZANU-PF headquarters – an assault by party thugs on reporters in the township of Mbare, the supreme court's rejection of an activist's constitutional challenge, another verbal attack by Mugabe's main henchman, George Charamba, on an MDC member bidding for the deputy prime minister's seat. These were some of the things listed in the next day's newspapers that the party's secretary for information and publicity might have wanted to investigate for himself. Whatever the reason, we had been asked to return later in the week.

Gumbo, it turned out, had played a starring role in *Reliving the Second Chimurenga*. Fay Chung had first met him as a young revolutionary in 1973, shortly after he'd completed his master's degree in Canada, and had arrived in Lusaka to enlist. Appointed ZANU's head of information – a position he would hold again as an old man, although now with the added portfolio of 'publicity' – Gumbo's erudition had caught the bookish young woman's eye. The relationship lasted until 1977, the year their daughter Chipo was born in Dar es Salaam. Of the break-up, Chung had written in her memoir that while Gumbo was involved in a 'ferocious leadership struggle', she was being used as a scapegoat by the movement's ascendant right wing, who'd condemned her on the basis of race. 'It was in this situation that I realised that I was not going to receive any support from Rugare,' she'd recalled.[40]

It was clear from her memoirs that Chung didn't entirely *blame* Gumbo – she appeared to accept that he was fighting for his political life, that it was 'a period of violent turmoil' when 'personal relations came under a great deal of stress'. No, if blame lay anywhere in her book, it was with the system. 'ZANU was formed in opposition to the Ian Smith regime,' she wrote. 'It united all forces that were against the Smith regime. One of the constant dangers it faced was that of fighting fire with fire, that is fighting racism with racism, fighting violence with violence. It constantly faced the danger of becoming a mirror of the colonial racist regime.'[41]

We had seen Chung's mirror everywhere. We'd seen it at Hero's Acre, the towering national monument situated on a hill above Harare, where one of the most prominent murals depicted a Rhodesian police dog attacking a Mashona woman – and where just about everything else, from the inscriptions to the North Korean architecture, was defiantly and triumphantly aimed at the vanquished white oppressor. We'd seen it in the colonial-era laws, initially devised as 'tools of segregation and social exclusion', that Mugabe had used to implement Operation *Murambatsvina*. And we were seeing it again now, on the day of our rescheduled appointment, when at precisely 11am a tea boy in a doily hat arrived in the ante-room of Comrade Gumbo's offices bearing a pot of Earl Grey and a trayful of cucumber sandwiches.

'The official position of the party is that we are doing business with our friends,' said Comrade Gumbo, for the third time, when finally we found ourselves face to face. 'Nobody can stop us dealing with the Chinese. If the West were interested in developing Africa, they would have done so a long time ago. Think about it. France and the British did nothing for this continent, the people are still living in abject poverty.'

This, we knew, was the standard line, the boilerplate spin. Robert Mugabe, added Gumbo, 'couldn't care less' what the international community thought about his Look East initiative. 'In truth, Zimbabwean policies opened up opportunities for the Chinese here. And in typical fashion, they grasped them.'

But if Look East was a wedge that further separated Africa from the West, if it provided new openings for old friends to secure new economic relationships, what did that mean for the Zimbabwean *people*? How would *they* benefit from the disruption? What plans were in place for fundamental economic reform, given that the United Nations had estimated a decline in the economy between 2000 and 2008 of more than 50 per cent? What about the allegation that four out of every five jobs were informal? What about the widespread reports of torture of political dissidents? The massive brain drain, the high mortality rate, the food shortages that had only recently been addressed? What about the country's place at or near the bottom of the governance and corruption indices for *the whole of Africa*?[42] And what about those diamonds?

Rugare Gumbo indulged us with an avuncular grin, and stuck to

Rainbow Vistarama, Mutare, February 2011

his message – which was that our information came from Western organisations, Zimbabwe's enemies all. He had a series of questions of his own. Did the land seizures really destroy this former breadbasket of Africa? Was the white Rhodesian really the most efficient farmer on the continent? Had Fast Track Land Reform really been an unmitigated disaster? Recent independent studies had answered these questions in the negative, pointing out too that the *actual* beneficiaries of land reform – not Mugabe's so-called 'war veterans', but almost 250 000 of the country's rural poor – were beginning to revitalise the economy by pushing agricultural yields up to levels unseen since 1990.[43]

Gumbo reminded us that after the American dollar became Zimbabwe's de facto currency, following the trillion per cent inflation

117

hikes of 2008, the economy eventually stabilised. He said that the old white masters had been booted from their manors, and that Zimbabwe was free to do business with whomever it pleased. He vowed that ZANU-PF would sweep the coming elections, at that point tabled for October. The future, insisted Gumbo, was luminous; any negativity was Western bunk driven by shame and humiliation.

HOW GREEN IS MY MONOPOLY

We pointed the truck southeast and headed out over the Christmas Pass, through the city of Mutare, and on towards our final appointment. The Marange diamond fields lay just west of us as we passed through the town, but there was nothing to be gained from risking a surprise visit. As a photonegative of Marange, as the *anti*-Marange, as another Zimbabwean funhouse mirror, we had set up a weekend at what we'd been told was the country's 'most progressive' infrastructure project. From there, on the banks of the Save River, it was a morning's drive to the South African border. We were relaxed enough to pick up a hitchhiking policeman as we approached the district of Chisumbanje.

It was just as we'd been promised. The Matibwe catchment was Chisumbanje's highest point, and below us, far as the eye could see, were fields of sugar cane as tall as two men, a landscape of leaves nodding in windblown eddies. On the horizon, set against a wall of approaching rain clouds, an ethanol plant rose like a rocket gantry under construction. Lights blinked on its columns until swallowed by the storm.

'We may get wet,' said Graham Smith, the plant's general manager.

Earlier, he'd warned us that if it rained the black loam would become so gelatinous it would suck the shoes clean off our feet. An experienced farmer, Smith had been brought up in Que Que by a strict Calvinist father who he remembered setting out for the Bush War with a rifle slung over his shoulder and a barked 'be good' – and while he now shared an easygoing secular outlook with his Jewish wife, Judy, even he couldn't help calling this 'God's country'. It was an incontestable assertion if you happened to be a sugar cane farmer, and one we were sure would meet the approval of Smith's boss: Muller Conrad 'Billy' Rautenbach, one of Africa's most notorious white business moguls, and co-owner along with ZANU-PF of all we surveyed.

A year and a half prior to our arrival, a delegation of Chinese dignitaries had huddled exactly where we were now standing. The cane was not as high, the fields were thinner, the plant was only a set of blueprints. Smith had painted for them a picture of this very scene, but it was an oratorical exercise rather than a business pitch. Rautenbach had seen no point in sharing with the Chinese what he felt he could achieve alone. 'A full value chain ethanol producer,' said Smith, 'from processing the cane to marketing to distributing the fuel to the end-user.' An ambition we would have considered most laudable, were it not for the Rhodesian-born ex-racing driver at the wheel.

How colourful was Billy Rautenbach's career? Try this for a resumé. Back in 2009, he had admitted in court to bribing South Africa's former police commissioner a considerable sum to get rid of his 'problems' in the country.[44] Those problems included, but were not limited to, his trucking company having incurred debts of well over $100 million in the late 1990s, when he was sought on fraud charges for cheating customs and stealing from his own till.[45] Rautenbach had handed convicted South African drug trafficker Glenn Agliotti the $100 000 cash bribe at a landing strip in the Democratic Republic of the Congo, where he was back in favour after having previously been removed from his position as head of Gécamines, the state-owned enterprise that accounted for a large chunk of that particular country's mineral wealth. He would be kicked out of the Congo for a *second* time in 2007, and so was now rebranding himself in the land of his birth. A rebranding we had been invited to witness by the office of Rautenbach himself.

Green Fuels Limited, a joint venture between the state-run

Agricultural and Rural Development Authority (ARDA) and a pair of Rautenbach-controlled entities called Rating Investment Limited and Macdom Investment Limited, had broken ground on the plant in early 2010. Work had progressed quickly, with shifts operating around the clock, and Rautenbach's PR people were now punting the March 2011 launch as both 'a breakthrough for the African energy sector' and 'a boon for the local economy'. In terms of the savings it would mean on fuel imports, as well as its potential to generate revenue and create jobs, the project had been pitched to us as a gift from Rautenbach to the good citizens of Zimbabwe – a clean energy initiative of which they could all be proud; a promise that they would never have to suffer empty fuel pumps again.[46]

'Come,' said Smith, heading for his four-by-four as the first drops started to fall. 'Let's get out of here. Tomorrow, we go look up close.'

◆

The $600 million plant, the only new piece of industrial infrastructure for hundreds of kilometres, was astounding. We were walked through each of its four components; shown where the cane would be fed into the mill for crushing, where the bagasse would be fed into the boiler, where the steam would be fed back into the generating plant, where the ethanol would be fed out from the distillery. We climbed the stairs to the roof of the boiler frame, the structure that had resembled from afar a rocket gantry, and were told by Smith that it had been shipped across the ocean from Brazil. As we looked down on the construction workers below, we were informed that 3 500 employees were currently on the books. We learned that the plant had a daily capacity of 350 000 litres, that it was financed by Rautenbach and government loans, and that the company aimed to build more plants so that it could meet more of Zimbabwe's fuel needs. We heard Smith say this: 'By the end of the process, Zimbabwe will be the regional leader in ethanol production.' It was all very convincing, because we could see it, and because Smith was a convincing tour guide. But what we were seeing, we knew, was not the issue.

120

As far back as 2008, shortly after Rautenbach had been deported from the DRC, ARDA's chief executive had been fired for refusing to sanction the project. While the details of his dismissal had been murky, it was widely believed that he'd objected to a scheme whereby hundreds of peasants would be illegally removed from their land. This belief would later be given credence by an allegation, made by the leader of the MDC-affiliated National Constitutional Assembly, that although ARDA had only 5 100 hectares of land available to deed to Macdom, Rautenbach had simply gone ahead and forcibly seized a further 8 000 hectares from local villagers.[47] Fast Track Land Reform, albeit with a twist.

The best estimates, surprising as they were to some, were that only 5-10 per cent of the farms seized during the land reform process had been handed to Mugabe's cronies.[48] Rautenbach, it's safe to say, did not figure in this equation. He couldn't, because although he was definitely a crony – a Wikileaks cable would reveal that he hated the month of January, as that was the time ZANU bigwigs asked for 'help' with their kids' school fees[49] – he didn't fit the category. He wasn't a ZANU police general occupying the tobacco plantation of a white Bush War vet, he was a white businessman occupying the plots of rural peasants, 247 of whom would be forced to relocate to Mozambique.[50]

For Graham Smith, the best medicine was to get the job done – eye on the prize, build the plant, 'do some good for the economy'. The project's general manager did not want to talk about land grabs. He let slip that his own farm had been invaded in 2000, but that was all he would say. Was his badly mangled leg, which caused him to walk with a pronounced limp, a result of the attack? We didn't ask. He said that he found the concerns of his fellow white Zimbabweans 'self-pitying and pointless'. He felt it was in everyone's best interests to simply move on.

After the tour, we were invited to sit with Graham and Judy on their veranda. An exercise bike was aimed at the swift-flowing Save River, and between the shrieking of hawks we could hear distant clanging from the plant.

'You know, we tried moving to Australia,' said Judy, still wearing her workout gear. 'We did six weeks there, travelling from town to town. It felt like a bloody police state it was so highly regulated.' Added Graham: '*Ja*, this is what we're used to. Things have changed but they haven't changed, if you know what I mean. It's the same old place, Zimbabwe.'

◆

Indeed it was. In 2013, arguing that the Ian Smith regime had done the same in the 1970s, the Zimbabwean government would unilaterally introduce mandatory blending of unleaded petrol and ethanol – first at a ratio of 95 per cent to 5 per cent, then at a ratio of 90 per cent to 10 per cent, and finally at a ratio of 85 per cent to 15 per cent. Despite the fact that a motorist would take the government to the Constitutional Court, stating that he had no desire to use blended fuels and that his right to freedom of choice had been violated, the government would up the ethanol count at all Zimbabwe's pumps once again in 2014, to 20 per cent. Green Fuels would remain the sole supplier, effectively placing Billy Rautenbach in control of the country's energy sector, allowing him to charge up to 25 per cent more for his product than any other supplier anywhere in the world. The fuel bills of ordinary Zimbabweans would rise dramatically, Nissan Zimbabwe would withdraw all warranties on its fuel systems, and Rautenbach would announce plans to build four more plants. All talk of Green Fuels setting up its own marketing and distribution networks to service the private consumer would be forgotten. The company would talk instead of exporting surplus product and developing 46 000 hectares of land for commercial cane. It would not say how this land would be acquired.[51] Graham Smith, for all his hard work and sincerity, would turn out to be just another money funnel into ZANU-PF's heart.

And so the anti-Marange was, in fact, Marange – except here, instead of diamonds, was ethanol. Happily for Rautenbach, his product did not require a global market to be of value, at least not in the early stages. Had there been a reason for him to cut a deal with that Chinese contingent, those dignitaries that had visited the plant 18 months before us, the analogy would have been complete. In our search for a more plausible explanation for the Zimbabwean story, there was still one voice missing: the voice of Fay Chung's 'new Chinese'.

BEGGING WITH A GOLDEN BOWL

Liu Guijin, special representative of the Chinese government for African affairs, was not the sort of person to demand a luxury suite. Cresting into old age, he was slight to the point of alarm, and his too-big spectacles and limp grey suit revealed absolutely nothing about his influence – in the high-stakes geopolitical chess game played between four dozen African capitals and Beijing, Mr Liu was a grandmaster.

On a chair to his left in this humble Cape Town hotel room sat Dr Martyn Davies, hair slicked back, thumbs flying over his Blackberry. It was May 2011, three months after we had left Graham Smith at Chisumbanje, and the end of the first day's proceedings at the World Economic Forum on Africa. Davies, who had so far proved our most generous China-in-Africa source, was something of a one-man onramp for businesses and governments seeking a seat on the Sino-African expressway. Frontier Advisory, the consultancy firm he'd launched in 2008, organised forums, seminars, breakfasts, lunches, dinners, banquets, meet-and-greets. If Davies had a defining outlook, a vision statement, it resided in a quote attributed to Senegal's then-president Abdoulaye Wade, one he often splayed on the opening slide of his PowerPoint presentations: 'The Chinese model for stimulating rapid economic development has much to teach Africa.'

This, as we would soon learn, put him slightly at odds with Mr Liu, but the South African had earned his stripes in the Tiananmen-era trenches, which meant that establishment figures like the special representative took note when he spoke. As an undergraduate in his early twenties, Davies had been drawn to the achievements of the Asian Tigers. He would eventually complete a doctoral thesis at universities in Taipei and Seoul, but as he'd once told us, his 'heart was always in Beijing'. In 1992, after finagling himself a visa, he had made his way from the capital to the rapidly growing city of Shenzhen, which Deng Xiaoping had just visited on his historic southern inspection tour. Barely two years after the Tiananmen massacre, this Johannesburg boy had travelled a country in the throes of an acute existential crisis. China was isolated, reeling under the weight of economic sanctions, questioning the liberalisation policies instituted when Deng had first risen to prominence in 1978.

The reformist sage had emerged from seclusion to show the country the light, and had chosen as the site for his sermons China's burgeoning southern coast. In Davies's eyes – eyes, it's fair to say, that the rest of the world would soon see through – this was the moment that changed everything. Deng had minted many quotes on that inspection tour, but the most famous was one he never actually uttered. *To get rich is glorious.* Martyn Davies had taken the apocryphal axiom to heart. He'd been profoundly moved by the idea that here, in Deng's philosophy, lay the path for African development. Productivity equals stability; pragmatism over ideology; growth before democracy.

It was an idea that Davies would expand upon, deepen and nurture; eventually, it would form the bedrock of his business. His commitment to it would bring him into contact, and often into lasting friendships, with Beijing's foreign ministry mavens.

'Hey, Mr Liu,' said Davies, following the formal introductions. 'I've been singing your praises to these guys for months. Before we get into the tough stuff, maybe they want to hear about your background from *you.*'

Liu turned to us, smiling diffidently. 'What is there to say? I am just an ordinary worker, and I joined the foreign ministry in 1972 because that's what I was *told* to do.'

Although delivered in less than five minutes, Liu's story, as promised by Davies, was anything but ordinary to us. One day Liu was being de-polluted in a rice paddy, his back bent double in service of the Cultural Revolution, the next he was belted into the seat of a CAAC jet, his education suddenly valued by the Party, bound for Africa's capitals. He served 10 years as diplomatic courier, and in 1981 was deployed as attaché to the embassy in Nairobi, which was followed by a stint as political councillor in Addis Ababa. From 1995 to 1998, he was China's ambassador to Zimbabwe, and in 2001 he assumed the top post in South Africa, a natural step on the road to being named President Hu Jintao's 'special representative'. In between his ambassadorial appointments, he headed up the Africa department in the Beijing foreign ministry. 'All those years,' offered Liu in summation, 'something like 40 years, Africa has been my career. And I could see all that time that the continent is so abundant with natural resources, with energy, with forestry. So how come it is poor? We from China say that Africans are actually begging with a golden bowl.'

It was a line that startled even Davies, who looked up from his Blackberry and chuckled. 'Good one,' said the South African, 'gotta remember that one.' For our purposes, the line was a perfect segue into our agenda – because what we wanted to glean from Mr Liu, before we got into the specifics of Zimbabwe, was how Beijing believed it was filling the bowl.

The diplomat nodded, and then proceeded to turn the question on its head. 'Why is Africa still regarded by some scholars in the West as *lost*,' he asked, 'when it was the West's own structural adjustment programmes that caused all these problems, these wars, these coups d'état? China has *never* painted or seen Africa as a dark continent.'

What China saw instead, insisted Mr Liu, was opportunities. As someone who had lived through the Great Leap Forward and the Cultural Revolution, he felt he understood better than most how an awful set of policies could be overturned with stunning speed. In almost every way that counted, Liu was a product of his generation, a propagator of the changes wrought by Deng. He wanted us to know that the scale of China's growth was forcing the world to recalibrate, not just economically, but also ideologically. His country, he said, was pushing the West further into a corner of its own making, compelling it to entrench the neoliberal position – open market economies, regular elections, continuing deregulation – just as this ideology was losing its lustre in the wake of the financial collapse. Where African leaders once listened to the IMF and the World Bank, suggested Liu, today they ignored.

For Liu Guijin, in terms of the golden bowl, it was less an issue of *alms* than *outlook*. Never mind the billions of dollars in trade that had flowed between China and Africa since the first Forum on China-Africa Cooperation in 2000 – an initiative, incidentally, that Davies swore had been engineered entirely by Liu himself[52] – never mind the foreign direct investment, the infrastructure projects, the concessional loans, what China had really given Africa was *an option*.

'It doesn't matter if the cat is black or white,' mumbled Davies, para-phrasing Deng's immortal maxim (the one he did actually utter), 'it matters that it catches mice.'

'Precisely, Martyn!' yelled Liu. 'So African countries outside of their own willingness have been forced to adopt a multi-party system. The problem is that this multi-party system is not quite adaptable to the soil of Africa. Whenever there are elections, normally there is violence.' But then, with us barely hanging onto the mast, he changed tack midstream. 'Gradually, the multi-party system has provided the kind of chances, kind of opportunities, kind of ventilation, for pressure, for people to express their dissatisfaction. They don't need to go protesting – no! Maybe, if they choose, they can express themselves by voting.'

Once again, without looking up, Davies played the foil. 'I'm a bit confused, Liu. Given that you come from an ostensibly successful single-party state, how is it that you view a multi-party system in Africa as a positive?'

'Yes!' yelled Liu, banging his palm on the desk. 'Because we from China think whatever system, whatever social model, whatever devel-opment path, whether a one-party system or a multi-party system, it is the *Africans* who have a right to decide. China does not have a say, China does not wish to intervene. Because I think that is an ideologi-cal kind of consideration. And since China opened its doors in 1978, there's a process of what I call *de-ideologicalisation*. And now in our foreign policy you cannot find any hint of an ideology.'

◆

There he was, Deng's man in the flesh, arguing on the one hand that China had nothing to teach Africa, and on the other that it had everything to teach. He reconciled the paradox for us by claiming that where China did not insist or dictate, sometimes it cajoled or implied.

'An example,' he said, pre-empting our very next question. 'So, when I was ambassador in Zimbabwe, the land problem was brewing up, becoming hot. I met with the Zimbabwe authorities, including with their minister of agriculture, Kumbirai Kangai.[53] I told him, "Minister, you cannot copy what China did in 1949, when we liberated the country. At that time we had land reform, we just simply grabbed land from the landlords. Sometimes, the landlords even were executed. But that was over 50 years ago, now you can't simply do that! I give you advice – could you try to impose a land tax?"'

What Liu had in mind was raising the tax on land to such an extent that white farmers would either start cultivating their vast tracts of undeveloped acreage, or, as was more likely, hand it over to the government' for redistribution. 'Not that drastic revolutionary way,' he said, 'just to grab the land. Of course, later on, they took a very drastic revolutionary way. I think the effect, really, was horrible.'

But was it? And for whom? The Zimbabwean situation, we knew, had provided Mr Liu and his government with an opportunity to force a wholesale re-engineering of the global status quo by vetoing, along with Russia, the UN Security Council's attempt to impose sanctions following the election violence of 2008. As Beijing was well aware, Mugabe's oft-cited enemy, a Britain with neo-imperial designs on its lost colonial object, was nothing more than an old man's dinner table fulmination. Richard Dowden, an Africa hand no less seasoned than Mr Liu, had stated the point clearly: 'Zimbabwe's crisis showed that Mugabe was wrong: Britain no longer had power in his country or in Africa. [The] veto, cast on July 11, 2008, marked the end of the Western predominance in Africa that had existed since the end of the Cold War.'[54]

A continental shift, which, in Liu's own words, largely came down to the following: 'Whether you regard it as more corrupt or less corrupt, we don't mind about that. Because it's up to the Africans, the African governments, to address their own problems.'

Liu leaned back in his seat. 'I love Africa. The people. They are so enthusiastic, so optimistic. Even today without something to eat, they can dance and they can sing and tomorrow maybe they can find something. So I have some advice. "Don't be like us, don't be like China! Be like yourself!"'

At this exhortation, we felt it was time to get to the crux. What if 'being like yourself' wasn't good enough? What if the hands-off approach became a form of enabling, the equivalent of investing in a bar managed by an alcoholic friend? Why hadn't Beijing yanked the chain on Sam Pa and his CIF? And why, as we'd been led to believe by Ray Ndlovu, was the Exim Bank financing companies implicated in the Marange debacle?

Mr Liu stiffened as we spoke, and then fully withdrew his diplomat's sword with all the dexterity of a *wushu* master. First, he slashed away at the CIF with several quick parries. 'I don't know these people. It's a private fund in Hong Kong, which is a special zone. And it does not pay a single cent of tax to the central government. But one thing I can assure you, that has nothing to do with the Chinese government. And some of our government organisations feel really a headache, some kind of headache, with them.'

On the second point, Mr Liu's sword slashed more swiftly still. 'They say that Chinese companies are supporting corruption. That is not true. Corruption is everywhere. In China, in Europe, in the United States, in Africa. No country can claim that they don't have corruption. China's aid has been tied closely with the *projects*. It's not like the case with Western governments, because they give money directly to African governments. *No*. The idea is that the Exim Bank is responsible for lending, and the Chinese companies get the money from the Exim Bank, and they use the money to work.'

By Liu's reasoning, if the Anhui Foreign Economic Construction Group was allowed *by the Zimbabwean government* to benefit from the Marange diamond fields, then what exactly was the problem? Wasn't this the very essence of pragmatics before ideology, the very essence of non-interference, the very essence of Deng? Zimbabwe's version of land reform, as Liu had suggested, resembled Mao's version of land reform: in both countries, a violent purging of the old imperialist order had made way for the new national order. Beyond that, once enough new national orders had taken hold, what you had was a new *world* order.

In April 2015, President Robert Gabriel Mugabe, recently having celebrated his ninety-first birthday, arrived in Pretoria on his first state visit since 1994. The tour felt more like the lauding of a liberation hero than a dry diplomatic excursion, although it was that too. And while the UK's largest daily free-sheet was publishing '19 Horrifying Facts' about him,[55] South African journalists were being treated to press conferences in which the world's oldest president came off as sharp, hilarious, indefatigable. He was the chairman of the African Union and the head of the Southern African Development Community. Back home, the brain drain was reversing and tobacco production was up 235 per cent against 2009 – the crop was once again up with the best on the market, and was being sold at a premium to the Chinese.[56] As for Marange, the alluvial deposits were running out and the easy money was gone; the stakeholders would have to professionalise if they hoped to remain productive.[57]

None of this erased the enormous injustices visited upon the Zimbabwean people; none of it ameliorated the autocratic tendencies of their president. But if we had visited Zimbabwe in order to learn about what commentators said was a failed state, instead we had found something far more complicated: a ruling party financed by diamonds linked to a global market defined by the new world order. Calling Zimbabwe failed was ridiculous. In the Zimbabwean hall of mirrors that reflected this new world order, in Mr Liu's African era of 'be-like-yourself', ZANU was simply being the best ZANU it could be.

By the time you read these words, Robert Mugabe may well have succumbed to nature's most immutable law – and from where we are writing, in Johannesburg in mid-2015, it seems likely he will die exactly as he was inaugurated in 1980: an African hero. There is, after all, a powerful and growing school of thought that understands his Zimbabwe as the only truly liberated country on the continent; not a place that copies models, but a place that serves as one.[58]

Ganyesa iv

Ganyesa and its sister villages of Tlakgameng and Morokweng are not your typical South African townships. Our work has accustomed us to those places, to the dormitory communities built to deliver black labour to adjacent white cities – to the rows of low brick hostels, the shacks tumbling against lean-tos, the one-room houses laid out in regular grids.

Ganyesa may be daubed here and there with these elements, but it contains little of the township's terrible architectural logic. For one thing, it is 70 kilometres from the nearest major hub. For another, it is organic, haphazard, growing at will into the Kalahari. Still, the region's history suggests that Ganyesa and the township are kin, birthed by the same species of hallucinatory racism.

In the early 1950s, members of the apartheid regime, believing that they'd found the solution to the country's 'ethnicity problem', began legislating a series of gerrymandered tuislande, or homelands. When all was said and done, in the late 1950s, the borders of 10 black Bantustans were scrawled into the country's least forgiving earth. Comprising about 13 per cent of South Africa's landmass, these homelands were nations within a nation, unrecognised by the international community, desperately corrupt and desperately poor. Ganyesa sat in the Republic of Bophuthatswana – home of the Tswana people – a fiefdom belonging to President Kgosi Lucas Manyane Mangope, who belonged in turn to the apartheid regime. The village had a dual purpose: to house the farmhands working on the vast white-owned cattle ranches, and to keep blacks from migrating to the cities. Ganyesa's two or three shops were owned by those same whites; any black businessman was either an entrepreneurial genius, or somehow related to the Mangope clan.

As it happened, Bophuthatswana was also where white political domination on the African continent breathed its last. In early 1994, with democracy looming, Mangope had lost his sponsors in Pretoria, and with them his power base. As he floundered, the Afrikaner Weerstandsbeweging (AWB), a white separatist militia, invited themselves into the territory to 'protect' white South African nationals from anti-Mangope violence. Travelling in convoy, members of the far-right group fired indiscriminately on the streets of Mmabatho, Bophuthatswana's capital. The enduring image of this debacle remains Kevin Carter's famous photograph: an AWB member named Alwyn Wolfaardt pleads for help, two comrades slumped beside him, moments before he receives a bullet from a black man's gun.

The AWB was reduced to a freakshow, Mangope was brushed aside, and Bophuthatswana was rolled into Nelson Mandela's Rainbow Nation. Officially governed by the province in distant Potchefstroom, the Dr Ruth S Mompati District is now properly overseen by a 12-member tribal council housed up the street from where we sit. Flush with patronage, Ganyesa, population 20 000, grows by the day. The people we meet on our trawl through the strip malls – Tswana, Afrikaner, Pakistani, Bangladeshi, Chinese – allow that growth has come at the expense of homogeneity.

In this frontier town on the edge of the Kalahari, the old laws of segregation have become meaningless; new ones have arisen to take their place.

FIVE

NIGERIA

Things Fall Together: Nollywood's Simple Secret

'Our determination to survive can often be outweighed by our will-ingness to accept our fate.'
— Nollywood box office smash *Last Flight to Abuja* (2013)

OF OIL FIELDS AND RED CARPETS

We had assumed that the 2013 African Movie Academy Awards, which claimed a guest list that included some of the busier people on the continent, would start and finish on time. Not even close. We were in the middle of the Niger Delta, the centre of Nigeria's oil-producing region, watching stars alight from SUVs. Crowds of onlookers had gathered behind the security cordon, and were calibrating their screams according to the fame of each face. Nollywood, we knew, had always trafficked in glamour, not least because it belonged to a media ecosystem that nourished celebrity tabloids, TV chat shows and gossip websites – a shadow industry almost as significant as the one it purported to cover.[1] Still, as with most occasions steeped in glamour, the details soon revealed the lie: broken tiles in a filthy bathroom; a fray at the edges of the red carpet; sequins missing from a starlet's gown.

'Ah, *oyinbos*, white guys,' said a voice behind us, as we were taking all of it in. 'Let me get a picture with you.' His name was Solomon, and he was the latest of many that night to confuse our paleness for star-dust – why else, the logic seemed to run, would *oyinbos* be here? Our sudden status as celebrities had become an impediment to our work, and so we politely declined. It turned out, however, that Solomon was head of the ceremony's security; in exchange for a photograph, he could offer us a seat at the governor's banquet, to be held after the show. We were provided with his mobile number, and ushered by his deputy into the upstairs gallery, where he would be sure to come and fetch us.

Red carpet, AAMAs 2013, Yenagoa, Bayelsa State

A few days before, back in Lagos, we'd heard that Yenagoa, capital of Bayelsa State, was going to be flush that night with two of Nigeria's less acknowledged commodities: exceptionalism and hard-nosed optimism. Indeed, our purpose in the country was to investigate the industry where these commodities were being mined in abundance, the thousands of filmed entertainments generated under the neologism 'Nollywood'. Although the name itself had recently raised the ire of no less a personage than Wole Soyinka,[2] Nigeria's Nobel literature laureate, we'd guessed that such bitterness was the privilege of an older generation. Exceptionalism and optimism being the province of the young, we'd discovered that some of the nation's freshest literary talents had been fully buying in. And we were now sitting in what we'd been told was the industry's youthful heart. 'Nigeria's "Oscars",' an insider had informed us. 'If you guys want to meet the players, you should forget what you've read about the Delta and get on a plane.'

And so we did. The annual African Movie Academy Awards, known to all as the 'AMAAs', had become – like the Nigerian export sector it celebrated – something of a test case for our continental peregrinations. If Nollywood's future tracked with that of the Africa it so efficiently entertained, we wanted to know whether its practitioners were content to accept the status quo, or whether they were planning to aggressively annex more eyeballs and wallets in Benin, Botswana, Brooklyn and beyond. Africa, as the criticism so often ran, produced nothing but holes in the ground – here was an industry that had gushed forth without anyone sinking a shaft; without the assistance of Chinese or Western multinationals, or international aid. Here was an authentically homegrown phenomenon that was generating *stuff* in enormous quantities, a private sector explosion, a free market fundamentalist's dream. Were there lessons to be learned as far as other nascent African sectors were concerned? Moreover, did Nollywood offer a roadmap for creating an export market of indigenously African, eminently international products? The AMAAs, we hoped, would go some way to answering those questions.

But patience would be required. Five hours past the scheduled start time, as we watched from Solomon's designated perch, the AMAAs opened with a stand-up comedy set delivered by a Christian entertainer named G-Bones. 'I've got God in my bones,' he explained.[3]

Then, the speeches began. An enormous man in a white silk tunic and black fedora, Governor Seriake Dickson took to the stage to remind the audience that Bayelsa State was known as 'The Glory of All Lands' –

a tagline endorsed by Big Oil. The governor was quick to point out that the AMAAs, as much as the African film industry for which they spoke, were a core component of the state's revitalised branding strategy. Instead of associating Bayelsa with the worst of the petro-state's depredations, he suggested, we should all come to think of it as the home of Nollywood.

'In any knowledge-based economy, creativity is the greatest collateral,' said the governor. To that end, he invoked the fame of Omotola Jalade Ekeinde – @RealOmoSexy to her legions of Twitter followers – the actress who'd recently been included in *Time* magazine's '100 most influential people' list.[4] A phalanx of praise singers ululated as he listed the investments being made in tourism, agriculture and manufacturing, his preparation of the state for 'life without oil' (it was as bound to run out in the Delta as it was anywhere else) and his sanctioning of the plans for a PGA golf course 'where a major tournament will be played'. The governor's masterstroke, however, was his announcement of a film industry trust fund with an initial disbursement of $16 million, which would function in tandem with a pledge of just under $200 million from the federal government in Abuja. In addition, he promised to build an underwater imaging facility, and a film school for the training of technicians within a larger Bayelsa Film and Arts City.[5]

To those in the know, the subtext was as clear as a Nollywood plotline – with Delta native and former Bayelsa governor Goodluck Jonathan at the time serving as the nation's president, Nigeria's power-base ran through the region like a steel spine.[6] Just as Hollywood had come to be associated in its political affiliations with the Democratic Party in the United States, so too were Jonathan and Dickson attempting to consummate a marriage between Nollywood and the then-ruling People's Democratic Party (PDP) in Nigeria. The parallels were as remarkable as they were explicit. 'In acknowledgement of the contributions of Nollywood,' said Dickson, nearing the end of his speech, 'we will make plots of land available for stars to build residences, so this great city will one day resemble Beverly Hills.'

Whether the promise symbolised his misaligned priorities or his visionary leadership depended, we thought, on what one made of Beverly Hills as a developmental model. For her part, AMAA chief executive Peace Anyiam-Fiberesima appeared a little underwhelmed. After a cursory thank-you to the government for its generosity, she outlined what she saw as some of the more structural obstacles to the growth of African film. 'The theme this year is *Africa One*,' she said, her voice cracking with overuse, her face marked – in the unflattering camera close-up – by the sleep she'd lost in getting to this night. 'Because we are, in fact, not yet united, because we ask ourselves for visas when we cross borders. *No one* is going to tell our stories the way we can tell our stories. We *want* to bring together the diverse African filmmaking communities across the continent. We *need* to start taking over the continent financially. We *need* to take on Bollywood and Hollywood, and to fight piracy internally and externally.'

The chief executive's speech was essentially Nigerian in character: a plea for the Kenyan, Senegalese, Ghanaian, Beninese and – most significantly – the Nigerian and South African filmmakers in the audience to understand that they were agents of their own destiny. Government handouts notwithstanding, hope for Anyiam-Fiberesima lay in the continent fully integrating as a distribution and financing bloc. In the rapidly advancing digital age, online consumption was a matter of years from predominance. But would African film be around to satiate the demand? Without expanding both markets and financing opportunities, she said, Nollywood and its continental cousins would be crushed by Hollywood, Bollywood, and any number of 'woods between. In stressing the slow pace of intra-African cooperation, the AMAA organiser had, unwittingly or otherwise, echoed the complaint of just about every other local industry on the continent.

◆

In late March 2013, while we were waiting for our visas to come through, Nigeria was mourning the loss of a legend. Throughout his long life, Chinua Achebe had displayed a genius for appropriating and subverting the West's dominant literary forms. *Things Fall Apart*, hailed an instant classic on its publication in 1958, had endured as a devastating comment on the arrogance of the European tradition, its moral force located in its unprecedented portrayal of the African's interior world.[7] The year before he died, Achebe would reflect on his processes in an autobiographical lament for Biafra, his short-lived Igbo republic. 'When I saw a good sentence, saw a good phrase from the Western canon, of course I was influenced by it,' he admitted. 'But the story itself – there weren't any models. Those that were set in Africa were not particularly inspiring. If they were not saying something that was antagonistic toward us, they weren't concerned about us.'[8]

Culture evolves by its own rules, and while we had no reason to believe that Achebe looked with greater compassion on Nollywood than his contemporary Wole Soyinka, we couldn't help but identify his legacy in the movies we'd seen playing the length and breadth of the continent – on the home players and smartphones; in the bars and buses and airport lounges, and any other public space where one could stare up at a flickering screen. These were African stories told by Africans for Africans, and in Nollywood's unwritten decree we'd detected glimmers of Achebe's distinctive outlook, if not exactly – or not quite yet – his peerless standards.

To audiences familiar with American or Indian cinema, Nigerian video films could appear hopelessly slipshod: scenes dragging on interminably; lighting and camerawork amateurish; melodrama turned up to 11, music to 12. Scores of artists and intellectuals had dismissed the industry in the strongest possible terms, most notably the French New Wave cinéaste Jean Rouch, who'd once called it 'the AIDS of the film industry'.[9] And yet because over the years audiences had been only too happy to get infected, a small core had lately started to emerge that believed in raising the game. 'Our histories and cultures are oral,' the actress and producer Najite Dede told us, 'so there's a lot of talking in Nollywood – people talking endlessly. But things are changing. Now we are learning *craft*, we're learning how to *show*. It is happening, and it is truly African in the organic way. You throw corn in the bush and three weeks later, boom!'

Lots and lots of corn had been thrown in this bush. Details on

Nigerian cinema's fecundity had largely been derived from a disputed UNESCO study commissioned by the government of Quebec and published in 2009. Researched over the course of 2006, the report had looked in detail at the film industries in 99 countries, and had concluded that India had produced 1 091 feature-length films, Nigeria 872, and the United States 485,[10] with the rest of the world lagging behind by leagues. Official but not necessarily accurate figures were also available from Nigeria's National Film and Video Censorship Board, stating that between 1994 and 2006 – Nollywood's 'first wave' – 8 868 films had been legally distributed in Nigeria, 761 of which had been made in 2006. In 2008, as many as 1 711 films had apparently been produced,[11] and while the industry had levelled off somewhat in the intervening years, the best estimate was that by 2011 about 50 features were being filmed a week,[12] providing employment for 300 000, and generating anywhere from $286 million to $600 million a year in revenue.[13]

By contrast, the most recent figures had Hollywood pumping $16 billion into California's economy per annum, with Bollywood generating around $2.5 billion. Nigeria had never been able to boast anywhere near an equivalent to Disney's Marvel Studios, where filmmakers could run up a $200 million production bill, and the marketing department might spend a further $200 million on a global campaign. But while almost every other film industry on earth had for years been receiving massive injections of capital – otherwise known as subsidies – from their respective governments, Nollywood had until 2013 been driven by a uniquely Nigerian laissez-faire. The average Nollywood flick could cost between $15 000 and $75 000 to produce, take as little as a week to shoot, and after a speedy turnaround move anywhere from 20 000 to a million units – at $1 to $2 a pop – out of hawker stalls across the continent. Cinemas had only recently returned to Nigeria, and distribution had always relied upon what an insider had once described as 'the cancerous Alaba economics',[14] Alaba being the Lagosian warren of alleys lined with stalls from which Nollywood films and their pirated doppelgangers would be flung into the atmosphere at prices that dipped and dived with meteorological caprice.

About half the movies were being scripted in English, a third in Yoruba, and the remaining percentage in Hausa and other local languages. Hausa films, catering to the Muslim north, bore an uncanny resemblance to Bollywood musicals and were thus vastly different from their southern counterparts (based in Kano, the industry had been termed – what else? – Kanywood). With remarkable agility, the Nigerian film industry had taught itself to cater to the fragmented local market, the diaspora abroad, and the pan-African English-speaking audience that numbered over half a billion.[15] The stories were about many things, but above all they concerned *change* – they depicted a society caught between modernity and tradition, governed by witchcraft and betrayal, transformed by fast money, and by oil. In Nigeria's extremes, Africans had found versions of their reality.[16]

Blackberry Babes Reloaded; *Friendly Scorpion*; *Kiss and Tell 2* – the titles, plotting and imagery were so lurid that Canadian documentary, *Nollywood Babylon*, had fetishised the industry as a rambunctious evangelical Holy Roller's club.[17] In practice, however, the sector was on most days more akin to bricklaying or textile manufacturing. As Don Pedro Obaseki, filmmaker and first president of the Filmmaker's Cooperative of Nigeria, had put it, 'For many people, cinema isn't an art. It is something of an assembly line.'[18]

No doubt, Nollywood appeared to provide the model for how any vibrant, free-flowing and unencumbered African industry might develop, or *not* develop, as the case may be. Nollywood resisted structure, courted chaos, and in its resilience resembled a Big Boy's bulletproof Mercedes Benz. And while it would be wildly inaccurate to say that it thrived in *opposition* to the state,[19] it had since its inception in 1992, and throughout several of the more oppressive regimes the continent had known, remained largely independent of Abuja's ministrations; if it was a mess, it was a mess of its own making. Where the state could help, especially regarding the implementation of intellectual copyright laws to tamp down piracy, nothing had been forthcoming.[20] Nollywood had thrived as an indigenous African industry, shorn of affect, capturing the dreams and nightmares of almost a billion people in a manner that was at once disquieting and thrilling, garish and titillating – and if Soyinka and his ilk thought to argue that it had no right to exist, [21] it was doing all this while generating hundreds of millions of dollars in the process.

◆

It was now midnight, and nary an award had been bestowed. The remainder of the AMAAs made an Oscar broadcast seem pithy by comparison. We filed out of the State Council Theatre at 4 am, dizzy with exhaustion and hunger, dreaming of the spread at the governor's banquet. But it wasn't to be. Solomon hadn't returned to his seat in the gallery, and his mobile phone was going straight to voice mail. We waited in vain for him by the theatre doors, too tired even to fob off the camera crews who wanted nothing more at this hour than to capture on film a pair of *oyinbos*. 'We're glad we came,' we said into their microphones, 'we're sure these awards will do good for the Delta's image. But again, guys, we're no experts.'

Two hours later, as dawn broke, we spanned the black waters of a Niger River outlet. Barefoot, rag-wearing children picked their way along the embankments, while clouds of bugs swarmed the blinking lights atop cellular towers. The occasional burp of a gas flame was visible downriver.

'Six months ago, I would not have taken people like you,' our driver had told us the previous day, when we were negotiating the return-trip price from Port Harcourt. 'Now, it is fine.'

The Niger Delta, with Port Harcourt's airport as its gateway, had long provided ticker fodder for Western news bulletins. This, after all, was where 2.4 million barrels of oil gushed from the ground every day, and a further $3.1 trillion worth of crude burbled in reserve.[22] If the situation in one of the planet's more active kidnapping zones was calmer in 2013 than it had been in previous years, travel agents remained unpersuaded. Tourism, extreme or otherwise, was non-existent.

Many millions of years before our arrival, on its final run to the sea, the Niger River had exploded into the network of outlets that satellite photographs would one day portray as a giant, bloodshot eye – a symbol, some might say, of the region's almost incurable hangover. *Oyinbos*, who'd been pumping the system with toxins since the start of the slaving era, had properly come into their own in 1956, when oil was first struck in commercial quantities in the small town of Oloibiri. Over the ensuing half-century, although their villages would literally ooze with spilled crude,[23] the people of the Delta would see very little return on this natural wealth. By April 2013, when government forces had begun to gain the upper hand in their campaign against MEND, the violently retributive Movement for the Emancipation of the Niger Delta,[24] there were still 31 million Nigerians living here on a combined average of less than $2 per day – meanwhile, the Delta was generating 80 per cent of Nigeria's revenues, and a staggering 95 per cent of its foreign exchange earnings.[25]

Despite the desecrated landscape outside the cab's windows, most analysts understood that through a trick called 'rebasing' Nigeria would overtake South Africa as the continent's largest economy by 2014.[26] And yet while the country may have been growing at 7.5 per cent per annum, it was stubbornly refusing to develop – unemployment had only *increased* along with the GDP figures, from 21 per cent in 2010 to 24 per cent in 2011.[27] Ngozi Okonjo-Iweala, Nigeria's celebrity finance minister,[28] had calculated that a minimum growth rate of 7 per cent would need to be sustained between 2007 and 2015 if poverty was to be cut in half. 'Anything less,' she'd noted in her book *Reforming the Unreformable*, 'would mean stagnation or worsening of the incidence of poverty.'[29] In other words, 7.5 per cent was bare bones for a nation that promised to expand from roughly 170 million souls in 2013 to 440 million by mid-century.[30]

There were other problems. The country produced less than half the electricity of North Dakota for 249 times more people.[31] There was the Boko Haram insurgency in the Muslim north, a low-level civil war in which scores of people were being killed every day. There was the looming 2015 general election, which would pit Goodluck Jonathan's PDP against the eventual winners, former military dictator Muhammadu Buhari's All Progressives Congress.

On the upside, 440 million people was an enormous audience, and Nigeria had plotlines to service every last one of them.

Niger Delta, April 2013, Bayelsa State

THE RELUCTANT MISTER NOLLYWOOD

Chief Eddie Ugbomah's first film, *The Rise and Fall of Dr Oyenusi*, was released in 1977, two years after he'd returned to Nigeria from England, to find a nation ravaged by petroleum and the gun. Born

143

in Lagos to parents from the Delta, Chief Eddie had always fashioned stories from the circumstances of his life. To read his self-published autobiography is to go on a picaresque journey through post-liberation Nigeria, with Chief Eddie the rogue-as-hero, and his films the plot points in the country's violent maturation. 'My mother gave me to my uncle ... [who] sold me to some Ijaw fisherman,' he recalls of his own unhappy coming-of-age, 'but being a clever boy, I jumped into the luggage cabin and covered myself there.'[32] By 1960, when he was 19, he had made it out of the cabin and all the way to London, from where he would watch Nigeria declare independence while learning the craft of filmmaking. *The Rise and Fall of Dr Oyenusi* is set in a venal landscape without opportunities for its young men, a group of whom the eponymous Dr Oyenusi leads on a campaign of maiming and looting. The film's poster art is reminiscent of the vibrant Lemi Ghariokwu artwork that made Fela Kuti's album covers so distinctive, and is very much in line with the maestro musician's rage-inflected politicking. Lagos's Bar Beach, the stretch of sand that would one day come to be frequented by dope-smoking area boys, was at the time employed as an open-air execution arena by the junta – Chief Eddie, in a bold attempt at *cinéma vérité*, had insisted on filming there.[33] So Dr Oyenusi's urchins meet their fictional end alongside the decidedly real corpses of petty criminals, a finale that announced the arrival of a filmmaker who cared a great deal about Nigeria's truth.

'I *am* Nollywood,' said Chief Eddie, now 72, in answer to our impromptu request for an interview. Our return flight to Lagos had been indefinitely delayed, we had managed to talk our way into the room that served as the Port Harcourt airport VIP lounge, and the chief was only too happy to educate us further on the exigencies of the local industry. 'Nigeria is number two in the world in cinema? To me, we're number one in the world in junk making.'

We knew it was more than irony informing the thread of Chief Eddie's thoughts. The Lifetime Achievement Award he'd received at the previous night's AMAAs, together with his standing as chairman of the Board of Trustees for the Nigerian Directors and Producers Guild, meant to us that he was entitled to call himself Mr Nollywood if he wanted to. The irony, of course, was in the fact that he didn't really want to – if Chief Eddie was going to proudly claim ownership of anything, it was of a time when Nigerian cinema had tracked with the country's political realities.

From London, where his memoir has him moonlighting 'as the first ever black model in England',[34] Chief Eddie had looked on as the optimism of the liberation era soured. The country had been wrenched into colonial form in the earliest years of the twentieth century, when the British arch-colonist Frederick Lugard convinced a conglomeration of Islamic emirs and caliphates in the West African Sahel to submit to his faraway Queen. In 1914, Lugard had sutured this Muslim protectorate onto a second vast region in the south, home to the Christian Yoruba and the Igbo. And so during the independence process, which began as a 'partial' event in October 1960 and ended with the signing of the Declaration of Independence in 1963, the British had divested themselves of the most populous nation in Africa, with 250 ethnic minority groups, and 200 linguistically distinct communities living in the northern climes alone.[35]

The Tenth Parallel, the line of latitude that partitioned the Muslim north from the Christian south, had formed the basis of the British rule by division gambit, and had promised to render an independent Nigeria ungovernable.[36] Unlike so many liberation-era countries, there was no possibility in Nigeria of a unifying political party that spoke, however narrowly, of a national esprit. As the 1960s progressed, a series of crises threatened to split the country apart. On the bloody night of 15 January 1966, the so-called 'Nzeogwu coup', named for the major at its helm, threw the young country forever off course.[37] Instituted by a cabal of largely southern officers, who slaughtered the country's northern Hausa leadership almost to a man, the uprising came to be interpreted as an Igbo play for power. Following a spate of retaliatory pogroms, there was a move towards secession in the oil-rich Igbo east, and in 1967 the Republic of Biafra came into being. The civil war that followed left around two million dead.

The war over Biafra was the world's first televised conflict, one defined by images of corpse-strewn villages and babies misshapen by kwashiorkor. British Prime Minister Harold Wilson was unwavering in his support for General Yakubu Gowon, the military government leader whose tactics included mass starvation of Igbo civilians,[38] primarily because Whitehall wanted a Nigeria reunited with its eastern oil fields. Wilson's cynicism was met with energetic protests by British leftists, and destroyed what remained of Chief Eddie's Anglophilia – in this story there were few good guys, and the crude made the bad guys even badder.

After his return in the mid-1970s and the release of *Dr Oyunesi*, Chief Eddie redoubled his efforts to portray the country as he saw it first-hand. Nigeria was bedevilled by a succession of juntas, interrupted occasionally by coups, all of it an indirect result of Lugard's colonial-era attempt to concertina what were *at least* three countries into one monster state. Chief Eddie's ambition to capture this all on celluloid was further complicated by the Second World Festival of Black Arts, otherwise known as FESTAC, which kicked off with enormous fanfare in January of 1977. The month-long festival was designed to mimic the durbars celebrated by British administrations in India and Nigeria, and so queasy colonial connotations remained indelible despite FESTAC's pan-African rhetoric and professions of black solidarity. FESTAC instantly devolved into an unholy mélange of 'cultural tradition', whatever that meant, and 'fast capitalism', the meaning of which was only too clear. Lagos's modernist National Theatre, built to headquarter the festivities, resembled from certain angles the hat worn by the country's military officers, an accidental but nonetheless potent architectural manifestation of the junta. Nigerians found that they were not celebrating art so much as a utopian interpretation of the centralised state, paid for by the Niger Delta's ever-flowing munificence. 'Oil for dollars, art for dollars, the equivalence was confirmed by the spectacular scale of the festival itself,' wrote cultural anthropologist Andrew Apter.[39] Blackness, African-ness and 'tradition' had now joined the global flow, but observers couldn't be blamed for feeling that FESTAC was an attempt to pressgang artists into the service of the country's military rulers. Leopold Senghor, Senegal's poet-president and liberation hero, abdicated his position as the festival's co-patron in disgust.

Despite the best efforts of Chief Eddie's fellow pioneer, Ola Balogun,[40] the festival never premiered a worthy Nigerian film. At odds with both the bitter nuance of FESTAC's more articulate detractors and the oil-jacked triumphalism of the state, Chief Eddie prepared his unambiguously titled *Oil Doom*. At the time of the film's release in 1979, with the cultural wound of FESTAC still suppurating, Nigeria was the sixth largest oil producer in the world, and the Delta was delivering over $24 billion worth of crude a year.[41] President Shehu Shagari's regime was a sinkhole of corruption, a government of contractors for contractors, where kickbacks comprised 50 per cent of the cost of doing business.[42] In keeping with this dismal reality, *Oil Doom's* main character, Uwa, was forced off his land by a leadership in collusion with the oil companies. Uwa fought back, and died long before the credits rolled.

Chief Eddie shot several more films, but Nigeria's brief flirtation with socially conscious celluloid cinema ground to a halt during the succession of military regimes and economic implosions of the 1980s and 1990s. Cinema culture had already begun its decline pre-FESTAC, when the Casino Theatre in Yaba, Lagos, had been the target of a home-made bomb, a casualty of the Biafran war. At the turn of the 1990s, cinemas were either dead or deserted, and locals sated themselves on state-made television serials such as *Mega Fortune, Checkmate* and the Ken Saro-Wiwa-scripted *Basi and Company*.[43] Although Chief Eddie's financing had come on the back of the oil boom he'd so vigorously criticised, the structural adjustment programmes instituted during the Ibrahim Babangida regime in 1986 would choke off all means of funding. The Nigerian film industry, such as it was, withered and perished.[44]

◆

'*Last Flight to Abuja, The Contract, The Meeting*,' said Chief Eddie, reeling off a list of recent Nollywood smashes. 'I don't call those movies, I call them soaps. They're not in the class of what you call a movie. They're fighting hard to keep the industry going, and I support them for it. But if they don't want to grow, what can I do?'

Since we'd sat down with him, Chief Eddie had been working away at a plastic half-jack of whiskey. Like us, he'd gotten very little sleep – his eyes were rheumy, and his thin frame was beginning to shake. His daughter, who was his chaperone on the trip, was proving an immense irritation to him. She was picking up the suitcases, putting them down, sighing heavily when the lone airport official had no answer to her question about departure times, which she would ask again every five minutes. 'Stop it, already!' barked Chief Eddie. 'Can't you see I'm talking to these men?'

This, we guessed, was part of the problem. Either his daughter had heard it all before and was slowly being driven to distraction, or she didn't want him to go on record. Whatever it was, Chief Eddie didn't care; he was now fully warming up to his theme. 'The industry is dead!' he spat. 'Not dying – dead! But it can be woken, within a month!'

The veteran filmmaker's observations dovetailed with those we'd heard at the AMAAs, from the mouth of Peace Anyiam-Fiberesima. They both believed that the Nigerian film industry required a wholesale reconfiguration – one that would reflect, if not presage, a few of the changes Nigeria's leaders needed to make if they wanted the country to develop. 'So the president of Nigeria is giving us $200 million,' said Chief Eddie, 'and nobody can access it because we aren't organised. We don't have records, we don't have good foreign partners.'

By 'foreign', Chief Eddie wasn't referring to Americans or Europeans. In his conception, Nollywood – or rather, a continental cinema industry with a financial base in Lagos – had to be an entirely African endeavour. 'We should team up and tell Hollywood to go to hell! We've got the market and we've got the stories! I don't know if it's the arrogance you have in South Africa or the stupidity we have in Nigeria, but we don't do it!' The quality issues that had dogged Nollywood since its earliest days had, in Chief Eddie's opinion, now become terminal. Weak production values were killing new markets and damming up potential streams of financing, and indeed, no Nollywood film had until that point played in a mainstream South African cinema. It was one thing to make a film for $25 000 and sell a million copies on the street, said Chief Eddie, it was altogether another to spend $1 million and blow the roof off cinemas across the continent.

Which of course was the crux: did Nollywood *really* not want to grow? Although we could've taken Chief Eddie's word for it, we knew that the industry was too diffuse – too febrile and chaotic – to be represented by any one man. What we *could* take from Chief Eddie Ugbomah, as from Peace Anyiam-Fiberesima, was the fact that the problems were structural and that the structures were deeply embedded. Nollywood, as any of its spokespeople could tell you, had first been served up to Nigeria in 1992, during the second military junta, a year prior to the indefensibly vile Sani Abacha taking power. This was a time when civil service jobs were worthless, when pensions offered little reassurance, when the currency was a national joke. Crime was tearing through communities like inclement weather, and thus keeping millions of citizens indoors. It was no accident that video films rose in prominence alongside Pentecostal Christianity and fundamentalist Islam – they were the only choice of salve.

So *Living in Bondage*, credited as the first pureblood Nollywood production, hit reeling Nigeria like a cultural A-bomb. The precedent to the film's 1992 release was *not* the celluloid scene within which Chief Eddie had crusaded, but a mash-up of pulpy Onitsha market literature – hastily produced, mega-selling pamphlets with titles like *Chief Awolowo and the Bitterness of Politics* – and Yoruba travelling theatre, which brought to the mix an established genre tradition. The market gap that allowed such influences to meld had been the sudden cancellation, in the late 1980s, of the TV serials put out by the Nigerian Television Authority: the non-payment of advertising shares to filmmakers had, on the one hand, deprived countless households of their daily fix, and, on the other, left a constellation of stars without a means to shine. Needless to say, it was a gap that would have meant nothing had nobody felt the urge to seize it.

Nollywood lore has it that some time in 1992 an Igbo electronic goods salesman by the name of Kenneth Nnebue was sitting on a large consignment of blank videotapes, a shipment that in the economic climate was quickly becoming dead weight. The lore is less clear on whether Nnebue hit on the idea himself or whether he caved in to the badgering of his colleague Okechukwu Ogunjiofor, but either way a plan to move the units was hatched – they would fill the tapes with the big celebrity names of the day, including Kanayo O Kanayo, Francis Agu and Kenneth Okonkonwo. Of course, these out-of-work actors couldn't just stare into the camera and smile: they would need to be placed in a story. And who knew what kinds of stories Lagosians liked better than Igbo electronic goods salesmen? The movie, about a man who gets sucked into a money ritual in which sacrificing his beloved wife brings him untold wealth at the expense of everlasting happiness, was an instant and unprecedented smash. 'To an extraordinary degree,' wrote the film scholar Jonathan Haynes, 'Nnebue's *Living in Bondage*, the film that started the Nigerian video boom, contains the seeds of almost everything that followed.'[45] Although it was by no means the first example of Nigerian video, after *Bondage* the sections of Lagos that had once sold blank videotapes and discounted video players, most notably Nnamdi Azikiwe Street and Ereko Lane in Idumota, became outdoor film markets.

Later, as the industry evolved, rules of a sort took shape. Much of the financing came from eastern-based Igbo 'marketers' – more properly, distributors – a detail that would endow Nollywood with both its unmatchable vitality and its potentially fatal flaw. These salesmen would double as producers, churning out as many films as they could as fast as they could, with scant thought for the craft of filmmaking and no thought at all for the art. Technicians would be drawn largely from the Delta region, and writers and directors, at least initially, from TV serials and Yoruba theatre. After Sani Abacha's death and the re-institution of democracy in 1999, Nigeria had suddenly emerged as one of the planet's more prolific centres of film production.

It was an arrangement that bred its winners and losers, and the man sitting across from us in the Port Harcourt airport belonged firmly in the loser category. Celluloid had officially perished in Nigeria decades before it perished in the rest of the world[46] – Chief Eddie, who'd shot his entire oeuvre on 16mm film, had never been willing to make the shift. Nollywood's ontological instigators were relatively cheap video cameras and VHS cassettes, followed by even cheaper digital cameras and video CDs imported from Singapore, Taiwan and, eventually,

China's south coast. For the idealists, this represented the democratisation of an art form long commandeered by foreign-educated snobs. The snobs saw it as the hijacking and debasement of an art form by illiterate hacks. But wherever one stood on the spectrum, Nollywood as a phenomenon appeared to have arrived at a crossroads. On that point, Chief Eddie wanted to say one last thing about the president's $200 million – and specifically, about the possibilities it heralded for intra-African co-productions.

'If I see crews who want to work in Nigeria and they have the know-how, I will present their case to the government,' he told us. 'But the government wants guarantees that they're dealing with established people who have collateral. The equipment, the director, the lighting and cameraman – *all* of those count as money. Then the Nigerian side brings the cash and the cast, the South Africans produce, and we shoot the film. That is what I would call the "New Nollywood", which is what the president *wants*.'

Chief Eddie put the empty half-jack aside and started in on a bag of oranges. 'But we're not ready,' he said. 'Africans are too stupid.'

MAD BUDDIES TO THE LAST

In 2012, the South African popcorn movie icon Leon Schuster released a film, his fourteenth such effort, entitled *Mad Buddies*. Schuster, whose career began in the 1980s with the *You Must Be Joking!* hidden camera franchise, had remained the highest-grossing African filmmaker of all time. *Mad Buddies* was a mash-up of slapstick gags, a story that saw Boetie (Schuster), your stereotypically fat Afrikaner, reluctantly team up with Beast (Kenneth Nkosi), your stereotypically fat Zulu, in order to unsuccessfully complete a road trip. Although the film was an obvious send-up of South Africa's racial divisions, it had occurred to us on the flight from Johannesburg to Lagos, as our screens served up images of Boetie and Beast slamming into tree trunks and pulling beehives from their pants, that it read as a metaphor for the dysfunctional relationship between sub-Saharan Africa's two giants. Everyone we met in Nigeria, down to the last interview, emphasised the importance of the Nigerian-South African connection. As Chief Eddie had noted repeatedly, South African filmmakers could claim a technical expertise on par with their counterparts in France and the US – and certainly, while *Mad Buddies* might have *aspired* to lousiness, it was still superior in production values to just about anything that Nollywood had until then offered up.

But this wasn't the half of it. In the same breath that Nollywood veterans uttered 'South Africa', they also mentioned AfricaMagic, the pay television channel that in the mid-zeroes had descended on Nollywood like a conquering army. AfricaMagic formed part of an empire comparable to Rome's, with Jacobus Petrus 'Koos' Bekker its Caesar.

In the mid-1980s, when apartheid was uttering its death grunt, Bekker joined the newspaper conglomerate Nasionale Pers (Naspers), a pillar of the Afrikaner establishment. He promptly started Africa's first pay TV channel, which he called M-Net. Come 2012, and the company's massive share of the South African media market was but a blip on its bottom line. It held a 1 per cent share of Facebook, a 35 per cent chunk of both China's Tencent and Brazil's Abril Group, and dozens of other investments in media ventures across the world. The conglomerate netted over $5 billion in revenue in 2012, and was valued at the time at $23.5 billion.[47]

MultiChoice Africa, the Naspers subsidiary that delivers digital satellite television to the continent under the consumer brand DStv, is thus a giant fist attached to a muscled arm. Operational in all but four of the continent's 54 states, it launched in Nigeria in 1994, and had since grown to over 1.6 million local subscribers – many of whom, as per articles and surveys in the Nigerian press, believed they were being 'exploited'.[48] Bekker and his lieutenants believed otherwise. 'Our group helped to modernise Africa,' the media baron told veteran South African journalist Anton Harber in 2012. 'One day DStv arrives and connects you to thirty of the best TV channels in the world ... One day you are just plugged into the global village.'[49]

Over the course of our travels, we had encountered DStv sales booths in the main square in Kenya's Indian Ocean town of Lamu, at a road-side mall in Namibia's Atlantic Ocean town of Swakopmund, and in dozens of places between. We had watched South Africans play rugby on screens from Bentiu, near the oil fields of South Sudan, to Mufulira, in the heart of the Zambian copperbelt. And aside from DStv's signature bouquet of SuperSport channels, which were mostly driving subscriptions off broadcast rights to the world's football leagues, we had spent many idle hours watching AfricaMagic – the so-called 'first dedicated TV channel made in Africa by Africans for Africans', which was the other ace up the Johannesburg-based corporation's sleeve.

According to a press release put out by the company in November 2013, to mark the occasion of AfricaMagic's tenth birthday, this channel had been 'relentlessly pioneering'. From a single offering at launch, it had hived off into a catalogue of eight sub-channels, including AfricaMagic Swahili, AfricaMagic Yoruba and AfricaMagic Hausa. Out of its offices in Lagos and Nairobi, it had initiated master classes for locals in TV production. It had introduced the first Nollywood-themed weekly magazine show *Jara*, created the *Great Africans* documentary series, and had inaugurated, in 2011, the AfricaMagic Viewers' Choice Awards. In September 2013, building on this foundation, the channel announced its 'Original Film' initiative – the astonishing aim of which was to create 80 West African movies and 56 East African movies in a single year.[50]

Chief Eddie, we can safely assume, wouldn't have been too impressed by the last point. Original or not, an output like that would only have justified his concerns. 'Forget AfricaMagic!' he'd beseeched his fellow Nigerian filmmakers, via the medium of our notebooks. 'Don't give them your film! Maybe five, six, ten years later, yes, but don't shoot a film Monday to Friday and give it to AfricaMagic for a few hundred dollars on Saturday.' He claimed to have been present when a contingent from AfricaMagic met with a guild of Nigerian producers, fixing a price of $2 500 per film with a year's moratorium following release. The deal broke down, he'd told us, when AfricaMagic negotiated directly with a prominent producer and took his entire 150-film library for about $1 000 per title, thus flooding the market and

shattering the sales price. After that, Chief Eddie had said, many producers did the same.

For her part, Caroline Creasy, MultiChoice Africa's general manager
for corporate affairs, could neither confirm nor deny the allegations.
Given her PR problems in Nigeria, and notwithstanding the fact that we
visited her at group headquarters in Johannesburg, it was understand-
able that for much of the interview she appeared to be on the defen-
sive. 'We're not the bad guys,' she told us. 'If you look at the growth
of Nollywood, AfricaMagic played a major part.' But how major was
major? While Creasy stressed that MultiChoice was a *provider* of content before it was a *producer*, and that contrary to popular opinion the
space was open to whatever other pay-TV providers wanted to play,
she said that as far as Nollywood was concerned her group had always
been involved in skills sharing. Which, we knew, was true – in 2004,
struggling to programme an abundance of films with unintelligible
dialogue, the South African company had sent two sound specialists
out to Lagos, and had been training local technicians ever since.

The key, of course, was in the word 'abundance'. AfricaMagic hadn't
grown into a bouquet of eight channels by punting Nollywood's upper
end. The content it served was the same content you could buy on VCD
in the Alaba or Idumota markets, and although it was certainly staked
in raising quality there, it wasn't about to start backing the big budget
co-productions of Chief Eddie's dreams.

For the numerous Nigerian filmmakers who decried the influence of
AfricaMagic, believing it had brought TV sales prices down to unsustainable levels, the channel seemed to exemplify just how lopsided the
relationship between South Africa and Nigeria had become. In this
sense, Koos Bekker's company was at the front of the firing line – it
was taking inordinate heat for a much bigger problem.

◆

During our time in Lagos, the extent of the 'Mad Buddies' relationship
between Nigeria and South Africa was articulated by none so clearly as
by Kola Karim. The chief executive of Shoreline Energy International,

one of Nigeria's largest privately run energy conglomerates,[51] Karim was stout with handsome features and an expensive pair of spectacles that only emphasised his wildly expressive eyes. At 44, he was a ranking member of the Davos scene, a designated World Economic Forum 'young global leader'. To our amazement, given that the rivalry between our two nations was increasingly resembling an England/ Germany football match, he had placed an example of South Africa's sporting prowess on his otherwise bare office walls: the framed game jersey worn by Springbok rugby hero John Smit, when he had captained the side to a World Cup victory in 2007. Regarding the item, Karim told us that his family had received a call from Warner Brothers, the studio responsible for *Invictus*, Clint Eastwood's dramatisation of the Mandela-inspired 1995 World Cup win. 'They were offering stupid money,' he said. 'We just didn't want to take it, we're not hungry.'

The Karim family may not have been hungry, but neither were they complacent. Shoreline had in recent years benefited from a drive to 'indigenise' swathes of the Niger Delta, in which pipelines and projects that had historically belonged to international oil companies were being offered for sale to viable local outfits. At the same time, the company was buying up energy projects elsewhere in Africa, most notably in Ghana, Uganda and Kenya, and was offering reciprocal turnkey services for those looking to invest in the Nigerian market. The four Karim brothers had transformed their mother's import-export business into a billion-dollar concern, and while year-on-year growth was dazzling, there remained an abrasion or two, the scabs of which Karim was only too happy to pick away at.

Karim's grievances were a riff on the keynote speech we'd heard at the 2013 AMAAs: the lack of effective cooperation between the continent's economic powerhouses. He used as a launching point for his disquisition the stupidity of a recent flap over yellow fever vaccination certificates – the documents Africans must lug with them when travelling across borders. In March 2012, customs officials at Johannesburg's OR Tambo airport had denied entry to 125 Nigerians, including a senator, claiming that their certificates were invalid (this despite the fact that the last confirmed case of yellow fever in Nigeria was recorded in 1995). Diplomacy being reciprocal, the same courtesy had been extended to 28 South Africans newly arrived in Lagos.

According to Karim, the enmity was reckless, alarming and lousy for business. There were, as he pointed out, over 100 South African companies active in Nigeria, including the cell phone megalith MTN, which claimed a local base of over 46 million subscribers. Bilateral trade, although it had remained largely petroleum focused, had grown from a disastrous $16.5 million in 1999 to a more robust $3.6 billion by 2011.[52] Meanwhile, said Karim, 'Twenty years after apartheid, and there's not one Nigerian business thriving in South Africa.' When Shoreline made a bid on a South African power line contract in 2006, he told us, the government asked the company to present evidence that it had a Black Economic Empowerment partner.[53] 'I was stunned,' he said. 'Last time I looked, I *was* black.'

Part of South Africa's reticence could be explained by the reputation Nigerians bore throughout Africa as drug dealers and scammers,[54] part played into the larger issue of South Africa's entrenched xenophobia, and part was due to the struggle for power and influence at multilateral bodies like the UN Security Council – on which both countries had wrestled for a lone permanent seat in 2005[55] – and the African Union, where it was becoming more and more unclear which horse to back: the galloping but easily spooked Nigerian stallion, or the plodding but reliable South African nag. Nigerian-South African relations were, it seemed, based on a zero-sum game, and therein lay Karim's, the Nigerian business community's, and Nollywood's exasperation.

We found it remarkable that Karim made the same case for a successful, growing energy corporation that most enlightened Nigerian film and video producers had been making for their own sector – the liberalised, global outlook that defined South Africa as a powerhouse to outsiders, they argued, should be applied equally to her sister countries on the continent. 'So, you get into South Africa as a Nigerian and first have to prove that you're not a criminal,' said Karim. 'I don't intend to do that! I go to Kenya, and the guys are welcoming. The amount of Nigerian businesses now going into Kenya, you'd be shocked. Kenya has scrapped visas for Nigerians. Uganda has no visa restrictions. Business is good there. We're employing people. Do you see the difference?'

We did. In order to properly grasp the subtleties, however, we were advised to consider how the financial sector had changed in West Africa over the past several years. After Nigerian banks had tightened up their balance sheets and instituted single obligor limits – 'the maximum amount a bank is allowed to lend a single borrower in relation to its total shareholders' fund', Karim explained – they'd become among the more reliable lending institutions in the world. This new regulatory environment meant that large loans had to be cobbled together from multiple banks across the continent: South African institutions had entered the Nigerian space and were now banking the country's most successful businesspeople. 'Still,' he said, 'South Africa as a market remains closed to us.'

Karim was more than willing to concede that Nigeria was infested with corruption on a grand scale – after all, there were few nations on earth that had disappeared such untold billions over the course of a five-decade resource boom. But he offered a fascinating spin on what had transpired when the corruption met with these new regulations. Whereas the rape of Nigeria's oil wealth had once brought the country to the brink of penury, dirty money was now fuelling both local construction and consumption, to say nothing of local industry, Nollywood very much included.

'You see,' he said, waving his arms expansively, '9/11 brought the idea to the world that we needed to go after the movement of cash, of capital, to stem terrorism. Today, I transfer $10 000 to your bank account, the bank is going to call and say, "what's this money for?" So think about it. People need to spend the money, either stolen or acquired legitimately. And they can't move it to Europe. So it's fuelling a local boom here. Which in itself is not such a bad thing, because it's creating jobs. If I am the governor and I stole a billion dollars, it used to find itself in a Swiss numbered account. Today I will build a stadium. You're actually *creating jobs by doing bad!*' Nigeria, according to Karim, was so flush that the biggest problem it had was how to invest in a manner that stimulated the development of a more robust, diversified economy.[56]

As for his own investments, Karim obviously took great pleasure in amassing sports souvenirs that South Africans would kill for – and the irony, given the subject of our conversation, was sublime. How, he asked, were African multilateral bodies supposed to agree on the brand of coffee in the communal kitchen if the continent's heavy hitters couldn't present a united front? While we knew that in May 2012 the Nigerian-South African Bi-National Commission had met for the first time in four years, and while this had resulted in a softening of the cross-continental stare-down,[57] it wasn't happening quickly enough for the likes of Karim. The same shortsightedness that hamstrung Nigerian film producers was thus hounding the CEO of a billion-dollar energy conglomerate, a man with significant pan-African ambitions and access to hundreds of millions of dollars in financing from all over the global south. His problem: the African chain bore broken links.

For Karim, if anything was going to fix this, it wasn't going to be government led. Echoing the views of many members of Africa's emergent business class, he saw the solution in the smartphone penetration that was expected to double on the continent within the next four years – in the technology that currently lived in the pockets of almost 100 million Africans. These were people, he said, who were informed, vocal and impatient, and their outlook would ultimately prevail. In the mid-1990s, he reminded us, no one in the Niger Delta had heard a phone ring. Now, the ringing didn't stop. 'It's about *connections*,' Karim insisted. And Nollywood, as he saw it, was an industry at the vanguard.

THE GODS ARE STILL NOT TO BLAME

She would talk, began Chimamanda Ngozi Adichie, about what she called 'the danger of the single story'. It was mid-2009, and her message to the packed auditorium in Oxford, an audience comprising mainly students and dons from the esteemed university, was that, although she had started to read at the age of four, she did not know that people like her 'could exist in literature' until she came across the works of Chinua Achebe.[58] As most in the audience understood – it was, in fact, the reason they were there – Adichie's 2006 novel *Half of a Yellow Sun* had won her a reputation in the West as Achebe's successor; it had taken the Orange Prize for Fiction, been named a *New York Times* notable book, and had earned the praise of the master himself, who'd admired it as 'fearless' and 'wise' in its portrayal of the horrors of the Biafran war. The achievement was such that not even a shallow Hollywood interpretation could have seriously damaged the author.

But *Half of a Yellow Sun* never did make the journey to California. Instead, in the words of its executive producer, Yewande Sadiku, it became a 'made-in-Nigeria' product.[59] Sadiku, who had jumped into the industry from the relative safety of investment banking, wanted to be as careful in her fundraising as Adichie had been in her promotion of the book. She wanted, she said, to apply the principles of 'formal financing' to the project. It was a strategy without precedent in Nollywood.

In order to cover the $8 million budget, a number that pushed the industry into an entirely new tax bracket, Sadiku appointed a trustee to oversee the 73 legal agreements governing individual and corporate investments. A 'completion bond', offering insurance against everything from catastrophic weather to a star's undisclosed drug habit, was secured to protect investors and guarantee a finished film. Beyond these assurances, what Sadiku promised her investors – 80 per cent of whom turned out to be Nigerian – was a slice of a prestige product, a movie that would co-star British-Nigerian Chiwetel Ejiofor, of *12 Years a Slave*, and Thandie Newton, Tom Cruise's love interest in *Mission: Impossible II*. Established international producers Andrea Calderwood and Gail Egan would be brought in to assist first-time director Biyi Bandele, and the production would be headquartered in Calabar, on Nigeria's coast, where the mostly local crew would learn a range of technical skills.

And yet made-in-Nigeria though it certainly was, the film's non-Nigerian connections presented an existential problem. In 2012, a petition was drawn up to protest the casting, with bi-racial Newton causing most of the handwringing. Newton, the protesters asserted, didn't look Igbo, didn't sound Igbo, didn't behave like an Igbo – and her role should be recast with someone who did.[60] *Half of a Yellow Sun,* which debuted to middling critical reception at the Toronto International Film Festival in 2013,[61] raised a few of the more troubling questions that filmmakers aspiring to 'quality' could expect to confront. As more investors were placated and ever larger budgets raised, would films become less African? Would more stars need to be cast whose features, like Newton's, were less of a mirror than a cypher? Would the industry become beholden to a fuzzy international mean, and thus begin to leave local audiences cold?

Despite Adichie's warnings in 2009 about 'the danger of the single story', *Half of a Yellow Sun* was in fact less Nollywood, or even Nigerian, than it was middlebrow 'world' cinema, designated for theatres in the United States, the United Kingdom and elsewhere. When she'd crunched the numbers, Sadiku had realised that the Nigerian market couldn't deliver anywhere close to breakeven for her investors. Again, this was largely the result of a distribution model that didn't include a lucrative cinema run: while the US had 100 cinemas for every million people, and India a dozen, Nigeria had a depressing 0.4 per million.[62] To service the local audience, Sadiku would need to play the game according to its own entrenched rules – which is to say, she would need to throw a VCD onto the street, hope for enormous sales, and then watch the pirates swoop in and skim the top off of her profits.[63] Because of these issues, *Half of a Yellow Sun* became a Nigerian film that was not intended for Nigerians.

It seemed, then, that the industry wasn't only at a crossroads, it was also in a cul-de-sac. Chief Eddie's conception of the 'New Nollywood', a self-contained *strictly African* film sector with Lagos as its commercial hub, would never have its moment if the supporting structures didn't allow. Regardless of the quality of the films, there could be nothing new about Nollywood if its only objective was export. That, we thought, would be to undermine the very thing we had visited Nigeria to parse – this rich homegrown product, generated by Africans and consumed by Africans, this phenomenon whose enduring value was that it existed sufficient to itself. Obviously, for there to be more to the phrase than hype, New Nollywood would need to appeal to Africans first: the export market, if the films were good enough, would follow.

Lagos street scene, April 2013

'Look, like I say about New Nollywood, there will always be the rest of the industry,' we'd been told by Kate Henshaw, an actress who lived the conundrum in her bones. 'You need them for the lower-end type of market, for people who just want to keep making movies, for people who don't want to spend too much money. But the New Nollywood, they want to go to the cinema. They want the big time.'

◆

161

Henshaw, we knew, was eminently qualified to talk to us about the big time. As one of Nollywood's very first ingénues, she did not appear, at 42, to have aged a day since her 1993 debut – which saw her playing a country girl in the industry classic *When the Sun Sets*. Like so many veterans we'd met, Henshaw had come to acting by accident. She was studying medical microbiology at the University of Calabar when, on a whim one day, she'd auditioned for a modelling contract. A week later she was the African face of Shield Deodorant, and by the mid-1990s she had emerged as a Nigerian star, making $150 per film and amassing dozens and dozens of credits. In 2008 she would win an AMAA 'best actress' for her efforts, although by then her priorities had started to shift. 'I try not to do too many films these days,' she told us. 'I want to do quality work – after 20 years, you have to be picky.'

Picky for Kate Henshaw meant becoming the African ambassador for Samsung Electronics, the face of Onga Seasoning, the host of a cooking show called *Onga Time Out*, the co-host of *Nigeria's Got Talent*, the voice of Project Alert on Violence against Women and Children and, soon, a candidate for the PDP in the coming general elections.

'The *only* Galaxy S4 in Nigeria, actually,' she said, with mock gravitas, when we enquired whether the not-yet-released gadget on the table beside her was one of the first in the country. This was followed by a deep laugh that reverberated through Cactus, Lagos's Lebanese-owned waterfront patisserie. Henshaw, who was wearing a species of tight, hi-tech denim that cowboys might have fantasised about, and whose nails were painted a perfect purple sheen, was more than comfortable in her role as roving billboard – if an increasing number of global brands believed that 40 million middle-class Nigerians was too alluring a prospect to ignore,[64] and if they further believed that Nollywood could help influence consumer affections, who was she to deny them?

As Henshaw explained, the income from her endorsements had freed her up to pour all of her creative energies into a single passion project. Originally entitled *Ceremony*, and later changed to *Lagos Wedding*, the film was an adaptation of a play by Sefi Atta, a writer who'd done as much as any of her generation to define the contemporary Nigerian voice.[65] Henshaw, who would star as lead, had been involved in fine-tuning the script. With Nollywood legend Ego Boyo producing, and rising auteur Akin Omotoso at the helm, the project, according to the actress, had been in development for close on two years. 'Which,' she said, 'is roughly two years longer than the average Nollywood production.'

Did this, we wondered, make it New Nollywood? Did the pedigree of its names? It was a tag that Henshaw, for one, didn't reject. More to the point, she stressed that for the film to be properly Nigerian, it would need to speak to audiences at home. Cinema culture, as far as Henshaw was concerned, was making a comeback in Nigeria, and she urged us to visit a Lagosian theatre where she expected the film to screen.

The following afternoon, with modest hopes for the local title that we'd picked from an online movie guide, we left our lodge in Ikeja and set out on a familiar walk.

◆

Given the notorious difficulties that Lagos presents to the stranger tasked with navigating it, the Ikeja City Mall had become, on its opening in December 2011, a haven for travellers and expat contractors. Aimed squarely at the wallets of the same consumer class that Kate Henshaw had been recruited to empty, it exuded an efficient ubiquity that left no potential sale to chance. For our purposes, after days of trying elsewhere, the mall's ATMs had been kind enough to accept our credit cards, its mobile outlets decent enough to provide working SIM cards for our phones. And yet occupied as it was by South African mainstays like MTN, Shoprite and Woolworths, the Ikeja City Mall, which at first had soothed us with its familiarity, had lately become a place to avoid. Its sanitised corridors had nothing to teach about the perpetual hustle on the streets outside, except perhaps that our country-men could help the winners spend their coin.

As could the Silverbird Group, which owned and operated the mall's five-screen movie theatre, one of the city's newest and finest cine-plexes. Since 2004, we had learnt, when the Silverbird Galleria on Lagos's tony Victoria Island had first reunited the country with its cinemas, the Nigerian media conglomerate had built state-of-the-art theatres in Abuja, Port Harcourt and Uyo, a string of successes that had led to a multiplex in Accra, Ghana, and to this second Lagosian development, on the mainland. At the time of our visit, although followers like Ozone Cinemas and Genesis Deluxe had been doing their best to catch up, Silverbird's standing as the region's leading cinema chain was undisputed. In less than a decade, with its tickets costing many times the price of the average VCD, it had amassed a portfolio of 50 theatres. All indications were that here was a model with promise.

But if Silverbird was the pioneer that the more ambitious of Nigeria's filmmakers had been waiting for, its high-end facilities had mostly exposed their shortcomings. 'Sound awful, picture unwatchable, embarrassing,' the producer Najite Dede had warned us. For better or worse, it was her words we remembered as we dropped into the seats of the Silverbird Ikeja, to watch *The Gods Are Still Not To Blame* – a 2013 reformulation of the Odysseus myth that, if not quite New Nollywood in execution, had once probably aimed to be. Although the characters were more than vivid enough to thrust the story forward, we were forced to concede to Dede on the film's technical finish.

It's impossible to know whether New Nollywood would have come into being had Nigeria's cinema house culture remained dormant, but this much was certain: arriviste tastes had put many African services and industries under pressure, and those that hoped to thrive would need to move closer to international standards. In Nollywood's case, the possibility of bigger returns meant securing bigger budgets, which in turn bought an uptick in production values. This, in a nutshell, was New Nollywood, and its icon was the filmmaker Kunle Afolayan, whose 2009 thriller *The Figurine* was the first properly successful example, earning $200 000 at the box office and more in residual markets. That said, Afolayan had spent $350 000 making *The Figurine*, and claims that the film never turned a profit[66] – a fact that must have influenced *Half of a Yellow Sun's* internationally minded business prospectus.

For the moment, the catch-22 maintained its logic. But as Kate Henshaw had put it to us, her manicured hand waving her country's first Samsung S4 in the air, 'Oh, you have to reinvent yourself, or you just get left behind.' She was saying, in effect, that the situation would inevitably be resolved. Irrespective of how far short the industry fell of Hollywood's technical standards, New Nollywood was setting quality benchmarks where none had existed before. Skills acquired on big-budget productions were trickling down to the mid-range, which would result in more films worthy of a cinema run. As of this writing, most Silverbird cineplexes were splitting their screens between Hollywood and New Nollywood, with a few Bollywood titles here and there. For the ratio to tip in Nollywood's favour, and for the cinema chains to reach the sort of critical mass that could offer properly meaningful returns, mall culture – which was to say global middle-class culture – would need to fully take hold in Nigeria's cities.

The joker in the pack was Kate Henshaw's phone. When that S4 became a relic, which was about a year away, would Nollywood be more or less of a master of its technological fate? Were the 'cancerous Alaba economics' compatible with Nigeria's smartphone revolution, or was the market moving beyond the Igbo marketers' control?

LAGOS GETS HER CLOSE-UP

Perhaps this is the moment for a few more words on Lagos, the city that brings to mind the act of sucking on the tailpipe of a MiG. Lagos has been, over the course of its three centuries, a slave-trader's harbour, a scholar's fetish object, an example of extreme urban blight, and a glimpse of humanity's urbanised endgame. With 21 million people howling into the face of its fury on any single day of the week, at any random given hour, there is no element of life in this city that does not exist cheek by jowl alongside its polar opposite. Simply, Lagos *is*.

In the 2006 *New Yorker* piece that introduced the city to a certain class of reader, the American journalist George Packer made the curious decision of opening his essay, entitled 'The Megacity: Decoding the chaos of Lagos,'[67] with a migrant teenaged prostitute who lived in the city's most abject slum – curious because migrant teenaged prostitutes living in poverty are one of the few constants to be found in *any* city, from Calgary to Hong Kong to Kinshasa. Still, the reader was at least prepared for the encounter via a few richly descriptive paragraphs that explained what makes Lagos *Lagos*: its size, its pace, its unparalleled fecundity. This is a city that exhales the hot breath of its traumas, one whose *sui generis* history impacts in a thousand ways on the present. A slaving station turned colonial afterthought turned military killing field turned barely governable postmodern *thing*, its essence is in the sheer volume of lived life that subsists and strives between those data points.

Lagos, we reflected, felt like the twenty-first century's default setting. And although thinking and writing about Lagos may have become something of a cottage industry, that didn't make *being* in the city any easier. For instance, Idumota market on a sweltering Thursday afternoon. If Nollywood's producers and directors based themselves in the comparatively calm 'brain centre' of Surulere, Alaba and Idumota made up the industry's central nervous system, sending thousands upon thousands of new movies out into the continent every year. These were the gunked-up alleyways jammed with people and VCDs, from the latest Nollywood to unreleased Hollywood to fatty porn. But as vibrant, as Lagosian, as Idumota may have been, we knew it was a living fossil.

Which was largely thanks to technology, although the Internet entrepreneur Jason Njoku will end up taking much of the credit. Njoku, who has repeatedly been described in the press as the most confident man on Earth, once performed a succinct self-summary in an op-ed for a Nollywood website: 'My wife always tells me to ignore the negative drumbeat and focus on building awesome.'[68] We would meet him some months after our trip to Nigeria at a media conference in Johannesburg where, despite his having been born in London, he would reveal his unmistakably Lagosian personality. With a head the circumference of a soccer ball, he spoke in highly articulate fusillades that jammed essays' worth of information into seconds of speech. Njoku's frame, all of six foot seven inches and covered in muscle, was not nearly enough human real estate for such a boundless presence.

In 2007, broke and bereft and having moved back into his Nigerian mother's London council flat, this University of Manchester chemistry graduate noticed something that would change his life – his mother wasn't glued to her television set any more, instead she was hoovering up ten-minute clips of Nollywood movies on YouTube. Njoku, then 28, soon saw the business opportunity: Africa's Netflix.[69] He soon founded his film and music online distribution company, Iroko Partners, with a small amount of start-up capital provided by a young German named Bastian Gotter.

African business favours first movers, a fact that anyone at the South African mega-corp Naspers would be only too happy to confirm. Njoku arrived in Lagos in 2009, and hit Alaba with wads of cash and a chequebook in hand. He was stunned by the lack of regulation, the absence of record keeping, the paucity of vision. 'No one in Alaba was thinking the long game,' he told us. 'Absolutely *no* one.' He wanted to stream films legally, which meant securing contracts and a legal chain of title. As he pointed out to wary distributors, the bulk of his market was in the diaspora, and his company represented a brand new revenue stream. Before long, he had acquired a library of 200 movies, which grew exponentially. His website Nollywood Love streamed them off a YouTube channel, and within a year, Iroko Partners was earning between $50 000 and $60 000 a month off Google advertising alone.

Njoku and Gotter ran the numbers, and came to the realisation that YouTube would not allow them to reach $100 million a year in revenue under any circumstances. When the hedge-fund outfit Tiger Global Management ponied up $8 million dollars in a capitalisation deal, at the time the largest international funding package for an African tech outfit, the partners created Irokotv, their own proprietary streaming site. All Njoku would tell us in late 2013 was that he had 'less than fifty thousand' sign-ups at $5 a month, which was either deliberate coyness or an admission that subscription had yet to take off – with Njoku, it was impossible to be sure. His competition, of course, was the dozens of producers who'd dumped their films on YouTube looking for the quick buck, a tactic he despised. 'I *revere* DStv,' he told us. 'Whatever price they offered for films, Nollywood producers could've said no. But they didn't. Always thinking small, man.'

By way of contrast, Njoku was planning decades ahead. He believed that it would be about 10 years before Africans routinely consumed

Ikeja, Lagos, before a storm, April 2013

content on their smartphones – and he, like many in Nigeria, didn't think that a tech company servicing Nigerians could as of yet be established in the country. Start-ups, he had often noted, were inhibited by wretched Internet infrastructure that left final mile connectivity dangling, a spotty power grid, and a bleed of talent to the more stable and remunerative oil industry. The stigma of 419 scams tainted every Nigerian IT venture, regardless of how anodyne, and raising capital was an enormous challenge. It was therefore no surprise, and somewhat tragic, that the bulk of companies looking to take Nollywood into the future were based *outside* of Nigeria. But Njoku did not see Irokotv as another in a long line of exploitative endeavours aimed squarely at the country's vast market, endeavours that ultimately left Nigeria poorer. With offices in Lagos, London, New York and Johannesburg, Iroko was by necessity global, although its raw product – its rubber, its cocoa, its petroleum – was Nollywood film.

And not *New* Nollywood, either. 'Listen,' Njoku said to us, 'popular is what popular is.' He didn't see production values as critical to the industry's future success, but *stories*. What's more, he had the numbers to prove it – his servers spat out algorithms that told him exactly what movies constituted a hit, his biggest title being 2012's *Miss Somebody*, not a film anyone would confuse for a Cannes contender. And while Iroko and its competitors were destined to wipe Alaba off the map by 2025 if not before, Njoku planned to retain the market's ad hoc pulse-taking. 'We have to be really specific about what our product is,' he said, suggesting that Africans *needed* to see themselves on screen, and that they needed to do so often. 'Africans want what Africans want,' he shrugged. Which was of course Nollywood's simple secret.

◆

As far as Jason Njoku was concerned, Nollywood was one of the very few authentic cultural industries to be found anywhere in the world, one that existed without the benefit of protectionism or subsidies, and its primary risks were the upward pressure of wages and the downward pressure of pricing. With Iroko paying a minimum of $5 000 for a licence, stars were demanding as much as $15 000 per film (a trend that marketers had tried to obviate by blacklisting), and budgets were becoming unmanageable. There was always the chance that another African country – a Ghana, a Kenya, a Uganda – would start doing what Nollywood did for less. That said, built into Nollywood's success was a star system, a massive local consumer base, a rich compost of local media, and an intangible Nigeria-ness that nourished it all. Could there be a Nollywood without Nollywood? For our part, we were less than convinced.

As we shuffled through Idumota, the industry roaring around us, we found ourselves at a loss for comparisons – next to this place, Johannesburg was as good as underwater. And like Lagos, whose GDP was twice that of Kenya's, Nollywood's size and speed were inherently disruptive. There were compelling theories: if Lagos's boundaries were to continue to encompass more and more African real estate, eventually engulfing Abidjan in Côte d'Ivoire and Accra in Ghana, Lomé in Togo and Cotonou in Benin, it would mean a contiguous urban zone taking shape.[70] An unprecedented African city-state, it would mean English becoming the spoken tongue in Francophone Côte d'Ivoire and Togo, and it would mean borders being erased by asphalt. This would not occur at the behest of the Nigerian federal government, but *despite* it, in opposition to it. If Abuja could not sort out the hyperactively violent Boko Haram insurgency in the north, the city-state wouldn't care – insulated by its own vitality, it would continue to ignore the problems of the larger state. 'Lagosian' would become the collective identity, the term 'Nigerian' applicable to someone else.

As for those who hoped to win the Nollywood sweepstakes, like Jason Njoku, their success would depend upon certain contingencies, broadband penetration not least among them. Their model, in the long run, seemed a sound one – content consumption would almost certainly migrate to mobile devices. Should the unlikely happen and 'Kampalawood' one day became the centre of production, it would make no difference to the Njokus of the world: after all, 'popular is what popular is'. Nollywood had transcended its origins and had become a connecting force, a common language, a necessary African resource. That alone made it unique. As the continent knitted together, the culling would become ever more ruthless, and the competition would either drive standards up or uncouple entire industries, countries, regions. Jason Njoku had taken the imaginative leap that Peace Anyiam-Fiberesima had insisted was necessary when she'd spoken at the 2013 AMAAs in Yenagoa. '*Africa One,*' she'd said – imagining the 54 disparate, occasionally warring, seldom compatible African nations as an intertwined entity, as a single organism.

We see him at the same time. We have left the last of Ganyesa's Pakistani stores, and we are standing on the verge of the highway, breathing in fumes. He stands on the verge opposite, arms folded, legs rooted in place. He watches us watching him.

His name is James Yu. He offers a pantsula handshake – fingers up, fingers down, thumbs snapped – that he could only have learnt in a local township. He nods when we tell him our purpose in Ganyesa, that we have come to find out why four Chinese shopkeepers died in a fire.

'I did know those people,' he says. 'My shop, it has only been open four months. But I did know them. We did some business.'

'What do you think happened?'

He grins, and signals for us to follow him into his shop. In many respects, James Yu's supermarket is a typical southern African grocery store. The aisles are wide and clean, most of the brands are recognisable. This, we soon discover, is entirely James's doing. His English is flavoured by South African-isms; he has absorbed and adapted and understood. There is nothing in the supermarket that would unsettle a South African.

James tells us that he left the coastal city of Xiamen for the coastal city of Port Elizabeth in 2003. He worked retail, he worked wholesale – he learned everything there is to learn about the trade. Four months ago, he says, he received a call from a friend.

'He tells me he has this supermarket in Ganyesa. The town is growing, growing. He got the shop from a white man, who was let us say "confused" about security. So the white man is out, and I am here to help.'

Over the course of the conversation, James makes it clear that he does not share the former owner's confusion.

'Here in this town there are tsotsis,' he says, using the vernacular for 'thug'. He makes a stabbing motion. 'I give them some punishment, I give them some lessons. If I am beating them the cops can lock me up, but I don't care. Here, it is robbing and stealing, robbing and stealing.' He shrugs. 'I am used to it.'

'And the fire?' we ask.

James offers us his smile again, which is not really a smile at all. 'I will tell you,' he says. 'Some guys say it is accident of electricity. But I don't think so. I say it is some guys.'

171

SIX

DEMOCRATIC REPUBLIC OF THE CONGO

Gold into Lead into Gold: The Alchemy of War, Reformulated

'I don't want to see the fucking fight. You can go somehow, Ralph. I don't know how, but watch it on television or something. We didn't come here for that. We're doing something else. I'm trying to find out where the money came from to put the fight on. Not the fight itself. That's not important.'

— Hunter S Thompson, Zaïre, 1974

CHAUFFEUR

From our vantage point beneath the radio tower, we took turns with the binoculars. The hill to the immediate southwest, where Louis Watum was pointing, had recently been cleared of huts, as we could see from the squares of flattened earth that ran up its slope. Watum's finger dropped to the hill's base, indicating the portal to the underground shaft, which was being swarmed over by construction workers. Although geologists had identified this hill as the obvious site for the main opencast pit, the gold was known to run a lot deeper than the surface. 'The deposit is so rich that we literally don't have the means to get to the bottom of it,' said Watum.

The parlance he used was 'elephant deposit', which was another way of saying it was one of the largest ever found in Africa, with the potential to do for the local economy what the discovery of gold on the Witwatersrand had done for South Africa in 1886. 'There's a perception here that we can build Johannesburg overnight,' he said.

We shuddered at the thought; the inevitable despoiling of the virgin jungle by concrete jungle seemed especially profane up in humid hill country. But the rhetoric did give us a sense of what Watum's current employer, the South African-managed, Jersey-headquartered, NASDAQ and LSE-listed Randgold Resources, was trying to do in this remote corner of the Democratic Republic of the Congo. In the company's literature, and at mining indabas around the world, Randgold was promising both current and future investors that the eastern DRC, still an active conflict zone, was 'open for business' – the risk, they insisted, was less risk than it was a species of opportunity, one that required the company to innovate solutions with one of the more maligned governments in Africa. In this, Randgold had been touting the project as 'the largest corporate social responsibility initiative on the continent'. We were here to see what that meant.

Born in Kinshasa in 1962, Watum could have passed for the ungainly progeny of a basketball pro and reclusive professor. He had left his homeland in 1993 to study metallurgy at the University of the Witwatersrand, and it was his internationally protected patents, which he'd put together on behalf of the Anglo American Corporation while still living in South Africa in the late 1990s, that had made his reputation as a mining star – if such a designation existed.

The Kibali gold mine, named for the river that forms near the northeastern border with South Sudan and eventually flows into a tributary of the fabled Congo, demanded every last one of Watum's considerable talents. Like much of the chaos in this vast country, its troubles could be traced to King Leopold II of Belgium, who had run his Congo Free State – 'his' in the sense that from its founding in 1885 to its dissolution in 1908 it remained his private property – with a savagery unmatched by any single landowner on the continent before or since. The closest Leopold would ever come to actually *seeing* his possession was in his map room in his palace in Brussels, but, in service of the extraction of the territory's riches, his agents could act as they pleased. The slaughtering of entire villages whose men failed to meet the rubber quotas; the slicing off of hands for minor infractions;

the cracking of a whip of hippopotamus hide known as the *chicotte*. The final death toll, when accounting for disease, starvation, exhaustion, exposure and plummeting birth rates, would be estimated at half the territory's population at the time, or 10 million souls.[1] In the first six months of 1920, 17 years after gold had first been discovered in the Congo's far northeast and 12 years after Belgium had annexed the territory from the aging king, the *chicotte* would cut more than 26 000 times into the backs of the African miners of Moto (the site of the modern-day Kibali), a sum equivalent to eight lashes per miner.[2] The technique for recruiting these miners had been passed down from the era of the regent: a local chief would be recompensed for delivering the prearranged number of men; if a man tried to escape, a member of his family would be locked in a cage.[3]

'The Belgians,' said Watum, as we sped through the bush to the next stop, 'knew exactly what was in the ground here. Their maps and records were excellent. We have studied them all.'

It was not, we would learn, a habit of Kibali's general manager to talk about *how* the Belgians had mined from these hills more than three million ounces of gold. He had returned from South Africa to focus on the Congo's development, and he was directing his energy towards a minimisation of the potential for conflict. To that end, his most important task was to manage the relocation of the locals who'd been eking out a living here as *orpailleurs* – artisanal miners – since the late 1990s. Finding some 17 000 villagers on the land when they'd taken over in 2009, Randgold had outlawed artisanal mining in the so-called 'exclusion zone', and had made a decision that everyone be removed. In a neighbourhood where the wealth that lay inside the earth's crust had long meant displacement and devastation for those who happened to live on top of it, such decrees were likely to have consequences. But then Randgold felt they were well aware of the sensitivities, which, again, might have been why Watum never mentioned the *chicotte*.

'That,' he said, braking to a hard stop, 'is our first new village. We have named it *Chauffeur*, because it is the driver.' We stood on a mound of gravel that brought us just about eye-level with the general manager, and looked out over rows of box-like if not entirely unattractive houses. Watum explained that each of the houses came with a title deed to its 30-metre by 20-metre plot, and that these families were now property owners for the very first time. He pointed to a larger building at the southern edge of the settlement, which would accommodate the local administration and the police; to the left of that, he indicated what would become the communal vegetable garden. 'Resettling people like this is not just a numbers game,' he said. 'It's about providing an entire lifestyle.'

With these words, Watum placed the Kibali project at the heart of the African development paradox. Did these people actually *want* an entirely new lifestyle? Under what conditions did foreigners get to *tell* locals what they wanted? Was Kibali a model for making the continent's vicious cycles virtuous? Could the wealth in the ground be spread? If Congo or the rest of Africa was ever going to turn its resources into improved living conditions for the bulk of its people, Kibali for us was a microcosm of the binaries that would need to be reconciled – innovation against tradition, global against local, the incentives of private enterprise against the integrity of the state. Before we returned to the compound, Watum told us that one of his biggest worries was that Randgold would assume a 'paternalistic' role; as per the terms of the deal, he said, the maintenance of these new villages was *not* the responsibility of the mine. 'Every time we speak to the government in Kinshasa,' he informed us, wiping the sweat from his prodigious brow, 'we remind them that we're building 14 schools, seven health centres, five public recreation areas. These things need to be serviced and staffed, they must be properly run.'

We asked him whether Kinshasa was listening, but the big man could only shrug and smile. In a country like the DRC, his gesture stated, it was impossible to know.

◆

The next afternoon we were seated on plastic chairs on the verandah outside the Kibali compound's boardroom, and Jean-Pierre Mbuluyo, or 'JP' as he was known to his colleagues in senior management – his underlings couldn't bring themselves to call him anything but 'sir' – was giving us a précis of a life that mirrored the postcolonial history of the Congo at large. JP had joined us during our trip to Chauffeur where Louis Watum had introduced him as the Kibali camp manager and regional government liaison. 'You must sit with him,' Watum had said. 'You can't hear our history better than he tells it.'

JP was born in 1960, the year of independence from Belgium, and he was less than a year old when liberation hero Patrice Lumumba was murdered in an infamous collaboration between the Central Intelligence Agency and Belgian foreign agents – a gambit designed to wrench the country out of the Soviet orbit, and one that confirmed the inauguration of the Cold War in Africa.[4] He grew up in Isiro, a town 300 kilometres to the east of Kibali. His father, a former officer in the Belgian colonial forces, had a distinguished military career that extended well into the era of the US-backed big man Mobutu Sese Seko, and so was able to send JP to technical college in Kinshasa. As a qualified electro-mechanical engineer, the young man took a series of jobs with various transport and trucking companies; in 1989 his skills took him to Générale des Carrières et des Mines, or Gécamines, the country's most important state-owned enterprise, which operated in Katanga province in the south. There, he watched up close as the copper and cobalt company imploded, an event that would lead to the government going bankrupt in 1991. The causes of the implosion could be traced back to Mobutu's 'Zaïrinisation' and 'radicalisation' drives of the early 1970s.

Buoyed by his nationalisation of the giant copper industry, President Mobutu introduced as law the concept of *authenticité*, an ideology whose name would soon be changed to 'Mobutuism'. Aside from the fact that it propped up a single national party with Mobutu as its sole guide, the defining feature of the ideology was this official name-changing itself. The Republic of Congo, which the country was named in 1960 when Belgian Congo no longer seemed appropriate, became Zaïre; the major cities of Léopoldville, Elizabethville and Stanleyville became Kinshasa, Lubumbashi and Kisangani; ordinary citizens with

Christian first names were ordered to become nominally Africanised; and, leading by example on the last point, Joseph-Desiré Mobutu became Mobutu Sese Seko Kuku Ngbendu Wa Za Banga, meaning, 'The all-powerful warrior who knows no defeat because of his endurance and inflexible will, he who leaves fire in his wake as he goes from conquest to conquest.'[5]

In 1973, when JP was on his way from primary school in the gold-rich province of Orientale to high school in diamond-rich Kasai, Mobutu was pulling a move that would match King Leopold II for pure extractive audaciousness. Under the guise of taking back Zaïre from the colonisers, he seized without compensation some 2 000 foreign-owned companies, registering them in the names of himself and his family.[6] He amassed a portfolio of plantations and ranches that encompassed three-quarters of the country's total cattle head-count and one-quarter of all its rubber and cocoa production.[7] And he appointed himself the largest shareholder in Banque du Kinshasa, upping his income through the 1970s to one-third of the national revenue. Now a significant portion of the takings from the state-owned mining houses, which were required to bank at Banque du Kinshasa, flowed into his personal account.[8]

When JP started out at Gécamines, yearly output was just short of a record high of 470 000 metric tons, but mismanagement and equipment obsolescence had rendered the company extremely sensitive to price shocks.[9] As Gécamines had never accounted for less than 60 per cent of total exports, Zaïre's GDP graph had become tethered to the international market for copper and cobalt, and crashes in 1975, 1981 and 1986 had exposed the vulnerability of the government's books.[10] This hazardous correlation would ultimately prove fatal in 1990, when, in the midst of a cobalt boom, the roof of the Kamoto mine – the largest cobalt mine in the country – caved in. Gécamines was too weak to sustain the blow, and from 1991 the national coffers were too depleted to pay the salaries of soldiers and civil servants. Between 1988 and 1995, copper production would drop by 90 per cent; in 1993, the year JP left the company to take up a position as technical advisor to Mobutu's minister of internal affairs, cobalt production was at 20 per cent of its 1988 level.[11]

Back in Kinshasa, JP witnessed the complete disintegration of the state. He observed with alarm the hyperinflation, the freefall of the local currency until 110 million units purchased only one US dollar, brought about by the government printing money to support its debt and the lifestyles of the Mobutu clique. He watched as one after another the banks shut down, a direct result of the bankruptcy of the Central Bank, whose policymakers had proved powerless in the face of the spiralling crisis. On his walks through Kinshasa, he observed the devastation that had been wrought by rioting soldiers, the empty husks left after the *grands pillages* of the capital's factories and shops. Once the government could no longer meet its debt obligations to the utility companies, JP saw the lights go out and the taps run dry. And how was he, an engineer who specialised in transport infrastructure, supposed to 'advise' the minister now that the country's vital rail and river networks were no longer functioning? By the end of 1995, when JP was grappling with the challenges of his next posting, internal cargo trade in Zaïre had fallen by 90 per cent.[12] Thanks to the domino effect brought on by the implosion of Gécamines, income per capita was at one third of its pre-independence peak.[13]

Still, while he had by nobody's measure returned a man of wealth, JP had come home to Orientale province a man of much experience. He had seen first-hand how the collapse of a single mine could start a chain reaction that crippled an entire country, and he was determined that what had happened to Zaïre's copper would never happen to its gold. As the engineer in charge of maintenance of machines for L'Office des Mines d'Or de Kilo-Moto, or Okimo, the state-owned gold-mining company that Mobutu had formed alongside Gécamines in 1967, JP knew that his current employer suffered from the same capital depletion that had led to the crumbling of Kamoto. But he also knew that Okimo operated nothing close to a mine of that scale or importance, that the fields of Kilo-Moto had been lying more or less fallow since the year the Belgians had fled.

'Okimo was going down,' he told us, 'productivity was only 5 or 10 kilograms a month, and the CEO wanted new engineers. When they were almost bankrupt, they went looking for international partners.'

In 1996, he said, the Canadian Barrick Gold Corporation came in, only to turn tail the following year.

'Were you ever tempted to run as well?' we asked him.

Louis Watum, who had been translating for us from the French, chuckled as he repeated the question. 'Only when it was very hot,' JP said. 'Maybe for a day or two.'

◆

We were speeding once more across the savanna, pockets of woodland reminding us just how close we were to the endless rainforest to the west and south, and Watum was telling us about the time he oversaw the mass exhumation of the bodies. 'We always recognised the need to do it,' he said. 'People here tend to bury their loved ones in the yard, so there were graves everywhere, also in the mining zone. We had to find a way to do it with dignity and respect, and that meant including all the chiefs and elders in the process.'

JP, Watum went on, had been present when many of the graves were dug. 'During the wars, thousands were killed here. How he survived those years was a miracle.'

In the Ituri district of Orientale province, which bordered the Haut Uélé district in which the mine was located, the fighting was still ongoing. This had been confirmed earlier in the day by Kibali's security manager, Smith Kombo, whose job it was to monitor all activity within a 300-kilometre radius – 'If the heat comes within 10 kilometres of this mine, I'm late,' he'd told us. A more immediate danger than the Ituri rebels, Kombo had explained, was Joseph Kony's Lord's Resistance Army, which was operating in the Garamba National Park about 330 kilometres to the north.[14] But while both of these threats could be linked back to the mind-bending factionalism that had endured after the official end to the Second Congo War in 2003, for now it was the exhumation story that brought the complexity of Randgold's challenge alive.

'Identifying the bodies in those graves was a tedious process,' Watum said. 'There was no paperwork, we had to wait for the relatives to return from Kisangani or Kinshasa.'

Two thousand graves were finally identified, he told us, and the day of the event announced. As the ranking manager on site, Watum was in charge of planning and implementation; he engaged the villagers through a series of workshops, and hired consultants to ensure his staff were technically and emotionally prepared. Early on the appointed day, the chiefs performed the symbolic rites, the church leaders conducted the services, and the traditional healers appeased the ancestors. Only then did the teams move in with their gas masks, biohazard suits, disinfectant and shovels.

'Everyone was sweating,' said Watum. 'Some bodies were so decomposed there was almost nothing left. But you just had to remind yourself why you were doing it. You had to focus on why you were here.'

THE GREAT WAR OF AFRICA

The Second Congo War, which sucked into its vortex some nine African countries and 30 local militias, was as incomprehensible to the international media as it was to most of the combatants. But as for Jean-Pierre Mbuluyo, he had one simple objective – it was all about the equipment. If he could just keep the bulldozers, backhoes and diesel that belonged to Barrick Gold out of the hands of the fighters, then maybe, when all of the killing was done, there would be something left for the Congo to build on.

It took hours for JP to talk us through the intricacies of the war, but he wanted us to remember that no matter how dizzying the array of acronyms and war parties, it came down to individual humans doing their best to remain alive. It was therefore only with the support of the local community that his plan could work. 'We explained to them that the development of this area depends on the investors who will come back,' he told us. 'If they come back and don't find their machinery, they will be discouraged.'

How did it all start? It started, said JP, with the First Congo War. How did history choose Laurent-Désiré Kabila as victor – the same man who in 1965 had been dissed by Che Guevara as lacking in 'revolutionary seriousness',[15] and whose primary occupations three decades later remained 'smuggling a little gold, doing a little gunrunning, and organising the occasional kidnapping'?[16] Initially, during the first weeks of his campaign to unseat Mobutu in 1996, Kabila's triumphs were as much of a surprise to JP as they would have been to Che. But the Okimo technician soon suspected what history would later bear out. This *libérateur*, who dressed in black and wore a cowboy hat, was a proxy in another man's war.

The aftershocks of the 1994 Rwandan genocide had been reverberating beyond that country's borders. Paul Kagame, the former military commander of the Rwanda Patriotic Front, had led his Tutsi forces to victory in Kigali and was now the national president. He knew that among the 1.5 million Hutu refugees in the camps of eastern Zaïre were *génocidaires,* backed by Mobutu, in the process of regrouping.[17] In order to get rid of the *génocidaires,* Kagame needed to get rid of Mobutu. Everywhere he looked, it seemed, he found willing allies: Mobutu's regime was broke and desperately trying to fill its coffers by selling off the mines to foreign concerns; the United States had grown tired of the old strongman's profligacy now that the Cold War was over; the window of opportunity, which opened out onto some of the planet's richest mineral deposits, had never looked so inviting to the neighbouring African states.

Determined to prevent a repeat of the circumstances that had claimed between half a million and a million lives in 100 days in 1994, and yet reluctant to attack the *génocidaires* under the Rwandan flag, Kagame needed a foil – he found one in the Banyamulenge, the ethnic Tutsi who had been living across the border for generations. Over time, this term, meaning simply 'the people of Mulenge', a town in the highlands west of Lake Tanganyika, had become a pejorative, a catchall phrase for the 'tall, dirty herders' who had settled in the Congo during the years of Belgian rule. By the mid-1990s, no longer Rwandan and unwanted in Zaïre, they had assumed the role of scapegoat. In October 1996, when the deputy governor of South Kivu, cheered on by Mobutu, ordered all Banyamulenge to vacate Zaïre or be 'exterminated and expelled',[18]

Poster by Tricontinental Organisation in Cuba (Organisation of Solidarity for the People of Asia, Africa and Latin America, or OSPAAAL), undated, unsigned

Kagame had his excuse. He had in the interim created the Alliance des Forces Démocratiques pour la Libération (AFDL), under the command of Monsieur Kabila – not exactly a Tutsi, but a former anti-Mobutu rebel and, as Che had intuited, a committed opportunist.

The force at Kabila's disposal was formidable. Aside from Banyamulenge volunteers, who had been trained by Kagame's newly formed Rwandan Patriotic Army, it included Ugandans who had helped Yoweri Museveni to overthrow Milton Obote, and Eritreans who had been hardened in battle against Ethiopia. The AFDL's core, however, was made up of the skilled soldiers and officers of the Rwandan army itself. As the head of the invasion force, James Kabarebe, a young protégé of Kagame's, had begun to fill out the ranks with *kadogos* – child soldiers conscripted under duress – which was the first outward sign that the Rwandan president's motives weren't entirely pure.[19] The second sign came in the war's opening days, when Hutu refugees in the camps of Uvira, Bukavu and Goma were targeted as a matter of principle, prefiguring an ethnic slaughter that some estimates would place at 230 000 dead by war's end.[20]

The conflict had come to JP in waves. First there was word that the AFDL, who had rounded Lake Kivu, had split into columns and were marching north to the Kilo-Moto goldfields for spoils. Then there were the advanced platoons of the troops themselves. Then there was the great abandonment – everyone who could run did, including Barrick, and JP was left alone with his diminished community to protect the mine's equipment. As a representative of Okimo, and therefore a Mobutu man, when the soldiers arrived there was nothing he could say. They sacked the mine's equipment stores, leaving little more than grease stains. Shortly after they swept through, in May 1997, Kabila took Kinshasa. Mobutu was expelled from the country, and would die of prostate cancer in Morocco in September of that year. The First Congo War, which lasted six months, three weeks and one day, was now over.

But where did the mine stand? As it turned out, Barrick had hit a magical reset button, and in 'February or March of 1998,' JP told us, he had watched in astonishment as the Canadian conglomerate returned with new equipment. Meanwhile, following his presidential inauguration at the capital's soccer stadium, where Kagame and Museveni were among the guests of honour, Kabila began to outline his mining strategy.

In 1995, a desperate Mobutu had reversed his nationalisation policies and signed with Western multinationals in order to privatise the destitute state monopolies.[21] Kabila's response had been to renege on the deals; now, step-by-step, he was reinstating in his own name the structures that had existed during Zaïrinisation. In October 1997, Kabila formed the Banque du Commerce et de Dévelopment, in which his ministers and dignitaries from the AFDL's supporting states all had major shares. This bank was promptly conjoined with his own private company, the Compagnie Mixte d'Import-Export.[22] When Kabila then ordered all foreign companies doing business in the Congo to deposit their funds with the entity, and set up a new monopoly for the buying of diamonds and gold,[23] the reversion to 1973 seemed complete. Kabila may have renamed the country the Democratic Republic of the Congo, but here again were all the tactics of the deposed Mobutu, who had in turn taken his extractive inspiration from King Leopold II.

Kabila's invasion force had now become the Congolese national army – the Forces Armées Congolaises, or FAC – and the Rwandan Tutsis in its upper ranks an increasing threat to his presidency. In Kinshasa, where the old phobias about the Banyamulenge were stirred by sounds of Kinyarwanda on the streets, Rwandan officers were enforcing their own moral codes on ordinary Congolese civilians via a reintroduction of the *chicotte*.[24] On 26 July 1998, in a public broadcast, Kabila thanked his people for 'tolerating' the Rwandans and ordered all foreign troops out.[25] Back in Kigali, James Kabarebe, the FAC's expelled chief of staff, met with Kagame to plan a second march west.

It would become known as the 'Great War of Africa', partly because of the number of African nations that got involved, partly because it would be the deadliest conflict since World War II, and partly because at the time of this writing it is still ongoing.

◆

JP wasn't buying the theory that international mining capital, abetted by the governments of Canada and the United States, funded the Second Congo War. But nor did he dismiss it as stock conspiracy theory. Most of those *for* this theory cited the West's obvious incentives to oust Kabila, who had forgotten not only that the Clinton administration had supported the AFDL, but that its withdrawal of support for Mobutu – which brought to an end a 30-year love affair – had been a direct function of the post-Soviet age. If the Washington Consensus no longer needed Mobutu as a buffer against African socialism, it certainly didn't need someone who broke almost all of global capital's new rules. Did it mean anything to JP that former US president George HW Bush served on Barrick's advisory board, or that former Canadian prime minister Brian Mulroney was a company director? This, after all, was how the world worked. He aligned himself more with the *against* camp, which saw a contrary truth in the post-Soviet age: the 'evident' reality, as proven by the *Black Hawk Down* saga in Somalia in 1993, that a single unopposed superpower could no longer impose its will on even the poorest of African states.[26] Indeed, it was no secret that the renewal of the conflict did not advance the West's interests. Thanks to the Second Congo War, privatisation of the Congolese mining industry would be delayed until 2005[27] – Canadian conglomerates, including Barrick Gold, would lose more than $15 billion in mining claims in 1998 alone.[28]

If JP felt that Laurent Kabila might have made a mistake when he betrayed the Rwandan officers who'd been his loyal proxies and king-makers, he wasn't the only one with such misgivings. For 10 days in the middle of August 1998, many of the inhabitants of Kinshasa were entertaining the notion too. On 2 August, James Kabarebe once again led his troops over the eastern border, with the intention, once again, of toppling the regime in the capital. The difference was that where in the First Congo War it had taken the Rwandan commander almost seven months to reach the west, now it took less than a week. Kabarebe had hijacked a few planes in Goma, filled them with Rwandan-assisted rebels, and had simply hopped across the jungle to the military base of Kitona on the shores of the Atlantic.[29] From there, he had overrun the river port of Matadi and the Inga hydroelectric plant, which had allowed him to squeeze, at will, the veins and capillaries of Kinshasa. It was only the intervention of troops from Zimbabwe, who arrived on 19 August, and more troops from Angola, who entered the Congo on 22 August, that saved Kabila from the siege.

What did Zimbabwe's Robert Mugabe and Angola's José Eduardo dos Santos have to gain by coming to the aid of a man who, by most accounts, was still behaving like a dipsomaniac rebel gunrunner? In the case of Angola, as the Belgian author and historian David van Reybrouck would put it, there was 'a distinct possibility that, in order to bring down Kabila, Rwanda would this time support UNITA'[30] – meaning that while Rwanda had initially done Angola a favour by ousting the UNITA-supporting Mobutu, the equation for Luanda's power elite in its own civil war had now changed.[31] For Zimbabwe, on the other hand, the motives were a little more clear-cut: Mugabe was after the copper in Katanga.

JP refused to comment on the objectives of Angola, Zimbabwe and Namibia, the last of which had also entered the fray on the side of Kabila. Neither would he say anything to us about Sudan, Chad and Libya, which had offered support to the president from the north. While Namibia's involvement appeared ridiculous to us, it made at least a modicum of sense that Sudan would oppose the Rwanda-Burundi-Uganda alliance, seeing as Uganda's Museveni had for many years backed the southern Sudanese rebels. As for Chad and Libya, aside from wanting to show Khartoum some Afro-Arabic solidarity, we were equally stumped. Perhaps the only regime that did not conflate ideology or strategy with opportunism was Mugabe's. When we discovered that Muller Conrad 'Billy' Rautenbach had been named chairperson and managing director of Gécamines in November 1998, we were reminded that for a really big continent the characters tended to get around – this was, after all, the same Billy Rautenbach who was gaming Zimbabwe's energy sector. Mineral loot for boots on the ground: an equation that in the end would go down as the most honest summation of the war.

◆

JP was now in the midst of the largest armed conflict in Africa's history. Since the Ugandans had arrived in August 1998, claiming Kilo-Moto for themselves and chasing corporations like Barrick Gold out, local *orpailleurs* had been press-ganged into service on the industrial mines. They were forced to either pay the soldiers a fee on entering or to hand over a portion of their ore on leaving, and were regularly beaten for failing to deliver the expected quotas of gold[32] – in this, the Ugandans appeared no different from the Belgians who had occupied the area 80 years before. To up the takings of ore, the Ugandans soon began using explosives stolen from Okimo warehouses, a practice that led to the collapse of the Gorumbwa mine – and the death of a hundred *orpailleurs* – in late 1999. JP knew by now that confronting the soldiers directly was a potentially fatal move: a few months after the Ugandans had swept into the district, his boss had been publicly beaten for daring to open his mouth.[33]

But if he couldn't bear arms, there were other things JP could do. 'What we have here is our future', his banners read in English, so that the Ugandan soldiers could understand. 'It is the future of our children. Taking this means you are killing us. While we are alive, you will not take it.'

He erected the banners during the second stage of the war, after the Lusaka agreement of July 1999, when France and the United States had pushed for all foreign armies to withdraw their troops.[34] They had done no such thing, of course, and the map of the Congo, as Van Reybrouck would write, was 'frozen in place': to the west and south, Angola and Zimbabwe leading the pro-Kabila camp, with the Zimbabwean forces rushing in to 'protect' the diamond concessions around Mbuji-Mayi; to the north and east, the Rwandans and Ugandans leading the anti-Kabila camp, with the diamond town of Kisangani becoming the source of their own internal split.

JP told us that it must have been the hand of God keeping him alive. There was a full Ugandan brigade stationed in the area, he said, while he and his men were stranded, cut off from reinforcements and supplies. To pay his men, on those miraculous days when some money came in from Kinshasa, JP would ride an old motorcycle between the units. The Ugandans had their eyes on Barrick's fuel, over 500 drums of diesel at 200 litres each. In the end the soldiers managed to take it all, a haul that amounted in JP's estimate to

$2 million. But they never got a single dollar's worth of hardware, which JP ascribed to two reasons. First, he had removed the starters and fuel pumps from the larger machines and had locked the smaller equipment in containers; second, he had mobilised the local population to the cause – the words on those banners, although written in English for the benefit of the Ugandans, were repeated in French and the vernacular, person to person, across the length and breadth of Haut Uélé.

Between July 1999 and December 2002, when South Africa's then-president Thabo Mbeki would prove his mettle as an African peace-broker and initiate the Sun City agreement[35] – which would lay the foundations for a reunified country under a transitional government, but do nothing to end the conflict in Ituri and the Kivus – Paul Kagame and Ugandan president Yoweri Museveni would fill their coffers with Congolese bounty. Like so many, they would not stop making a play for the country's riches *after* December 2002, although from then their ability to do so without hindrance would be reduced.

In 2001 the United Nations Panel of Experts on Illegal Exploitation in the DRC announced that Ugandan officers had been involved in abuses and looting around the town of Durba, a few kilometres from where JP was based. He wasn't surprised when a follow-up commission of inquiry, appointed by the Ugandan government, led to zero arrests.[36] In September 2004, almost two years after the Sun City agreement, the transitional Congolese government would demand $16 billion in compensation from Uganda – although Kampala would refuse to pay a single cent to Kinshasa, Ugandan officials would acknowledge in newspaper reports 'some responsibility for the killings, plunder and looting the DRC suffered at the hand of their troops'.[37]

As for JP, he had successfully protected, at great risk to his life, Barrick Gold's machinery. When it became obvious that Barrick wasn't coming back, that they were going to take the insurance payout off the declaration of *force majeure* and call their Congo venture quits, he had wondered for a moment what it had all been for. But then the Damseaux dynasty, a Belgian Jewish family that had bankrolled Okimo since the Mobutu era, saw in the concession an opportunity to collect on the debt: with Barrick out of the picture, Okimo all of a sudden had a major asset. In 2003, in a sublime demonstration of their deal-making skills, the family approached the Australian-headquartered Moto Gold – 'a bunch of guys', according to Louis Watum, 'who were small and hungry and adventurous enough to dig in the jungle' – and convinced them to buy access to the concession in the form of bundled Okimo debt. The genius of the deal was that where the Damseaux books had for two decades reflected the unrecoverable loans, now they had equity in one of Africa's most coveted gold deposits. And yet not even the Damseauxs, who would end up making tens of millions off the deal,[38] could predict what would happen next. 'Moto didn't expect to find any machinery when they got here,' JP told us. 'They were very surprised and they were very happy, because it meant they could start drilling immediately. The discovery time was shortened by many months.'

Largely in recognition of this, two years later JP would be promoted by an ordinance of the state president to the board of directors of Okimo. In 2007 he would be promoted again, to acting CEO. He would meet and befriend Louis Watum, who had returned to the Congo in 2006 to serve as executive director at Moto Gold. The two men, as large in stature as they were in experience – while JP had been staring down the Ugandan army, Watum had been honing his craft at the Yatela goldmine in Mali – would find their ambitions uncannily aligned. Both wanted to forge a Congolese first: an industrial-scale mine in northeast Orientale that delivered substantial tax revenues, and hence development capital, to a post-independence, democratically elected government.

In the DRC's attenuated state of chaos, was such a dream even worthy of being dreamt?

SECRET MOUNTAINS, WAITING DRAGONS

The software was designed to illustrate, in a navigable mock-up, what

$24 trillion in mineral reserves looked like in three-dimensional space. That it failed to convey the scope of the reserves was understandable. Their monetary worth alone was equivalent to three-quarters the combined GDP of Europe and the United States.[39] Still, given that we were in the Kinshasa complex of the United Nations Organisation Stabilisation Mission in the Democratic Republic of the Congo (MONUSCO), we could see why the attempt had been made.[40] We stared at the screen, the UN official guiding us over and around features that resembled icebergs, inverted mountain ranges, giant geological formations that might have made the Congo one of the wealthiest nations on earth, and we listened as she gave us her unsanctioned take on why it was still one of the poorest.

'Everywhere in the world you find a peacekeeping mission,' she said, 'you will find natural resources.' It was because of such statements that the UN official preferred to remain anonymous. They came at the rate of around two a minute, each an expression of her cynicism, which, she admitted, was the only honest response to the futility of her job. Starting out in Katanga province, she zoomed in on the uranium deposits near the Zambian border, stopping at the Shinkolobwe mine, whose ore had been used in the Manhattan Project and the atomic bombs of World War II.[41] Although this mine had been shut in 2004, she reminded us that French president Nicolas Sarkozy had visited Kinshasa in 2009, ostensibly to praise the government for allowing Ugandan and Rwandan troops to assist in the fight against rebel forces, but mainly to secure a deal that gave Areva, France's state-owned nuclear energy company, a monopoly over the DRC's uranium reserves. Then, navigating up the eastern border and into the Kivus, the UN official showed us the rock formations that were believed to hold as much as 80 per cent of the world's coltan, the precious columbium-tantalum blend without which the aerospace industry would have no superconductors and the electronics industry no capacitors – during the Second Congo War, she said, when there was a rush on the mineral for use in next-generation cell phones and Sony's Playstation 2, Rwanda all of a sudden became the major supplier, exporting almost $500 million worth in two years. 'The UN is

191

now trying to regulate the trade with a tagging system,' she went on, 'which has basically killed official exports. If any Congolese tantalum *does* make it onto the world market, it's been smuggled through Burundi or Rwanda by rebels or corrupt government soldiers.'[42] Staying in the northeast, she guided us through the rich tin deposits of North Kivu, which were likewise the domain of rebel groups and corrupt officers of the Forces Armées de la République Démocratique du Congo (FARDC), as was the gold of Ituri in Orientale province. In the diamond fields around Mbuji-Mayi, which she reached in one practised sweep down to the southwest, she insisted that the development potential was being squandered by artisanal mining. 'Now,' said the UN official, 'maybe you are beginning to see why the DRC has a national income per capita of around $230.'

But she wasn't close to done. As she moved the cursor southeast from Kasai and returned full-circle to Katanga, she mentioned the names of Dan Gertler, an Israeli billionaire who got his start in diamonds, and Ivan Glasenberg, the Johannesburg-born CEO of the all-powerful commodities trading house Glencore. This pair, she alleged, had been the masterminds behind a secret bargain-basement sale of three state mines, two of which, Kansuki and Mutanda, were expected to jointly account for 40 per cent of the world's cobalt production in the next few years. 'They convinced the government to give them away for next to nothing,' she said. When we asked why the government had agreed to the sale, she clicked a bookmark on her computer that led to a photograph of the Israeli at the recent funeral of Augustin Katumba Mwanke, who had been the de facto powerbroker in the Congo since Joseph Kabila had taken over as president following his father's assassination in 2001 – Kabila *fils*, who assumed office at the age of 29, would prove a lot more politically durable than Kabila *père*.[43] 'Katumba *ran* mining in the DRC,' said the UN official, 'and Gertler gave him what he wanted.' She suggested that proceeds from the Glencore sale funded Kabila's 2011 re-election campaign, an allegation that the UK activist group Global Witness would repeat less than two months later.[44]

While she couldn't know in March 2012 how things would play

out, the information provided by our UN source would turn out to be remarkably robust. In May 2012, Global Witness would cite Gertler as a 'key intermediary' and 'also a partner' in a 'secret and possibly corrupt' deal that saw Glencore acquire stakes in three Katanga mining ventures valued at $4.6 billion. The report would note that the 'sales prices of all these stakes were far below commercial valuations attributed to them by financial analysts, resulting in the loss of billions of dollars to the Congolese state'.[45] As to the potential reason for the sale, the report would point out in the first paragraph that Gertler remained 'a close friend' of President Kabila, adding in the fifth paragraph that '[some] of the proceeds of mining sales in 2011 were used by the Congolese government to cover costs related to the 2011 election'.[46] In June 2012, perhaps sensing that he needed to address the charges, Gertler would spend three days with *Bloomberg* journalists in Israel and Congo, insisting, with regard to the allegations of kickbacks and below-market rates, that the lies were 'screaming to the heavens'.[47] His spokesman had already protested his innocence in the Global Witness report, stating that Gertler had always acted with 'utmost honesty, integrity and fairness', and that 'President Kabila has never been directly or indirectly involved in any deal or negotiations.' As far as Glencore were concerned, there had never been any 'material breaches of any applicable law or regulations' regarding its work in the DRC. Gertler would not deny the Kabila connection outright, however: according to the *Bloomberg* article, they had first met at Kinshasa's InterContinental Hotel in May 1997, when Joseph had just been made deputy chief of the army; they had gotten on so well, he said, that a year later he was introduced to Laurent, who granted him a monopoly on all DRC diamond sales in exchange for a war fund donation of $20 million in cash.[48] The *Bloomberg* article would be published in December 2012, the same month that the International Monetary Fund, citing a breach of its transparency terms, would suspend a $532 million loan programme with the Democratic Republic of the Congo.

It was now time for lunch, and our lengthy interview had earned us a meal at the UN canteen. Emerging into the sunlight of the MONUSCO headquarters yard, we noticed a sign that placed the 'Threat Assessment Level' in the country at 'three' out of a possible 'five'. We ordered a meal and returned to the outdoor tables to eat. 'Nope, I wasn't drunk driving last night,' we overheard a UN worker tell his colleague at the next table. 'But I sure was drunk walking.'

◆

Think of it as a city that stumbles, a city that learns to walk by a process of perpetual falling. We drove the length and breadth of Kinshasa with a young Congolese who went by the *nom de Facebook* Sedrick Fils de L'Homme (Sedrick, Son of Man), and stared at the passing street scenes as he did his best to explain the place into something approaching coherence. Why would that never happen? Because Kinshasa, we would learn, was a reflection of the country beyond its ever-expanding limits. Twelve million people by the most conservative counts, all of whom were contributing to making it the fastest-growing city in Africa in absolute terms. 'The locals call this area *Chine Populaire*,' Sedrick told us, as we snaked through the traffic in Commune de Masina, one of the city's largest slums, and headed back towards the river. On our left was the Marché de la Liberté, the market built and presented as a gift from Laurent-Désiré Kabila to the residents of Masina in 1998 for the loyalty they had shown to his cause. Fifteen years on, that market was overrun by cheap Chinese product; the locals, as Sedrick put it, were 'still suffering and even poorer', and the extended entourage of Kabila's son was eating at the finest restaurants in town. One of those restaurants, we knew, was called Limoncello, where the pasta was peerless, and the bill so impressive that we were considering having it framed.

Is there another city in Africa as culturally ferocious? On one typical day we went from hearing the famous Kinshasa Symphonic Orchestra finish up an al fresco rehearsal just as we arrived at the zoo, to watching bereft and underfed big African cats pacing their tiny cages, to over-indulging on comped vodka cocktails while a DJ played Parisian techno at a rooftop club.

The city's nightlife was weighing heavy on us as we woke the next morning for a meeting at State House. Our lodge was in the riverfront suburb of Gombe, opposite the InterContinental Hotel, where, during the buildup to the Ali-Foreman 'Rumble in the Jungle' of 1974, Hunter S Thompson had famously emptied a dustbin-bag of marijuana into the pool.[49] We regretted little as we walked out of the lodge's gates and turned left towards the river. On the Avenue Des Nations Unies, we passed by a national army tank with a portable radio on its turret, the crew sitting in the shade, heads nodding to the rhythms of *kwassa kwassa*. The beat faded as we continued on, tracing the Brazzaville skyline above the far bank, still in thrall to the idea that this was the only place on earth where the capital city of one country could be seen from the capital city of another.[50]

Wenge wood logging on the Congo River, Stanley Pools, March 2012

'So, you guys are sporting guys, huh?' said an officer of the Republican Guard at the western gate to the Palais de la Nation, the complex in Gombe that had once housed the Belgian governor general and a statue of Leopold on a horse. Clearly, they weren't used to visitors who came underdressed. Given that the complex was now the residence of the president, with 'Papa' Kabila's mausoleum standing in place of the statue of the king, we felt we ought to explain ourselves. But as we were telling him why we hadn't packed our suits, the officer broke into a smile. 'South Africa, yes? Me, I was living in Durban for eight years.'

And so, once again, although it had never failed to surprise us, we were about to be saved by our accents. '*Afrique du Sud!*' the officer shouted to his colleagues as he scanned the guest book for our names. He hurried us through the gate, practising his English, saying how he wished he could go back, how Durban was 'much, much better than this place'. The surprise, as always, was in the contrast; in the gap between the way South Africans conceived of their country and the way the country was conceived of up north. Soldiers in Kabila's Republican Guard may have gotten paid regularly, they may have enjoyed working conditions vastly superior to the ordinary soldier, but *this* young officer spoke of our country in terms of true deliverance. Was he the exception? We knew by now that he wasn't: throughout sub-Saharan Africa, in every village and town and city where we had come across a community of strivers – which was to say, everywhere – *deliverance* had been rendered inseparable from *development*. If a government was starting to provide even the rudiments of the latter, if it was offering its people at least *some*thing more than it had offered the year before, there was generally reason for hope. Somewhere in the grounds of the Palais de la Nation, we had been told, was a man who fully grasped the connection.

Kimbembe Mazunga wore a tailored black suit over a Chinese collar. The initials 'KM' were stitched, in blue silk, onto his shirt pocket and cuffs, and were repeated again on his cufflinks. He was completely bald, with a deep bass voice. 'You know the problem,' he said, as he removed his jacket and invited us to sit on the opposite couch, 'is that when I was a boy of about twelve, I realised Congo was potentially rich. Now, I became a government minister, I became the mayor of this city, I became the special advisor to the president.

I said to myself, "When are we going to transfer these potentialities to riches?"'

For Mazunga, who earned a degree in civil engineering and went to work at the Office de Routes in 1986, the measure of Congolese development was first and foremost its roads – when the Belgians left in 1960, he explained, the nation could claim a world-class road network of 145 000 kilometres; by 1965, when Mobutu came to power, that had dropped to 55 kilometres; and by 2002, when Mazunga was serving as public works minister in the younger Kabila's transitional cabinet, there were all of 30 kilometres of paved roads in a country roughly the size of Western Europe. 'Joseph Kabila asked me to get the roads back to the level of the Belgians,' he said. 'The question, of course, was *where do we get the money?*'

It was here that Mazunga gave us his inside take on what became one of the largest deals in Sino-African history, a 2007 resources-for-infrastructure swap that was finally supposed to make something of the wealth in the ground. The deal had been initiated by the state-owned Chinese company China Railway Engineering Corporation (CREC), which had failed to secure concessions in Latin America, and so had turned to the DRC in 2006. At the time Mazunga was governor of the city-state of Kinshasa and his experience had made him a natural member of Kabila's advisory team. The decision to go ahead, he told us, had been based on a simple process of observation. 'We saw that our southern neighbours Angola and Zambia were developing, Gabon to the northwest, Brazzaville across the river, all because of cooperation with the Chinese government. After 2006, we decided to do the same thing.'

But Mazunga was careful to point out that the deal was not signed with the Chinese government *per se* – and in the context of the barrage of criticism it was destined to attract from the West, we could appreciate why. With his Mont Blanc pen and a sheet of paper, he sketched us a map of how it worked. In the left-hand column, he wrote 'DRC' and beneath it 'Gécamines'; in the right-hand column, 'China Exim Bank' and beneath it 'CREC/Sinohydro'. He then joined the two columns in a new entity called 'Sicomines', an abbreviation for Sino-Congolais

197

des Mines. As a classic Sino-African joint venture, Sicomines had been divided into two broad shareholdings, with the Chinese partners awarded 68 per cent and the DRC government, through Gécamines, the remaining 32 per cent. The venture had been granted the rights to mining concessions in Katanga province holding over 10 million tons of copper and 600 000 tons of cobalt, a monumental reserve with an estimated worth as high as $100 billion.[51] To earn such a haul, Mazunga said, the partnership had initially agreed to invest $9 billion into upgrading – and building from scratch – Congolese infrastructure, with $3 billion earmarked for mining capacity and $6 billion for roads, railways, housing, hospitals, universities and hydroelectric plants.

What, then, was the West's problem? On the surface, the answer was obvious: this was the most alarming evidence yet of the arrival of the new world order in Africa. But while the Western donor community would protest that the deal was *léonin*, or skewed in favour of the Chinese signatories, and that its terms weren't concessional, in that the interest rates weren't low enough and the repayment period not long enough to qualify for the concessions usually granted to poorer countries, we didn't need Mazunga to remind us that deeper forces had been at work. The previous day, we had been told by the UN official in MONUSCO headquarters that due to the 2008 financial crisis, the International Monetary Fund had been badly spooked by the original Sicomines deal, and she had urged us to read a paper authored by Danish researcher Johanna Jansson. Published by the South African Institute of International Affairs, whose work in the Sino-African field we had found consistently enlightening, the paper was available online, its contents as revelatory as promised. In a narrative that provided detailed background to the eventual visit of the IMF's then-managing director Dominique Strauss-Kahn to Kinshasa in May 2009, Jansson articulated why Sicomines stood for both change *and* continuity in the DRC's relationship with the outside world:

> Change, since it reflects how the power configurations of the global political economy have shifted and that China's position as a foreign policy actor is now consolidated. Continuity, since the 2009

amendment of the agreement, which came about partly as a result of China's ambitions to take up an active role in the [IMF], was to the benefit of the policy preferences of the IMF and the World Bank.[52]

China, in short, was not going to 'save' the Congo; as ever, the Congo would have to save itself. And yet as counterbalance to the weight of this reality, the Congo now had more say over its destiny than at any point since Leopold had drawn the national boundaries. Although Beijing may have been pulled into a larger game by the 2008 financial collapse, a game in which it could increase its authority in the IMF by exploiting the West's weakness, it is inconceivable that President Kabila didn't see the opportunity to play both sides. He surely understood that the only bargaining power left to the West was the DRC's external debt, the $13.1 billion that had accumulated in interest and deferrals off the loans granted to Mobutu in the 1980s, and he likely foresaw that the IMF would write down the debt if he gave in to certain of their demands. Indeed, when Strauss-Kahn arrived in Kinshasa in May 2009, it became clear that the IMF's major gripe was the 'collateral' clause in the Sicomines contract, which, in the event that the copper and cobalt reserves turned out to be less profitable than expected, guaranteed the Chinese shareholders the value of their investment – a guarantee, said the IMF, that had never been offered another foreign investor, and one that ran the risk of plunging the country further into debt. The final contract, signed in October 2009, could therefore be read as testament to the nous of Kabila and his team: the collateral clause was removed; the value of the infrastructure projects was dropped from $9 billion to $6 billion; and the DRC's repayment obligation was set at a maximum $3 billion. In July 2010, the IMF and World Bank announced that the DRC qualified for $12.3 billion in debt relief.[53]

No small thing, given that the number was $1.1 billion more than Congo's 2009 GDP.[54] But Mazunga had an even simpler equation with which to measure the worth of Sicomines. 'Up until now,' he said, 'we have got 500 million from Exim Bank to spend on road infrastructure, and Sicomines has not produced one ton of copper. If there is a war tomorrow, and it all stops, the Chinese are down half a billion. So tell me, who is losing?'

It was a good question, albeit a rhetorical one, and it might just as well have been asked about Randgold and Kibali. *Was* there a way for a miner to come out on top in the Congo? And if the man who practically ran the Palais de la Nation was cavalier enough to mention the ever-present threat of war, then perhaps it took something else – a quality we hadn't yet identified – to wind one's way through the heavily armed acronyms to the 'potentialities' beyond.

THE POLITICS OF RISK

Of the five elements that Mark Bristow, Randgold's fearsome chief executive, held up as Kibali's 'five commandments', security was the one that could sink all the rest. Not that the remaining four – infrastructure, community relations, power generation, further prospecting – were less important, just that they were less dependent on Randgold's core area of expertise. At the time of our week-long visit to Kibali, Bristow was in Mali, assessing the threat to the group's Morila mine. Mutineering soldiers had just attacked several locations in the capital Bamako, and Morila was only 280 kilometres to the southeast. Like its newer sister mine in the DRC, Morila was a three-way joint venture between Randgold, the Johannesburg-headquartered AngloGold Ashanti, and the national government. On Kibali, the foreign companies held 45 per cent each, as against the 40:40:20 split on Morila. Might this be because Kibali had been viewed as the greater investment risk? Willem Jacobs, Randgold's chief operating officer and Bristow's second-in-command, dismissed the question with a wave of his Nicaraguan cigar.

It was 25 March 2012, a sweltering afternoon on the verandah outside the Kibali compound's boardroom, and Jacobs was multitasking: he was preparing for a budget review with AngloGold, checking his phone for updates from Bristow, and speaking in the gaps to us. 'You asked me a few days ago how South Africans perceive risk on this continent,' he said. 'I would say most of us perceive it as an opportunity, with your English-speaking South Africans a little better equipped to deal with ambiguity.'

An unusual compliment from an Afrikaner, we thought, particularly since it wasn't aimed solely at his boss. The previous week, we had met Jacobs in Kinshasa's Memling Hotel, where he had laid out for us his business philosophy. The ability to 'think local', he'd said, was the difference between success and failure in Africa; he had talked up the South Africans, French and British, while talking down the Chinese. 'And I'm Afrikaans, so I hate the fukken British. But I just can't see the Chinese succeeding in Katanga. They can't work in a foreign culture, and their lack of transparency and openness is going to fuck them in the long run.'

Now, after replying to an SMS from Bristow – 'That's a hard man,' is all he would let on – he was back onto Sicomines. He was aware of the contention, as per the Jansson report, that CREC and Sinohydro had entered into the deal without a proper feasibility study.[55] It was, he insisted, just further support for his thesis. As the bearer of five degrees, including a pair of master's and a PhD, Jacobs placed great store in his education, which informed at least half of his discourse. 'China *can* be a game-changer in Africa,' he said, in the context of his doctoral research into the impact of culture on business strategy, 'if they ever work out the formula. But I haven't seen anything in the history books that tells me they will be open to local conditions.'

Then there was the other half of his discourse, which, although he was a man of 62, had possibly been informed by his rugby career. 'God didn't plant this gold 20 kilometres outside Paris,' said the former flank forward, who had risen to just one level below Springbok glory,[56] 'he planted it *here*, and that comes with its own share of shit. In order to operate in the Congo, the people need to benefit. Otherwise, the people will take the fukken mine back from you.'

It was a bravura performance, each point punctuated by a stab into the air of his fat cigar, each tangent rounded back to his theme. What the Chinese *couldn't* do in Katanga, Randgold *would* do in Orientale;

where CREC and Sinohydro were in it ultimately for *China*'s growth, Randgold was first and last for *Africa*. In the Jacobs monologue, there was scant allowance for contradiction, almost no acknowledgement that sometimes the facts were at odds – was this, we wondered, because he really had transcended doubt, or because there was simply no room for doubt given the levels of risk? The acquisition of the Kibali gold mine, he told us, which cost $568 million in payments to Moto Gold and Okimo in 2009, had thus far cost a further $219 million in development capital; after Randgold and AngloGold earned their capital investment back, he said, the government would take 52 per cent of the profits. 'Randgold has zero debt and $500 million in the bank,' Jacobs added, 'and for *exactly* this reason we can afford to work in risky places.' He said that companies with a 50 per cent debt ratio couldn't work in such places, and that beyond this what you needed was a good relationship with the government, with men like Kimbembe Mazunga, who put their country's needs before their own. But then where, we asked, quoting Mazunga's calculation about winners and losers on Sicomines, would Randgold be if war broke out? 'This country will not go through a civil war again,' insisted Jacobs. 'The people are fukken sick of it.'

If his selective appeal to the history books, the same history books that he'd used to rubbish the chances of the Chinese, was what got Jacobs up in the mornings, who were we to argue? Besides, we were about to learn that his faith in stability and growth wasn't all talk.

'Come see,' said Jacobs, as Louis Watum tapped him on the shoulder to indicate it was time for the meeting in the Kibali boardroom to start. 'Just sit down,' he told us, 'and shut up.'

Seated around the boardroom table were five nervous-looking Congolese contractors. The previous day a vicious storm had blown through the area, and had ripped the roofs off dozens of houses in the new villages. Jacobs had called them all in for a pow-wow.

'We had a catastrophe yesterday,' he said, pointing his finger at each one in turn. 'You are going to build neater, do you understand? Zero tolerance. We will fix all our fuck-ups.'

He remained standing, and waited for Watum to translate into

French. 'Your name is on every house you build,' he resumed. '*Your* name. It's *your* country. I want to be *very clear* about this.'

◆

Randgold's policy on mine security, like its policy on housing and the provision of social and infrastructural amenities, was in theory a non-negotiable: in the final analysis, it had to be the responsibility of the state. In practice, however, the state was barely functional. The distance between these two points, we found, was consistently reflected in the management styles of the senior executives; for instance, where Watum was concerned about coming across as overly paternalistic, the default style of Jacobs was the very essence of paternalism. To our minds, this push and pull could be read as symptomatic of the fact that Watum lived on the mine full-time, while Jacobs, whose duties extended to Randgold's assets throughout the continent, flew in and out – his real accountability was to the board. And on that board sat directors of AngloGold, which, much to the South African's discomfort, had a record in Orientale province that made a mockery of his corporate social responsibility-speak.

'We don't believe in private armies,' Jacobs had told us when we'd met him in Kinshasa. 'If we have to protect ourselves to do business, we won't do business.' As it turned out, Kibali's security personnel were indeed unarmed – the men with the AKs and bowie knives, who had followed us on our tours of the concession, were government forces, called in whenever the security manager deemed extra precautions necessary. But in this part of the world 'private armies' did not refer only to armed private bodyguards; the term was equally a euphemism for rebel groups funded and supplied by the region's numerous players, *including* mining houses. 'Look, so rebels arrive on your mine with guns,' Louis Watum would tell us, by way of evasion. 'What do you do?'

According to a 2005 Human Rights Watch report entitled 'The Curse of Gold', what AngloGold did was establish relations with 'an armed group responsible for serious human rights abuses including war crimes and crimes against humanity.'[57] The group was known as the Front des Nationalistes et Intégrationnistes, or FNI, and had been founded in 2002 to protect the interests of Ituri's ethnic Lendu, who'd been waging battle for control of the gold fields with the ethnic Hema, represented by the Union des Patriots Congolais, or UPC. The big prize in the ongoing conflict between the two groups had been the gold mining town of Mongbwalu, situated about 150 kilometres south of Kibali, which in an 18-month period had passed from UPC to FNI control a total of five times, resulting in the execution, rape, torture and displacement of thousands of civilians. In late 2003, when AngloGold were beginning exploration activities in Mongbwalu, FNI combatants were returning from a campaign of ethnic slaughter in the nearby villages of Drodro, Nizi, Fataki, Bule and Largo, 'where they had left some of their victims dead in the streets with their arms tied, sticks in their rectums, and body parts cut off ...'[58]

Watum, we suspected, knew there was more to it than AngloGold simply giving in to the extortionist tactics of the neighbourhood bullies. In fact, according to the evidence gathered by the Human Rights Watch researchers, the South African company had initiated the meeting with Njabu, not the other way around. Lending credence to this claim was the allegation (subsequently denied by the mining company) that AngloGold Ashanti's corporate predecessor had approached the UPC's commanders in mid-2002, during the months that the Hema had been in control of Mongbwalu.[59] At a press conference following the release of the Human Rights Watch report, AngloGold's then-chairman Bobby Godsell, while describing the allegations as 'unhelpful', would not deny them in their entirety. He would admit to taking payment of $9,000 from FNI 'under duress', which, he said, was a 'breach of principle' that the company 'regretted'. He insisted, however, that company management had not met with any of the rebels to secure tenure at its exploration site at Mongbwalu.[60] Either way, what seemed to make the 'association' so striking was the timing – when Ashanti Goldfields had offered their alleged sweetener to the UPC, the transitional government in Kinshasa had not yet been established; in late 2003, when AngloGold gave in to the FNI's pressure, the new government under

President Joseph Kabila was being hailed worldwide as a central component of the peace process. The FNI, which had rejected the call for disarmament, was *not* part of this transitional government, and so could not be a legitimate spokesman for Okimo, the only government agency with which foreign mining corporations in Kilo-Moto were mandated to negotiate. In bypassing Okimo and dealing directly with the FNI, AngloGold wasn't just providing material benefits to a group that was at the top of the watch-list of the International Criminal Court, it was giving the middle finger to Kabila, the United Nations, and any real prospects for peace.

Did Jacobs and Watum get the irony? Did they see that AngloGold could be held partly responsible for the fact that, in Ituri at least, the Second Congo War hadn't yet ended? As Kibali's security manager Smith Kombo had told us, the situation in Ituri required constant monitoring – in 2012, the Hema and Lendu were still locked in mortal combat, with the mineral riches of the region the prize. In November 2012, eight months after our departure from the fields of Kilo-Moto, a United Nations Security Council report would cite the names of Hema and Lendu combatants who were generating profits for themselves and their respective rebel movements through the illegal taxation and direct sale of gold.[61] The FNI and UPC may have been disbanded in the interim, but new movements had emerged in their place, and these movements had as little inclination to submit to the wishes of the Congolese government as their predecessors. To our thinking, even if AngloGold had long since broken off contact with the rebels, the corporation had contributed to President Kabila's enduring inability to police the region – a contribution (and here was the real irony) that could now be linked back to Kibali's engorged security budget, given that Mr Kombo needed a total of 280 trained staff on his team.

The president certainly had his problems, but in a milestone election, the largest ever organised by the international community and the first ever for the country, Kabila had emerged victorious in 2006. He had ushered in a new mining code, a new parliament, a new constitution, and had been re-elected in 2011. Yes, there had been violence, yes, the Second Congo War hadn't really stopped, yes, the death toll from the war was now well above five million[62] – if you really looked at it, however, Kagame of Kigali and Museveni of Kampala had a lot more to answer for than Kabila of Kinshasa.

Here was the crux: in the neighbouring district of Ituri, Rwanda's defence minister James Kabarebe and senior officials of the Ugandan government were still supporting armed groups hostile to Kabila; in the two Kivus, they were doing the same. Within days of our departure from the DRC, the M23 rebels, with a chain of command that culminated in Kabarebe himself, would emerge as the next great threat to Congolese sovereignty.[63]

When Randgold and AngloGold bought out Moto Gold in 2009, JP and Louis Watum's dream of a functional mine in a functional community in a functional mining sector was suddenly possible. If either of them were scandalised by the 45 per cent holding in the new joint venture of a conglomerate that had once helped the governments of Uganda and Rwanda to pillage their country, they were keeping mum – they had accepted positions on the new management team, which perhaps spoke for itself. We were learning that the politics of risk in the DRC was a politics of contingency, a politics that morphed, a politics that happened on a scale: there was no everlasting good, no everlasting bad. As Randgold's chief operating officer Willem Jacobs had said to us in Kinshasa's Memling Hotel: 'You need to know, for instance, who do you call if you get taken into custody here and you have to pay someone $10 000 in cash. You can't be legal *all* the time. You can't be a fukken virgin.'

TELLING UP FROM DOWN

There was, however, such a thing as movement in the *right direction*, which it was our professional duty to parse. During our daily passage up a portion of the road that led from the Kibali compound to the Ugandan border town of Arua, a vein of freshly graded earth that connected the mine to the ports on the continent's east coast, we were lulled into thinking that this task was simple – what, after all, could articulate the ideal of forward movement in the DRC, the ideal of *progress*, better than its new network of roads? Refurbished in 2009 at a cost of $8 million, the new Arua road had shortened the travelling time to the border from more than a week to less than three hours. Where once six-by-six trucks had been undone by the mud and slime, now a 125cc motorbike could complete the journey in a single afternoon.

Still, as local lore had it, the smoothness of the road did not guarantee the success of the trip. 'Crazy *boda-boda!*' our driver would shout, often within minutes of leaving Kibali's gates. 'Why doesn't the government come here and make him get a licence?'

Those 125cc motorbikes, cheap imports from China and India that in Kinshasa were known as the *wewa* – for the precocious noise they made – but out here went by the East African *boda-boda* – for the trade they had long facilitated between the Kenyan and Ugandan checkpoints at Busia – were apparently notching up as many deaths in Haut Uélé as had previously been claimed by the war. While there was no way for us to confirm the numbers, we had every reason to take the locals at their word: almost none of the riders wore helmets, almost all overtook on the blind bend or rise, and only a handful appeared to have any respect for the outer limits of traction.

And yet Jacobs and Watum were adamant, the road was a generous gift. There was, we were told, no plan to recover the $8 million; the company had not even scored a tax break. The fact that it was a *national* road, as Watum had stressed, made it a freebie of almost unprecedented proportions. 'If you consider that until 2009 the market here ran on a barter system,' he'd said, 'and today runs on Congolese francs, you begin to see what our road has done for the economy.' We did consider this, of course, and when we visited the market we saw that most of the goods were likewise from China and India, that the region, cut off for decades from the outside world, had been opened through Mombasa and Dar es Salaam to the distinctive products of the East. Neon mobile phone covers, plastic shoes, Double Happiness cigarettes; at the entrance to the market, a live goat strapped to the pillion of a metallic blue Bajaj – modern Africa, we marvelled, had landed in the rainforest with a flourish. But modern Africa, astonishing as its advance seemed, had predictably brought along with it a surge in drug abuse and prostitution, plus an opportunity for criminal

Watsa market, March 2012

syndicates to extend their reach. 'Do you think I look like wildlife in a park?' a gold trader demanded of us in rapid fire French. 'Then you must pay for that photograph!' Our driver translated while dragging us away, explaining that the man bought his gold from recalcitrant *orpailleurs*, and that to him Randgold was the enemy. The new Arua road, it turned out, had broadened his client base in Uganda.

Later that week we took the road the short distance to Durba, the same town the United Nations had once deemed the site of Uganda's most serious wartime offences, a town that – until Randgold arrived – had been a hub for working artisanal miners. Our driver and guide on this trip was Serge Mubilulu, a young Congolese national who had a degree in sociology from the University of Johannesburg and the unenviable job of 'Resettlement Coordinator'. Serge parked the truck on the outskirts of town, near a group of men playing cards in the shade of a tree. 'But *you* are the company!' the men yelled at him, after he'd tried to placate them with the promise that employment was available to every former *orpailleur*. 'Where is your promise, where is the real work?' The nub of their complaint, we suspected, was in the word *real*. When we asked the men whether they'd prefer a return to the old ways rather than a life of breaking rocks for Kibali, the answer was a resounding '*Oui!*' 'If you are a man,' their spokesman said, 'you would rather rely on yourself.'

This demand for a respectable livelihood, for a not merely *masculine* but essentially *human* freedom, was – or so we'd guessed – why Kibali needed to hire people with sociology degrees. As Louis Watum had explained, Randgold knew well before taking operational control that implementation of an exclusion zone would be its most difficult first-stage challenge. That said, the company had not anticipated that Okimo, a 10 per cent equity partner in the mine, would make a tough job even tougher: many of the state-owned corporation's mid-level functionaries, it transpired, were unwilling to forego their regular payoffs from the *orpailleurs*. So in mid-2010, according to Watum, Randgold had called a meeting with the Okimo bureaucrats and representatives of the *orpailleurs*, and had invited along Governor Médard Autsai Asenga of Orientale province. Autsai had sat at the head of the table, and had spoken not in French but in Lingala, letting everyone know that the artisanal miners would be compensated for being moved off their land, and that the Kibali operations were happening whether they liked it or not. 'That, for me, was the best proof yet that the president wanted Haut Uélé to develop,' Watum had recalled, before going on to tell us that a follow-up meeting with the governor had taken place in February 2012. At the latter meeting, he'd said, progress on the key points had been confirmed – Okimo (now called Sokimo, for Société des Mines d'Or de Kilo-Moto) was no longer straddling the fence, and as many as 2 000 *orpailleurs* were earning a replacement income. Their new livelihood involved breaking the region's boulders into rock aggregates, for which the mine paid them per weight.

'These are the lazy ones,' said Serge, when we got back to the truck. 'They can earn $200 a month, but all they want to do is play cards.' We were reminded by this lament of the card players we had encountered the year before in Botswana, who'd seemed desperate enough to accept *any* work – difference being, where they were stuck in Selebi Phikwe, a mining town past its prime, Durba was on its way up. Another difference, as evidenced by the pile of banknotes on the ground, was that the Congolese game was a money game, which perhaps meant that 'lazy' wasn't the most appropriate word. Were these the guys supplying that gold trader in the market? It was entirely possible, admitted Serge. But he wanted us to know that if the men were working the old pits at night, they were relics of a fast fading past. Kibali had built their new homes, he said, it was giving them food and taking care of their hospital bills. And if what they wanted was *respectable* employment, the mine was offering that too – a professor from Makerere University in Kampala had been contracted to teach the people agricultural skills; Serge took us on a quick tour of the fish ponds, the vegetable gardens, the pig pens. 'International standards of resettlement *don't* require a mine to provide jobs,' he told us, 'and yet look how far we've gone beyond that. These schools weren't here before. We're giving them electricity for the first time since the Belgians left. So far we have employed 1 000 on the construction project and 400 in the brick factory. For the others, we spend up to $100 000 a month buying rock aggregates. Kibali is the best thing to happen here in living memory. While it's true that we will always be a focal point for dissatisfaction, I think most of the people know what we bring.'

On our second to last day on the mine, we took our final trip up the Arua road. Our destination was the Catholic Church in Watsa, a beautiful structure with deep verandahs and red brick arches that had been built in the 1930s by the Belgians. In the priest's quarters, at the end of a palm tree-lined drive, was the room that housed Radio RTCB, Haut Uélé's new FM station. It was a tiny space, with a torn linoleum floor and broadcast equipment that might have had its heyday in the 1980s. The presenter and only permanent member of staff, a man in his mid-sixties named Akwila Konziwa, waved at us from behind the mike. He was wearing a T-shirt with the imprint '*Kokiza Joli Joli*' – the same phrase we'd seen throughout the week on billboards, a message that branded the main resettlement village 'nice, nice'. When Mr Konziwa was done reading the news, he programmed in a *kwassa kwassa* medley and signalled for us to enter. We pointed at his shirt. 'We thought the station was independent,' we said.

'It is,' he laughed. 'Two years ago a local MP gave us the money to start it, Kibali only pays for public service announcements.'

'So you really do believe everything is *joli, joli?*'

'Listen,' he said, 'my signal goes out at least 70 kilometres in every direction, sometimes up to 200 kilometres if the village is on a mountain. My audience has never had contact with a radio station before, but they send me messages all the time by SMS. The messages are mostly talking about the new opportunities from the mine. There is lots of discussion, because more than 100 villages now have radio clubs where they get together and debate. They know they are getting real information from me, not gossip. I can tell you, the people are starting to trust.'

Which, it struck us, was about as close as we would get to our answer – this altogether unfamiliar notion of trust, this feeling that maybe there *was* a reason to hope. On Watsa's high street, where we saw a family of pygmies who had come in from the forest to buy wares, our driver pointed to a sign on the side of a bus. '*La vie est un combat,*' it read, life is war. The bus, we were told, belonged to Mr Lenguma, a local entrepreneur; there were 30 others just like it, all leaving regularly for Kisangani, Goma and Kampala. Mr Lenguma, our driver said, had started his business within days of the Arua road's upgrade.

◆

On a Tuesday in late September 2013, more than two years ahead of schedule, a pair of Congolese miners would pour Kibali's first gold bar. By the close of the final quarter of 2013, the mine would deliver to market 88 200 ounces of the metal, at a profit before interest, tax and depreciation of $68.3 million. At the mine's official opening ceremony in May 2014, an event presided over by the DRC's minister of mines, Martin Kabwelulu, Mark Bristow would venture the opinion that 'successful development' of Kibali could herald the birth of an economic region in the far northeast to rival the copper fields of Katanga. To us, following the event in the press, these words of the Randgold CEO would read as uncharacteristically coy: as the company's latest annual report had shown, Kibali had so far met with *nothing but* success. Since reviewing and updating Moto Gold's feasibility study in 2011, geologists had demonstrated that there were at least double the reserves in the ground than had originally been assumed; the Kibali board had consequently doubled forecasts, and had guaranteed shareholders an average output of 600 000 ounces per annum over the next 12 years.[64] All indications were that Kibali would recoup its capital costs, forecast to top out in 2016 at $2.5 billion, well inside the breakeven date. What's more, the mine was almost certainly going to deliver the 550 000 ounces it had promised for 2014. And now Bristow was *hedging*?

But we didn't know what everyone at the ceremony knew. For years, the Congolese government had been considering revising the 2002 mining code, and the latest draft of proposed amendments had once again ignored the private sector's input. The government, as per the draft, appeared intent on raising the taxes and royalties it had been levying on foreign companies, while at the same time cutting back on exemptions and introducing a new tax on windfall profits. As Bristow was aware – he had in fact said as much to a journalist who'd flown in for the event – most of the miners in the Congo were operating *outside* the code, so such measures could have limited upside for the treasury.[65] Translation: instead of penalising the legally compliant conglomerates, thereby dis-incentivising foreign investors and hampering long-term growth, go after the Rwandans, the Ugandans, and the downright corrupt.

Regarding the last category, Bristow would also have been aware that in April 2013 the international board of the EITI, the all-important Extractive Industries Transparency Initiative, had temporarily suspended the DRC for failing to meet certain 'full disclosure' requirements. This had been the EITI's polite way of saying that the secret sale of state assets to anyone, no matter how powerful and connected, was an unconscionable breach. And yet in January 2014, following the release of two very positive reports, the EITI had been quick to point out that progress in the broadest sense had been made. The reports had demonstrated that a record $1.4 billion in revenues had been collected from the Congolese oil, gas and mining sector in 2011, up 60 per cent on the year before.[66] The improvement had reportedly been the result of the DRC's implementation of the 'EITI Standard', a set of best-practice guidelines aimed at transparent government auditing, increased accountability of tax collecting agencies, and ramped up policing of conflict minerals.

For Mark Bristow, as for Louis Watum, Willem Jacobs and JP Mbuluyo, this general contradiction in the EITI's outlook would not have come as a huge surprise: if anyone understood the vagaries of operating in a country like the DRC, it was them. But given what they'd done to get their own operation to 'first gold', none of them could have been blamed for taking a *specific* contradiction to heart. Randgold would make its true feelings felt in a presentation entitled 'Review of the Mining Code in the DRC ... risks and advantages for private mining companies', in which it would argue that high administrative costs, infrastructural deficiencies, tax compliance burdens and extensive capital payback periods still rendered the Congo one of the most unattractive investment destinations on earth. At a time when such barriers were just beginning to be removed, the company would add, raising taxes was the 'completely wrong' approach – it would, in their opinion, kill the economic potential brought on by the 'multiplier effect' from the development of new mines.[67] Interestingly, Randgold would *not* mention the security threat in their assessment, perhaps because they'd always taken it as a given, but more likely because they didn't want to terrify investors. Indeed, while record copper exports from Katanga would help the Congolese economy grow by 8.5 per cent in 2013, even that story had not been without its risks – in March 2013, five people had been killed by secessionist Mai Mai rebels in the relatively 'safe' Katangan capital of Lubumbashi, and in January

Framed image of Sister Marie-Clémentine Anuarite Nengapeta, first beatified African woman, born Haut Uélé district, Belgian Congo, 1939, died 1 December 1964. Photograph taken in Grimari Catholic Mission, Central African Republic, August 2014

2014 a further 26 would be killed in an eight-hour battle between these same rebels and government troops.[68] Meanwhile, Sinohydro and CREC, the Chinese partners in the massive Sicomines joint venture, had temporarily lost the backing of China Exim Bank, and although the bank would resume its loans in early 2013, it was obvious that

Beijing's appetite for risk in the DRC was waning.[69]

As we sat pondering all of this at our local pub in Johannesburg, we couldn't help wondering whether Kimbembe Mazunga and Willem Jacobs remained friends. Did they still meet for dinner at the Memling when the South African was in town? Did the former rugby player wave his cigar in the air and notify the presidential advisor, as he'd once notified us, that 'a government's bureaucratic sophistication rises in proportion to the number of new conglomerates it attracts'? Did he offer the quip that 'commercial traders don't build roads in Africa, industrial miners do'? Did the elegant consigliere shrug, sip his whiskey, and reply that since Randgold had now figured out how to mine one of the world's most coveted gold deposits, perhaps it could afford the extra tax? We liked to imagine the two men smiling, clinking their glasses, and agreeing to stake the middle ground.

Which was where, precisely? We had visited the Democratic Republic of the Congo to discover what 'open for business' meant in such a context. We had gone there to see what it took to be a 'responsible' corporate player in an active war zone. We had learned that 'business' was a mutable term, and that occasionally your partners made it into the pages of Human Rights Watch reports. We had learned that 'responsibility' was a type of cultural currency, pegged more to your own needs than to the needs of the community you professed to serve. And yet, in the conjoining of business and responsibility, we *had* found development. Not the sort preached in NGO booklets and government vision statements, but a rougher, a meaner, a less naïve sort. 'There's a perception here that we can build Johannesburg overnight,' Louis Watum had told us in Kibali the first day we'd met. That wasn't true. They were building something unprecedented. Something unrecognisable.

It turns out that Josim Uddin Miridha, the name we read in the newspaper report that brought us to Ganyesa, is a misspelling of Hossin Redoy. And he is not from Pakistan, but Bangladesh. We have discovered this fact thanks to James Yu, who has accompanied us back across the highway, and has introduced us to a man who was one of the first on the scene.

The young Bangladeshi, when he's told of our business, when he hears that we are journalists, almost weeps. It's as if he wants us to recuse him, as if he needs to be absolved.

'Yes,' Hossin says, 'after the store begins to burn, I get a call on my cell phone.'

He holds up a battered Nokia, and we are surrounded by four more Bangladeshi men, all clamouring to speak.

'The call was from inside the store. They are begging us, "please come help". You see, we have a deal to help each other in case of problems.'

What we are able to glean, amidst the interjections, is that it is after two o'clock in the morning when the call comes through. Hossin and his 13 companions – some his brothers, some his cousins, all escapees from the slums of Sylhet – are asleep in a single room. He wakes everyone with a shout, and, expecting the worst, each picks up a baton, a cricket bat, anything to fend off the suspected attack. They race the 500 metres to the fire. En route, they pass Mi Zheng, who's running, yelling, 'My brother, my brother Chen, he's inside!' Hossin is still on his cell phone, speaking with Chen. 'Where? Where are you?' he asks. 'In the kitchen room!' screams Chen, 'We are trapped!' As he runs, Hossin keeps the phone to his ear; he hears women coughing, shrieking, wailing. Then – nothing.

'So we get there and I go around the back,' Hossin tells us, ignoring the incessant interjections, no longer in English but in rapid Sylheti. 'All the brothers, we shake the burglar bars until they are coming loose. Then I push my body inside, but there is too much smoke. I call the fire department. They come with only two people and their hose is too small. I call the police. The police don't arrive.'

One of Hossin's brothers, reverting again to English, says they saw broken glass beneath the kitchen window. No, he says, it was not an accident. Hossin snatches back the narrative: 'Many hours after, I told the police. I told them somebody threw a petrol bomb.'

'And are the police investigating?' we ask.

'I don't think so,' says Hossin. 'I don't think they care about us foreigners. We are all afraid.'

We will learn, over the course of our time in Ganyesa, that thugs have recently delivered a vicious form of vengeance upon two Bangladeshis who have dared to resist a burglary: the beating of the man senseless, the wrapping of the body in a blanket, the dousing of the blanket in petrol, the striking of a match.

Now, as Hossin shows us around his premises, we begin to get an inkling of his fear. A guard dog is tied on a chain to an iron peg outside the living quarters; alarm locks are affixed to all the doors; in the single room, scattered between the mattresses on the floor, are dumbbells and barbells and a machine for the strengthening of pectoral muscles.

We have one more question for Hossin before we leave. 'Mi Zheng,' we say, 'Chen's brother. Is he here? Can we speak with him?'

Hossin considers the request. 'He is in Ganyesa,' he says finally. 'He works in the shop next to mine, that one over there. Maybe I will tell him about you. And then if you come back tomorrow, I can help.'

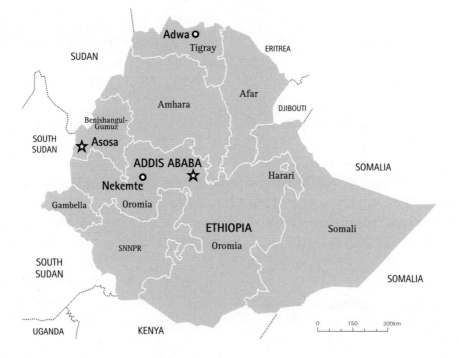

SEVEN

ETHIOPIA

Food Security & the All-seeing Eye

*'We all wish to live. We all seek a world in which men are freed of
the burdens of ignorance, poverty, hunger and disease.'*

— Emperor Haile Selassie

THE HUNGER

The Ethiopian economist Eleni Zaude Gabre-Madhin found her purpose
in life during a food fight in Cornell University's mess hall, midway
through one of the darkest periods in her nation's 3 500-year history.[1] The throwing of victuals was an established tradition at Cornell,
a celebration of American bounty. But Eleni was not American, and
11 000 kilometres away her people were being wiped out by a calamity
that seemed unprecedented in its scope.[2] Over the course of 1984, 14
million Ethiopians would be at risk of starving to death, and by 1986
more than a million would have perished. Images of the country's
malnourished children were already the most marketable item on the
international news menu, and Bob Geldof was about to gather together
his friends for the recording of 'Do They Know It's Christmas?'[3]

And so that night, as she dodged dinner rolls and tapioca pudding,
something inside of Eleni snapped. Her family had left Ethiopia in
1974, shortly after Emperor Haile Selassie had been deposed, and she
remembered home as a civilisation crafted by countless generations of
proud culture, not as some shameful Third World backwater. Strong
women, Eleni had been taught, formed the bedrock of her family.[4]

Her great-grandmother, Imahoy Saba Yifat, had been one of the few women to take up arms during the Battle of Adwa in 1896, when Ethiopian forces had repelled an Italian advance and thereby saved the country from the colonialists. Eleni's mother, Bizuwork Bekele, had grown up in the legendary city of Harar, next door to where the renegade French poet Arthur Rimbaud had once lived.[5] As a young girl, Eleni had marvelled over hundreds of such historical footnotes, all sculpted and recorded by the Ge'ez alphabet, one of the oldest writing systems in continuous use anywhere in the world.

Due to her father Zaude's decision to flee the post-Selassie regime, Eleni would get an extreme close-up on the Africa of the 1970s – an era in which notions of gender, race and ethnicity were becoming entangled in the fast-fading liberation dream. Zaude had secured a job as a senior official at the United Nations, and following a stint in New York City had taken the family along to postings in Rwanda, Togo, Malawi and Kenya. 'I grew up all over the continent,' Eleni would tell us many years later, 'and I got to experience how things were run. I knew Africa very, very well. I understood it.'

It was all but fated, then, that with Cornell's evening meal splattered across the mess hall floor, Eleni – short, preternaturally intense, her brown curly hair cascading onto her hunched shoulders – would leap onto a table and start screaming. 'I reminded my peers that while they wasted food, children were dying in my home, my country.' As the year wound on, Eleni would watch awestruck as Ethiopia became a *cause célèbre* with its own soundtrack, a fame that would contribute to famine relief in 1984 and 1985 but do nothing to stop ensuing famines after the world had turned its gaze elsewhere. Before Eleni fully understood that a sack of grain could be used as a weapon of war, and before she realised that a plate of food in Africa had as much to do with geopolitics as it did with nutrition, she made a vow to herself: she would dedicate her life to ensuring that Ethiopians never again went hungry. Her ambition was nothing short of turning the world's largest recipient of food aid into a regional food basket, and she didn't yet know that to achieve it she would have to unravel one of the abiding mysteries of agriculture on her continent – with over half of the world's arable land, and almost 700 million people farming it, why were so many Africans dying with empty bellies?

◆

One thing *was* clear to Eleni, even in those early days: the Ethiopian famine of 1984 was not a biblical catastrophe, ordained from above. Although drought would eventually contribute to the misery, Eleni believed that Ethiopia's problems could largely be blamed on how its crops were packaged, sold and distributed. After all, nobody at Cornell had ever starved to death because of a dry spell on the American prairies – the very thought was absurd. So following her outburst at Cornell, she enrolled in every agricultural economics class she could find. She earned a BSc at Cornell, and a Masters at Michigan State. In the first year of her second degree, Eleni came across a paper that told of a food surplus in western Ethiopia during the 'hell years' of 1984 and 1985. 'It was one of those eureka moments,' she would later tell us, 'but it needed a close reading of history if you wanted to understand.'

Ethiopia, Eleni knew, was less a nation than a tapestry – a nation of 'nations, nationalities and Peoples', as the compilers of the 1994 constitution would later note.[6] In the northern highlands of what is now the Ethiopian region of Tigray and the independent nation of Eritrea, running south into the towns of Welo, Gondar, Shewa and Gojar, the Tigray and Amhara had for centuries belonged to the parishes of the Orthodox Church, whose mythic origins were said to stretch back to King Solomon's Israel. There were the Cushitic-speaking Muslims of the Afar, Saho and Somali regions, while the Oromo, who formed the country's majority, were themselves split into 12 cohorts spread over 10 provinces.[7] In amongst all of this, Eleni had learnt, were a few historical rules of thumb: the emperor reigned with the tacit consent of the church, while both liturgy and administration were conducted in Amharic. That said, retaining the unity of the empire had always depended upon the consent of these disparate groups, an imperative often achieved by violence, sometimes by suasion, and occasionally by sheer accident.[8] A few of the empires had lasted days, others centuries.

Before the arrival of the Europeans, imperial Ethiopia's fortunes had been largely determined by the Arabian Peninsula across the Red Sea, and by those Arabs who'd trekked south from Egypt and northern Sudan to trade in coffee, teff and human beings.[9] But while Ethiopia had never been Arabic, neither had it ever been typically African. Through the millennia, it had carved out – and perpetually reaffirmed – its own distinct world.

For medieval Europeans, as Eleni had discovered, this world was so distant and alien that it became a palimpsest on which myths were written. The most remarkable of these concerned Presbyter Johannes, or Prester John, a Christian king who ruled over Muslims in a land roamed by fantastical beasts. Prester John's secret weapon, the story went, was a mirror through which he could examine all the realms of his kingdom at once – the so-called 'magical speculum' that served as a symbolic precursor to the postmodern surveillance state.

Outsiders' misconceptions, and their resulting blunders, did not dissipate over the course of time. As Eleni's family rose to prominence in the 1880s, Ethiopia became a buffer zone between French Somaliland (now Djibouti) and British interests in Egypt and Sudan. Fitawrari Gebremedhin, Eleni's grandfather, had served as an official in the sprawling administration assembled by Menelik II, and had watched as the emperor fused the country around men exactly like himself – the strategy was to develop an administrative web based on patronage, supported by a large army wielding the latest in European weaponry. If it was obvious to the day's Africa hands that such technological advancements would exact their price, it's doubtful that many of them pegged the suppliers as the eventual losers. The Treaty of Wuchale, signed with Italy in 1889, promised Rome territory in modern-day Eritrea in exchange for financial and military assistance. When the treaty failed to hold, the wheels were set in motion for one of imperial Europe's most fatal head-on collisions. On the first day of March 1896, in the mountains north of the town of Adwa, Ethiopian forces routed four Italian brigades, wounding 1 500 and killing 7 000.[10] Avenging the humiliation would motivate Mussolini's Fascist project, with legions of Italian soldiers being sent back to the Horn of Africa in 1936. Ras

222

Teferi Makonnen, who'd been crowned Emperor Haile Selassie in 1930, fled the country to spend the onset of World War II in bitter exile. He arrived back in Addis in May 1941, after the Italians had been routed in Ethiopia for a second and final time, their ultimate defeat delivered courtesy of the Allied forces.

Across the world, Emperor Selassie now emerged as an icon for a liberated Africa, his rectitude and rhetoric affording consciousness movements their true north. In far-off Jamaica, members of the burgeoning Rastafarian faith claimed the emperor as an incarnation of Christ. But ordinary Ethiopians, not without reason, rejected the deification of their leader – by almost any measure, Ethiopia was one of the poorest countries in the world. As the Selassie administration became increasingly sclerotic, his subjects starved through famines in the 1950s, 1960s and 1970s. The pain was by no means shared, and in 1974, as Selassie imported grain into an insulated Addis, the northern regions of Wallo and Tigray buried their dead by the tens of thousands.[11]

Students, Marxists, Muslims, labour unionists and members of the military rose up in disgust. In late 1974, after months of unrest, Selassie was powerless as the 'Coordinating Committee of the Armed Forces, Police, and Territorial Army', comprising 100 or so men in open mutiny, placed him and his family under arrest. The committee bore the revolutionary standard 'without blood', a slogan that proved hollow when Major Mengistu Haile Mariam took over the chairmanship at the age of 36. Mengistu and his men would enter the annals of African ignominy as the Derg.[12]

Modelled after a Stalinist/Leninist workers' party, but in effect a communist-themed fascist junta, the Derg were one of those twentieth century 'modernising' projects always destined to end badly. Shortly after they assumed power, Eleni's father, a career official in the Selassie administration, learnt of the murder of 60 high-ranking imperial loyalists – it was not unreasonable to assume that the same fate awaited him. Many hundreds of thousands would die in successive Derg purges. The committee's lasting contribution to African development would be award-winning photographs of infants with distended bellies, flies in their nostrils, mothers powerless to help.

The teff harvested to make the *injera* that Ethiopians ate with almost every meal, the coffee beans roasted in intricate ceremonies served between those meals – such were the traditions that tied the nation's psyche to the land. Mengistu knew this, which was why the corner-stone of the Derg's inevitable nationalisation programme was called 'Land to the Tiller'. As one of the more radical land reform drives ever conducted, so deadly that even Mengistu's backers in Moscow were horrified, the rural resettlement campaigns had as their core objective the breaking of the millennia-old ethnic ties. 'Land to the Tiller' secured some early popular support, mostly because it dismantled the feudal systems of tenancy that existed during successive imperial regimes. But before long, it became clear that the Derg's policies were nudging the country toward starvation. In fields denuded of activity, in peasant-run 'villages' desperately short of co-operative expertise, the road to 1984 was being mapped out in the dust.

◆

Eleni was reintroduced to the sounds and smells of her childhood in 1995, after three decades in exile, when her Stanford PhD gave her an excuse to book a return flight. Mengistu's Soviet-backed regime had fallen four years before, the Western-supported Ethiopian People's Revolutionary Democratic Front (EPRDF) was firmly in power, and she was at last in a position to confirm her long-held theories. Eleni knew from her studies that the Derg had deliberately hidden food in order to starve the north into compliance, but she had remained steadfast in her belief that this was not the sole cause of the famine. As she rat-tled around the rural areas in the dented Ladas that served most of the country's transportation needs, she spoke with hundreds of peasants who told her of a shadowy cohort of brokers that traded during rau-cous morning markets. These men, lumped by Mengistu in the same camp as the feudal landlords, had suffered terribly during the Derg, but had not disappeared entirely – mostly because they bought and sold almost everything that non-farming Ethiopians ate. Eleni wondered how this was still possible in a country obsessed with centralised, statist oversight.

African countries, Eleni was now certain, had a double problem with farming. The first could be described as an issue of scale. 'Most Africans are farmers,' she would later explain in a much-downloaded 2007 TED Talk. 'Most are small farmers in terms of the land they operate, and very *very* small farmers in terms of the capital they have at their disposal.' As late as the mid-zeroes, the same talk would make clear, only 7 per cent of African land would be irrigated, as opposed to 40 per cent in Asia. African farmers would use about 22 kilograms of fertiliser per hectare as compared to 144 kilograms in Asia. Road density would be six times greater in rural Asia; Latin America would have eight times as many tractors, and Asia three times.[13] In short, Africa's subsistence farmers would continue to battle climate change, exhausted seeds, disappearing soil, terrible infrastructure, zero access to credit and pervasive government indifference, which would consistently result in harvests less than one quarter the size of the worst yields anywhere else in the world.

Eleni had been influenced in her thinking by Theodore Schultz, the Nobel Prize-winning theorist whose specialty was the economics of agriculture. Schultz had once noted that farmers were as rational and profit-minded as the rest of society, but rarely possessed the 'human capital', the education or technical skills, to make good on their ambitions. Policy makers didn't understand this, and were instead intent on increasing production so that high yield figures would make agricultural ministries look good, resulting in invitations to Davos and other talk shops to punt Africa's incipient 'green revolution' – a buzz term that had almost no limitations on how often, and in what context, it was employed.[14] But high yields one season meant plummeting prices the next. Loans for the previous year's harvest could not be repaid, fertiliser use dropped in order to save on costs, and lo! – the following season, no one had anything to eat. This was raw market economics, and farmers felt the effects even if they did not grasp the mechanics.

In 1995, as Eleni travelled Ethiopia accumulating data, she repeatedly encountered what she considered to be Africa's second – and far more serious – farming problem: the agricultural market was an abomination. Every time grain changed hands, which it did five or six times before it was sold, it changed sacks, which led to handling fees that increased prices by 26 per cent. Almost 67 per cent of traders faced regular contract defaults, but could pursue legal recourse only 4 per cent of the time. In all, a farmer took home about 30 per cent of the final cost of his produce. To describe the agriculture market in Ethiopia as medieval, thought Eleni, would be to insult medievalists.

As she familiarised herself with the logistics, Eleni found that the archaic nuances of buying and selling were primarily understood by that small corps of brokers who gathered at rural markets at six in the morning to buy and trade food for a population (at the time) of around 80 million. Many years later, she would evocatively describe the scene in an essay for an agricultural think-tank:

> [O]n any given day of the week, traders, farmers, labourers, house-wives, and donkeys would be jostling in front of rows of stalls, white polypropylene sacks of maize, sorghum, wheat, barley, and teff, would be piled high in the back, and in front of each stall a trader would be weighing all sales and purchases on an old Italian-made scale. At the ends of the muddy lanes between the stalls, truck horns would be honking as diesel fumes filled the air, drivers would lean out of their windows to buy a cob of roasted maize to munch on as they waited to load or unload crops, and goats would stand by to nibble the fallen grain as the sacks were hoisted in the air.[15]

Eleni spent hours committing this prehistoric Nasdaq to film. When she replayed the footage for her PhD advisor back at Stanford, he said, 'Yup, this looks like a commodities exchange.' He encouraged Eleni to study the advent of the Chicago Board of Trade and the London Metals Exchange. She did as suggested – and thereby took delivery of her next 'eureka' moment.

In 1848, Eleni learned, 82 grain merchants and farmers had gotten together in what was then a booming transportation hub on the shores of Lake Superior. The idea was to mitigate the immense risks farmers faced if, while transporting their grain by barge over the Great Lakes, prices happened to drop. They devised an innovation called futures contracts, which locked a price for grain *in time*, while an independent body simultaneously graded that grain by an established set of criteria. The Chicago Board of Trade allowed farmers and traders to exchange a product without having to visually inspect it, which resulted in less handling and better price security. As Eleni would later put it to us, 'If we were going to enable traders from anywhere in Ethiopia to efficiently coordinate with each other, meet each other through some trading platform, trade knowing the quality of the product – and all of this with farmers getting paid on time – we *had to* set up a commodities exchange. Basically, my thinking from then on was totally focused on this.'

By 2001, Eleni was living in Washington DC. She had established herself as an academic superstar, working for the World Bank's rural department as a senior economist for the Africa region, while writing carefully crafted papers for the International Food and Policy Research Institute (IFPRI), an NGO with a high profile in the agricultural wonko-sphere. That year, following a second season of bumper harvests, the Ethiopian agricultural ministry came to IFPRI for help in decoding a conundrum: prices across the country were plummeting, and the countryside was starting to go hungry. The organisation rushed Eleni to Addis, where she met with panicked officials. 'They were like, "We need help! What happened, Eleni? Why are the prices collapsing?"' In what would turn out to be a lasting lesson in how NGOs function in a reality removed from the one in which people starve to death by the village load, IFPRI commissioned a training symposium. Just as the results of the various panels were about to be published, in July of 2002, the Ethiopian government announced the advent of another famine. Fourteen million people were at risk of starvation. It was 1984 all over again.

'I just freaked out,' Eleni would tell us. 'How could there be no food? Where had the surplus gone?'

Others shared her incredulity. She was contacted by an ex-*Wall Street*

Journal correspondent named Roger Thurow, who had worked the famine beat since the 1980s, and had been responsible for breaking stories of the surpluses that had served as Eleni's original eureka moment. As far as Thurow was concerned, something similar was indeed happening. But it was worse than either he or Eleni could have imagined: this time, it wasn't government malevolence that was exacerbating the crisis, it was government cluelessness. Over the six months leading up to the latest famine, Ethiopian farmers had allowed over 300 000 tons of grain to rot in their fields because prices had dropped so low that there was no point in harvesting. US food aid trucks were arriving with over a million tons of grain grown mostly in the American prairies, all of it rumbling past warehouses stacked with *locally grown* teff and grain.[16] Fields in certain regions of the country were lush and verdant.[17] Africa had coined another terrible new phrase: green famine.

Eleni was no longer content to play wonk in Washington. She now understood her subject as well as anybody else alive, if not better: she was an expert in something that had the potential to save her people from ever again going hungry; something that could change not only the way her people stored food over time, but how they transferred that food across time and space. 'Either way, it's a *market*,' she would tell us. 'You buy low, you sell high – this is how the rest of the world works.'[18]

In November 2002, the World Bank decided to hold a big food security conference in Addis Ababa, where Eleni was scheduled to speak about commodities markets. She anticipated the usual agglomeration of junior ministers and miscellaneous suits. But on this day, one of those suits contained the most august personage in the Federal Democratic Republic of Ethiopia. 'Completely by coincidence and by great surprise,' she would recall, 'the prime minister was in the room. I was facing Meles.'

Meles Zenawi Asres: the Tigrayan officer who, in May 1991, had rolled into Addis Ababa on a tank in order to destroy what was left of Mengistu's regime. By 2002, he had become an international statesman of significant repute, one of the most important men in Africa. According to his supporters, Meles was a philosopher king who backed

228

up his erudition with precision-sharp political instincts; according to his opponents, he was a nightmare reincarnation of Prester John, as evidenced by his all-seeing speculum. Tapping phones, curtailing Internet use, sending his security forces into rural villages by moonlight – Meles was everywhere, all of the time, and he was watching.

But as far as Eleni was concerned, she was facing the one man in Ethiopia who could acknowledge her policy recommendations as sound. This was her moment. 'I did not stumble over a single word,' she would tell us.

I HAVE GIVEN UP ON THIS LIFE

'Traffic, traffic,' said our driver, Mohammed, when he arrived at last to fetch us. 'Too much traffic.'

There was no need to tell him where to go. Today, 29 January 2012, there was only one possible destination. Addis Ababa was gridlocked, locked down, frozen, the entire city subject to the inauguration festivities at the newly constructed African Union headquarters located in the centre of town. Mohammed managed to sneak his Corolla through back alleys barely wide enough for a donkey, under rising towers braced by ironwood scaffolding.

'You see that building over there?' he asked, pointing at a rack of concrete bones dominating the vista to our left. 'Two years ago, this was a place you would come to buy goats.'

Mohammed, we'd learnt, enjoyed pointing out the surreal incongruities brought on by change. The Addis on the ground belonged to a different era than the Addis in the sky; elevators doubled as time machines. This was largely due to the fact that the Ethiopian economy had been growing at around 10 per cent year-on-year, one of the steepest rates anywhere in the world, and certainly the fastest-growing non-oil economy in Africa.[19] And yet, according to Prime Minister Meles Zenawi, the construction sector was not the focus, much less the point, of Ethiopia's ascendancy.

Bole Road in flood, Addis Ababa, August 2014

'Rapid and sustained development in African countries will crucially depend on agriculture,' Meles had written in a 2006 paper presented to Columbia University's Initiative for Policy Dialogue, a project founded by Nobel Prize-winning economist Joseph Stiglitz. 'It is the dynamism of agriculture which is going to determine the dynamism of the non-agricultural sector and the economy as a whole.'[20] In other words, everything we saw around us was driven by what was happening in the countryside, a green revolution – that term again – that suppos-edly accounted for almost half of Ethiopia's GDP, and four-fifths of its employment. According to Ethiopia's Central Statistical Authority, cereal production in the country had increased by more than 12 per cent year-on-year between 2004 and 2007. A study of private peasant holdings in the rainy season had claimed that the estimated cropped area and volume of production had grown by 2.2 per cent and 7.4 per cent respectively over the 2010 season.

Yields – the national obsession. Meles ascribed the uptick to 'democratic developmentalism', a statist-driven alternative to the neo-liberal policies that were, according to him, 'incapable of bringing about the African renaissance.' But in the context of all that Eleni would tell us later, and according to reams of contrarian data – such as a 2012 IMF report which claimed that Ethiopian growth was 'fuelled in part by heavy public investment in infrastructure' – we might have wondered whether the prime minister was overplaying his hand. Did Eleni's fortuitous meeting with Meles back in 2002 have anything to do with Ethiopia's ecstatic growth figures? Or was something more complicated, and comparatively more sinister, at work on the country's GDP?

As it happened, we were on our way to see the prime minister. We would not be speaking with him directly – he possessed such disdain for our profession that, under the pretext of a far-reaching 2009 anti-terrorism law, he had jailed more of our colleagues than any of his African counterparts.[21] Rather, we were on our way to watch him in action in front of an international audience, doing what he did best: high-grade geopolitical dissembling.

Mohammed had finally negotiated us through the worst of the gridlock, and drew the Corolla to a halt before twin oil drums and a weighted boom.

'Here,' he said. We stepped out, and a soldier in wraparound shades and brown fatigues stepped forward. His features suggested the Maghreb, Morocco maybe. He was similarly curious.

'Where are you from?' he asked. We handed over our passports.

We noticed the flag on his uniform – not Morocco but Tunisia. Glancing at our documentation, he scrolled through his mental map of the continent, working his way down the eleven or so nations that separated us, and arrived at the inevitable.

'Mandela!' he exclaimed.

'Mandela,' we agreed.

He nodded us onwards. The street, a minor but otherwise busy artery in central Addis Ababa, was deserted, so quiet that we were able to hear the high keening whistle of kites as they rode the thermals overhead.

Every 10 metres or so another soldier, there to protect Africa's most important men and women from the people beyond the booms. According to Meles and his generals, pre-emptive enforcement on this scale was entirely necessary. In July 2012, during the AU summit that would follow these inaugural celebrations, thousands of Ethiopian Muslims would flood the streets around the headquarters, protesting the government raid on a mosque in the bustling Mercato neighbourhood. Thirty-four per cent of Ethiopia's 94 million citizens were Muslim, a number roughly equivalent to the population of Canada, and they were chafing under the constant harassment.[22] Indeed, much of Meles's international backing was linked to his stance on the Horn of Africa's 'Muslim problem' – he was a Christian leader in an ocean of Islam, and he was more than willing to serve as regional policeman. Ethiopia had become a bulwark against Somalia's Al-Shabaab insurgency, Sudan's intransigent Omar al-Bashir regime, and numberless renegade Islamists along the Red Sea littoral. The country's own Muslim minority had interpreted Meles's iron fist as another historical instance of Christian rulers treating them as second-class citizens, with at least one (banned) opposition movement decrying the 'trends that make use of our ethnic, religious, and cultural differences as a means of achieving myopic and short term political gains'.[23]

All of which played into Meles's overarching local and international strategies, as evinced by the compound that awaited us at the end of the road. The new African Union headquarters, built at a reported cost of $200 million by the Chinese government, was apparently the largest project that the People's Republic had completed in Africa since the 1970s.[24] But this was not a building so much as a *rebuilding* – at the same moment that the tallest skyscraper in Addis came into full and uninterrupted view, we got our first sighting of the *old* African Union headquarters, built by the Germans and inaugurated in 2003. The three-storey structure was a squat and altogether uninspiring articulation of the West's enduring involvement in Africa; much grander pronouncements were made by the glass and concrete structure that rose

African Union Headquarters, Addis Ababa, November 2012

99.9 metres into the Ethiopian sky.

We followed the throng of delegates up the ramp and around the back of the tower, to where all 54 flags of the nations of Africa were flying, including the flag of South Sudan, the union's youngest member. And yet the most prominent flags at the 18th African Union Summit were the flags that loomed distinct and apart, the flags with yellow stars against a red background, the non-African flags. 'AU Conference Centre and Office Complex donated by Chinese Government', read a placard affixed to an outdoor stage.

Beijing, it was plain, did not want anyone to forget.

◆

Mid-afternoon, in a huddle of conference delegates, their aides, and their aides' aides, we were ushered into the sun-dappled atrium, the abundant light bouncing off the mirrored windows and brushed steel fittings. The auditorium itself was a rush of pine falling in an arc towards the presidium, its fragrance a mix of fresh leather and varnish. We found seats in the press box, and from our perch listened to the diplomatic peacocking of UN secretary-general Ban Ki-moon, AU chair Jean Ping, and special guest Jia Qinglin, then the fourth most powerful statesman in China.

The show properly kicked off when Meles took the mike. A short and owlish figure, he spoke in the reedy voice of the quintessential professor, his moustache, spectacles and balding pate all complementing the effect. As anticipated, his address was rigged with intellectual bear traps, stuffed with provocations. Its geographical setting was the space we now occupied – this swathe of real estate that the Ethiopian government had donated to the African Union.

'This magnificent edifice,' the prime minister began, 'is built on the ruins of the oldest maximum security prison in our country. People in Ethiopia used to call that infamous prison *Alem Bekgne*. Loosely translated it means "I have given up on this world, this life".'

Officially known as Addis Ababa Central Prison, or *Kerchele* in Amharic, the will of three successive regimes had been enforced here. For many Ethiopians with the old atrocities fresh in their minds, the AU compound represented an inexcusable historical elision: this was, after all, where Mussolini's proxies had murdered members of the Ethiopian elite during an orgy of violence in 1937, and where the Derg had done the same to members of Selassie's court in 1974. So what about a plaque in honour of those cruelly dispatched dead? Where were the monuments, the commemorations?

In conjuring the ghosts of *Alem Bekgne*, Meles the autocrat was – no doubt unconsciously – reminding his audience of an abiding psychological truism: the liberator eventually behaved just as his oppressor once did.[25] But in transforming the house of horrors into a world-class office park, Meles the statist was – no doubt *consciously* – resetting the narrative. His message to us was that through his erasure of all traces of

234

the prison, he was clearing a space for a better story, a story where, no matter the circumstances, the heroes did not give up. 'Naturally,' Meles continued, 'the people and leadership of Africa could not give up on Africa and did not do so.' Since *The Economist* magazine had famously written off the continent at the turn of the millennium, Meles went on, China and India had emerged as major economies, commodities prices had risen, and the cost of consumer goods and new technologies had nosedived. The free market fundamentalists, who with exasperated *noblesse oblige* had once imposed their theories on weak states, had taken a well-deserved beating in the wake of the financial collapse. Suddenly, Africa had its choice of dance partners. 'We are now seeing the results of our struggle for survival,' Meles said, as he stared into a sea of brigadiers, finance ministers, and presidents. Between torture chambers and office compounds, between hopelessness and opportunity, between Afro-pessimism and Afro-optimism, this was the dawn of Meles's self-achieved Afro-realism.

And if there were those in the audience expecting bashfulness in the face of the AU having accepted a $200 million gift-wrapped facility from the Chinese, the Ethiopian head of state was not about to satisfy them. 'It is therefore very appropriate for China to decide to build this hall, this hall of the rise of Africa, this hall of the African renaissance,' he said. When the West turned its back on Africa, China stepped forward with a 'win-win partnership', and therefore the AU compound was not an example of an outsider *imposing*, but of Africa *allowing*. It was a middle finger extended at all those who had once pronounced the people within this auditorium 'hopeless'.

There was a drawn out moment of silence, followed by cascades of applause. It was impossible to know what the few Westerners in the audience were thinking as Meles shuffled back to his seat, but if any of them were familiar with the term 'chutzpah', it likely came to mind. In Amharic poetry, we remembered, there was a tradition called 'wax and gold' which, as the journalist Helen Epstein had recently noted, markedly influenced modern Ethiopian doublespeak.[26] For the poet, 'wax' referred to the superficial, outside meaning, while 'gold' was the deeper, inner meaning. In the case of Meles's speech, the gold was in the fact that his country was then one of the world's largest recipients of foreign aid – by the close of 2011, Ethiopia's total aid package would amount to $4 billion, a haul netted chiefly from the stores of the World Bank, the United States and the United Kingdom.[27] In a building awash with symbolism, the most powerful was its tribute to Meles's expert trawling of two planetary tides at once.

GROW WITH US

'Does Ethiopia need a commodities exchange?'

This was the title of the talk that Eleni gave in 2002 to the audience that included the prime minister.

'I had to explain what a commodities exchange was,' she would tell us, 'because nobody present really knew.' So she spoke about the hundreds of interviews she had conducted for her PhD: how she had measured transaction costs, how 60 per cent of the time traders had no clue what prices were outside of their immediate market, how contract failure was endemic, how the risks were too high for people to try to sell to markets far away.

Eleni knew well the art of 'wax and gold', and she enlivened her story through character. Her protagonist was a young Muslim trader named Abdu Awol, whom she had first met in 1996 in Nekemte, dead in the centre of Ethiopia's maize belt. Abdu had seemed hardworking and industrious; his trading business had been passed down to him from his father, who in turn had inherited it from his grandfather. When Eleni had asked Abdu why he hadn't sold grain to the hungry Tigrayans, he'd said that a few months earlier he had indeed found a buyer from the region. He'd negotiated an amount, arranged a meeting place almost equidistant between their two hometowns, and had set out in his truck.

Abdu's journey to the village on the Sudanese border was only 900 kilometres, but had taken almost three weeks to complete. He'd been stopped around two dozen times, had paid bribe after bribe, had risked his life on the terrible roads. 'And when he got there,' Eleni told the

crowd, 'the buyer said, "Hey, this is not good maize. This is pretty rubbish! I'm cutting the price in half."' Abdu had realised right then that
he was ruined. 'Our friend went bankrupt because of the deal,' Eleni
concluded. 'He never traded outside of Nekemte again.'

The prime minister was clearly intrigued. He asked Eleni question
after question, quizzing her on the minutiae of her methodology for
close on 45 minutes. Obviously, the elegance of Eleni's theory appealed
to both the authoritarian and the statist in him: the key to ending
starvation was in formalising and regulating the commodities market.
'Today we have just learned something that we have never thought
about before,' Meles announced to the assembled dignitaries, thereby
bringing to an end the question-and-answer session. 'This country has
to do something about its markets. We have not paid any attention to
this issue. And from now on, that's going to change.'

Ethiopia, Eleni was aware, was not alone among African countries
in never having made the decision to create a commodities exchange.
African leaders were happy to create stock exchanges and start listing
companies – in the case of some countries, *a* company[28] – but outside
South Africa, Kenya and the Maghreb, there were almost no formalised
commodities markets to speak of. 'I knew that this could be the start of
something very, very big,' she would tell us.

It would take enormous personal sacrifice. Eleni's family had been
closely associated with the imperial regime, and it was unthinkable
that she would return to help a government that most in the Diaspora
considered dictatorial and fraudulent. 'But I just felt that this was what
I'd been working for most of my adult life, since 1984, and this was
the moment I'd been given. So I had to go.' By late 2004, Eleni had
left North America; she was fully installed in Addis under the auspices
of IFPRI, her old think tank, when she was asked to set up a research
programme that would work directly with the PM's office. Her first
assignment was to write a short paper that encapsulated her ideas,
which she handed to Deputy Prime Minister Addisu Legesse, who at
the time was in charge of the agricultural and rural development portfolio. Upon reading the paper, he insisted that Eleni lead the task force
that would design the exchange.

'Now, this is not what an academic does, build a commodities exchange,' Eleni would tell us, 'so it was another big struggle to get IFPRI to agree that it would be the appropriate thing for me to be doing.' IFPRI finally agreed, and this being Ethiopia, international donors hosed money at the idea.[29] Eleni assembled a small team, and told them that the plan was to create a full-trading ecosystem – all the way from the holding warehouses to the computer terminals in remote rural areas that would allow otherwise unwired farmers to check prices. They would institute quality grades, issue warehouse receipts and market information, while coordinating trading, payment systems, and contract enforcement. In response to their blank stares, Eleni took the team on a study tour across the globe.

'There were things,' Eleni would remember, 'that we learned just wouldn't work.' In 2005, Ethiopia registered less than 5 per cent mobile phone penetration, while barely 1 per cent of the country used the Internet. Electronic trading was therefore out of the question. 'This exchange was not for the suits – people who have computers, who have systems, who came from Harvard business school.' The government sponsors wanted something for small farmers and traders, an institution that catered to the informal sector, and with 95 per cent of the market in the hands of men who couldn't read or write, their rationale made sense.

But Eleni, the deputy PM and the agricultural ministry could not have disagreed more about ownership. Eleni wanted the buy-in of the private sector; the EPRDF were still deeply suspicious of anyone who could loosely be labelled a capitalist. Meles in particular made it known through intermediaries that futures contracts would, in his opinion, lead to unchecked speculation. There were shouting matches. 'I was fearless,' Eleni would tell us. 'I don't know why, I guess I had nothing to lose. I was there because I wanted to be there. I had already given up almost everything personally.'

On this, the EPRDF were unbending. 'You have to remember where we come from,' Meles told her. 'Our background is revolutionary social-ism. We are trying our best to understand.'

Similarly, the international community was trying to fathom how

Ethiopia's 2005 national elections, which were supposed to be the country's official democratic coming-out party, had suddenly devolved into a bloodbath. The EPRDF had called elections for the middle of that year, and by Ethiopian standards the process was relatively free and fair, which is to say that while there *was* significant intimidation and vote rigging, the opposition polled big numbers, especially in Addis. This baffled the EPRDF who, according to political analyst Hallelujah Lulie, 'were very confident that they would get the votes ... and they didn't.' Almost 200 people were killed in post-election violence, a state of emergency was declared, and Ethiopian democracy's summer in the sun proved to be a violent and short-lived anomaly.[30]

The European Union and the Americans were, of course, shocked by the carnage, and had little choice but to hold out on the billions they were pumping into the Ethiopian treasury every year. But the stick approach had never worked with Meles. 'It just meant that in the post-2005 period,' Hallelujah told us, 'the EPRDF turned their eyes toward China.' Faced with losing influence over their most valuable regional ally, the Western powers conceived of another way to keep Meles happy. 'Very simply, they diverted the aid they were giving to the Ethiopian treasury into regional bodies or organisations,' said Hallelujah, 'so although the amount they gave didn't change, it wasn't *officially* going to Ethiopia, and looked like it was going to the Ethiopian people.'[31]

Having thus discarded the fig leaf of democracy, and under enormous pressure from allies both at home and abroad to do *something* to improve the lot of the average Ethiopian, Meles decided to double down on development. The commodities exchange happened to be one of the flashier projects in the government's arsenal. Suddenly, everyone was in a rush. The deputy PM made it clear that the exchange was to be designed no later than December 2006.

Eleni quickly compiled a task force of politicians, bureaucrats and traders. In just 35 harried days, it was determined that the new facility would trade food-grains, oilseeds, pulses, and coffee, while Soviet-like financial sector policies were to be tweaked to include provisions for formalised trading. The recommendations were reviewed and accepted almost immediately.

Next, Eleni organised another field trip. Along with six senior government officials, including the deputy prime minister, and six private-sector industry leaders, including representatives of the Coffee Exporters Association, the Oilseeds and Pulses Association, the Grain Traders Association, and private banks, she hopped aboard a flight to India. There, her team took extensive notes on the workings of the Multi Commodity Exchange (MCX) and the National Commodity and Derivatives Exchange (NCDEX). The parallels between the two countries were remarkable: rampant poverty, lousy infrastructure, a ragged system of informal markets, tens of millions of small farmers and small traders. The Ethiopians watched in wonder as it was all smoothed over by the technological miracle of the high-tech market.

In the 200-page final design paper that Eleni compiled following the trip, she stripped the Indian concepts down to their foundations – as archaic as the subcontinent's challenges may have been, they were space-aged in comparison to Ethiopia's. She handed the completed document over to the prime minister's office on a Friday in June 2006. It was a crushingly technical paper, detailing, as Eleni would tell us, 'minute, tiny stuff, like how we're going to build a clearing house, what the central depository will do, the warehouse receipt system, what will be the basis of trading, what are the laws that will need to get written, all of it.' A meeting was scheduled for the following Tuesday. What with Meles running a country in crisis, Eleni figured he wouldn't have time to go through the paper, so she prepared a 15-minute briefing.

'I get there, right, and he takes out the report. *Every page* is marked up. There's circles, there's arrows pointing to other things, there's scribbles on the back! I'm thinking, holy cow, this man has read every single page!'

Not only had Meles read the report, he had pondered its implications and conducted further research on his own. He spoke to Eleni about the Chicago exchange; he spoke about London's history of trading commodities. 'He'd spent the entire weekend coming up to speed on this,' Eleni would tell us, 'and absorbing it, and becoming, you know, an expert.'

And so once again, Meles reminded Eleni that he did not want anyone to get rich off the initiative. 'I want to ensure that this is going to help the small farmers,' he told her. 'This is the only reason why we want it. This is *not* to just move money around the economy.'

To which Eleni replied, 'Absolutely, absolutely, that's why I'm doing it too.'

◆

There was, unfortunately, a catch – and not a small one either, given that it had been enshrined in the constitution. In the conception of a new Ethiopia, drafted by the EPRDF in the early 1990s, the countryside was seen as the spearhead of development policy. If anything defined just how carefully the Ethiopian authorities would institute their own market reforms during an era of unfettered global neo-liberalism, it was Article 40 of that document, the third clause of which read as follows:

> The right to ownership of rural and urban land, as well as of all natural resources, is exclusively vested in the State and in the peoples of Ethiopia. Land is a common property of the Nations, Nationalities and Peoples of Ethiopia and shall not be subject to sale or to other means of exchange.[32]

Article 40 made sense in a historical context: it upheld the tradition of Ethiopian monarchies and governments owning both rural and urban land, and dispensing that land at will. Although certain of its clauses *implied* an improvement for small-scale farmers as compared to life under the Derg – peasants were constitutionally protected from summary evictions, and could sell produce at market prices whenever and wherever they saw fit – the constitution did not guarantee land tenure. The EPRDF's opponents had quickly seen that there were few incentives for farmers to upgrade the land, and no collateral for them to borrow against should they wish to do so. The countryside, these critics insisted, would be locked in terminal stasis, with farms divided into smaller and smaller lots as fathers bequeathed to sons, until Ethiopians were literally farming on top of each other. The events that followed appeared to bear this out: the average per-capita landholding had dropped from a quarter of a hectare to less than a tenth of a hectare between 1970 and 2000, with per-capita food production falling by nearly half over the same period.[33]

Meles and the EPRDF dismissed these criticisms, believing that state ownership of land would protect the countryside from market forces and function as a buffer between rapacious developers and desperate farmers during times of difficulty. The EPRDF's nightmare was a massive migration from farms to the cities, as had occurred across Africa during the structural adjustment campaigns of the 1980s. The government was also hoping to avoid the problem of tenancy, where farmers worked the land for errant landlords (badly, in most cases), the inevitable result of which was exploitation and plummeting production.

In short, the EPRDF's policies bucked every Clinton-era economic trend that was being promulgated across the developing world – and not only had Meles earned himself a pair of master's degrees to back his theories up, he had won the support of the 'discontented globalist' himself, the economics Nobel laureate Joseph Stiglitz.[34] Still, millions of Ethiopians remained unconvinced. What if, underneath all this talk of migration and tenancy, Meles's real view on the land was no different from his predecessor's? What if, to the mercurial PM, land was simply a political tool, to be pulled Derg-like from under a peasant's feet should his loyalty be found wanting? The government assured its critics that the practice of land registration and certification, which guaranteed peasants the rights to farm their plot in perpetuity, if not the rights to sell that plot, offered all the tenure that one could reasonably hope for.[35] The constitution also promised free land via a land grant, so long as the applicant lived in the area and derived a livelihood from agriculture.

No, Meles was not about to slough off the cloak of socialism, no matter how loudly his detractors were baying for him to do so. And yet, as the years wore on, Ethiopia's land policy would evolve. The Federal Rural Land Proclamation, amended in 2005 – around the same time as the hellish election debacle – included provisions for a properly commercial agriculture sector:

> Private investors that engage in agricultural development activities
> shall have the right to use rural land in accordance with the investment policies and laws at federal and regional levels.[36]

What this meant was that Ethiopia was now open for agricultural business. But it wasn't socialism with a new face, it was an unholy marriage of collectivist farming and industrial-scale capitalism. It was also a deft and cynical move: in an otherwise closed and tightly regulated economic system, there was now a way in for desperately needed foreign capital. By the close of 2011, the amendment would lead to a planned 3.5 million hectares of land being transferred to domestic and international investors with the wherewithal to buy in. In Gambella, Ethiopia's westernmost state, the worst fears of Meles's critics would be confirmed – the Anuak people would complain of forced removals and resettlement in 'villagisation' campaigns that recalled the brutal excesses of the Derg.[37] Had Meles therefore proven himself a better educated, more articulate Mengistu?

To most in the diaspora, he had. These vast tracts of farmland, awarded through a central land-leasing bank based in Addis, were to them an inevitable result of economic policies that left Ethiopia short on foreign currency reserves and long on debt. Unlike other sectors of the economy, agriculture became almost deliriously pro-business, with the government offering financial sweeteners, tax breaks and discount rates to investors. Under legislation instituted in the mid-zeroes, corporates were suddenly entitled to better social protections than small-scale farmers – the very notion of 'citizenship' in an agricultural context was upended. In some isolated cases, the results of land expropriation and villagisation were indeed as devastating, disruptive and violent as they'd been under the Derg: farming practices, however imperfect, were replaced by the sedentary life of the 'village', and cultures were shattered and reformed under the watch of the surveillance state.[38] In the Lower Omo Valley, the construction of the Gibe III

243

hydroelectric dam would, insisted the government, bring electricity to a region that was badly in need of it, while generating enough for export to neighbouring Kenya. But the dam had a second function – to provide irrigation infrastructure for 245 000 hectares of state-run and commercial farms downstream of the Omo River. Over half a million people would be directly affected by the Gibe III project, many of them by forced evictions. What's more, the West would end up paying for most of it. In 2011 alone, USAid and the UK's Department for International Development (DfId) would jointly disburse over $800 million for development initiatives just like Gibe III; both agencies would tour the Lower Omo in January 2012 and, perhaps unsurprisingly, find no evidence of wrongdoing. And while the United States Congress would put an end to all funding of forced evictions in early 2014, and thus retroactively admit culpability, the Brits would remain in denial. 'It would be stretching credulity beyond reasonable bounds to believe DfID's claim that no UK money is being used to finance [the evictions],' David Turton, an Oxford University anthropologist with over 40 years' experience in the Lower Omo, would say.[39]

Of course, from the vantage point of the EPRDF government, the pain had all been worth it: these macro-farms had ushered in a much-needed bump in technical skills, infrastructure and investment.[40] 'Even though [the Lower Omo] is known as backward in terms of civilisation,' the prime minister had declared in 2011, 'it will become an example of rapid development.'[41] Some of the industrial farms may have been focused on biofuels, others operated by Indian multinationals producing commodities for their own domestic markets (in India taxes were so much lower on food imports than they were on locally grown food that it didn't pay agribusinesses to produce on the subcontinent), in the end it made no difference – local food security was always part of the plan.

A plan, the agricultural ministry believed, that would blaze the trail for Ethiopia's *real* green revolution: custom-made for the unique challenges of the African continent; a state-managed private-public development-focused approach. While there were short-term winners and losers in rising economies, Meles had argued, in the long term everyone came out ahead. Hadn't Eleni, in her paradigm-shifting talk of 2002, reminded the Ethiopian technocracy that producing food wasn't the problem, that distributing and paying for it was? This, then, was arable Africa's future. That it at times looked like the past was, insisted its supporters, little more than an unfortunate accident of optics.

◆

'Grow With Us!' exhorted the ECX's 2008 recruitment drive.

What Eleni loved about this payoff line was that it spoke as much to prospective clients as it did to employees. A year earlier, she had left IFPRI and become the company's founding CEO, and her first task – after okaying the branding pitch, whose sexy 'X' placed the Ethiopian Commodity Exchange in the same conceptual space as India's MCX and NCDEX – had been to convince circumspect brokers and traders to purchase membership seats. Her critics took great pleasure in pillorying the $5 000 asking price, a small fortune by Ethiopian standards, and one that seemed to undercut everything Meles had emphasised regarding universal access for farmers.

Defending the cost-per-seat, however, was by no means Eleni's biggest challenge. If she had been wary of government bureaucracy before this experience, waiting on the drafting of two essential new laws – one legalising the exchange, the other establishing the regulatory framework under which it would operate – made her dream of a universe governed by Milton Friedman. She flipped vertiginously from the virtual to the actual, overseeing the design and beta testing of the IT network, and ensuring that the 17 concrete-brick holding warehouses in the countryside would not leak or topple during the rainy season. She visited dozens of small offsite trading centres, all to be used by a population who had no idea what 'off-site trading centres' were. It was one of the more radical moments in Ethiopia's modern history; a moment an economist of the future might conceivably look back on as the beginning of a new phase.

The ECX team's spoonful of sugar was the motto *'Yichalal!'* – *It can be done!* – as borrowed, with gracious thanks, from Ethiopia's world-beating Olympic marathoner, Haile Gebrselassie. Again, this motto applied as much to Eleni's staff as it did to those who would one day make use of their services. At a national forum covered by a breathless press, the ECX unveiled a vision statement – 'to transform the Ethiopian economy by becoming a global market of choice' – accompanied by a mission statement – 'to connect all buyers and sellers in an efficient, reliable, and transparent market by harnessing innovation and technology, and based on continuous learning, fairness, and commitment to excellence'. The exchange, it transpired, had become Ethiopia's favourite news story.

By April 2008, six months ahead of schedule, the ECX was registered as a commercial entity, with 67 members having purchased the initial run of seats. In order to close the narrative loop, Eleni went looking for Abdu Awol, the maize trader from Nekemte. She wanted him to be there for the opening bell, wanted to show him what she'd built for him and for those who shared in his hardships. But Abdu had disappeared, and no one in Nekemte could tell her what had become of him. Eleni would have to console herself with a less momentous, although more serendipitous, joining of her dots. 'We issued the very first warehouse receipt on 18 April 2008, in our Addis Ababa warehouse, to a man called Hagos Worku,' she would later write. 'Hagos happened to be a grain trader from Nekemte.'

On 24 April 2008, television crews from across the region jostled for position on the ECX trading floor. They filmed cutaways of the sellers in their green vests and the brokers in their cream vests. The bell rang like a clarion call from the future, and the cameras zoomed in on the first trade, conducted between the Lumme-Adama Farmers' Cooperative Union, from rural Mojo, and a private trading company called Seid Yassin PLC, based in Addis. The deal was sealed with a high five. It was a new day for Africa.

And like most new days, it was coldest at dawn. Eleni was immediately forced to defend her creation against attacks on its integrity. '[There is] the perception that because the government of Ethiopia sponsored ECX and fully owns it,' she would write, 'ECX cannot be a free market, that it must be an instrument of control and a typical, bureaucratic, state-owned enterprise, and that it must be a monopoly.' The founder wanted to make the point that things were no longer so simple. 'In my view, we have moved from the era of African marketing boards in the 1960s and 1970s, when governments tried to do everything, to the period of structural adjustment in the 1980s and 1990s, when governments were told to do nothing, to an emerging "third wave", when governments and the private sector are forging a path together.'[42]

But the time for theories was long past – somehow, the agonies of modernisation weren't that different in texture or intensity from the pains of primitivism. Within weeks of the opening day's trading, the ECX began fighting for its life.

OPEN SESAME

In 2014, six years after the exchange opened and tottered and all but fell, we boarded an Ethiopian Airways Airbus and flew west, in our own small way honouring Abdu Awol's trip to the Sudanese border. At a cruising altitude of 36 000 feet, we tracked his passage from Nekemte to Gimbi to Dongoro, onwards through Mendi, and up past Asosa and beyond. The aircraft circled back to land in countryside that evoked the ocean in the midst of a storm, hills rising like swells, emerald foliage cresting in wind-whipped whorls. The scene, we agreed, was a master-class in natural abundance – and yet few regions in Ethiopia could better articulate green famine's grim privations.

In the airport parking lot, as promised, waited a phalanx of acronym-emblazoned Landcruisers; we ran through the rain to the one that said 'CHF', for Canadian Hunger Federation. 'It will seem strange to you that people starve in this place,' said Damte Dagnew, the organisation's regional director, from the vehicle's front seat. 'But for many years nobody knew what to *eat*, never mind what to plant.'

The town of Asosa, capital of the vast region of Benishangul-Gumuz, was little more than a grid of muddy tracks lined by makeshift coffee

The road to Sadel, Benishangul-Gumuz, August 2014

houses and northern hemisphere-funded NGO outlets. Our first objective was a rare exception to the rule, a warehouse compound ringed by mango trees that stood a few dozen metres off the main drag – this concrete-brick structure, owned by ECX, functioned as the storage and shipping facility for local farmers and brokers. In these parts, or so we'd heard, the Derg had been particularly successful at conflating ignorance with modernisation, and the consequences had endured well into the Meles era. 'When we started, the people here couldn't even conceive of the *idea* of a market,' Damte confirmed. The CHF had therefore set up the $20.5 million Benishangul-Gumuz Food Security and Economic Growth Programme, which, using the ECX as the connective tissue, was designed to link sesame, honey and apricot farmers with the outside world. 'In 2010, when we began, we were at less than zero. There was no formal or informal education, literacy wasn't even 30 per cent. We had everything to do, and I mean *everything*.'[43]

Damte, a handsome 35-year-old with the kind of eyes that suggested his passion was more than just an act, was a popular figure on the streets of Asosa: the easy way in which he greeted the townsfolk soon had us joking that he was a born politician. Indeed, he laughed, he was now in the first stages of preparing for a mayoral campaign – in ideological terms, he was hoping to use Asosa as a launch pad for a career inspired less by Meles's authoritarian ego than by his technocratic id. Damte had come of age in the nearby town of Wombera, and having witnessed whole villages starve to death due to a particularly African form of isolation, had retained an abiding faith in the power of expert-driven change. 'The people had no connection to anything outside,' he explained again. 'No knowledge, no technology, no ability to sell their surplus. They were alone. I wanted to link them.'

But if Damte had once been naïve about the pitfalls of his globalist worldview, the events of 2008 had matured him. At the beginning of that year, along with most educated Ethiopians of his generation, he'd been cheering for Eleni and the ECX when all of a sudden food prices across Africa and Asia had spiked. By April, the price of wheat had increased 200 per cent to a record $10 per bushel, and riots had broken out across the developing world. As if on cue, drought had then swept the Ethiopian hinterland: the Meles government estimated that 4.5 million citizens would require food aid.[44]

Stoked by a combination of record-high fuel prices, changing middle-class consumption patterns in China and India, increased biofuel production in the American Midwest, and declining world stockpiles, the global food crisis was another of those 'failures of the system' that seemed to bloom like nightshade wherever you looked. One school of economists believed that the price hikes were largely brought on by a demand for more resource intensive food – a kilogram of beef, for instance, required seven kilograms of feedstock. But there were others, including academics in IFPRI, who believed that the trouble was the result of rampant commodity speculation.[45] A conclusion that, if it achieved nothing else, certainly upped the volume on the static that Eleni was already hoarse from shouting above.

The ECX did *not* deal in speculative financial products, its founder insisted, meaning that Wall Street gamblers did *not* set its prices. It was 'the only exchange in the world,' she wrote, 'that [had started] out as a spot exchange with the intention to later develop futures contracts,' a decision that in hindsight had played 'very much to [the ECX's] favour.'[46] In the end, although government legislators would step in to save the ECX – by compelling the coffee industry to use its trading pipeline, which would theoretically provide stability through volume – the episode served as a reminder that not even the most committed of statists was exempt from global forces.

Still, as far as Damte was concerned, the principles behind the ECX remained sound. The true genius of Eleni's concept, according to Asosa's wannabe mayor, was in how it employed ancient mechanisms of social control to create economies of scale. 'In Ethiopia,' Damte said, scrawling a diagram into one of our notebooks, 'the village has always been called the *kebele*, a cluster of villages is the *woreda*, and the region is called the ethnic division, or *kilil*.' In Benishangul-Gumuz Region, a chunk of land almost double the size of Belgium – with less than a tenth of the population – individual farmers banded together to form *kebele*. These were assembled into *woreda*-level co-operatives, which then formed unions, out of which partnership trusts were created. Price information, technical expertise and equipment poured *downward* to the farmer, who in turn supplied *upward* for the market. This two-way flow had been coaxed and nudged and cajoled into existence by the will and wisdom of Eleni, although NGO handouts and the buy-in of the government hadn't hurt. At the topmost level, it had all been woven into the EPRDF-mandated national development strategy, a blueprint that had designated Benishangul-Gumuz an 'emerging region'.

Asosa's salvation, it turned out, was the humble sesame seed. Damte guided us into a musty warehouse, empty except for several roosting pigeons and three wooden pallets bearing sacks of the ancient crop.[47] Before the CHF programme, the sesame produced in the region was graded 'five' – meaning it was largely indistinguishable from garbage. Now, the locals produced grades two and three for the international market. 'How did we do this?' asked Damte. 'We changed the mindset of the poor people, equipped them with knowledge and expertise and some seed capital, and an understanding that micro-enterprise is the only way for development. We educated them about market orientation.'

He pointed emphatically at the sacks. 'Sesame is a cash crop, along-side coffee in terms of micro-indicators, worth roughly 3 725 birr or nearly $200 per *quinta*, and as much as 4 200 birr during the high season.' Wheat, so often left to rot in the fields, was worth less than one hundredth of that. 'Before, they just simply planted,' said Damte. 'Now, they plant with calculation.'

According to the warehouse manager, a sullen ex-government bureaucrat named Mezgebe Meja, the process was a little more compli-cated. Getting the sesame into the warehouse meant cracking the cabal of brokers who still worked side markets, selling contraband sesame over the border to the Sudanese. By furiously regulating the market, and by grading the sesame in an on-site laboratory, the ECX had man-aged to squeeze the brokers into a quasi-legal grey market. 'We have had great reluctance,' Mezgebe said, 'because the sellers know that from the old brokers they get money straight, and then the brokers sell to us here and make a big profit.' To close this loophole, a receipt from the *woreda* agricultural office was now required in order to sell through the warehouse. The ECX, in the eyes of those who opposed it, had become not an agent of change but a standard-bearer for the regime's grasp on Ethiopian economic life.

◆

In mid 2014, as we were travelling west on the highway out of Asosa, readers of *National Geographic* were being treated to a cover story that sought an answer to the following question: 'Can Africa's fertile farmland feed the world?' In the magazine's inimitable way, the piece was illustrated by a series of photographs that left the reader in no doubt as to the contested nature of the term 'fertile': an aerial per-spective on a 3 500-acre banana plantation known as 'Bananalandia', which, having helped to turn Mozambique from an importer of the fruit into an exporter, had recently become one of the nation's largest employers; a wide-angle shot on the hillside plot of a female Rwandan smallholder, who had been given seeds, fertiliser and training in the belief that equal access to the aforesaid for women could increase local yields by as much as 30 per cent; a portrait of a leprosy-ravaged Ethiopian peasant, who had been forcibly relocated to a community in Gambella as part of the EPRDF's 'villagisation' campaign. In the online version of the story, just above the image of this elderly peasant, was an image of an 11-year-old Ethiopian girl – she was 'scavenging', as per the caption, in a desiccated cornfield that belonged to the Indian multinational Karuturi Global. After 'displacing villagers and cutting down native forests,' the caption noted, Karuturi was 'deeply in debt and struggling to avoid bankruptcy'.

Like all writers with even a passing interest in agriculture on the African continent, we had of course *heard* of Karuturi – they were a company with a formidable reputation, vast and inviolable, akin in power and influence to the largest state-owned enterprises of the Chinese. Naturally, we had been waiting for an opportunity to test the myth, and that opportunity was now. But the cover story had dampened our enthusiasm: if Karuturi's failures had been exposed in a publication as mainstream as *National Geographic*, we could hardly see the point. What we *did* see, however, was how its inclusion in the mainstream reaffirmed Karuturi's global context. 'The next breadbasket: Why big corporations are grabbing up land on the planet's hungriest continent' – the magazine's headline showed why the stakes didn't get any higher. Humanity's forecast 9 billion population mark by 2050; Africa's millions of acres of fallow land and its plentiful water for irrigation; the continent's average 5 per cent economic growth since 2000 and its improving profile as an investment destination; the fact that small farmers (read subsistence farmers) comprised 70 per cent of the African labour force: all of the inherent tensions of *Homo sapiens'* looming food saga were there. And *National Geographic*'s conclusion? 'Whether Mozambique's future farmers will look more like industrial farmers in Iowa or the small but productive rice farmers of Vietnam remains to be seen,' the publication ventured. 'But all sides agree on one thing: The status quo is unacceptable.'[48]

An evasion, no doubt, albeit a tolerable one, a revealing one, perhaps even a transcendent one – because the highway on which we were now travelling was *likewise* a lesson in the limits of perception. When, we wondered, will the bounty and starvation reconcile? It was Eleni's question made manifest: why do so many Africans starve when they have so much at hand?

'This is the land of sesame,' said Damte, as we crossed the Dabus River, the de facto border between Benishangul-Gumuz and the *kilil* of Oromia. It was a statement made with a straight face, and yet, we sensed, not to be taken at face value. Although sesame grew in these valleys like a weed, the local farmers had produced only desultory harvests, hulled in filthy conditions, packaged in filthy sacks, sold in filthy side deals across the Sudanese border. The hills were lousy with *Acacia senegal* and *Acacia seyal*, but the trees were tapped for gum arabic by migrants from the north – until very recently, nobody in Oromia knew that tapping gum arabic was such an easy way to make a living. Meanwhile, back in Benishangul-Gumuz, the locals weren't just producing grade two sesame, they were learning how to produce and package a range of sophisticated commodities. The further down the highway we got, the more careful we had to be of falling prey to its conceptual tricks: a task that went counter to what we saw out there in plain sight. Because if the gap between the neighbouring regions really could be closed by a formula, if know-how and good intentions really could turn scarcity into abundance, NGOs like CHF would have fixed Ethiopia long ago.

After several hours' hard driving we turned off the highway and onto a gravel track that led down into a valley within a valley. Marble outcrops pierced the greenery like shards of bone, and trucks laden with slabs of it rumbled past us up the hill. 'These vehicles belong to Al Amoudi,' said Damte, his congeniality now tinged with bile – he was referring to Sheikh Mohammed Hussein Ali Al Amoudi, the Ethiopian-Saudi billionaire, the famous and dear 'friend' of the regimes in Addis and Riyadh. 'Whatever marble leaves the ground, the locals don't see a cent.'

The Sheikh, we knew, was the country's largest miner, hotelier, oilman and tyre manufacturer. More to the point, he was one of Ethiopia's largest landowners and industrial agriculturalists, with a reported half a million hectares at his disposal. Al Amoudi's state-sanctioned mega-farms, which seemed to be faring a little better than Karuturi Global, were one way Ethiopia was mapping its agricultural future; Damte and the CHF were the diametrically opposed other.

Having looped back into Benishangul-Gumuz from neighbouring Oromia, the Landcruiser pulled to a stop in the village of Sadel, a settlement of mud-brick, bamboo and tarpaulin lean-tos. The community, according to Damte, was growing, transforming itself into a production hub for the region's best-kept secret. We stretched our legs and were introduced to a beekeeper named Solomon, who led us to a shack with a heart etched onto its lintel. Behind the door, we made out five large plastic vats swarming with smoke-dazed bees. Solomon handed us a pair of teacups, dipped a ladle into the nearest vat, and dished out the golden contents. We chased the bees off with our teaspoons and dug in.

Later, we would agree that the honey, with its notes of peat, moss and applesauce, wasn't quite the best thing we'd tasted on our travels – mainly because that honour belonged to the coffee we were chasing it down with. We sipped, and Damte spread his arms, raised his eyebrows, smiled. '*Can you see what we have here?*' his gesture asked. It was as unnecessary for him to speak the words as it was for us to respond to them.

AFTER CAMP DAVID

The last time Eleni saw Meles was the day she told him she was done.

It was the first quarter of 2012, and while the ECX was by no means running itself, the graphs were all trending upwards. Trading volume of 138 000 metric tons for 2009 had increased to 508 000 for 2011, trading value had risen from $293 million to well over $1 billion, and membership had jumped from 2 407 to 7 917. Judged in purely numerical terms, the ECX was a ripping success. But would it, as Eleni had hoped, function as a catalyst for a market-based revolution that would end hunger in Africa? Another question entirely.

In early spring, Eleni had bumped into Meles at a Camp David food security luncheon hosted by President Barack Obama. It was an intimate affair, with four African heads of state and another three members of the private sector present. These sorts of events were meant to reinforce the fiction of a fair global marketplace, one that – were Africans only smart and technologically savvy enough – they'd plug into via mechanisms *exactly* like the ECX. Meles had been warm and gracious, and had invited Eleni to Menelik Palace on their return to Addis.[49] They had both known that the meeting would be something of a break up.

On a public holiday afternoon, the entire capital in slumber, Eleni and Meles spoke for two hours. Between them sat Eleni's resignation letter and succession plan. 'I basically told him how I was ready to go and launch a company that would start exchanges all over Africa, and I sort of reflected on what I thought we'd done right with the ECX, and what things I would have liked to have done differently.'

Eleni, ever the American-trained theorist, urged for full privatisation and the implementation of futures trading; Meles, ever the Marxist-Leninist freedom fighter, balked. 'I'm really nervous that we do not have the sophistication to know how to regulate those products, because the private sector will always outsmart us,' the prime minister said. 'We need to build our capacity, even the Western governments have been unable to cope with how their markets have gotten out of control. I could see this exploding very easily.'

They agreed to disagree, and Eleni walked out of the meeting and into her next life. She would launch Eleni LLC in early 2013, a venture financed by Morgan Stanley and the International Financing Company to the tune of $7.5 million in start-up capital. Her intention, she told us again, was to incubate and build commodities exchanges across the continent. 'I cannot think of a better time to develop this business in Africa,' Eleni stated in a press release. 'Africa is the world's last frontier for agriculture, with only one quarter of its yield potential achieved and 70 per cent of its farmland as yet unused.' Notably, the company was registered not in Addis, but in Nairobi.

◆

Eleni was now one of the most famous self-made businesswomen on the continent. Still, nobody who takes on African hunger leaves the field unwounded, and she had collected her share of scars. She had stared into the eyes of the starving, felt the bloated emptiness of their bellies, sat down in the dust with them in an attempt to honour their despair. These experiences had all left their blemishes, but to our eyes the most prominent scar was the one that marked Eleni's faith. Her belief in the free market had been tested: not just by Meles and his regime, but by the system itself. And the system's blind spot, its slight yet cruel betrayal, had unfolded from the incident that took up most of her exit interview with the prime minister – bringing coffee online in 2009.

By the end of the first decade of the twenty-first century, as Eleni reminded us, coffee had become an incredibly intricate commodity, with hundreds of varietals and thousands of taste profiles. The Ethiopian market had until then been governed by a brokers' auction, and a new law had shifted the selling of beans into the rubric of the exchange. Local coffee brokers were alarmed, but more disturbing for the ECX was the realisation that international buyers wanted nothing to do with a professionalised Ethiopian coffee industry, mostly because they didn't want empowered sellers. Despite Starbucks' insistence otherwise, coffee buying had not suddenly sprouted a conscience – at a 2009 Specialty Coffee Association of America (SCAA) event held by the same hustlers who promised 'fair trade' and 'organic beans' for Americans who paid five dollars a cup for the privilege, Eleni had been heckled off the stage. The world's high-end do-good baristas saw her as the enemy. On the long flight home, enraged and humiliated, she'd written an open letter to the SCAA and various other buyers. 'Change is good,' she'd noted. 'It can even be seen as necessary. Or, as we learned in the wonderful Symposium closing lunch session, innovation is love, and love can move the world.'[50]

In mid-2013, when Eleni told us about it, her memory of the incident seemed to have lost none of its original sting. And a year after that, during a short stopover in Addis, we got a deeper perspective on why that might have been – the pervasive doubt about the ECX, the paradox that appeared like Schrodinger's cat to render Ethiopia a land of scarcity *and* abundance, was about to be decoded for us by a man who lived on the ever-shifting fault line.

'What is the song of the NGO world today?' asked Salfiso Kitabo, country director of the CHF (Damte's immediate boss) as he laid out the honey jars he'd brought back from a recent trip to Sadel. 'I'll tell you. Climate change, pro-poor, market-led.'

Salfiso explained how the benevolence industry had transformed over the past decade or so, its priorities shifting towards connecting farmers with markets. In Ethiopia, he said, that coincided nicely with the advent of the ECX. But there were 90 million citizens in this country the size of Portugal, Spain and France, and the majority of them were desperately out of touch. 'How must someone know that we make this honey?' Salfiso asked. 'I'm not just blaming the outside world, there are those in Ethiopia, in Addis, who do not know the countryside and do not know this stuff exists!'

He leaned forward and gathered his fingers into a meaty circle. 'The ECX made a pipe. Everything flows through it, bringing us to the outside world. That woman single-handedly changed the game.' The playing field, however, was skewed – Benishangul-Gumuz, which to us looked so unspoiled, was apparently sick with deforestation, topsoil desecration due to poor farm management practices, all the usual blights of development. While our cameras lauded the beauty, they were mute on the hidden devastation. The land, to an outsider, remained unreadable.[51]

But Salfiso, it turned out, had been educated in a rural missionary school by Seventh-day Adventists, and he told us of their emphasis on connecting the head and the hand with the heart. 'I really loved that,' he said, suggesting that it spoke to what Ethiopian agriculture *required* – a government linked to the farmers linked to the market. Capital, innovation and regulation would irrigate Benishangul-Gumuz's vastness, leading to an enormous uptick in growth: in short, Salfiso was endorsing Eleni's Third Wave.

And then at drinks after sunset, in the blurry neon of his favourite pub, he took it all apart again. He knocked back triple-shots of Johnny Black and soda, bemoaning Ethiopia's 'pride' at never having been colonised. 'The Kenyans understand the market because they *were* colonised,' he said, his mouth twisting into an ironic grin. 'They were *taught* the market. But no, Ethiopia is a *special* African country.'

Yes, the ECX was a great idea, a 'game-changer' and all: yes, its problems were still as plentiful as the bubbles in Salfiso's drink. 'It's expensive, it's imposed from above, it's ineffective, it's too bureaucratic. The government should have total buy-in, sure, but then educate the public about it at the grassroots.' If only a select few – the lucky, the educated, the elite – knew about the ECX, it became a tool only for them. And what was their motivation to share?

'Zero! Think about it. When you get rid of the middle man' – by which he meant the brokers – 'where is he going to go? He's going to join the producer or the buyer. He has to.' And so brokers continued to exploit farmers by buying below market rates, largely because they could. The ECX remained un-policed and un-policeable, even if it was the only legal option. 'I should be able to sell coffee to whom I bloody well want,' said Salfiso, 'and I should have access to market information *outside* of the ECX system. They should be competing with someone else. Why should they have the whole legal market?'

Depending on how one looked at things, over the course of six short years, the ECX had either become the wallpaper on the country's poorly conceived and highly extractive agricultural policies. *Or*, it offered a way forward for government and private sector partnerships across the African continent, a means of bringing the small producer or trader into the economic conversation, a technocratic marvel that marshalled the best-trained economists and agriculturalists in the world in an effort to eliminate hunger through expertise.

Nobody was quite sure which: that, we surmised, was what really bugged Eleni. She was, after three decades of *living* the problem, back where she started. Big farm, small farm, it didn't really matter.

Looking out from Meskel Square, Addis Ababa, November 2012

◆

Two months after Eleni handed in her resignation, Meles disappeared. He did not attend the AU summit in July of 2012, and was said to be undergoing treatment for an undisclosed illness in Belgium. Two months after that, on 22 August, his body was repatriated on an Ethiopian Airlines flight. He had died, his handlers said, after contracting an infection in a Brussels hospital.

The reaction to Meles's passing was remarkably muted – there was the wax, and there was the gold. The wax was that a highly intelligent man, who had run Ethiopia for 21 years, had passed away at a critical time in the country's history. The gold was that it was *always* a critical time in Ethiopia's history, and that Meles's death offered an opportunity to free journalists and political activists from prison, roll back the surveillance state, modernise the banking sector, wipe away the vestiges of Derg policies in the countryside, and institute a system in which civil society and opposition parties were allowed to contribute to the body politic. Hailemariam Desalegn, a sanitation engineer about whom outsiders knew little, officially became prime minister on 21 September 2012. Under his watch, as of this writing, not much has changed.

On return visits to Addis, we saw that the entire city had turned into a shrine for the dead leader. In Meskel Square and elsewhere, Meles's visage looked down on us with its signature mix of intelligence and violence. Another corner, another poster. Even from beyond the grave Meles, like Prester John, was watching.

Ganyesa vii

We leave Ganyesa and check in to Vryburg's International Hotel, where after dinner in the bar we get talking to a pair of local women. They have identical haircuts, dyed an identical shade of black, and they wear the same smart-casual uniform: denim, draped blouse, bedazzled flip-flops. One is tall, the other petite; one forthcoming, the other aloof. They have of course heard of the dead Chinese shopkeepers. They have their opinions on the matter.

They take us to a bar called Stetsons, the name a salute, we presume, to the region's agricultural corollaries with the southern United States. The five other drinkers are enormous Afrikaans men.

'Hello meisies,' says one as we enter, feeding coins into the jukebox. Hello girls. By his sideways glance, we are meant to understand that the greeting applies to us too.

Tequilas and beers are ordered. The younger of the two women downs a shot in preparation for her disquisition, which she will deliver mostly in Afrikaans.

'Okay, fine,' she says. 'Everyone knows about those Chinese people. They come here and they sell cheap what the blacks need. But they must know that if they are playing games, then they can't stay. The blacks must also make a living. What do they need these Chinese for?'

We have heard all this before; it's late, we're tired.

'When you come from another place,' continues the woman, raising an eyebrow in such a way as to remind us of our own uitlander status, 'you must have respect. No one likes death. But can you blame the people in Ganyesa if they put those people on fire? Can you blame them? Maybe it is a message. But really, we are not upset here. No one likes death. But we are not upset.'

We do not finish our beers in Stetsons. We take them back to the hotel and drink them on the balcony, watching transport trucks thunder down the main road, hauling their wares into the Kalahari and beyond.

261

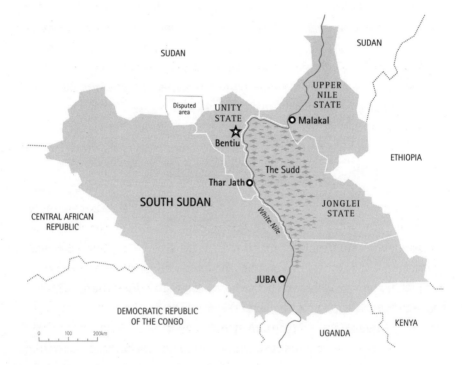

EIGHT

SOUTH SUDAN

The Newborn: Realpolitik in the World's Newest Country

'In the absence of justice, what is sovereignty but organised robbery?'
                                                    – St Augustine

AFRICA'S MORALITY PLAY

It was called, unselfconsciously, the Quality Hotel. It was run by a family of Eritreans – perhaps the family weren't used to guests like us, perhaps it was their policy not to talk to anyone at all, but we never would find out from them why they had fled or how they had come to this place. There was the mother, who managed the operation; the son, who manned the front desk; and the three daughters, who prepared the food, brewed the tea, scrubbed the tiles in the pit latrines. They had one local in their employ, a tall Dinka who sat in the dust by the gate, his AK-47 reflecting the sun as it arced through the sky overhead. From the roof of the hotel, two floors up, you could see beyond the wall to the Kali-Ballee mosque, the idle oil trucks, the power lines that hadn't delivered electricity in months. Bentiu, capital of Unity State, Republic of South Sudan: in November 2012, it was already more than half a year since the regime in Khartoum had last dropped its 'dumb bombs' on the town. People were saying that soon the oil would start to flow; people believed that the world's newest country would soon be allowed to heal.

James Adiok Mayik, for instance, the man who had installed us in the Quality Hotel, with the apology that the Greater Nile, where he was staying, was full. 'President Salva Kiir,' said James, 'his focus is on peace. We must build peace before we build anything else. Let all the soldiers who have been traumatised, let them all cool down. There is no other way.'

But which soldiers? The soldiers who were fighting last year? Ten years ago? Fifty years ago? Two hundred and fifty years ago? In the political conception of our interlocutors, the history went as follows: once there was a region called Bilad-al-sudan,[1] then there was an outpost called Sudan, then there was a colony called Sudan, then there was a country called Sudan; as of 9 July 2011, thanks largely to American evangelicals and Chinese technocrats, there was one country called Sudan and another country called South Sudan. This latter country had been born out of the longest civil conflict in Africa's history, two rounds of civil war spanning close on 40 years, but in truth its people had been at war for over half a millennium – with Arab slavers, with successive regimes in the north, with European colonialists, with raiding pastoralists, with themselves.

How, we wanted to know, could a coherent state be created out of all of this conflict? And if one *was*, would nationhood prove the panacea that everyone wanted it to be? There were another two questions, which seemed even more pressing. What if the government of the Republic of Sudan, the Arabic regime in Khartoum, continued at every opportunity to play spoiler? And what if the Dinka and the Nuer, the two main ethnic groups in South Sudan, continued to pretend to have such radically different interests? The answers to all of these questions, we knew, lay as far down in the darkness as they lay in the light. They lay in the interplay between what was most base in human nature, being greed and lust and all manner of power-fuelled vampirism, and what was possible at the most refined edges of human aspiration, being a politics that worked for the empowerment of all. Our answers, in short, lay in the duelling forces that we were here to witness up close.

We were up on the hotel's roof, sipping warm imported beers. James had brought along his cousin, Peter Riak Monchol, who clearly wasn't on his first drink of the day. As a US military veteran, a former infantryman

Main road, Bentiu, Unity State, November 2012

in the Third Brigade's combat division, Peter had served two tours of duty in Iraq, and like thousands of his countrymen – like James himself – he'd returned to South Sudan soon after independence had been declared in 2011. James and Peter were both 'Lost Boys', members of the generation who'd been old enough in the 1980s to survive the trek to the refugee camps on the eastern border, children young enough at the time not to have to fight in the civil war.[2] But where James had parlayed his Catholic mission schooling into a master's degree in education from the University of Portland, Peter had taken his US asylum papers and become a fighter anyway. The ironies in where they were now read like the script of a morality play: James, who might have become one of South Sudan's two million illiterate, was being paid by the government to teach teachers how to teach; Peter, who might have volunteered

265

when he was old enough for the rebel forces, was unemployed, barred from joining the south's brand-new national army.

'I'm the wrong ethnicity,' he slurred, 'they won't accept me. I'm more responsible than them, you see, I was trained in America. My path is strictly defence.'

James, we sensed, was beginning to regret that he'd invited his cousin. The discussion was going the way of tribal conflict, calling up the demon that had been haunting the south's main vector for independence, the Sudan People's Liberation Movement (SPLM), since the day in 1991 when it had split into two ethnic factions – one Dinka, the other Nuer. This event had been a godsend for the common enemy to the north, the government in Khartoum that had for just under four decades (or five centuries, depending on who you asked) subjugated the people of the south and treated them as second-class citizens. The north was inhabited by Arabic Muslims, the south by Christian/animists, but those were only the most obvious divisions, and they split into smaller and smaller factions from there.[3] In this farrago of conflicting identities and selves, and as returned Lost Boys – rural Nuer herdsmen who happened to have resumés that could secure them middle-income salaries almost anywhere in the United States – James and Peter were supposed to stand for the values of cohesion, forgiveness, progress.

'Before 2005,' said James, referring to the Comprehensive Peace Agreement, or CPA, which had marked the end of the second civil war and laid the groundwork for the eventual secession, 'Bentiu was run by military interests. People like Peter and me, we would have been *disappeared*. Killed for our clothes and education.'

Peter smirked, drained his beer, and slammed the can on the table. There was only one way we could interpret the gesture: not much had changed in this borderland petroleum province, where the Greater Nile Oil Pipeline began its journey through northern Sudan to the Red Sea.

◆

In order for us to be sitting here with James Adiok Mayik and his cousin, we had flown over country that was entirely empty, save for the oil installations outside the muddy Thar Jath landing strip on which we had finally touched down. But just because Unity State was empty did not mean it was *tabula rasa* – the slate, historically or otherwise, was far from clean. Could James's hopes come to fruition here, in a place that had killed so many and for so many reasons, where forgetting and remembrance appeared to erase each other in nanosecond micro-cycles?

Welcome, then, to 'the Sudd', the ecological wonder that had taken its name from the Arabic word for 'barrier'.[4] The wetland's inadvertent role, through its three-storey-high papyrus reeds and acres of water lilies and giant crocodiles and venomous snakes, had long been to protect its inhabitants from the slave-raiding kingdoms to the north, west and east, preventing as it did any permanent Arab settlement of the region below Malakal.[5] As the world's largest wetland, the Sudd had likewise curtailed the human-trafficking exploits of the Egyptian viceroy Muhammad Ali – the man who, on behalf of the greater Ottoman Empire, had invaded the Sudan in 1820 and set up Khartoum as its capital in 1822.

History had not been as kind to those on the Sudd's fringes. The decline of Christian Nubia and the expansion down the Nile floodplain of Islam, at the end of the thirteenth century, had led to the spread of slave raiding and the adoption of Arab protectors by the native communities of the river valley. The rule of the *kashif*, Mamluk military leaders who were technically answerable to the pasha in Cairo but who ran their tax-collection and slave-trading operations like desert lawmen gone rogue – which, from 1517 until Muhammad Ali's arrival in 1820, is essentially what they were – magnified the problem. From 1504 to some time in the late eighteenth century the non-Muslims of the floodplain had also to keep an eye out for raiding parties from the Funj Empire, the so-called 'Black Sultanate' that at its height extended from the Nile's third cataract to the edge of the southern rainforest. The Sultanate of Darfur, the Sunni kingdom to the west that lasted from 1604 to 1874, had also been filling its coffers off the capture and sale of non-Muslim slaves. And so, by the time Muhammad Ali came along, it was an open secret that his sole reason for pushing into the

267

Sudan was to fill out his fledgling army with a people known in the north by the pejorative *el abeed* – slave.[6]

Initially, Ali sought to achieve his quota via raids into the established harvesting regions of the Nuba Mountains, the Upper Blue Nile, and Darfur – it was only after these efforts had failed to deliver the numbers that he sent his men into the ancestral lands of the Dinka.[7] As evidence of the viceroy's desperation, a rare twentieth-century study of the period would reprint a bill of fare that had first appeared on the streets of Cairo in 1837: 'Dinka grown males' going for around a tenth of the price of 'Ethiopian boys'; 'Dinka grown women' going for nearly a fifth of the price of 'Ethiopian girls'.[8] While this same study would not bother to comment on the price disparity, perhaps assuming that the racial context spoke eloquently enough, it would point out that Ali had aborted his project in the late 1830s, when he had chosen to focus instead on the trade of gold, gum arabic and ostrich feathers.

But this was just the beginning of the troubles for the people of the Sudd. For the next 40 years, the slavers would be private merchants from Europe, the Middle East and Sudan's north, men collectively known as 'Khartoumers', who would make use of advances in navigation technology to penetrate into the deepest reaches of the wetland. Their raids would extend as far south as the basin of the Uele River in modern-day DRC (the same vicinity, incidentally, in which most of the action in this book's Congolese chapter takes place), and would eventually be brought to an end by one Charles 'Chinese' Gordon, who in 1873 had succeeded the explorer Samuel Butler as the British governor of Equatoria province, and who in 1877 had been named the governor-general of the entire Sudan.

Could the Sudd's pastoralists therefore look to Britain as a saviour? Hardly. For the Dinka, Nuer and Shilluk, it would matter little that Britain had muscled in on the territory of the Turks, and neither would it matter that in 1885 'Gordon of Khartoum' was proclaimed a warrior-saint for his martyrdom during that city's infamous siege.[9] The role of the newly built Suez Canal in piquing British interest in Egyptian affairs after 1869; the rise of the Muslim mystic Muhammad Ahmad and his self-anointment as *al-Mahdi* in 1881; the subsequent 18-year

reign of the *Mahdiyah*, Sudan's pioneering experiment with the politics of what would later be termed 'Islamofascism'[10] – while all of it
culminated in Britain's re-conquest of Sudan in 1899, this wouldn't
change the lives of the wetland locals for the better. The so-called
'Anglo-Egyptian Condominium' kept the remote provinces of the south
in a condition of sustained neglect, and it was only after World War I,
when the Foreign Office retrained its sights on British East Africa,
that Sudan's southern region was introduced to anything resembling
the technologies of the modern world. Whitehall blatantly applied the
divide et impera maxim throughout the 1920s, 1930s and 1940s, and
His Majesty's Government did not just administer southern Sudan as
though it was a separate entity, it also closed off the region to travellers from the north, actively inhibited both the spread and practice of
Islam, and steadily relocated all Arab merchants and officials until
there were hardly any left. 'Finally,' as the United States Library of
Congress would note in its country study on Sudan, 'a 1930 directive
stated that blacks in the southern provinces were to be considered a
people distinct from northern Muslims and that the region should be
prepared for eventual integration with British East Africa.'[11]

A plan, of course, that never came together. Instead, delegates at the
Juba Conference of 1947 were informed that Britain's policy regarding
the future of a self-governed Sudan would henceforth be one of uni-
fication, and an attempt was made to convince the southern elite that
their interests would be well protected by a common legislative assembly. *Another* plan that never came together – instead, in August 1955
the ethnic divisions that had been exploited by the British for the previous 50 years, which in turn had simply built upon and exacerbated
the ethnic divisions exploited by various slave-raiding kingdoms for
the previous *500* years, would achieve their apotheosis in a rebellion
of southern soldiers in Equatoria province. Only four months before
the scheduled independence of the Republic of Sudan, the first of the
country's two civil wars had begun.

For years, the people of the north fought the people of the south, and
they died by the thousands in the marshes of the Sudd. Then, in 1978,
oil was discovered; five years later, the fighting would begin in earnest.

269

◆

On our second morning in Bentiu, we piled with James and a driver into an old Toyota four-by-four and reversed out of the Quality Hotel's gates. We were on our way to the source of the Sudd's latest downfall and the site of its potential salvation: a compound of the Greater Nile Petroleum Operating Company (GNPOC), a facility about 40 kilometres outside of the city. Along with 900 wells and the pipeline itself, the compound had been inoperative since January 2012, when the SPLM had halted all production in a kamikaze move during negotiations with Khartoum. The apparent deal-breaker had been the pipeline transit fee, the gap between the $32-per-barrel Khartoum wanted to charge and the $1-per-barrel Juba was willing to pay. Ugly as the fee dispute was, its true cause lay in South Sudan's inheritance of the majority of the nation's wells at independence. The government of Omar al-Bashir, which had drawn 57 per cent of its revenues from oil prior to the south's secession,[12] had suddenly been landed with a budget crisis. Did al-Bashir really 'steal' $815 million worth of South Sudanese president Salva Kiir's crude in the last few months of 2011? This had been the contention of the SPLM, and the party's secretary general had gone public with the threat that the Juba elite would rather suspend production – and thereby forego their own revenues – than leave another drop of oil vulnerable to raids from the north.[13]

Still, given that the Republic of South Sudan had itself earned 98 per cent of its income from the resource in 2011,[14] the tactic was reckless in the extreme, a ploy that could have crippled the infant state before it had learned to crawl. Accepted by some as proof that such tactics nevertheless paid off, the two parties had returned to the table around the time of South Sudan's first birthday. In late September 2012, six weeks before our arrival in Bentiu, Juba and Khartoum had signed a series of cooperation agreements on a range of issues from oil revenues and border demarcation to security, migration and trade. According to these agreements, the south would pay the north $11 per barrel to use the Unity State-Port Sudan pipeline, both sides would cancel their claims to any oil-related arrears, a demilitarised zone would be established along the de facto border, and an existing pledge not to support rebel groups in each other's territories would be upheld.[15]

Which, we guessed, was why the owner of the Quality Hotel had been more than willing to rent us her Toyota SUV, and why the regional security chief, whose compound was just down the road, offered no objections to the trip.

'The situation is normal,' he said, 'If you take one soldier, you may go.'

We already had our soldier, the tall young Dinka who'd been spending his days by the hotel's gate. The soldier folded himself into the Toyota's rear hatch, James reclaimed the front passenger seat, the

River bridge, Rubkona outskirts, Unity State, November 2012

driver stubbed out his cigarette and got behind the wheel, and we climbed into the back. On the outskirts of town, as James was pointing out where the pipeline ran beneath the swamps to the east, we slowed down to wait for a wedding procession to pass: ululating, dancing and clapping, the lowing of dowry cattle. And then we were crossing the river bridge that connected Bentiu to the market town of Rubkona, the same bridge that on 23 April that year, at ten minutes to nine in the morning, a pair of Mig 29s had attempted to bomb. We pulled over to inspect a crater, which gave nothing away – just a hole in the dirt, a reminder that al-Bashir's pilots had missed. But had they? The *Sudan Tribune* had wasted no time in publishing a photograph of burnt stalls in the marketplace, and an AFP stringer had reported seeing the charred remains of a young boy. Traders had placed the civilian death toll at three.[16]

It was now almost noon, and James suggested a restaurant in the market for lunch. 'Rubkona used to be beautiful when the oil was flowing,' he said, a statement undermined by the smell, by the flyblown meat and open sewers.

On James's advice, we ordered the yams, rice and salad. The meal was fresh, rejuvenating even, but we couldn't get over that word. *Beautiful*? If it was tough to reconcile it with the context, it was tougher to reconcile it with the facts. Since the discovery of oil in this region in 1978, the impact on the environment had been matched only by the impact on the local way of life. In the former case, the oil reservoirs had begun to seriously contaminate the drinking water in the wetland.[17] In the latter, as detailed in a 567-page report published by Human Rights Watch, 'corporate complicity' in Khartoum's abuses had included 'sponsored ethnic conflict' and 'forced displacement to clear tens of thousands of southern Sudanese from their homes atop the oilfields'.[18]

Beautiful Rubkona was not.

But just a few clicks out of town, the smell fading and the bridge receding into the background, the landscape got pretty. The roadside shacks melted off into subsistence plots, which abruptly melted off into flat virgin bush. It was a landscape no different from a dozen others we'd seen on our travels – the acacias and the birds and the brilliant luminosity of the clouds could have been set in the ranchlands of northern Namibia, the copperbelt of western Zambia, Samburu County on the plains of central Kenya. As always, it was the sort of landscape that calmed us, that left us reflective and self-contained. James, however, was troubled.

'Peter didn't come home to be a drunk,' he shouted, above the rush of hot air beating a rhythm off the half-open windows.

While James wasn't about to apologise for his cousin, he did feel compelled to explain. Peter had been unemployed for more than a year, he reminded us, with nothing to do but mope. Counting on the fingers of his right hand the reasons that a whole lot of returnees drank, James was getting angrier – the wind was making it difficult for him to hear himself, and he ran out of fingers too soon. But he needn't have bothered; we knew the score. Along with a host of top-tier Western NGOs, the Brookings Institution had recently put together a 'first anniversary of independence' compendium that outlined exactly what the situation was for skilled returnees. Peter, the document revealed, had left the wealthiest nation on earth for one of the poorest.[19] His inability to get a job in the army, in light of the bizarre fact that 28 per cent of the 2011 budget had been allocated for security against 7 per cent for health and 4 per cent for education, couldn't have made it easy for him to keep the faith.[20]

Less than 18 months in, South Sudan's trust in itself was teetering: the memory of the two million killed during the second civil war was pulling the country once again to the brink.[21] As it would later become obvious to almost everyone with an eye on the situation, it wasn't so much a question of the conflict between South Sudan and the Arabic north being exacerbated by the tribal divisions as it was a question of the north *manipulating* those divisions to destabilise the new country. Dinka versus Nuer, Nuer versus Dinka – this was already South Sudan's primary story. With the interethnic violence concentrated for the moment in Jonglei State, the Beltway-based Brookings was championing 'well defined property rights' as a fix for the problem, although it did acknowledge that this hardly addressed the much larger conflict that had been tethered, since 1978, to ownership rights over oil. Here, DC's most trusted think-tank was pushing for Juba to join the Extractive Industries Transparency Initiative, the global body that we had first encountered in the DRC. It was also expressing the hope that South Sudan and the Arabic north would respect one another's borders. 'As the saying goes,' Brookings had declared, 'good fences make good neighbours.'[22]

There were, James told us, many things that might drive a returned Lost Boy to drink.

For instance, this road to the compound of the GNPOC, which counted as its shareholders the China National Petroleum Corporation (40 per cent), Petronas of Malaysia (30 per cent), ONGC Videsh of India (25 per cent), and Sudapet of Khartoum (5 per cent), passed by a UN base. The United Nations Mission in South Sudan (UNMISS), so named by a resolution of the Security Council ratified three days before independence, was in the opinion of these locals more Janus-faced than most of the NGOs. Everybody wanted a piece of the oil-rich newborn.

'He must be late for lunch,' the driver said, as an UNMISS Landcruiser sped past us in the direction of Bentiu.

COLONISATION OF THE SKY

Lumumba Stanislaus-Kaw Di-Aping. It was December 2009 when the name, unforgettable as it was, finally made it into one of our conversations. Since our epiphany back in Angola in late 2006, we had been amassing a bucket-list of men and women whom we thought would make representative or enlightening interview subjects, but due to an unaccountable blind spot, Lumumba's name had failed to make the cut. And then one day there he was, his face on CNN, the man hated by all the most powerful people at COP15, otherwise known as the Copenhagen Climate Change Conference.

Barack Obama, Gordon Brown, Kevin Rudd, Stephen Harper – the heads of state of the Great White Nations hadn't been humbled like this at one of their own meet-'n-greets in years. 'What is Obama going to tell his daughters?' Lumumba had asked the African delegates. 'That their [Kenyan] relatives' lives are not worth anything? It is unfortunate that after 500 years-plus of interaction with the West, we are still considered "disposables".'

The date was 8 December 2009, and it was a couple of hours after the leak of a document that the media had dubbed the 'Danish text' – a proposal secretly drawn up by the US, UK and Denmark to keep the average global temperature rise to two degrees centigrade above pre-industrial levels; a *sub rosa* agreement that not only ignored two years of delicate north-south negotiations, but would condemn much of Africa to a rise of 3.5 degrees. Lumumba, who was the chief negotiator at the summit for the G77 bloc of developing nations, had broken with protocol at an ad hoc meeting of around 100 African representatives. Turning his microphone on in defiance of an official request to keep it off, he'd sat there in silence, tears streaming down his face, when it came his chance to speak. 'We've been asked to sign a suicide pact,' he had eventually said, excusing himself with the words that in his part of the world it was 'better to stand and cry than to walk away'.

Lumumba's part of the world was southern Sudan. One of us had befriended him back in 2003, when he was the SPLM's unofficial ambassador to South Africa. An economist with degrees from Yale and Oxford (and a professional resumé that included McKinsey & Co), he'd been intrigued by the thinking of Joel Netshitenzhe, then-President Thabo Mbeki's development mandarin – the friendship between us had been the result of a co-written profile on Netshitenzhe, which Lumumba had cleverly engineered.[23] Two years later, after the signing of the Comprehensive Peace Agreement and the formation of a Sudanese government of national unity, Lumumba had been offered the position of *official* ambassador to the UN. He'd left for New York with his new South African wife, the daughter of a retired apartheid-era police general, and had not been heard from since. Until, that is, that day in 2009.

The Danish text, it turned out, included a clause that proposed to placate poor country signatories with a check of US$10 billion a year for what was labelled 'early action' and 'mitigation readiness'.[24] As Lumumba told the press, 'This was nothing less than a colonisation of the sky! Ten billion is not enough to buy us coffins!' At the meeting, after noting that the industrialised nations were wilfully disregarding their own historical emissions – and thus looking to prolong their carbon-heavy consumption patterns at the expense of Africa's poor – Lumumba had said, 'I would rather die with my dignity than sign a deal that will channel my people into a furnace.' His Oxbridge eloquence, his heartfelt emotion, his familiar references to the hard facts of climate science had succeeded in galvanising the room – the continent's delegates had flooded out into the central hall, chanting 'Two degrees is suicide!' and 'One Africa, one degree!'[25]

But what really made Lumumba a Third World hero was less his aptitude for the informed incitement of his comrades than his talent for humiliating his enemies in the lands of their birth. In Sydney and Melbourne, voters were spitting up their flat whites at the news that Prime Minister Kevin Rudd was *not* the world-beating climate change progressive that Australian media had painted him as – in point of fact, although Australia was then the world's worst polluter per capita, Rudd had been a pivotal backstage supporter of the Danish text, and Lumumba's statements on 16 December to America's ABC radio would earn the Australian PM the moniker 'Kyoto killer'.[26] Two days later, when the UK's Gordon Brown would deem the putative Copenhagen agreement 'a success on five out of six measures', Lumumba would be quoted in *The Guardian* as saying: '[This deal expresses] the lowest level of ambition you can imagine. It's nothing short of climate change scepticism in action. It locks countries into a cycle of poverty for ever.'[27]

And so we were now determined, when the timing was right, to track our old friend down. 'It's great to hear from you,' read the email response in late October 2012. 'I hope you get your visas soon. Please contact Ambassador Paul Macui, who is our ambassador in Pretoria. He is a good friend and a great guy to introduce you to our new republic.'

◆

'There is no such thing as reconstruction in South Sudan,' said Lumumba, when at last we sat across from him, listening to the soft and deliberate monotone that was suddenly so familiar. It was nearly a week since we had arrived in Juba, and here was Lumumba in a sober suit, occupying an outdoor table at one of the capital's new office parks. 'In South Sudan, we have only construction,' he went on. 'We have no powerful vested interests that can impede a developmental state the way South Africa's transformation plan was scattered. Ideologically, we have no power struggles within our movement like you have in the ANC.'

No ideological power struggles within the SPLM? No vested interests? Had the Dinka and Nuer factions finally put all of their differences aside? For the last half-hour, since we had reaffirmed the friendship and established the ground rules for engagement, Lumumba had been spinning the terms of his new republic, not all of which aligned with what we had seen and read. The document he'd retrieved from his leather briefcase, entitled 'SPLM Manifesto 2012', was a blueprint intended to inform three things: all of South Sudan's development objectives; its entire process of state formation; the founding constitution itself. As the chief writer on a team of seven, the man tasked by President Salva Kiir with articulating the ruling party's top-line vision, Lumumba was in a rush to get the document endorsed and signed off by early December (less than a month away), which would then allow it to go public at the national budget in January 2013. But this was not going to be a straightforward class in Liberation 101. Lumumba wanted us to bear in mind the feeding trough that had bloated and despoiled Nelson Mandela's once-proud African National Congress, the endemic kleptomania that had knocked South Africa's own development vision off course. Then, he wanted us to juxtapose it against a liberation movement that had reconciled its internal factionalism at the moment of independence, one that had smoothed over the (manufactured) differences between Dinka and Nuer, and was ready to dodge the post-liberation potholes as outlined in Frantz Fanon's seminal *The Wretched of the Earth*.[28] This, insisted Lumumba, was the SPLM.

We would have to take his word for it. Western history books presented the 1991 split in the SPLM/A – the 'A' standing for 'Army', the movement's military wing – as the result of an ethnically driven coup attempt masterminded by Riek Machar Teny, a Nuer, against founder John Garang de Mabior, a Dinka.

For his part, Garang was the quintessential African liberation hero; an enormously charismatic, US-educated, Marx and Christian-fundamentalist influenced army officer who in 1983 had been sent by the government in Khartoum to quell an uprising of soldiers in the south, and had instead created the rebel movement that would later achieve southern independence. Garang's leadership philosophy may have been informed as much by his PhD in agricultural development from Iowa State as it was by his 11 years as a career officer in the Sudanese military, but his stewardship of the SPLM/A was informed first and foremost by his opposition to the autocratic Islamism that had taken hold in the north. The beginning of the second civil war would go down in history as July 1983, the date that Garang, having success-fully brought 3 000 rebel soldiers under his personal control, began to agitate for more southern army garrisons to mutiny.

Lumumba dismissed the relevance of Garang's Dinka ancestry, focusing instead on his ideology. He glossed over more than a dec-ade's worth of post-1991 intertribal bloodshed with these words: 'There were two main thrusts for the movement. The one that opted for what we call "the new Sudan vision", the transformation of the whole of Sudan, and the other that insisted Sudan cannot be trans-formed, given its characteristics, and so opted for self-determination, what we call "the separatists". Basically, we ended up with an unde-clared position.'

The way Lumumba was pitching it, there was on the one hand a united, multi-ethnic, democratic Sudan as envisioned by John Garang; on the other, a separate and standalone South, as articulated by Riek Machar – Dinka and Nuer didn't come into it. Machar's abortive coup attempt in August 1991, we knew, had led him to form a splinter group called SPLA-Nasir, named for the town close to the Ethiopian border where it was based. In 1993, this rebel movement had changed its name to SPLA-United, and from 1994 to 1997 it had been known as

SSIM/A, for the South Sudan Independence Movement/Army. But for all of his bluster about 'independence', that 500-plus page doorstopper of a Human Rights Watch report had revealed that Machar had been covertly relying on the funding and matériel of the National Islamic Front, Khartoum's ruling party, from the month of SPLA-Nasir's inception. Where Garang's SPLA had actively attempted to disrupt the oil industry, Machar had offered the NIF exactly what they wanted: control of the oil-rich regions of the south.[29]

Was there any point in calling Lumumba out on these inconsistencies? We thought not. Garang, who would die in a helicopter crash shortly after the signing of the CPA in 2005, had after all gotten his start in guerrilla life from Ethiopia's Mengistu Haile Mariam, the architect of Ethiopia's 'Red Terror'.[30] Granted, unlike Machar, Garang hadn't pimped for the SPLA's number one enemy but, to the best of our knowledge, a spotless record had never been a requirement for leadership of an African liberation movement. Besides which, there really wasn't anything to gain from a nitpicking session with Lumumba; the trajectory of Machar's career was there for all to see. In 1997, after acting as the key southern signatory to the Khartoum Peace Agreement, he'd been appointed an 'assistant' to President Omar al-Bashir, head of a new Sudanese political party called the United Democratic Salvation Front, and commander-in-chief of Khartoum's brand-new military arm, the South Sudan Defence Force. His dalliance with Khartoum had backfired when his own Nuer people had blamed him for a forced displacement of civilians from the Unity State region. In January 2002, he'd been compelled to merge what remained of his army with John Garang's SPLA, and had received a leadership position as his reward.[31]

'Look,' said Lumumba, when the issue of the SPLM's governance pedigree inevitably came up, 'what puzzles me about the West is they don't ask themselves, "How did it happen that in 20 years more than three million people perished here?" They vanished into the ground, and the West said nothing. And now they call us a failed state? Where are we going with this? I'm not talking about 10 000, 40 000, half a million – I'm taking about *three million people*. It's statistically, it's literally, about a quarter of a million people killed a year. So it is just fanciful to talk about a failed state. I mean, this is the new term, in vogue, but is it the reality?'

The in-vogue term, actually, was *pre*-failed state, and we'd been hearing it a lot in Juba's expat bars. As for the three million figure, it was one million more than the estimate we had been relying on, but the debate about who had done the counting (and *how*) was beyond our expertise. Whatever the truth, the scale of the catastrophe was enormous – and the catastrophe, according to Lumumba, meaning the second civil war, had been hijacked by outsiders to serve their own political ends. The behind-the-scenes wrangling as southern Sudan crested the signing of the CPA and lurched towards independence involved the cooperation of every traditional player in the neighbourhood, all of whom decided just this *once* to accept the dissolution of a colonial border: lines scribbled onto a continental map that had, since the Berlin Conference, remained largely unrevised.

South Sudan, then, was a *special case.* Had any country in Africa ever received such lucid, bipartisan attention from the US Congress? Had so many celebrities, State Department wonks, evangelical Christians, academics, successive presidential administrations and CNN documentarians ever found themselves on the same side of the nation-building fence? Since the 1980s, the idea of a separate southern nation for the Sudd's Christians had been an abiding American obsession, insofar as America *had* abiding obsessions in Africa. Billions of dollars in aid, both humanitarian and military, had been marshalled for the cause of democracy. Legions of Lost Boys were brought to America; phalanxes of advisors were sent to southern Sudan. And slowly, as independence appeared more and more likely, so too did the creation of an African democratic heartland that would serve as a buttress against the north's indurate Islamism.

Meanwhile, the Chinese looked on as a country in which they had invested upwards of $20 billion, in order to secure its oil, started to dissolve before their eyes. When the new sketches on the map became manifest, then-president Hu Jintao invited Salva Kiir to Beijing, where the two sipped champagne and discussed the reported $8 billion in oil sector capital the Chinese felt obliged to proffer the fledgling state. It was a near ideal situation – a tacit agreement between two world powers to *just let South Sudan get on with it.* All that was now required was for the Dinka and the Nuer to set aside their differences and play nice. If it wasn't for tribalism, or so the outside view went, South Sudan would be an oil-soaked, aid-drenched Shangri-La.[32]

In this, Lumumba was fiercely averse to what he described as the mainstream 'ethnic perspective' on his country, especially considering the fact that the original colonial borders were arbitrary, that they hadn't accounted for the intricate network of cross-cultural familial ties, and that the British divide-and-rule maxim had remained pretty much intact. Not that he denied the objective existence of the Arab-African duality that had maintained its geographical expression at the northern edge of the Sudd, just that he treated with deep suspicion all attempts to reinforce it and repeat it: in the vast majority of post-independence African societies, he said, the growth of the nation had been retarded by the congenital distortions, the 'various perpetuations', of the divisive colonial lens.

'So they say that I am first and foremost my tribe,' he scoffed, 'and *only then* am I a member of the state. In South Sudan, I am Dinka or Nuer. In South Africa, I am Zulu or Xhosa ....'

◆

Lumumba pushed back his chair, stood to his full six-foot-plus height, and loosened his tie. He removed his spectacles and rubbed his eyes like a man who didn't expect to be getting a lot of sleep in the coming weeks. Now that he had undone the 'ethnic perspective' with his own gentle brand of sophistry, he flipped through the pages of the manifesto until he arrived at a particular paragraph, which he invited us to read aloud. 'The mission of the SPLM is to construct a knowledge economy in South Sudan,' one of us obliged, 'and to build a nation and society that is inspired by peace, freedom, justice, unity, prosperity and progress. The SPLM will ensure democracy under the rule of law and good governance, to safeguard fundamental human, economic, social, cultural and religious rights and freedoms. Through the people, SPLM shall govern.'

The question all but asked itself: a knowledge economy in a country where barely a tenth of the population was able to read and write?

'The only way ahead for South Sudan is through a massive educational programme,' said Lumumba, sitting down again to pour himself a second cup of tea. 'This is the difference between where Africa went wrong and where the Asian tiger economies went right. You cannot think of creating opportunities when the majority of your people are illiterate. I don't care whose theories you've read, okay?'

According to Lumumba, its late admittance as an independent state had given South Sudan the chance to learn from the developing world's mistakes – and the most important thing it had learnt, he told us, was that where education had not been a priority, only suffering had been harvested. He rejected the assertion that his country lacked 'capacity', countering that, however the term was defined, no nation in history had ever started out with it. 'What we need,' he said, 'is the will and the wit.'

It was the country's vast pool of youth, he went on, that was at the core of the manifesto. South Sudan's returning exiles, those 'thousands of educated Lost Boys', had been earmarked to haul the rest of the nation up. It would be up to them, Lumumba said, to build what the SPLM recognised as its 'five pillars': mass education; effective petroleum and mining management; sustainable agriculture and climate-change policies; infrastructural development; financial and industrial growth. Men like James and Peter, returnees determined to put the trauma of the past behind them, would be essential in erecting these pillars, and in keeping them standing.

Later that evening, when we were taking cover indoors from a rainstorm, Lumumba explained the urgency of getting this vision squared away. 'We understand how the West plays the game,' he said, 'that's old hat. As for the Chinese, the only way you manage them is *after* you have everything spelt out. Otherwise? Otherwise they'll finish you.'

LIKE A MORGUE

When the four-by-four pulled up at the entrance to the compound of the Greater Nile Petroleum Operating Company in Unity Village, all was quiet. It was because of the heat, because it was a Sunday afternoon, because there were still a few issues to be resolved before the oil could resume its 1 000-mile journey to the sea – these were the reasons, according to James, that the compound was 'like a morgue'. James exchanged a Nuer greeting with the guard at the barbed-wire gate, and then we were through. In the recesses of an aluminium warehouse we found a man with sweat coming off his forehead in rivulets; he was the superintendent, he told us in English, and after hearing our story he signalled for us to follow. We were led back across the parking lot, up a set of stairs, down a disinfected corridor with whitewashed walls and 20 or so cheap wooden doors. This was where the expatriate staff of the GNPOC lived. The superintendent stopped at a door indistinguishable from the rest. He knocked, waited, and knocked again. And then we were shaking the hand of a man in his early fifties, a man in socks and briefs and a sleeveless white vest, a man who said we shouldn't have come.

'But they are looking for the Chinese in Africa,' said the superintendent. 'That is you!'

On cue, as the Chinese manager was shutting his door, two security officers appeared from around the corner. They marched us to their quarters, demanded our passports, and locked us inside. They returned after an interval, their manner markedly changed, their interrogation methods verging on friendly. Who were we? Why were we there? What was life like in Johannesburg? As concerned South Sudanese citizens, it seemed they wanted to give us access. As employees of GNPOC, men lucky to have their jobs, they needed to escort us immediately to our vehicle. Like almost everyone in Unity State, these guards were pawns in a geopolitical game whose masters were in Beijing and Khartoum and only lastly in Juba.

This was the pecking order that the SPLM had been trying their damndest to alter: their kamikaze negotiating tactics over the oil pipeline were the more desperate approach, Lumumba's development manifesto the saner. As always, history – whether remembered, forgotten or revised into intelligibility – had acted as a yoke. In February 1984, nearby Rubkona had been the site of an attack by southern rebels, an addendum to the civil war that had started the year before. Under the cover of darkness, a group of men from a faction known as Anyanya II,[33] which would soon be incorporated into John Garang's SPLA, had crept into the town and opened fire on the base camp of the American oil giant Chevron. The rebels' gripes had been Chevron's perceived collusion with the government of President Nimeiri in Khartoum, and specifically the latter's plan to build a pipeline that would pump the oil from the region's newly discovered fields up to the Red Sea coast in the north, thereby depriving the south of its rightful inheritance. In the attack, three Chevron contractors had been killed and seven injured, and although Sudan represented the company's greatest potential windfall, one which had cost a billion dollars to prospect and develop, when Nimeiri had refused to negotiate a political settlement in 1984, the company had all but fled.[34] As one of Chevron's advisors had put it, scraping the remaining gloss from the situation, '[Nimeiri] can forget about having his oil money.'[35]

The gap in development left Khartoum desperately short of the foreign exchange dollars it needed to pay off its debtors, ever more numerous in the wake of the global oil crisis and the subsequent and inevitable IMF-imposed austerity measures. As a sop to conservatives, who were baying for more power, Nimeiri instituted *shari'ah* law, the resultant beheadings and amputations further repulsing those in the south. Khartoum, once an easygoing if dusty trading town, became Riyadh without the oil money and the skyscrapers, five million dollars' worth of its booze dumped in the Nile during a ceremony announcing the formal arrival of the 'monolithic Arabic Islamic state' that John Garang had been warning against since the early 1960s.[36]

With each passing day, the rebellion in the south and the recalcitrance in the north dug a deepening trench along the Tenth Parallel, the line of longitude separating Muslims from Christian/animists.

Nimeiri clung to power for five tentative years after Chevron halted their drilling efforts, but on 30 June 1989, an obscure military officer led 300 of his American-trained paratroopers into the capital, relieving the president of his responsibilities. Brigadier Omar al-Bashir, trailed by his Revolutionary Command Council for National Salvation, did not remain obscure for long.

It was, of course, al-Bashir who had sent his MiGs to Unity State to do their dumb-bombing in 2012, and who had kept the city of Bentiu in a suspended state of terror since the disputes over pipeline royalties had flared into war. After being run out of GNPOC'S Unity Village by the two local guards, we paused once again at the bomb crater near the bridge adjacent to Rubkona. Not far from our vantage point, shimmering in the heat, we could make out the spaghetti strand of dirt under which the pipeline ran all the way to Port Sudan – the pipeline that southern Sudan's one-time rebels had tried so hard to inhibit until a fair deal was in place; the pipeline that those same rebels, now the government in good standing, had rendered dormant with so much wealth coagulating inside.

'They will need to flush it,' said James, one slender finger pointing accusatorily at the stretch of dirt. 'A costly, difficult procedure. Then, if they are lucky, it will work.'

◆

The four-by-four took us south, along a graded sand road through the dwindling wetlands. We were dogged for miles by the pipeline, until it eventually disappeared into the marsh and left us to our passage. James wanted to introduce us to another facet of life in the region, a place, he said, 'where the ebb and flow of the seasons still exist' – a place that was the inverse of Unity Village, but nonetheless existed alongside it, in the face of it, and was shaped by it. After 45 minutes of driving we pulled into a traditional Nuer village, a scattering of thatch huts shaped like giant Prussian helmets.

We hopped out of the truck, trailing James, who in turn was trailed by our SPLA soldier. Children ran up to us, curious but quiet. They wore the standard, ragged hand-me-down clothing dispensed by Western NGOs, the football club logos and cartoon characters clanging dissonantly against the way of life that James was now describing.

'Everything here has its place,' he said, drawing our attention to a pile of dung in the elders' communal clearing. 'Everything has its use. They will dry this dung, and burn it to chase away the insects. It is a beautiful circle of life when there is peace.'

For John Garang, James explained, village life represented a sacred link to the land. 'His philosophy was to bring the towns to the country, not the country to the towns.' James, we knew, was waxing lyrical on one of the more famous tenets of the liberation icon. 'When a hero dies in a village, the people cannot cry,' Garang had said at the signing of the CPA in 2005, adding that the agriculture-driven economy would have to be fuelled by oil – 'the building of dykes for flood control and canals and underground water development for irrigation will be priorities to guaranteeing crop production,' he'd vowed.[37] Garang's objections to urbanisation were hardly radical (he had a PhD from Iowa State University in agricultural economics), but he had articulated them so forcefully that Lumumba would incorporate them almost verbatim into the SPLM's 2012 manifesto, forming as they did the 'pillar' of sustainable agriculture policies.

As we followed James, shaking hands with the villagers, listening to his explications of local life, we quietly agreed that we had never encountered so enormous a gap between laudatory intentions and miserable results. Granted, the SPLM had had only seven years – if one counted the signing of the CPA as their initiation into governance – to marshal the Greater Nile Petroleum Operating Company into a force for the common good. But if the company seemed at times beyond the capabilities of either Juba or its own management to marshal, perhaps that was because the petroleum companies of the world were simply beyond marshalling.

In this, the Chevron attack offered both a window into the past and a vision of the future. Shortly after the Texans backed off, Khartoum began casting about for new suitors. In the early 1990s, after the Chinese had all but exhausted growth in their domestic Daqing oil fields, the China National Petroleum Corporation (CNPC), at Beijing's behest, began searching for oil properties in the world's unplumbed crannies. With much fanfare, CNPC picked up concessions in the regions Chevron had surveyed and subsequently fled, and formed GNPOC with a revolving door of partners – Canada's Talisman (eventually forced out by a vigorous human rights campaign), Malaysia's Petronas, Sweden's Lundin Petroleum, India's ONGC Videsh, their various subsidiaries and hangers-on, with Khartoum's interests represented by Sudapet.[38]

The Chinese-built pipelines that ran north from Bentiu and Heglig were unveiled in ribbon-cutting ceremonies that doubled as debutante balls for the Middle Kingdom's era of *Zôuchúqè Zhànlüè*, or *going out*. The pipelines carried 480 000 barrels a day, generating revenues averaging $5.7 billion a year between 2005 and 2010,[39] and they funded the towers that transformed Khartoum's skyline. But the engagement was transforming China too. When we had sat for a second time with Liu Guijin, Beijing's ranking Africa diplomat, in Johannesburg in April of 2012, he'd told us of 'informal chats' with Omar al-Bashir, in which he had asked the old brigadier to temper his attacks on 'non-Arabs' in Darfur.[40] The slaughter, of course, had continued unabated. China had therefore been forced to actively support South Sudanese independence in order to extricate itself from an awkward relationship – support that directly undermined their non-interventionist foreign policy, and altered their stance not only in the region but in the world.[41]

In the Nuer village, the distant geopolitical gamesmanship proved surprisingly resonant. Independence brought war, or rather *more* war, if war with a different context. 'You see over there?' asked James, pointing to an encampment across the road. 'That was an SPLA place, and al-Bashir dropped his bombs on it in April, killing three.' With every explosive shudder, the circle of life was further disrupted, driving from the village the 'vast pool of youth' that Lumumba had cited as his country's future. Off they went to Bentiu, or further afield to Juba, picking through the scraps of the oil economy.

'The wars smashed everything,' said James, as he walked us back to the truck. 'What good will come of people going to the city? What will they even do there?'

◆

That night, we ate a quiet dinner at James's hotel, the Greater Nile, under the light of a flickering television set. A news report told of a highway being built linking South Sudan and Kenya, with financing provided by China's Exim Bank – a second aspirational infrastructure project designed to integrate South Sudan with the East African community and finalise her divorce from the north. The first project, James reminded us, was an oil pipeline that would transport the country's bounty not to Sudan but to Lamu, Kenya, where the $24 billion Lamu Port South Sudan Ethiopia Transport, or LAPSSET, would finally culminate. And how would the pipeline be financed, given that it was unlikely South Sudan had enough oil reserves to justify a multi-billion dollar enterprise of this scale? 'We should approach a number of friends, a number of creditors, a number of people with good hearts,' urged Marial Awou Yol, deputy minister for finance and economic planning. 'Because up the road we have our oil in the ground. We can mortgage it to get loans. What's wrong about that?'[42]

This species of naiveté was becoming endemic in the SPLM, and in a land of magical thinkers, the man with the gun becomes king. After we'd finished our meal, James invited a civil society activist – an old friend of his – to join us for a beer. The situation was too dangerous for the man to go on record with either his own name or that of his outfit. We sat talking under the stars while a fly zapper punctuated his careful sentences. He had much to say about the magical thinkers in the SPLM, and those who used their fecklessness to advance an agenda of rampant rent seeking. As an example of such an official, the activist insisted, one needed to look no further than the governor of Unity State, Taban Deng Gai.

Deng, who spent most of his time outside Unity State, had landed in Bentiu the day before we'd arrived and had been whisked off to a hidden camp in the bush. Although we'd been cautioned against using the term 'warlord' in reference to men like Deng, our thesaurus offered no alternatives – the Unity State governorship was both his reward for services rendered and an enticement to lay down his arms.[43] 'I always talk about a report from the International Crisis Group,' said the activist, referring to a paper called 'South Sudan: Compounding Instability in Unity State', which had been published shortly after the gubernatorial elections in 2010.[44] 'It tells us how the voting was rigged, how Deng is leasing the land to investors, and how none of the money comes to the people.'

As far as the activist was concerned, there was no ideological back-bone to the SPLM whatsoever. 'The party is neglected,' he said, 'it is just a name.' At the root of Unity State's crisis, according to our source, was an errant governor with a long history of war atrocities who appeared to have no intention of developing his region into anything other than the extractive entity it had been during the wars. Examined in this light, Deng's gubernatorial post was the legitimisation of his wartime plundering. Although there was no way to objectively judge them, the activist's parting words stuck with us. 'He is not the most corrupt man in South Sudan,' he said. 'He is the most corrupt man in *Africa*.'

Later, after we'd said our goodbyes, and after we'd made our way back to the Quality Hotel by the glow of our cellphones, we climbed the stairs to the roof and listened to Bentiu's generators powering down. What struck us at that moment was the starkness, the raw-ness of the forces exerting their pull on the new nation. Everywhere, we'd encountered the archetypes: there was the light, represented by James Adiok Mayik and Lumumba Stanislaus-Kaw Di-Aping. There was the darkness, embodied by Riek Machar Teny and Taban Deng Gai. Between them, there lay the chasm of the country, a gulf that would somehow have to be bridged if South Sudan was to heal, grow, *survive*. We reached back into our boyhoods in order to find a corollary – the story we were jotting in our notebooks was as mythically taut as *Star Wars*. And frankly, we were rooting for the Jedi.

It was barely 10pm when the last generator went silent. We sat for a long while, the Milky Way as clear in the night sky as either of us had ever seen.

FREE AT LAST

Juba's architecture, if you could call it that, was synecdochal. The ministry of petroleum was a mirrored gangster palace-cum-1970s Baghdad nightclub with tight security and a consigliere in a fine suit who barked, when we entered, '*What is your agenda?*' At the ministry of industry and commerce, we found no security and compact, welcoming buildings. The ministry of wildlife was a bombed-out memory of what might once have passed for a safari bush camp.

In office after office, while we waited for interviews that would never happen, we were reminded of that morning's televised election. Barack Obama's November 2012 victory speech – 'You reaffirmed the spirit that has triumphed over war and depression, the spirit that has lifted this country from the depths of despair to the great heights of hope' – chimed out from someone's phone; it had already been downloaded as a ringtone. We had woken at 4am to watch the vote counting with the staff of a conservative American NGO called International Republican Institute; our Juba address, the Afex River Camp on the banks of the White Nile, was where George Clooney slummed it when he was in town, and the young Republicans had been installed here since independence. At around 5am Central African Time, when it was clear that Mitt Romney was going to lose, the NGO's security hack, a US army reservist and former psy-ops specialist, had yelled, 'Fuck it, I'm going to put in an order for a thousand rounds of ammo.' Now, the SPLM faithful in the capital's ministerial enclaves were celebrating the win of the candidate whose acceptance speech bromides, however empty, resonated with their own democratic aspirations. 'Ay, go home!' exclaimed a ministerial secretary at a mounted flatscreen as CNN replayed Romney conceding defeat.

The *sheer fragility* of South Sudan's peace was on our minds. Come noon we were seated at an outdoor table at the New Sudan Palace Hotel, where Juba's minister of defence was about to meet his counterpart from Khartoum. The *Sudan Tribune* had been reporting that the SPLA was on the verge of withdrawing its troops from the demilitarised zone on the border, and on this Wednesday November 7th, during the first few hours of Obama's second term, it was looking likely that President Omar al-Bashir would release his stranglehold on the flow of goods into the south.[45] We had a couple of hours before a second meeting with Lumumba, and seeing as the restaurant at the New Sudan was supposed to be the most popular eatery in town, we thought we would interview its owner.

'When I landed in Juba for the first time in 2005,' said Osman Abdelmoniem, who'd been born, bred and educated in Khartoum, 'there was one tarred road, and a tent in a camp cost me $350 a night.' A graduate of a Catholic school where many of his classmates were black, Osman had used the CPA as an excuse to visit his old friends, had seen the peacetime opportunities, and had beaten the logistical odds to turn a profit within six months.[46] This afternoon, doing his best to ensure that the peacetime opportunities would last, he was making sandwich platters for the delegations from the two Sudanese governments. Meanwhile, European and American aid workers were vying for table space with Chinese and Indian businessmen, some of them

Juba, November 2012

291

hoping to 'do good', some of them hoping to make a killing, everyone playing their pre-assigned roles.

'Don't get back on those *bodas*, my driver will give you a lift,' said Osman, when the SMS from Lumumba came through. We were grateful for the offer. In only a few of the African capitals we'd worked in had there been a need to rely on these motorbikes for transport – we had used them in emergencies, but never as our staple fare. Here, there was no option. The aid workers had their Landcruisers, the politicians and the businessmen had their drivers, and the locals, all 250 000 of them, were served by the unlicensed teenage riders on their badass *boda-bodas*, these sunglass-wearing touts on their made-in-Asia 125cc's.

Sure, you could hail a minibus taxi on a tarred main road. But Juba had boasted only one tarred road in 2005, and by late 2012 the number had still to reach double digits.

◆

The Republicans with whom we'd watched Obama's triumph, and with whom we'd enjoyed a breakfast of such mass it was as if the Afex Camp was a flagship outlet of Denny's, were in Juba in order to nudge along a constitutional process that had been underwritten by the United States Congress. But Lumumba, and by extension the SPLM, were refusing to be nudged. He made this clear during our second interview, which was conducted at another outdoor table at the same business park. This time Lumumba appeared less depleted, and more like the pugnacious diplomat who'd taken verbal swings at the Americans during the climate change negotiations in Copenhagen.

'Urgency?' asked Lumumba, after we'd pressed him to explain the time lag between independence and a working framework for the state. 'Urgency is a sense that is dictated by purpose. If you are not committed to a certain goal, you cannot have a sense of urgency. That has to be created. The SPLM has to have a clear vision as to where it's going, which will then drive the speed or the slowness as required.' On the one hand, then, as Lumumba had stated the day before, there was much urgency in getting the vision squared away

292

so as to fend off outside rapacity; on the other, no one was going to tell the SPLM what to do.

Which, as far as paradoxes went, was all fine and well – having now read through the manifesto, having scarred it with lines and question marks and exclamation points, our own most urgent issue involved the matter of how the SPLM would translate its shibboleths into principles of governance. How would South Sudan *be?* And how long was it going to take to get there, given that the peace was so tentative?

'A constitution is a manifestation of the will of the people to found a certain type of society,' Lumumba reminded us. 'Otherwise, we can go to Germany or South Africa and just delete references to those countries and put in South Sudan.' Again Lumumba was stressing specificity. But it seemed slightly dangerous, especially in light of the political instability of almost all oil states, that the manifesto, in trying to learn from and transcend all ideologies, expressed none. If the SPLM was without 'ideological power struggles', as Lumumba had previously argued, what exactly was the party agreeing upon in the manifesto?

He smiled a tight smile. 'The NGOs,' he said, drawing the term out as if it were a pejorative, 'in my humble view, did not understand the priorities of the movement. Our priority in the last five, let's say seven years, from the signing of the CPA, was to get the country independent. Was to implement the CPA, okay? That has taken massive, massive time from other priorities. I'm not saying that our effort is brilliant, I'm saying there are misconceptions and misunderstandings of what it is that we prioritised for.'

This was the slack in the rope that tethered liberation to statehood. Like so many movements of its kind, the SPLM was designed for a single purpose: independence. Free at last, its leadership was not so much in agreement as they were waiting each other out. The marked-up manifesto that lay on the table between two journalists and its principal author was meant as a stopgap against chaos. But the longer it lay on the table without being drafted into law, the more instability it courted.

◆

As afternoon approached evening, Lumumba sketched for us a country. South Sudan resembled Botswana at independence, he said, with oil substituting for diamonds. It would perhaps become a developmental democratic state, which described a statist model with a strong democratic component, unlike Ethiopia and more like Brazil. If there was a core to the manifesto, it was this: 'We have to engage in defining freedom in mutually beneficial terms,' said Lumumba. 'In other words, my personal freedom is not at the expense of anyone, whether economically or politically.' South Sudan, in this view, would become a post-tribal, post-traditional, democratic neo-cooperative. 'We do not want a situation where somebody thinks that they have freedom in the absolute sense,' Lumumba continued. The South Sudanese citizen would have to realise that they now belonged to 'the human family', membership of which demanded concessions, and exacted obligations. There would be support, but no handouts. There would be individuals, and they would constitute a people.

Although Lumumba demanded specificity, we were starting to believe that he possessed a genius for creating panoramas, much like the newly re-elected American president with whom he'd tangled in Copenhagen. It was now clear to us that Lumumba intended to drive a grand conception of society towards policy, rather than craft policy that would define a society. This approach favoured manifesto writing over governance, and it left Lumumba open to criticisms of naiveté, of magical thinking. And yet, it also proved that he was willing to debate, to guide, to forge consensus. In this, the manifesto was less a legal document than it was a work of performance art – an early example to his comrades in the SPLM that no matter how compromised their pasts might have been, their futures would be defined by negotiation, by engagement, and by ideas.

THE INVENTION OF GREY

When we sat down with Lumumba for a third and final time, the situation in South Sudan had degraded to such an extent that the

294

world's newest country could no longer properly be called a country. Over the course of 2014, we had followed the arc of a war between Salva Kiir and Riek Machar, watching from afar a catastrophe that only the most cynical of the 'pre-failed state' Cassandras could have presaged. Thousands killed, hundreds of thousands displaced, millions at risk of starvation. It was the old war in a new guise: Machar, who in South Sudan's brief flirtation with peace and reconciliation had served as vice president, versus Kiir, who in that same period had been consolidating his power like an old-school strongman. *No ideological power struggles within the SPLM? No vested interests?* Lumumba's words echoed across 12 months of unimaginable violence, and when we reached out to him in order to make some sense of the conflict, our emails echoed back at us too.

It was therefore a relief when a note finally came through on New Year's Day 2015. 'A Very Merry Christmas and Happy New Year to you,' wrote Lumumba. 'I hope it brings all humanity success and good health. I am sorry that I was not able to contact you as I was in a remote border town in South Sudan (Pagak) where there was no communication. I have just made it to South Africa where I am going to be for the next few days. I hope to hear from you soon.'

Two days later, we were sitting across from our old friend on white leather couches in a modernist mansion he and his family were housesitting in Johannesburg. When he finished a phone call and offered a welcoming embrace, it was clear that the intervening years had been hard on him. He was weary, ashen, with flecks of grey in his goatee. 'You have caught me at a moment of exhaustion,' he apologised. 'I suppose I need a bit of a break.'

In the brief silence after we'd finished sharing our personal news, Lumumba brought his hands together in a triangle, signalling that he was ready to start the interview. 'There was basically an explosion, or an implosion, in the party,' he began, 'and what followed was what seems to be the typical scenario of an African coup, ending up with effectively a civil war situation.'

While the violence wasn't in any way linked to the manifesto Lumumba had helped to craft, the document's unanimous acceptance at an SPLM extraordinary conference, which took place on 13 December 2013, was the last time the party would sit as an entity. The trouble had started six months before the extraordinary conference, when President Kiir had removed Taban Deng Gai as governor of Unity State, a move welcomed by civil society activists and human rights advocates until they had read the small print. Deng's removal was illegal under the temporary constitution, and his sacking was interpreted as an attempt to weaken Vice President Riek Machar's Nuer faction, with whom Deng was inextricably linked. But Kiir wasn't finished: on 24 July 2013, he had sacked Machar along with the entire cabinet, including Pagan Amum, the secretary-general of the SPLM who'd acted as Kiir's chief negotiator in the ongoing discussions over oil rights with the al-Bashir regime in Khartoum. Although a new cabinet would be in place by the end of the month, the Republic of South Sudan, which had only just celebrated its second birthday, was being dismantled from the inside out.

In this context, the manifesto's sign-off counted as a victory, one that had provided Kiir the conceptual tools with which to begin the much-delayed constitutional process. The following day, however, a cabal loyal to Machar withdrew from the conference, insisting that any draft of the constitution that Kiir proposed would invest all of the government's power in the presidency, with none of the federal diffusion that the manifesto had promised. Kiir interpreted this as the opening move in a palace coup, and on the evening of 15 December 2013 he ordered the commander of his elite presidential guard, a fellow Dinka, to disarm all Nuer members of the unit. According to the South Sudan News Agency, the unit's second-in-command, a Nuer, 'physically confronted' his superior in response, which prompted his 'fierce warrior' brothers to break into the barrack's stores and rearm themselves (from the language of the SSNA report, it was obvious where the writer's sympathies lay).[47] The next morning, after tank and artillery units of the SPLA had moved on the barracks and dislodged the Nuer force, soldiers loyal to Kiir swept through the neighbourhoods of Juba in what the country's interior minister was calling a 'clean-up operation'. As per the accounts of over 150 victims and witnesses,[48] the primary targets of this operation were civilian Nuer males – an estimated 500 were killed within four days.

After Kiir cried coup, the fighting spread throughout the country, quickly engulfing the northern oilfields. By mid-January, the International Crisis Group estimated that 10 000 had been killed.[49] Refugees began spilling over the borders into Kenya, Uganda, Ethiopia and Sudan. The UN stated that hundreds of refugees were entering Ethiopia every day, with 190 000 South Sudanese in camps in that country alone. The détente between the Dinka and Nuer, as embodied in a period of reconciliation that stretched from 2002 to early 2013, was now a thing of the past. Kiir dispensed the SPLA from Juba, and Machar his proxy troops from Nasir, his old holdout on the Ethiopian border. Just like that, it was all-out war all over again.

In the natural order of an African conflict like this one, liberation party politicians lined up behind their tribesmen – and the 'ethnic perspective', as Lumumba had once termed it, was made manifest as the country's prevailing truth. And so, when Lumumba's statements addressing the events of 15 December 2013 eventually hit the wires, they arrived as something of a shock. '[President Kiir], your legacy will come to naught,' declared Lumumba, using the *Sudan Tribune* as his loudhailer. 'History will remember and record you in its annals as the ... leader who charted the way to independence and delivered destruction to his people and country.'[50] His meaning was unmistakable: Lumumba, a Dinka, was criticising Kiir, a Dinka, in the harshest possible terms. 'Don't be misled by sycophants. Do the right thing for Christ's sake: embrace change, reform and embrace the hopes of our people. Or quit.'[51]

Kiir, of course, would do no such thing. And the clue as to Lumumba's next move lay embedded in his emailed New Year's greeting. Pagak, the 'remote border town in South Sudan', was about 100 kilometres from Nasir, Riek Machar's longtime base camp. Lumumba had joined the Nuer faction – or, rather, the SPLM-In-Opposition (SPLM-IO) – and in the simple act of doing so had transformed the situation in South Sudan from a tribal war into something ideological.

◆

Riek Machar's record had become only more tarnished over the course of 2014. 'Look, there was just something deeply disturbing and rotten about what Kiir did,' Lumumba told us. 'I could not stand by and be neutral.' But what struck us about our friend's choice was the fact that he'd made one at all – could he not have just sat this round out? There was the not insignificant matter of Machar's proxies, the so-called White Army, a militia comprised mostly of teenagers that had been implicated in the killing of non-Nuer civilians.[52] Even more disturbing, there was Machar's alleged partnership with the regime in Khartoum, allegations that were becoming as much of a factor in this conflict as they had been in the past.

All of which brought us to the point in the story where the narrative blocks, meticulously hewn by half a millennium of weathering, came tumbling into place; where all the players in the drama converged in order to make good on their Shakespearean arcs. The date was 31 August 2014, the setting a military college in Khartoum, and the players the 'palace dignitaries' – the core of Omar al-Bashir's court. The president was not in attendance, but was ably represented by his vice president, Lt General Bakri Hassan Salih, his most likely heir at the time of the meeting.

In one of those twists that have become a hallmark of the information age, the minutes of this gathering, a war-room powwow concerning the ruling National Congress Party's lead-up to the 2015 elections, were leaked. As the American South Sudan observer Eric Reeves noted in a lengthy post on his blog,[53] there was a chance that the minutes were a hoax – but there was a much larger case to be made for their authenticity, so much so that the burden of proof (or, rather, disproof) rested with the regime. Signed off by the security and military officials present, the 'South Sudan' item on the agenda read as follows:

> Assistance to Riek's rebel Sudan People's Liberation Movement in Opposition will increase and include tanks, artillery, intelligence and logistical training, as requested, said the Chairman of the Joint Chiefs of Staff, Gen Hashim Abdullah Mohamed, by Riek, Taban

Deng Gai and Dhieu Mathok Diing on a visit to Khartoum. The
NCP's explicit aim is a federal state of Greater Upper Nile – a bid
to regain the oilfields and to block the SPLM-North's route south-
wards.[54, 55]

The regime in Khartoum appeared committed to the creation of a sub-
country that would be governed by their puppet, a Greater Upper Nile
that would be comprised of the most lucrative oil-producing areas, its
borders embracing Jonglei, Unity and Upper Nile states, with Malakal
as its capital-designate. That city, brimming with local war history, had
served as a garrison town for the Sudanese Armed Forces during the
second civil war, and was more recently ground zero for the battles
between the SPLA and the SPLA-IO, the latter represented by the Nuer
White Army.[56]

Khartoum's abiding fear, and therefore its existential obsession,
was the 'New Sudan Project', the multi-ethnic, multi-party liberal
democratic Sudan articulated most forcefully by John Garang in the
years before his death. Lumumba's manifesto was, in no small measure, a means of bringing the New Sudan Project to life in the south.
We'd held the document in our hands and marvelled at its breadth,
its self-awareness, its swaggering insouciance in the face of what
its framers must have known would be derision from those who had
declared South Sudan 'pre-failed'. It was an attempt to build a dyke,
however flimsy, against the inevitable tidal storm that would slam
into the country in the first few years of independence. It was as if
Lumumba had kept Walter Benjamin's most famous image in mind
– that of the angel of history blown backward into the future, sur-
veying the past not as a chain of progressive events but as a pile-up
of catastrophes – with the manifesto an attempt to turn the angel
around to *face* the future, leaving the carnage in his wake. But it
hadn't worked.

The future in South Sudan had never looked more bleak, more like the
past it had been trying to transcend. In early 2014, all foreign nationals had fled Bentiu, the Eritreans at the Quality Hotel among them. The
hundreds of corpses that littered the city's streets were feasted upon

Kali-Ballee Mosque, Bentiu, Unity State, November 2012

by birds and dogs. Later that year, as we travelled through the western borderlands of Ethiopia, we encountered heavily guarded refugee camps full of traumatised South Sudanese – the present generation's Lost Boys, more lost even than those who'd come before them.

Salva Kiir, according to Lumumba, was no longer fit to rule. Whatever the NGO world's numbers, it was *his* contention that the president had slaughtered 20 000 Nuer within three days of the showdown at the Juba military barracks. 'My own father was a general in the SPLA before independence,' he reminded us, 'and when Khartoum found him guilty of fighting them, did they massacre tens of thousands of South Sudanese? Or did they arrest him and deal with him alone?'

The SPLM under Kiir was apparently worse even than the National

Congress Party under Omar al-Bashir – so bad, in fact, that in January 2015 his presidency would prove the catalyst for the formal end of China's non-intervention policy. Beijing would announce that it was sending 700 troops of the People's Liberation Army to Juba, a move that a member of the Chinese Foreign Ministry would later characterise for us as imperative: 'To *not* get involved would have been worse,' he would say. In the middle of 2015, John Garang's liberation movement would have its next (legitimate) leadership contest, in the run-up to South Sudan's first general elections. And just about the only South Sudanese politician without taint, without demonstrable tribal affiliations, without blood on his or her hands, and with the credentials to govern a nascent country in the first blush of its youth? Lumumba Stanislaus-Kaw Di-Aping.

Our friend's play was now mapped out for us, and it was a beautiful work of realpolitik. Straight down the middle, in an end run to the presidency. 'Yes,' Lumumba confirmed, 'I will put my name into the hat, and we will see what happens.'

And was he hopeful? Did he believe the country could right itself, could *be*? 'Hope is the only possibility,' he said, leaning back into the leather of the couch. 'But by that, I don't mean wishful thinking.'

Ganyesa viii

There is no sound in Mi Zheng's Ganyesa grocery store, save for the hum of a refrigerator and, out back, the braying of a donkey. Three Bangladeshi men have formed a protective mantle around the Chinese shopkeeper, a buffer of concern. As an introduction to his friend – a signal, no doubt, that we must tread gently – Hossin explains that the night of the fire that killed his brother, Zheng was inconsolable, 'crying from the heart.'

His demeanour, the tenor of his speech, makes plain that Zheng is still in mourning. 'My brother leaves four children,' he whispers. 'The big one is seven, the baby just ten months.'

Over the course of the next few hours, we will learn that Zheng was born in a third-tier city in Fujian province, called Fuqing. We will learn, also, that he was the second of six brothers, and that Chen's death has left him as the oldest surviving son. We will learn that in Fuqing, as in the shtetls of Lithuania a century ago, South Africa is spoken about as a place of rich promise – almost 100 locals have left, many for North West Province. We will learn that since he arrived in Ganyesa in 2007, Zheng has been trying to save money, but that he has lost most of it due to a string of misfortunes.

Several years ago, he tells us, on a road 50 kilometres south of Vryburg, he and a younger brother were driving late at night. He believes that this brother fell asleep at the wheel, sending them into the path of an oncoming truck. Now, the brother spends his days inert on a cot back in Fuqing. Zheng escaped with a mangled leg and a dead eye – left alive, he muses, only to witness a new familial tragedy, which took place outside the realm of luck, in a different sphere of human experience altogether.

The night of Chen's death was not the first time Ganyesa Fruit & Vegetables had been attacked, Zheng tells us. Six weeks before it went up in flames, four armed gangsters entered the store and stole R50 000 in cash.

We interrupt to ask why Chen was holding so much money, and Hossin, ever conscious of his role as protector, steps in. 'The black people here, they trusted him,' he says. 'Chen was the one who was giving them their government pension. That day was pension day.'

His voice faltering, Zheng continues to relate that Chen's wife and baby were in the store; that the attackers grabbed the baby and threatened to harm it if the money was not handed over. After the incident, Chen sent his wife and the baby back to Fuqing.

'They are only once more in Ganyesa,' he says. 'To fetch the ashes, and take them to my father in China.'

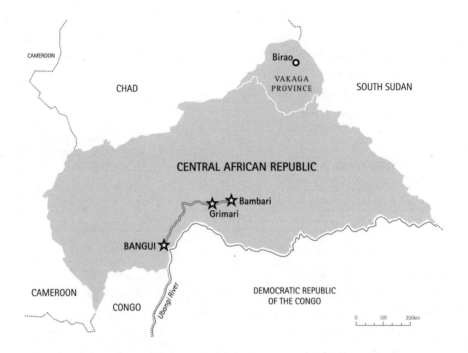

NINE

CENTRAL AFRICAN REPUBLIC

The Republic of Nowhere & the Limits of the Nation State

'Do you know where breathes today
The Christian spirit of France?
Of ancient Rome and Byzantium?
It's in Bangui, la Coquette.'

– Coronation ode, composed for the crowning of
Emperor Jean-Bédel Bokassa I, 1977

THE HAUNTING

'Just listen to the ghosts.'

We were offered the advice before leaving for the Central African Republic, but it turned out to be unnecessary. In the VIP lounge above Bangui M'Poko International's lone runway, the ghosts never shut up. For more than three hours now we had been waiting for Rodrigue – our fixer; the man who'd assured us he'd be holding up a big nameplate – in this room that evoked a dancehall by Le Corbusier. The clock was stuck at 2:20, the bottles of hard liquor were covered in dust, and the hall was empty save for a barman who kept us topped up on Nescafé. And yet, it appeared, everybody was here: dead presidents, French colonialists, fake diplomats, Asian oligarchs, rogue dealers with diamonds in their digestive tracts. To call oneself a player, we reckoned, to feature in this country's improvised, stream-of-consciousness narrative, a person would have needed to pass through M'Poko's open-air VIP lounge at least once.

305

As a breeze blew in off the Bas Oubangui, we outlined for each other in the centre of the dancehall the silhouette of Barthélemy Boganda. CAR's liberation hero, we'd read, had been the son of subsistence farmers who'd lived and worked in the Lobaye district, Oubangui-Chari colony, where the Compagnie Forestière de la Sangha-Oubangui had once held sway. The *compagnie* had practised a form of slavery called the *corvée* – forced labour in lieu of taxation – so as to make its aggressive rubber quotas. 'Their methods were not gentle,' noted a history of the period. 'They used the lash liberally to keep their "employees" on the move, and they punished insubordination with mutilation and death.'[1] In the late 1920s, after a *compagnie* official had thus killed young Barthélemy's mother, the pious M'baka boy had been whisked off to missionary school, soon to become the first ordained Catholic priest in the colony.

But God could do only so much for a black man in Oubangui-Chari, and Boganda had been urged to run for the French National Assembly, an institution to which he would triumphantly ascend in 1946. That said, like God, Charles de Gaulle too had his limits – Boganda would return to Bangui in 1949, in order to inaugurate the Movement for the Social Evolution of Black Africa, or MESAN. *Zo kwe zo* ran the party's Sango tagline, *Every human being is a person.* It had been Boganda's dream to create a multinational Francophone state in the middle of the continent, but in 1959, the year after CAR had achieved autonomy, his plane would explode magically in the sky. Boganda's people had called him the Black Christ, and many believed that he could walk on water. There had been much dismay when it transpired that he could not fly.[2]

Alongside Boganda, amongst the devils and the decent men, we traced the shape of David Dacko, who had replaced Boganda as leader of MESAN to become the nation's first president in 1960. Dacko would be pushed aside by his cousin Jean-Bédel Bokassa in 1966, who would be pushed aside by – yes! – Dacko again in 1979. Who would be pushed aside by André Kolingba in 1981, who would be pushed aside by Ange-Félix Patassé 10 years later, who would be pushed aside by François Bozizé in 2003.

Boganda Memorial, Bangui, August 2014

In the shadows' shadows, at the edges of the dance floor, lurked the Frenchmen who'd facilitated the pushing. That jowly one smoking the cigarette, that one circling, watching, determined to miss nothing? That was Jacques Foccart, de Gaulle's – and later Jacques Chirac's – man on all matters Africa.[3] Beside him was Jean Christophe Mitterrand, who'd maintained an Africa cell in his father François Mitterrand's presidential office. The spectres of men, but also the spectral boom of planes blowing up in the sky. It was so crowded in the empty lounge that we barely had elbowroom to drink the shitty coffee.

CAR was our last port of call. After four-and-a-half years of travel – eight years if you counted our first trip to Angola – we had landed in Bangui to take the measure of Africa's most dysfunctional country. Right in the continent's core, a brutal civil conflict had been gathering in pace, form and fury, spinning chunks of itself out into the African ether. Here was what CAR came down to: the government ran a few strategic streets in the capital, while two main rebel groups – the 'Muslim' Séléka and the 'Christian' anti-balaka – battled each other town by town for the scraps. Behind this mess was the *real* power: the French. The country was cracking in half, in thirds. In an age when we assume boundaries are dissolving, CAR suggested that they were in fact being further entrenched, and the country's multiplying divisions seemed to point to a terrifying future. Was this the vestigial remnants of Africa's past, a ghost roaming the halls to remind us from whence we had come? Or was it an intimation of the African tomorrow, a balkanised non-place on the brink of dissolution, a rent-a-country governed by masters and miners and bankers in foreign capitals?

We had arrived in Centrafrique in order to hear the final word, and we were hoping against hope that it was neither. We were hoping, since our concern was for the living, that the word would not be delivered by the dead.

◆

Rodrigue's mouth, when at last he appeared in the VIP lounge, four hours late and out of breath and meekly apologetic, was ringed by malaria sores. Our indignation, which had been building up all morning, was instantly defused. 'Shouldn't you be resting?' one of us asked – not only was it obvious what the lesions meant, his pallor was an extravagant shade of grey. 'It is not a problem,' he said.

This, we would learn, was Rodrigue's tagline, his own version of *zo kwe zo*, a statement infinitely variable in its inferences and just as indulgent of the country's ironies. We followed his short frame down the stairs and out into the carpark, where we got first-hand confirmation of some of the media reports we'd been following. The airport was less an airport than it was the headquarters of the French mission, named Opération Sangaris for the bright red Central African butterfly that adorned its logo.[4] France's recent military adventures in Africa, we'd discovered, had typically been named for adorable local creatures: the anti-Islamist Opération Serval in Mali and Épervier in Chad meant 'wildcat' and 'sparrowhawk' respectively. The tradition of nomenclature had been broken by Opération Barkhane, or 'crescent-shaped dune', for the 3 000-strong French force newly gathered in N'Djamena, Chad, in order to drone away the Islamists of the Sahel region.[5] Sangaris hadn't fallen under Barkhane's mandate, and thus got to keep its pretty butterfly.

On the apron side of M'Poko Airport, as Rodrigue fumbled with his keys, we saw orderly planters filled with violet and blue geraniums. On the Bangui side we saw the tents and tarpaulins of the refugee camp, the same camp that had housed around 100 000 people at the peak of the fighting in December 2013, the camp that was now home to some 38 000 souls. In CAR, a land of acronyms on a continent of acronyms, they were called IDPs – for Internal Displaced Persons. Almost a fifth of the country had been on the hop since war had broken out in December 2012, and a prominent response of the outside world had been to further perfect the compacting of human misery into three-letter combinations.[6]

Bangui la Coquette, went the motto. Bangui the Beautiful. But the city, when we entered it, was just sad. It wasn't anything as blatant as the fact that its old colonial centre had decomposed in the jungle heat – Bangui had never been one of Francafrique's masterpieces, and the 'old city' itself was so haphazard that it spoke only of exploitation, the country's abiding *raison d'être*. It was rather that the dominant architectural genre, a species of African modernism, recalled the euphoria of liberation. Our first stop, after checking in at our own hotel, was Bangui's landmark building, the Oubangui Hotel, which towered over the river that gave the city its name. Built in 1960 by a Greek tycoon, the 15-storey structure had been commandeered by Bokassa in 1966, shortly after his successful coup. Not content to merely seize them – even if he'd wanted to, there simply weren't enough to sate his appetite – Bokassa had erected scores of these handsome edifices for himself, buildings that were soon to become so removed from their time and purpose that the South African photographer Guy Tillim, referring to their equivalents in other African countries, would label them 'Floating Worlds'.[7] Bokassa's coronation and subsequent imperial ambitions were about to unmask his psychotic face; in an era of Big Man excesses, he would be deemed the biggest Man of all: Papa Bok, *le roi nègre*, the Negro King.[8] Still, in those early days, when CAR could still pretend, he had articulated worthy dreams in concrete.

Oubangui Hotel, August 2014

From a bench on the natural isthmus that extended out from the modernist pool deck into the river's ancient current, we considered our next move. We decided to head back up the airport road, to take a closer look at the neighbourhood of Combattants, where, as Rodrigue had explained, the country's war was being prosecuted in miniature.

For visitors, our fixer had said, Combattants functioned as something of a *dramatis personae*, an introduction to both the players and the played. Once again, we passed by the Sangaris forces in their blinged-up armoured trucks and full Kevlar battle gear; we passed by the Chinese-made pick-ups of the African Union's Mission internationale de soutien à la Centrafrique sous conduite africaine, known for short as MISCA; we passed by the decaying concrete base of EUFOR, the European contingent. Eight thousand seven hundred and fifty heavily armed men and women from two continents, all here to help France pay the price for inventing countries.[9]

The previous day, Rodrigue reminded us, a 'fight' had broken out in Combattants. The neighbourhood, he said, was run by one of the country's two main rebel groups, the nominally Christian anti-balaka, which had emerged as a counterweight to the nominally Muslim Séléka, themselves a coalition of northern rebel groups that had banded together for the purpose of taking Bangui. Within the anti-balaka, he went on, a Sango word that could loosely be translated as 'anti-machete', there were many conflicting objectives, and sometimes those objectives were local.

'The battle was a personal clash between an anti-balaka boy whose name is Andilo and a captain in FACA,' said Rodrigue, referring in the last instance to the mostly disarmed national army.[10] 'Everybody knows this *petit* Andilo,' he said – in the days ahead, our fixer would revert habitually to the diminutive when talking about (or to) members of the anti-balaka.

So how were these boys, these *petits*, who were ostensibly being policed by three – *three!* – international armed forces, allowed to discharge their weapons in broad daylight on the streets of the capital? How could a 'personal clash' between a leader of a rebel group and an officer in the national army be allowed to result in three deaths?

Answer: Combattants was called Combattants for a reason.

◆

CAR's latest conflict had achieved the status of an international event on 24 March 2013, with the fall of François Bozizé's government. At the time, it had been widely assumed that the president was a stooge of the French, but this had proved a costly miscalculation – Bozizé had been a stooge in search of a master, which meant that things were a lot more volatile than most outsiders thought.

Not that you could blame those outsiders for their assumptions. The ex-president, a military man, had a back-story that was fairly typical of CAR's post-independence era. One day, Emperor Bokassa had caught wind of the fact that young Bozizé had slapped a Frenchman for insolence, and so had promoted him to the rank of 'general'. With a natural flair for the intrigues of the game, a sublime talent for forging the best alliances, Bozizé would take the ultimate prize in 2003, courtesy of a coup staged in Chad. His regime, a family business referred to in Bangui as 'the Board', would hold onto power for a decade, and would then tumble quickly and spectacularly and for all the usual reasons – the sector of the population with the least access to representation and development would seek and find their own partners and benefactors, and would head for the capital with the aim of spilling government blood. In December 2012, when the Séléka had first knocked on Bangui's door, they'd been talked down by the Mission for the Consolidation of Peace in CAR, an organisation working under the aegis of the regional Economic Community of Central African States.[11] Bozizé had balked at the negotiated power sharing agreement, and when Séléka had once again advanced on the capital, in March of 2013, this time killing thousands, the president had looked around for his traditional allies – only to learn that now they had other fish to fry.

There would be no stranger battle in Africa that year than the Battle for Bangui. Back in 2011, the South African National Defence Force had deployed 250 soldiers to protect two small training teams appended to the Multinational Force of Central Africa. Now it would find itself on the front line.[12] Three thousand heavily armed Séléka insurgents would roll into the capital, having chased away a Chadian contingent posted in the northern town of Damara without firing a shot.[13] Meanwhile, the 200-strong French force at the airport would appear interested in holding only the airport. So the South Africans would lock and load, and over the course of almost 48 hours would fire off more bullets, rockets and bombs than they had during any single battle in Angola. Thirteen South African troops would be killed and 27 wounded; almost 500 Séléka bodies would pile up on the streets until the eventual signing of the ceasefire.[14]

By then, it would be too late for Bozizé. 'Where did I go wrong?' the ousted president would wonder.

> There are no political prisoners at the moment, the press is free. Why did they start raping, killing and hurting the Central African population? We gave them everything. Before giving oil to the Chinese, I met Total in Paris and told them to take the oil; nothing happened. I gave oil to the Chinese and it became a problem. I sent [a representative to] Paris for the Uranium dossier, they refused. I finally gave it to the South Africans.[15]

When we first encountered this statement, we were struck by the floating pronoun *they*. In his distress, Bozizé had clearly been referring to the French, whom he believed had betrayed him. He was likely also referring to the northern rebel groups, most of them Muslim, whom *he* had betrayed. And he was no doubt referring to the government of neighbouring Chad, which had almost certainly provided start-up arms and financing for these Séléka components. In Bozizé's conception, *they* seemed to serve as a catchall for a new and inscrutable force, a vortex that was sucking CAR into the inevitable and yet unknowable vacuum of its past, present and future masters.

Bozizé, we sensed, had not listened to the ghosts. When he'd sat in the airport's VIP lounge on his frequent trips abroad, he had paid no attention to what his predecessors were whispering. Did he flee to Congo-Brazzaville with only their laughter in his ears? Probably, we guessed, as Rodrigue performed a three-point turn to get us out of Combattants. But one thing *could* be said for the departing president: his bewildered, closing statement was a succinct précis of his country.

It was a place to be sold. Failing that, it was a place to be given away.

ALL TOMORROW'S COUNTRIES

'Although the Central African Republic has been a member of the United Nations Organisation since 20 September 1960, it remains the least known region in the world.'[16] This astonishing declaration opened Pierre Kalck's *Central African Republic: A Failure in De-Colonisation*, one of the few reference books available to us in English translation. Although first published in 1971, six years before Bokassa crowned himself emperor, the sentence – when we came across it in August 2014 – read as enduringly true. By almost any measure, CAR was unknown.

But unknown to whom? Kalck, on the surface, appeared to be writing for Westerners – academics and policymakers and people far enough removed from the mainstream to be interested in the subject matter. Nonetheless, as we studied his workaday volume, it occurred to us that Kalck was also writing for Central Africans. We soon collided with the opening line's equally astonishing qualifier: on the eve of independence in 1960, wrote Kalck, Oubangui-Chari 'had a population of about 1 200 000 scattered over some 206 000 square miles'. The reader thus learnt that the empty and cavernous Central African Republic – or the idea of a nation-state called the Central African Republic – had been largely unknown even to those who counted as her citizens. And if *they* were unaware of their citizenship, if they didn't want to be citizens in the first place, what did that say about the legitimacy of CAR's post-colonial condition?

Kalck maintained that there were compelling cultural and historical circumstances to explain this general reticence: the region had long been primed to ask uncomfortable questions about the utility and worth of nation-states, he suggested, especially in an African context. Over the course of thousands of years of history and into the era of

314

the French – periods linked by the terrible through-line of slavery (or 'forced labour' or 'military conscription', depending on the euphemism of the age) – Central Africa had been perennially peopled and depopulated, filled and emptied like a calabash gourd.

The country, it so happened, hadn't always been *nowhere*. It had once been the focal point of the continental axis, its importance as a crossroads intuited and understood. Dozens of tribes and ethnicities had moved through here, several claiming it as their ontological home. *O Centre Afrique, ô berceau des Bantous*, Barthélemy Boganda had crooned in 'The Renaissance', the national anthem he had personally composed – *O Centre of Africa, cradle of the Bantu.*[17] According to Kalck, the region used to be 'a meeting place of routes' that converged in from Tripoli in the north, Mombasa in the east, and Pointe-Noire in the west. The peaks of the northwestern Yadé massif had for generations been considered sacred by the Baya and Mboum, whose pilgrimage paths would in later years be used by slave raiders from Sudan. The Lobaye River, which sliced through the range, was key to the German colonial Mittelafrika project, a fascist-tinged blueprint for connecting Douala with Dar-es-Salaam.[18]

Yes, Central Africa was a wet place; her rivers were her highways to the world. The capital, and the river from which it took its name, were the domain of the Boubangui, a trading culture that had worked the waterway for ages. In the late 1800s, it was not uncommon to see 200-person canoes powering goods and slaves off into the Congo basin. Although Sango, the 'water language', would only be adopted as CAR's official tongue in 1964, it had provided the region with its cultural and linguistic ligature for much longer than the locals could say.[19]

Central Africa was a place of shifting alliances, of rising and falling families, of nascent empires – and of sultans moving down from the Sudan, slaving the interior relentlessly.[20] All of this downward and outward and inward pressure had created a vibrant region with highly defined social structures, *and with no borders to speak of.* And while the northern Muslims, who wore their faith lightly, were obsessed with territorial expansion and empire, the Baya, Banda and Sara in the south were opposed to even the vaguest idea of a state, having thrived in 'ordered anarchy' for centuries.[21] There existed in Banda lore a great chief named Ngakola who, after overextending his welcome as leader of the tribe, was put to death by his own people. Kings in these parts had an allotted time limit, usually the length of a military campaign, and those that developed a taste for power tended to lose their heads. Regicide was a local specialty; most cultures were profoundly suspicious of leadership as an end instead of a means.

Through it all, the region functioned as a filter – goods and people moved across and out, outsiders rarely moved in. The slaves that ended up at Atlantic ports were too traumatised to explain to white traders from whence they had come, and few slavers bothered to ask. But by the 1870s, the outside world was knocking with urgency. The Belgian King Leopold II identified the big blank spot in the middle of his Africa map as a treasure to be added to his Association Internationale du Congo, the academic organisation that had been created as a front for his rapacity.

For the explorers Henry Stanley, who served Leopold, and Pietro Paolo Savorgnan di Brazzà, stumping for the French, amongst the most tantalising of African prizes was this uncharted tributary of the Congo, the Bobangui's waterway over which Bokassa's modernist master-pieces would one day stand sentry. During the Berlin Conference, Leopold would hide from the French Stanley's reports of the Oubangui and the route to the Congo from Chad that it implied. The parties were therefore negotiating over a fake map portraying an imaginary terri-tory, a region that may as well have been marked 'There Be Monsters'. This time, however, Leopold did not get his way – in 1884 Oubangui-Chari became French at the stroke of a pen, relinquished by the Belgian regent in exchange for a loan.[22] Paris was now in possession of a dreamscape, the first official colony of nothing.

◆

In 1890, the Comité de l'Afrique Française, a powerful colonial busi-ness association, began encouraging French entrepreneurs to paddle down the Oubangui and make a go of it. An 'orgy of concessions' followed, and 39 of the dreaded *compagnies* started out for the centre of Africa, their forced recruitment of porters and practice of the *corvée* wiping out entire tribes in a matter of a few years. How did this pillage economy differ from the slave trade, which the French had outlawed in 1830?[23] According to Kalck, it didn't. Compounding the violence were outbreaks of sleeping sickness, yellow fever and malaria. While the contours of the map of French Africa were iterated by careful cartographic work, and while Centrafrique was becoming a place that its overseers could describe in familiar terms, the colony itself was devolving into an abyss.

As soon as Central Africa was won, it was placed in an expanding imperial jigsaw that could – and one day *would,* insisted the French – frame an enormous portrait of commerce in which Algiers was linked to Brazzaville, Rabat to Libreville, Bangui to Dakar. The country was thus ripped from its fluid traditional context and made to fit with France's unyielding Africa vision. It would now be connected back in time to events that had unfolded in San Domingo (the formerly French Haiti) a century before the Scramble, and would be connected forward in time to the horrors of Algeria and Indochina in the 1950s. Of course Bangui, as it became increasingly less 'exotic', would in return reveal a truth about France: the Third Republic, inaugurated in 1870, was now the embodiment of the very opposite of the values espoused during the founding years of the French Revolution.

France's imperialist agenda could be traced back as far as 1697, when the country signed the Treaty of Ryswick with Spain, and had thus gained the legal right to the western part of the island Christopher Columbus had annexed for the Spanish king in 1492 and named Insula Hispana, or Hispaniola.[24] The French West Indies was thenceforth wedded to Africa via the Compagnie du Sénégal, which had been established in 1673 in order to ship slaves out of Senegambia to the sugar plantations of the Caribbean.[25] 'In 1789,' wrote CLR James in his classic *The Black Jacobins*, 'the French West Indian colony of San Domingo supplied two-thirds of the overseas trade of France and was the greatest individual market for the European slave trade. It was an integral part of the economic life of the age, the greatest colony in the world, the pride of France, and the envy of every other imperialist nation.'[26] But 1789 was also the year that the Bastille was stormed, the year that the Declaration of the Rights of Man and of the Citizen was proclaimed in Paris by the Constituent Assembly (and the year, incidentally, that uranium was discovered by the chemist Martin Heinrich Klaproth, thus launching yet another arrow destined to lodge in CAR's back). The French Revolution was now fully underway, and inspired in part by its rhetoric the slaves of San Domingo revolted. In 1801, the political and military genius Toussaint L'Ouverture, an ex-slave himself, became governor-for-life of the first autonomous territory in the Caribbean.

Although L'Ouverture, the so-called 'Black Napoleon', would be removed from office by the soldiers of the original Napoleon in 1802, the Haitian Revolution would continue under the aegis of his lieutenant, and full independence would be achieved in 1804. As far as the brand-new concept of *liberté* was concerned, this was the beginning of the split – there would be one definition for France's citizens, another for her subjects. Still, the former had by then gotten the jump on the latter on the all-important battlefield of discourse. The language of the French Revolution had been woven into the imperial mission as early as 1798, when Napoleon had swept into Egypt with his pro-tractor-wielding boffins from the Institut d'Égypte, all but declaring the Second Empire the vanguard movement of the twilight decade of the Enlightenment. Napoleon and his Institut had been sent packing in 1801, but the civilising impulse had already taken up residence in the French soul; the impulse would reappear with renewed vigour in Algeria in 1830, and again in the 1850s with the initial forays into the Senegalese mainland. By the 1870s, after Napoleon III had been pounded out of Versailles by the Prussians, and France had been divested of Alsace-Lorraine and much of her dignity, Africa was where the country's new leaders believed that their national honour would be redeemed.

The Third Republic, which was supposed to be transitional but lasted until World War II, was many things, but in the colonies it was a prolonged (and sometimes successful) experiment in expediency: no two cantons were precisely alike, and while Alexis de Tocqueville believed that the colonial administration was a caricature of the metropolitan bureaucracy, he might have also argued that it was an avant-garde parody.[27] The difficulty of exporting values across the ocean and into the bush, where the whip often seemed more useful than the quill, meant that at every turn the French undermined their own *mission civilisatrice*, an ideology intended to reconcile the democratic principles of the Third Republic with the iron authority of empire. Indeed, 'civilisation' was a French concept, promulgated by the French, with its hub in metropolitan France and its spokes stretching out into the colonies. But as the French macheteed their way further into the tropics, the *mission civilisatrice* congealed into something approaching capitalist millenarianism. As an authoritative study of the subject noted, 'French imperial ideology consistently identified civilisation with one principle more than any other: mastery.'[28] Not mastery of Man over Man, necessarily, but of Man over unreason, ignorance, Nature. Driven by the business lobbies and the railway barons who worked the halls of the Quai d'Orsay with vulpine skill, the term *mise en valeur* – which bears many nuances, but is perhaps best translated as 'rational economic development' – became the official standard of the imperial cortege.[29]

By 1895, with the age of conquest on the wane, the new French *idée fixe* was 'constructive exploitation' of the existing colonies.[30] In Dakar, the governor general amalgamated the new super-colony called Afrique occidentale française (AOF), or French West Africa, encompassing territory that was nine times the size of France, and at least as ethnically and linguistically diverse as Western Europe.[31] A vast, epic expression of *mise en valeur*, the super-colony, along with the similar Afrique équatoriale française, or AEF, a second federation which included Oubangui-Chari,[32] was meant to pool resources, build railroads, string telegraph wires, engineer public health works – bureaucracy as salvation, trade as secular Enlightenment-era god.[33] The Third Republic did not, however, treat each colony equally. While the *originaires* of Senegal's Four Communes, the four towns that comprised the oldest of the French properties in Africa, were granted (most of)

319

the rights of French citizens, and while the governor general in Dakar proposed extending citizenship to 'an elite of nature', those who had 'evolved enough' to be worthy of the honour,[34] republican imperialism became more obviously a contradiction in terms – a nation comprised of *citoyens* could not, by definition, possess *sujets*.

Paris, for all its appeal to the deities of Reason, made manifest its own brand of magical thinking. Governors were tasked with breaking 'ancestral habits' and ridding the *cercles*, cantons and provinces of 'barbaric chieftains' who commandeered 'feudal villages'. But there were simply *no such things* as village or canton chiefs. As has already been observed, the Central African bush was ruled by families and clans who found the idea of leaders with open-ended mandates abhorrent. And so, just as they thought they were tightening the knots, republicanism's obdurate rationalists were undoing Central African society.

With the onset of World War I, the ropes were shredded entirely. The establishment of the Force Noire and the conscription of 200 000 African troops, 31 000 of whom lost their lives, filled the countryside with despair. These *tirailleurs*, often forcefully recruited under a quota system, met a different sort of Frenchman to the ones they'd become accustomed to – the sort that lit their cigarettes, called them 'brother', and in the mud and the blood of the trenches of Europe displayed the virtues to which the colonial officers had only paid lip service while whipping their clansmen with rawhide.

But the damage could not be undone: Centrafrique was ruined. In 1928 the legendary French investigative reporter, Albert Londres, wrote of Central Africans what would count as their epitaph:

> Their utter desolation seemed to have no name. They dragged along the railway-line like nostalgic phantoms. Cries and beatings could not bring them back to this world. As they dreamed of their distant Oubangui, they tried to grope their way to the grave.[35]

◆

Tired, sick and despairing as they may have been, at no point in the story did the inhabitants of Central Africa die without a fight. They were not short of inspiration: the long-ago efforts of Toussaint L'Ouverture; the honing and sharpening of *négritude*, the French version of pan-African black consciousness; and in Senegal, the efforts of the socialist politician Blaise Diagne, who'd been the first black African elected to the French Chamber of Deputies in 1914. The French themselves had over two centuries of anti-colonial discourse burbling in the ether, while André Gide's widely discussed *Voyage au Congo*, published in 1927, made the horrors appropriately visceral. In the bush, insurrection followed insurrection, culminating in the Kongo-Wara Rebellion, or the War of the Hoe-Handle, so named for the small battle charms handed out to the followers of the Baya warrior Karinou, who counted as many as 350 000 adherents before his movement was crushed in 1934.

The inter-war years were bitter: as the Third Republic tottered towards its final resting place in Vichy, attitudes towards France's black African subjects hardened. New and rising obsessions with eugenics, social hygiene and increased birthrates (for white citizens, of course) inspired a re-imagined version of Gallic race prejudice – there was less and less conceptual space for an *indigène* in the colonies to *become* French, because France had ceased to be an inclusive catchment for 'civilised' men. Frenchness had narrowed to a pinhole that would have baffled the white settlers of San Domingo who, two centuries earlier, had been encouraged to procreate with the islanders.

Then came World War II. Although the French West African administration chose not to join General de Gaulle and his Free French in resurrecting France's honour, French Equatorial Africa came on side in 1940 – a crucial turning point for de Gaulle's campaign. That same year, Félix Éboué, grandson of slaves from France's South American colony of Guiana, would be appointed the AEF's first black governor general. A firm proponent of *négritude*, Éboué nonetheless stood proud for the singing of *Le Marseillaise*. He could not abide France's permanent defilement by the Nazi scourge and their Vichy collaborators. Thousands of Central African men, including Jean-Bédel Bokassa, willingly signed up for the fight.

Indeed, across the region in the lead-up to the liberation era, it was hard to find a black intellectual advocating a complete split with France. It was understood that the post-war years would bring changes to the Empire[36] – no longer were the *indigènes* of the colonies willing to perform their duties without being granted their rights. As the scholar Frederick Cooper pointed out in his superbly researched study *Citizenship Between Empire and Nation: Remaking France and French Africa, 1945-1960*, Francafrique's revenant possibilities remained nestled between two quotes – the first delivered by an African giant, the second by the general himself.

'It is necessary,' said Mamadou Dia, the socialist firebrand who would become Senegal's first prime minister, 'that the imperialist concept of the nation-state give way definitively to the modern concept of the multinational state.' As if in agreement, in 1946 Charles de Gaulle declared that 'the future of the 110 million men and women who live under our flag is an organisation of federative form.' Dia and his peers – men as disparate as the Senegalese poet-president Léopold Sédar Senghor and Côte d'Ivoire's more conservative founding father Félix Houphouët-Boigny – trusted that federation would be African in nature, an arrangement Senghor described as a 'Negro-African Civilisation'. De Gaulle and his government were less than enthused on the point. Still, there was hope that the future of metropolitan France and her African satellites lay in a conglomeration that tied together local, regional and remote forms of governance in a way that would motivate every French-speaking person towards a functional tomorrow, hand in hand, members of an inviolable French Union.

For his part, Barthélemy Boganda refused to utter in public the word 'independence'. His wife was French, and he did not want to relinquish his status as a French citizen.[37] Nor did he want kinder masters. What he did want was an adoption of Central African common law, most notably communal property rights that trucked more closely with local mores. 'Justice comes before charity,' he reminded the French. 'The whole of Africa demands an end to the slave-trade, in all its myriad forms. Colonisation is slavery's eldest daughter. It has proved inhuman and must be outlawed forever from the vocabulary of the new society.'[38]

The new society. What would it look like? Who would it serve? As Boganda's career careened toward that final fated flight, he was thwarted by the colony's entrenched mining, coffee and business interests. The remnants of the old *compagnies* understood that the nation-state was the surest way to continue the plunder; for them, the chaos of ungovernable statelets wasn't to be avoided but actively encouraged. In a battle for the soul of the region, Boganda pitched a federation he called the Republic of Equatoria, which would act as a permanent replacement for French Equatorial Africa. But he was also thinking bigger: Les États-Unis de l'Afrique Latine, the United States of Latin Africa, a prize cut of the continent's western spine that ran from modern-day Angola in the south, through the two Congos, Cameroon and Gabon, to Central Africa and Chad in the north. It was fantastically ambitious, a concept that contained the added sweetener of providing a Francophone ballast to Anglophone southern Africa (in the late 1950s, it wasn't yet obvious that the racist polices which had built the formidable economic bloc of South Africa and the Federation of Rhodesia and Nyasaland would soon become a national embarrassment for Britain). What's more, the idea was no less unfeasible or unwieldy than independence for each lonely colony. Yet the old colonialists, especially in Gabon, foiled Boganda at every turn. When Oubangui-Chari was granted self-autonomy in 1958, Boganda wondered how 500 newly minted local 'politicians', all of whom were replacing colonial administrators, none of whom had any training or experience, would be able to run the country. He called them *mbounzou veko* – black whites. They rule to this day.

Boganda died on Easter Sunday, the symbolism of which was lost on no one. Months later, his successor David Dacko found himself ratifying an independence constitution in Paris. Dacko was terrified at how quickly it had all unfolded. 'We must take care not to miss our target,' he said timorously, 'and condemn the Central African people to live in fear or misery instead of independence and freedom.'[39] Even Dacko, who dug the strongman ruts that Bokassa would later cement, understood that some form of federation was necessary. He pushed hard for a Central African common market, the same concept that Kalck would insist '[was] the necessary basis for any sound economic policy in Central Africa'.[40] He got nowhere with it.

The disaster was thus foretold. In 1958 Algeria exploded. Indochina exploded. The Congo exploded. CAR's historical context burned off as quickly as the jungle mist, and Emperor Bokassa, who in an alternate reality would have fallen prey to the healthy local penchant for regicide, emerged as the punch line to the joke about African self-rule. Boganda's motto, *zo kwe zo*, was replaced by its Sango inverse: *mbi yeke qi kobe ti yanga ti mbi*.

I search for food for my own mouth.

METAMORPHOSIS

It didn't take much imagination to find in modern-day Bangui the results of this great undoing. But let's consider some numbers. CAR ranks 180th on the 187-country United Nations development index. Total per-capita foreign direct investment net inflow was a wretched $0.23 in 2012, by far the lowest in Africa. Life expectancy at birth was 49.1 years, as compared to 57.3 years in war and Ebola-ravaged Liberia. Gross national income per person had *dipped* since 1980, from $0.963 to $0.722. For every 100 000 live births, the maternal mortality rate was 890, double the rest of sub-Saharan Africa.[41] According to UNICEF, 10 000 of CAR's children were at war. As for how many people had died in the conflict, it seemed our guess was as good as anybody else's.

On our first morning in the country, Rodrigue picked us up from the Hotel Levi, Bangui's second-finest purveyor of rented rooms, and drove us to a residence about five minutes' walk from the river. There, in the darkened *majlis* within his fortified compound, we shook hands with Imam Oumar Kobine Layama. As our eyes adjusted to the gloom, we made out a Barbapapa tablecloth piled with religious texts, the faded upholstery of the lounge suite on which we sat, and nothing else by way of adornment. The imam, thin and hunched with a scruff of beard at his chin, was as spare as his home. He spoke so softly that we had to lean forward to catch his words. Over the past six months, as president of the Communauté Islamique Centrafricaine, the imam had buried 775 members of his community. He was precise on the number of dead, just as he was precise on another number he considered germane to CAR's predicament.

'We have many things for miners here,' he said, after apologising once again for the full body search at the gate. 'There are 488 resources in the ground.' As something of an inter-faith dialogue specialist, the imam had recently bunked with Bangui's archbishop in a house closer to the city, but he was now a resident of this hidden place in the outlying suburb of Ngaragba. Nearby was the site of Bokassa's infamous prison, which meant that not only had Ngaragba been adding fresh atrocities to its ledger, it had known outrageous violence in the past.[42] A few weeks back, the anti-balaka rebel group had come through here looking for Layama, hoping to impart their own views on inter-faith discourse. Even so, the imam wasn't buying the conventional Muslim-versus-Christian take on the conflict. In CAR, he said, the number of the resources versus the number of the dead was the only ratio that counted: the former were pulled from the ground, while the latter were dumped in to fill the void.

'In the history of our country,' the imam said, 'man was not known as a violent guy. But now, the Central African man has become a fighter, has become violent. I am not a politician; I am religious. So I am called on to tell this truth.'

The imam wanted us to know that only 19 per cent of CAR was Muslim, and that this division had never in the past been an issue. Indeed Bokassa, during one of his frequent fallouts with the French, and in order to woo Muammar Gaddafi and his oil money during the tumultuous mid-1970s, had converted to Islam, declaring himself Salah Addin Ahmed Bokassa, a reference to the Muslim Sultan who'd held off Richard the Lionheart and driven the Franks from Jerusalem. In a peculiarly Bokassian version of *cuius regio, eius religio*, those in his regime who'd joined him in facing Mecca were paid 20 million CAR francs for their prostrations.[43] Bokassa would soon drop his minted-in-Tripoli designation, leaving his minions to make their money the old way.

But Bozizé, in order to shore up his own power base, had extended certain promises to the northern Muslim communities, amongst which were guarantees that he would swear in a Muslim prime minister and fund a series of development programmes. Like almost all of Bozizé's promises, he had neglected to follow through. With the steady accretion of resentments that had built up over the course of his rule, CAR had drifted towards a condition that could most easily be described in the language of religious conflict.

'Bozizé made militia units,' said the imam, referring to the shady precursors of the anti-balaka, 'which were the enemy of the Muslims. The Séléka came about in some way to avenge that. But we have no relationship with Séléka, because they are a political party. They do not represent Muslims.'

So what was happening? Left to their own devices, would the newly divided residents of Centrafrique ethnically cleanse each other into oblivion? Were the French, as was implied in their press material, the only thing standing between the locals and another African genocide?

'No, not at all,' insisted the imam. He had met the heads of the French mission, and had informed them that they should leave. 'If you've noticed, the anti-balaka are backed by the French, who also support the Séléka, and this kind of practice fragments the UN resolution that asks them to disarm the fighters by force.'

This, we would learn, was only partly true. The French weren't 'backing' both rebel groups, they were trying to prop up the government and thereby sustain the fiction of a functioning state. But the imam was correct on the point that the French were failing to fulfil their mandate to disarm the rebels, and were instead paying much more attention to the resolution's usual mealy-mouthed 'support for the stabilisation of the security situation'.[44] Which was perhaps why, as far as the imam was concerned, the French were 'photographers, journalists'.

'They don't protect,' he said, 'they just report.'

And when they weren't reporting, he went on, they were digging – mineshafts or graves, to them it was all the same.

◆

It took us several seconds to figure out why, exactly, Lieutenant Colonel Pierre-Yves Sarzaud had abruptly stood to attention and was now rooting around in the pockets of his fatigues. Then it became apparent that we were being treated to a pantomime. The commanding officer showed us his hands, palms up, fingers splayed. 'See?' he said. 'No diamonds. Nothing! Not one!'

Lieutenant Colonel Sarzaud was in charge of communications for the Sangaris mission, a job for which a sense of humour may or may not have been a prerequisite. Either way, the French base, named 'M'Poko' for the airport it adjoined, was the sort of rapidly deployed, hi-tech, heavily armed tented city that had been made famous by the Americans in scores of films (a number of them comedies) about their own foreign missions. 'War is beautiful because it creates new architecture,' wrote the futurist Filippo Tommaso Marinetti in 1936, in praise of Mussolini's Ethiopian campaign. Sangaris appeared to have contributed to the aesthetic with sharp Gallic flair. The communications tent was outfitted with a detailed map of CAR placed on an easel, a jaunty retro prop in this age of the GPS; the patio furniture on which we were gathered was safari-chic canvas, the bottled water Evian. We were, despite ourselves, appropriately charmed.

For the French, Africa had long represented in military terms a *pré carré* – an exclusive zone of interest. Their strategy on the continent, constantly tinkered with by successive inhabitants of the Élysée, was one of 'prevention and projection', which in its application had resulted in small, mobile forces operating from tactical bases that could address flare-ups instantly.[45] If one were to chart Sangaris's fluttering path, it would begin with Operation Boali, which had fulfilled the terms of a series of defence and security agreements signed between Bozizé and Paris when the Central African general had first won power. Named for a town about 100 kilometres northwest of Bangui notable for its

327

waterfalls, Boali was the site of the country's only hydroelectric plant. The operation had maintained a force of 200 at M'Poko in order to 'protect' the main air route out and 'prevent' anything terrible from happening.

And yet terrible things did happen, and Boali was in part responsible. In November 2006, the Union of Democratic Forces for Unity (UFDR), one of the Séléka's founding organisations, had attacked the restive town of Birao, capital of the Vakaga prefecture. Ruthlessly slaved by the Sudanese in the nineteenth century, Vakaga's forests had been all but emptied of people, so much so that it now matched the continent's desert regions for population density, with an average of less than one person per square kilometre. What Vakaga lacked in human capital, however, it made up for in oil. Allegedly aware of this, the French had provided CAR's poorly trained army with air and logistical support, another way of saying that jets and helicopter gunships strafed rebel positions, killing hundreds and forestalling the fall of Vakaga's capital. But only by a year – in 2007 the UFDR would burn Birao to a cinder, forcing Bozizé to sign a series of agreements that would integrate them into CAR's national army, provide their leaders and fighters with amnesty, and pay them off with a million CAR francs apiece.[46] Remaining firmly in character, Bozizé would break all of these promises, and *voilà!* – Séléka, Sango for 'coalition', a mighty gathering of aggrieved groups bearing AK-47s, would arise.

It would have made it simple – or, rather, simpler – were the French the only foreign power meddling in this distant redoubt. But they weren't. Through an operation called Echo Casemate, the Americans had provided support to Bozizé's forces, to say nothing of the fact that Washington was Chadian president Idriss Déby's most committed and enthusiastic backer. And while the *New York Times* had reported that the US had no troops on the ground in CAR, the website TomDispatch, after scouring the Africa Command's own documents, revealed that 'a Lion Forward Team of army personal was indeed sent there'.[47]

Vakaga, it seemed, was CAR's tinderbox. Caught in a vice between Cameroon, Chad, Sudan's Darfur region, and South Sudan, it didn't take a military expert to see that it was a natural conflict zone. The latest conflict to flare up in the region had earned the rather grand designation of the Central African Republic Bush War, and had sucked in the Chadians and the Sudanese – who had long policed the region because CAR couldn't – and the Cameroonians – who had long feared the spread of Islamist-flavoured rebel action in the south. The French had tended to this mess with their various animal-themed operations, to which President François Hollande would append Sangaris in January 2014,[48] but only after receiving a mandate from the UN.[49] It was a limited mandate with many caveats, not all of them fully understood.

'Sure, sure, we have to be very clear about our mission,' Sarzaud said. 'Sangaris is *not* a mission to disarm forces,' he added, as though scolding by proxy the imam for his mistake. 'Phase One' – he raised a single slender finger – 'is to confine the warring groups to their barracks. We say, "go into your barracks with your gun, and do not come out." If he comes out with his gun, we have the right to take that gun.'

But what was the point of leaving armed men to stew in their barracks? And how did Sangaris soldiers differentiate combatants who had *come out from* their barracks from those who had *never entered* their barracks in the first place?

Pah, details. These questions mattered less than the implementation of phases two and three of the mission, which focused on clearing the roads into Cameroon and Chad. Roads that were used to ship goods, weapons and, of course, resources into and out of the country. Which, if you took a moment to think about it, made it seem as if the French really *were* here for no other reason than to secure the smooth passage of commodities.

'No, never,' insisted Sarzaud. 'Our aim is to save people. Nothing else. If you would see the mines, they are broken. You would say it is too much money to produce uranium or other things. It is not possible.'

The French line was simple: they had come to CAR to cut off a likely genocide at the pass, to ensure that the continent would not suffer a repeat Rwanda.

◆

By midweek the weather had turned, and we drove out to the neighbourhood of Gobongo in heavy rain. To our right, the Bas Oubangui was shrouded in mist; to our left was a line of baguette vendors, from whom we purchased two-dozen breadsticks. Our destination was the Bangui Golf Club, the sand traps and fairways, if ever they'd existed, buried for the last six months beneath the sprawl of the Séléka barracks. A MISCA tent stood at the camp's entrance, and a sergeant waved us down a track shaded over by mango trees. Between the trees, on rocks and overturned crates and on their haunches in the mud, sat the men and boys who'd been corralled here by the French.

General Issa Issaka Aubin, the leader of the camp and the ranking Séléka officer in Bangui, greeted us with suspicion; as per Rodrigue's say-so, the baguettes were a necessary icebreaker. The general was a youngish man in a new *jamba* and old Nikes, who came from the north, near Birao. His eyes were deep pools, best avoided. We sat on the veranda of a ruined colonial building – the dining hall of the ancient golf club? – and he told us that where he was born, there was zero infrastructure. 'Why do we have nothing?' he asked. 'That is why I decided to join the UFDR.'

General Aubin, who'd been at war since 2006, had swept into Bangui in March 2013 at the head of a Séléka column, chased François Bozizé out of town, and helped to install the leader of the coalition, Michel Djotodia, in Bozizé's stead. The first Muslim to hold the office (if we don't count Bokassa's brief flirtation with the faith), Djotodia, it was assumed, would quiet the Séléka and end the violence. He had suspended parliament and declared a transitional government, but while regional leaders were attempting to fashion an agreement from the ever-shifting demands, the bloodshed had escalated. In N'Djamena, Chad, in January 2014, after the anti-balaka had been formed to counter the Séléka, Djotodia had resigned. He'd been replaced by Catherine Samba-Panza, former mayor of Bangui, only the third female president in Africa's history.[50] Djotodia, who had retained the support of a handful of Séléka factions, would declare a breakaway state in the north called Dar Al-Kouti, a reference to an Islamic sultanate in Central Africa that had accepted a French protectorate in 1897.

This last detail was important, because it described a reality that could not be washed away by the rhetoric coming out of M'Poko. The country was apparently 'splitting along religious lines', an absurdity given a) how few people lived in it, and b) how small a percentage of those people practised Islam. Were four and a half million human beings really incapable of co-existing in a territory the size of France and Austria combined? CAR's meticulously stoked conflict was now at the point where men like the general were up against anti-balaka factions that were threatening to rid the country of Muslims – a weary, endless stream of ethnic-cleansing invective that was becoming (no surprise) self-fulfilling.

So, after killing many people, after risking his own life over and over again, the general was back roughly where he started: wondering how to get electricity and a flush toilet in his family home. 'Today we have no solutions,' he said. 'You see around you, we have weapons, we have soldiers, if we have a bad mind, we will cause war. We are children of this country, and so we do nothing.'

Yet General Aubin was in agreement with Imam Layama: this was *not* a religious war. He pointed to the men under his command, the handful of officers invited to sit in on the interview and share the breadsticks. 'Musulman, Chrétien, Chrétien, Musulman, Chrétien, Musulman,' he counted. 'It is only the politicians who say this is jihadist or Islamist.'

And what of the French? Fifty-five years after the colonisers first left, they were back, holding the airport, running the show. How, we asked the general, had this been allowed to happen?

Aubin rubbed his face; he was suddenly looking old.

'The French at the airport are just covering what they want from the ground. We don't see any change here. If we were the partner of Great Britain, it would be better than being the partner of France.'

Robert Mugabe of Zimbabwe would no doubt disagree with that statement. A country is, after all, a partnership between its people and its government, not between its government and *another* government. Was the general just tired, or was he being obtuse? There could be no partnerships here. Even the Séléka was dividing itself up into ever-smaller factions, balkanising in a way that mirrored what remained of

331

CAR. The general knew this. He'd felled one president, and hadn't protested at the subsequent felling of the man he'd helped to install, the man who in turn would declare his own breakaway state in the north.

After we shook hands and took our leave, we walked through the smoke and mud and ripped tarpaulin of the camp. We tried to imagine pulling a set of golf clubs through the weeds, the crack of a drive against a Titleist's sweet spot. But there was nothing to suggest that golf had ever been played here. Someone had filled in all the holes – which, we supposed, was what counted as the national sport.

THE CAPITAL OF MARS

If the war had found a home, a point of focus, it was no longer the capital, nor was it the border regions from where diamond miners smuggled out their stones, nor was it the empty horror of Vakaga. Instead, the conflict had burrowed its way into the city of Bambari, 380 kilometres northwest of Bangui – the centre of the centre of Africa. The road out of the capital ran through PK12 and its market, yet another version of the archetypal scene wherein the last of the world's junk was being dumped (at a price) on the world's poorest people. PK12 had only recently been the eye of the storm. The neighbourhood functioned as Bangui's Muslim enclave, and in 2013 it had been the location of a camp that had housed those fleeing the anti-balaka during the worst of the fighting. The UN had claimed that there were at the time some 13 000 Muslims in Bangui, a number since reduced to about 1 000 – numbers that to us seemed ridiculously low on both counts, thus reinforcing the theory that local communities had never really cared about the distinction anyway.[51] But whatever the statistics, PK12, which had once been a polyglot of Muslim traders from across the region, had been wiped of its character and characters. Friends were murdering friends; no one we spoke to knew what the hell had hit them. 'Since I was born, I've never seen this kind of thing in this country,' Zenaba Montre, a PK12 resident who had lost her home and her children, had said to *GlobalPost*. 'How can I stay in the Central African Republic?'[52]

Ethnic cleansing: this is what it looked like. We pulled up at the market's checkpoint, operated by the Séléka, watched over by Sangaris. A young French soldier leaned into the passenger window of our truck. '*Où allez-vous?*' he barked.

Rodrigue handed him our papers. 'Bambari,' he said.

The soldier rolled his eyes. He must have guessed that we were on our way to investigate claims made by the Séléka that during a battle a few weeks before, the French had disarmed Bambari's Muslims and 'allowed' anti-balaka fighters to perpetrate a mini-massacre, killing several hundred in the city's Islamic quarter. While the allegations were difficult to believe, they seemed to be shredding what was left of Sangaris's credibility. We had decided to investigate for ourselves, and after loading up a rented four-by-four with water, diesel and hellishly expensive tinned food from a Lebanese-run *supermarché* in Bangui, we were on our way.

Bambari, we'd been informed, was a vital market town sliced in half by the vital Ouaka River – the city was often paired with the adjective 'vital', we were learning, which perhaps was why so many people had died trying to defend it. The French referred to it as the 'fracture zone', a euphemism that hardly hid its association with the Tenth Parallel, the line of latitude separating the Muslim north from the Christian south that dissected the globe all the way from Africa to the Philippines. Twelve thousand kilometres of war, perfectly articulated by the Ouaka River's heavily fortified bridge. Almost all of PK12's Muslims had been escorted to Bambari by the French over the course of 2014, a fact that from our vantage point looked remarkably like a partitioning of the country along religious lines. Hadn't French president François Hollande, during his visit to Camp M'Poko in February 2014, insisted that Sangaris's primary mission was 'to avoid at any price the partition of the country'?[53] If so, why were PK12's terrified Muslims being shipped out like cattle to bleed in Bambari?

We felt we needed to know – and so we were a bit too quick to agree to Rodrigue's choice of vehicle. We were by no means certain that the Toyota our fixer had secured for us would manage the journey; its hindquarters dragged like a pregnant raccoon's, its tyres seemed to have been gummed by the world's largest toddler. Rodrigue had told us that after the town of Sibut, 188 kilometres from Bangui, the road was 'un-tarred and bad', churned up by the rain and the regular procession of military convoys. But if we hoped to visit Bambari, it was either this or the offer of a lift with an NGO. No NGOs had been forthcoming, and so here we were.

What did the countryside of one of the world's poorest nations look like? A swamp of lassitude stirred only by the blades of a relief helicopter? Not in the least. We saw old sedans crammed full of people and cargo, with more people and cargo piled onto roofs, bonnets and trunks. Every so often, we saw a cart laden with timber, CAR's primary 'official' export, being pushed along the verge by adolescent boys. We saw countless villages nestled up to the asphalt, mud huts and straw roofs and zero evidence of electricity or running water or social services – just families beneath the hardwood trees, subsisting off the land as they had always done, selling whatever surplus they could to the passing traffic.

Road to Sibut, August 2014

And then we saw the checkpoints, 'manned' (a grim misnomer) by the anti-balaka. All government-issued denials regarding the existence of child soldiers were rubbished here, within 45 minutes of leaving Bangui. The children were armed with machetes and World War I-era rifles called *bandaguikwa*, an Ngbandi composite that doubled as a proverb: 'a man's weapon can be the instrument of his own death'.

◆

We did not, of course, make it to Bambari on time; we counted ourselves fortunate to end the day 80 kilometres shy of the objective. The Toyota had breathed its last on a submerged rock, brought low by a third flat tyre. It was close on midnight, Scorpio brilliant in the jungle sky, when we were again dodging potholes and sinkholes and the worst of the mud – Rodrigue had returned from a foray into rebel territory with a pair of motorbikes, riders paid for and included. We rolled through the Grimari checkpoint at 2am, drawing the attention of Sangaris, the night suddenly awash in the halogen spotlights of a patrol. And so, as they had been doing to the natives of Africa for 150 years, the French were now aiming their canons at us.

CAR is big, but there were times when it felt no larger than a village. The commander of the Grimari base, although his men in the gun turrets took longer to follow suit, was disarmingly rueful, unable to hide his amusement – he called through to Bangui to check on our credentials with Colonel Sarzaud's aide, and after being satisfied that we were who our papers said we were, he invited us to get back on the bikes and tail his armoured cars into town. No one would give us a bed – not Médecins Sans Frontières, not UNHCR, 'regrettably' not Sangaris themselves – and our last hope was the Catholic mission, where a priest named Father Stefano Fazzion, rubbing sleep from his eyes, agreed to shelter us.

The mission abutted a church of red brick and corrugated iron. When we awoke the next morning and went foraging for breakfast, we found that mini-villages had popped up between the church and the mission's schoolhouses, with entire communities cooking or cleaning or fixing bicycles on school desks. Numerous NGOs had set up relief tents, and there was a line of bright UNHCR privies near the edge of the bush.

At around 10am we met with Father Fazzion on his porch. He was a prim man who sat with his hands on his knees, his goatee neat and square. We were informed that he had served Grimari's Catholics for all of eight years. For most of his tenure the situation had been peaceful, he said, but in December of 2012 things had changed. That was when Séléka came through town, helping themselves to the assets of the mission, stealing two vehicles. In the surrounding countryside they took cows and goats and set fire to the huts. Father Fazzion remembered that he was surprised by the quality of their equipment – their AK-47s, their rocket launchers and their pick-up trucks. 'Those come from Chad and Sudan,' he said to himself. He knew that there were no car dealerships or gun shops in the north, that there wasn't much of anything. He ran the political numbers, and soon arrived at the conclusion that Bozizé's old backers had deserted him.

Father Fazzion played reluctant host to the Séléka from January through to March of 2013, at which point the rebels received their orders to invade the capital. They returned several months later, but by this time the war had found its larger narrative: the anti-balaka were armed and ready. Just as in PK12, villagers who had lived together in harmony and mutual trust were now killing each other en masse, inflicting social wounds that Father Fazzion knew would take generations to heal. Four thousand six hundred people flooded into the mission, mostly from Grimari but also from Bria and Bakala nearby. Father Fazzion was obliged by his values to assist. His resources were stretched, he could not feed these people, he could only offer the cloak of the church. For the most part, it was enough to keep them alive.

There were, he told us, no Muslims in Grimari any more. The rage in town, the new Central African rage, was focused on Séléka and their foreign weapons. And yet Father Fazzion, as if quoting Imam Layama, insisted that this was not a religious war. 'The worst thing Séléka has done has been to separate people,' he told us. 'Always with the Muslims, with the Muslims, but this is *not* how Centrafrique has worked. For a long time, people did not see themselves divided in this way.' If Father Fazzion had once spent his time explaining the finer points of Catholicism to parishioners who were happily blending Christianity and Islam, he was now telling those selfsame parishioners that Muslims did not deserve to die just because they were Muslim.

The war, Father Fazzion said, was an economic war. 'A war about money and about power,' he said. 'Power and money. Religion came to justify. In the north there is oil, diamonds, gold, uranium. A lot of things.' Today, a Saturday in August 2014, the north belonged to the Séléka rebels and those that supported them. The violence had arisen out of the vested interests in which the independence of Centrafrique had been declared. For more than 50 years, the very idea of governance had run contrary to the *raison d'être* of the state. Chaos was not the *result,* said Father Fazzion, but the *point.*

Despite it all, Father Fazzion was going nowhere. He belonged to the order of Comboni, after the Italian priest Daniel Comboni, who had arrived in Khartoum in 1857 and had fallen in love with Africa. Comboni had set up two missionary institutes over the course of his African career; he was ordained a bishop in 1877 and would be canonised by Pope John Paul II in 2003. '*O Nigrizia o morte!*' he had once written in a letter home. *Either Africa, or death.*[54]

◆

Only such faith as Saint Comboni had would have seen us safely into Bambari later that day, and so it seemed to us, when we limped across the finish line in our patched-up truck, that the mission's grace extended to Jewish boys too. How Rodrigue had mended the tyres we knew not to ask; suffice to say that the last leg of the journey, the home straight of this voyage of discovery that had begun for us almost a decade before, was taken in a condition of complete surrender to unknowable powers. Whatever it was that got us there, Bambari's 'fracture zone', when it finally came into view, was no more than a bridge under which the Ouaka River shimmered in the afternoon sun. Foreign Legionnaires, backed up by the African Union's MISCA troops, scrutinised our papers. Dominated by a deserted red earth square, ringed by shrapnel-adorned, red earth-stained storefronts, Bambari might have passed for the capital of Mars.

Rodrigue had secured us mattresses at the MISCA base, and the truck delivered us into a camp operated by a regiment from Gabon. The commander, Captain Alex Cambot, was a man in his mid-thirties whose ramrod-straight bearing out-soldiered even the French.

'Our orders are to protect the civilians,' he said, gesturing down at the tents that formed the nucleus of the camp. From up at the MISCA headquarters, where we sat on a shaded verandah, we had an unob-structed view of the living conditions of the thousands of Christians who had come here to escape an early death. Like all instances of the type, the refugee camp exuded an air of lethargy and defeat, and we wanted to know from the captain whether he believed that the French had complicated matters in Bambari. More specifically, by disarming Séléka and allegedly giving anti-balaka free rein, were the French responsible for the bloodshed of the previous few months?

Captain Cambot smiled. 'It is difficult to know what happened. Sangaris good, Sangaris bad – only Sangaris can say.'

Well, perhaps. But Rodrigue had arranged an interview with the local Séléka spokesperson, Captain Ahmat Nedjad Ibrahim, who had very definite views on the subject. We met him in Bambari's Muslim quarter, in a dark room in a warren of teetering houses, not more than 10 minutes' walk from the MISCA camp. Captain Ibrahim was a fine-boned 25-year-old in an impressive *djellaba*, and he was exceedingly pleased to see us. He had studied information technology at the university in Bangui, he said, which was where he had learnt to appreciate the importance of the international press.

This intense young man – number three in the Séléka's hierarchy; the organisation's principal intellectual warhead – had been radical-ised the old-fashioned way. His monologue, delivered with an icy calm, was flabbergasting. 'It is for multiple reasons that I decided to join the Séléka,' he told us. 'During Bozizé's time, Muslims' lives were very rebuked. When I completed my studies I was on my way to a party and I was caught by Bozizé's children. They brought me 60 kilometres down the Douala road to a location unknown to me. There were three others like me. They put us in a bag – I did not know the other three. They put us close to a bridge and they started shooting. I was unconscious. Later a woman came and opened the bag and noticed I was the only one not dead. And after that fact I went back to Bangui to join the Séléka in order to have my revenge.'

Captain Ibrahim went north, where he was trained in the art of war. He was, he said, happy to finally be amongst members of the Peul tribe – 'my people', he said. Although the Séléka had habitually been dismissed as 'foreign', manned by Chadians and Sudanese, Ibrahim was not interested in addressing this criticism. *His people*, that was all that mattered. Enormously bright, he had moved up the ranks with ease, serving as Djotodia's de facto deputy defence minister in the months before the Séléka took Bangui, splitting with Djotodia after the latter had shot his way into State House.

But as we moved on to the issue of French complicity in the murder of Bambari's Muslims, Ibrahim's story began listing towards conspiracy, the measured detachment of his delivery lost. 'When we met with Sangaris, we told them, "We want this prefecture to be peaceful,"' he said, his gaze now shifting from us to his laptop. 'And yet they relocated the checkpoint in Grimari so that anti-balaka could come here without bumping them.' Apparently, when Ibrahim and his contingent had been due to meet with an anti-balaka leader named American John, Sangaris had attacked the rebel stronghold, disrupting the meeting. 'They don't want peace in this community,' insisted Ibrahim.

What if they were simply *incapable* of delivering peace? Ibrahim shook his head: in most things, according to him, there was evidence of France's bad faith. He mentioned instances of human flesh-eating, the old CAR cannibal libel re-upped for a new generation. 'In the market, the anti-balaka cooked and ate Muslim flesh,' he told us, 'in front of Sangaris and the television cameras.' This, we would learn, was *partially* true. According to Rodrigue, a lunatic named Mad Dog, claiming anti-balaka affiliations, had snacked on a human femur in front of journalists.[55] However, Mad Dog was now in prison in Bangui, and it was almost impossible to nail down any watertight instances of cannibalism. The label was nonetheless useful – it had been applied to Africans during colonial times, to Bokassa during the imperial era, and now to either the anti-balaka or the Séléka, depending on who was levelling the accusations. That said, there seemed to be no disputing the fact that anti-balaka forces in Bambari were determined to 'cleanse' the city, pushing all Muslims behind the fracture zone.

At the end of the interview, one of Ibrahim's charges brought into the room an AK-47 and a second laptop, the tools of the modern insurgent. Behind us, piled high, were DVDs and CDs and computer parts. On top of the pile there sat a *Commando/Delta Force* double DVD. It was tough not to feel a brief pang of nostalgia for those films, for their easily decipherable simplicity.

And then we were ushered out into the light, for pictures.

◆

On the equator night came on so swiftly it was as if the rebels had figured out how to blow up the sun. Keeping an eye on the plummeting orb, we strolled through red-hued Bambari, down to the bridge, where the men of the Foreign Legion stood sentry. On this side of the Ouaka River, the Séléka; on the far side, the anti-balaka – the story of contemporary CAR in 50 metres.

Our main interlocutor was a Moroccan sergeant, whose name was withheld for reasons soon to be revealed. 'The mission here is to make sure that nobody brings weapons over the bridge,' he told us. He was sweating copiously under the weight of his equipment – knives, guns, a Kevlar vest, more knives, a flashlight, gadgets of no palpable utility. He told us a little about his life in the Foreign Legion, explaining that he was three years into his five-year tour, and that only 18 per cent of Legionnaires renewed their contracts, which he considered a big loss. It was hard work, he said, and nowhere harder than CAR.

'In Afghanistan we have one enemy,' he said, 'the Taliban. Here we have I don't know how many.' Without any prompting, he proceeded to clarify the issue that had haunted Bambari and thus the entire Central African conflict: the issue of disarming the Séléka.

He shook his head wearily. 'We took guns from the Séléka but we did

Ouaka River, Bambari, August 2014

not have time to do the same with the Christians. Then the anti-balaka came from behind our backs and ...' – he made a slashing motion across his throat. 'Now we don't disarm any more. No way. We just try to stop guns coming across the bridge.'

One of the signature events of the conflict, the manoeuvre that had most harmed Sangaris in the eyes of the locals, was according to this Legionnaire a blunder, a mistake. 'They will kill you here because you have an extra mark on your face,' he said. 'One day they will try to kill you, the next day they will smile and they are your friend. It is complicated. So complicated.'

The country, it was obvious, was too broken to be fixed by standing guard over a bridge. The more we looked, the more CAR's story

341

appeared to be just another in the larger tale of a balkanising planet, a refutation of the flat-world theorists who peddled the lie that borders were disappearing. Only a fifth of CAR's population was Muslim, and until very recently they had lived in peace with the Christian majority. Like scar tissue developing over bad wounds, CAR was growing a new set of dividing lines. It was a defining tragedy of the modern world: those who had once lived together would now live apart. In this way, Bambari was not some atavistic hellhole in which a distant and meaningless war played itself out...

It was a perfect representation of a possible global future.

THE WITCH HUNT

It was morning in the MISCA compound, and a light rain muted the sounds coming from the refugee camp at the base of the hill. Captain Cambot greeted us wearing full dress uniform, his beret cinched over his brow. Today was Independence Day in Gabon, and he had prepared a speech for the troops. 'I will say some words to them,' he told us, 'in honour of the special occasion.'

The official tagline of the captain's government was 'Gabon Emergent'; indeed, the country functioned as a sort of anti-CAR, a photonegative. Two nations with interlinked histories and futures – how was it possible that they could be so different? Gabon's capital, Libreville, was mellow, growing, functional. The president, Ali Bongo Ondimba, had recently starred in a *National Geographic* documentary detailing his enormously progressive marine ecology policies; Ali's father, Omar Bongo Ondimba, had started the trend in 2002, with the creation of 13 national parks.

Once, long ago in 1964, in a reverse echo of the military operation that had ripped Bokassa from power in 1979, the French had descended on Gabon to reinstall the hated Léon M'ba, who'd been ousted in a series of popular protests. It was around then that Camp de Gaulle had been established on the outskirts of Libreville, a base that remains garrisoned by French troops to this day. After M'ba died, in 1967, in had come Omar Bongo. Although the elder Bongo's portfolio of high-end properties in France would earn him a place in the Third World Kleptocrat's Hall of Fame, something very interesting would happen during his 41-year tenure – he would affect a subtle yet profound shift in post-colonial power dynamics. Bongo, with his oil and uranium money, would buy himself not only dozens of French chateaux, but French politicians too. He would become a kingmaker; aspirants would fly down from Paris just to kiss his ring. He would make it his business to know everything about everyone who entered the Élysée. As with all great men, there would be a summary statement attributed to him, one that he may or may not have said: 'Gabon without France is like a car with no driver. France without Gabon is like a car with no fuel.'

Papa Bongo would die in 2009, his son Ali would win the next election, and Gabon would *not* assume the mantle of the ideal African state. But there was certainly cause, on this rainy day in Bambari, to celebrate its independence. In the tangled web of relationships that defined Francafrique, Gabon, which still hosted French troops on its home soil, was holding strategy meetings with the Foreign Legion so as to protect Central Africa from itself. Who was the puppet, who the puppet master? It seemed like a question for Albert Camus, or maybe Wole Soyinka.

◆

The grim comedy of the absurd, the meaningless tragedy of the avant-garde – the road back to Bangui provided both. Soon after clearing the Grimari checkpoint, we were flagged down by a man on a bicycle.

He spoke in Sango to Rodrigue. 'This man,' Rodrigue told us, 'is a pastor.' The pastor wanted to warn us that we were about to drive into a big band of anti-balaka, and to say that we must '*please, please*' not mention anything to the French. The anti-balaka had apparently captured a witch from the village of Poumayassé; this witch, they claimed, had killed two men by means of a spell. They had promised the pastor that if Sangaris came to find them, his neck would be next.

Sure enough, as we crested the hill, we made out more than a dozen figures on the road, walking three or four abreast. They were carrying *bandaguikwa* and machetes. We slowed to a stop and saw that there were boys in the group no older than eight. In a ditch on the right side of the truck a man was hogtied to a length of bamboo, his skull staved in, clumps of red earth clinging to his hair. He was not yet dead but dying, breathing into the mud in short shallow gasps.

The gang leader, who appeared to be in his forties, leaned into the truck to shake our hands. A muscled teenager in a tight vest and an impressive array of *gris gris* circled the truck in mock menace. As a collective, the band was pumped, ecstatic, tripping on the thrill of the hunt. The leader, pointing and smiling through yellow teeth, told Rodrigue that they were taking the witch to their own village, where the chief would pronounce on his fate.

Road from Grimari to Poumayassé, August 2014

And thus was delivered our final lesson on morality, logic and the law. How did we save the 'witch'? To inform the French was to condemn the pastor, to get out of the truck was to condemn ourselves. As the Toyota continued on, we mollified each other with platitudes. People were killed for witchcraft in CAR all the time ... Our job was to bag the story and return alive ... What good could we have done with our lungs and two pairs of fists, anyway?

◆

So where to for CAR? By now you've probably guessed. The country will fragment into a confessional, a little Lebanon in the middle of Africa – what the writer Kamal Salibi, quoting John 14:2, called a house of many mansions. In September 2014, the UN would step in to manage the management of the chaos, their 8 000-strong MINUSCA peacekeeping force armed and fortified and itching to keep the peace. Meanwhile, a UN panel of experts would discover that illegal gold and diamond smuggling was continuing to fuel the conflict.[56] No prescriptions from afar would really help CAR, mostly because those from afar would have too many of their own interests to protect.

Which is the perfect place to reiterate a point: like a number of African intellectuals of the time, CAR's founding father, Barthélemy Boganda, had plainly foreseen something when he had pushed for a regional confederation of states linked in some way to France. He knew that Oubangui-Chari was too small, too sparsely populated, too remote to go it alone. There were many reasons that the dream of federation died, and with it any chance of success in the middle of Africa, but the main reason was that the chaos suited the suits. You'd think it would be easier to make money in a regulated environment governed by the rule of law, and yet the deregulators and their henchmen had always known the truth – for those at the front of the queue, extreme disorder was the gateway to extreme wealth.

Perhaps there is still value in the idea of federation. Africa is not a country, but CAR reminded us that it should try to behave like one. The Organisation of African Unity, the African Union's predecessor, declared African borders immutable in the early 1960s. The organisation believed that this would prevent wars, and bring to bear something like a status quo that could be maintained and negotiated around. But in reifying the idea of nation-states at the expense of more flexible multi-national entities, the OAU had consigned large chunks of the continent to perpetual misery. As befitted the Republic of Nowhere, the French were simultaneously holding the country together and partitioning it along religious lines. Just as the OAU had once made holy the borders that had been set in Berlin in 1885, the Tenth Parallel was manifesting before our eyes as a fait accompli.

Why change now, simply because the ghosts in Bangui M'Poko International Airport were whispering 'genocide'?

The man under the green and gold rugby cap does nothing to hide the amused expression on his face. Throughout our interviews and investigations, our comings and goings amongst the stores along the highway, he has been watching, biding his time. Now, it is clear, he wants to talk.

He beckons us over to where he sits, on a concrete slab in the shade beside a tangle of metal donkey carts. His name, he tells us, is Lazarus Musimang. The carts are his; he makes them from scrap metal and sells them to villagers. His brother, he says, owns this strip mall – the one where the Bangladeshis and Mi Zheng rent stores.

'Ten, fifteen years ago,' he says, 'people started coming from outside, renting our shops. If us blacks manage the shops, people won't buy – they say, no, he is too expensive. But they will shop from the foreigners. In this way, some of our people are angered by the Chinese and the Bangli.'

Lazarus looks a decade older than his 42 years. He suffers from diabetes and a host of attendant infirmities; he struggles with his breathing as he talks.

In 2009, he goes on, in the aftermath of the xenophobic violence that wracked South Africa, leaving dozens dead in a spate of mob riots targeting foreigners, a truck rolled through the streets of Ganyesa. There were speakers in the bed, and men growled into a microphone. 'They say that there will be fire,' Lazarus recalls. 'They say that the Bangli and the Chinese must go.'

The initiative was funded, according to Lazarus, by a 'concerned group' of connected black businessmen who did not approve of the presence of outsiders. The group's problem, in a word, was the foreigners' 'experience' – their ability to offer lower prices and still turn a profit. So further meetings were held, where the central item on the agenda was a question: 'How can we set fire to their tuckshops?' The question then filtered down to the village's unemployed youth, whose answer was tacitly sanctioned. 'These young black guys, every day they started breaking in, smashing the Bangli, smashing the Chinese, wanting money, wanting smokes.'

In response, adds Lazarus, his brother and himself and another eight local black entrepreneurs created a group to safeguard the foreigners, who in their view were such efficient shopkeepers that running them out of town would destroy the local economy.

With the above in mind – and eager to see the documented evidence that Lazarus has promised – we pile into his pick-up, and hammer up the dirt roads that wind into the depths of the village. A series of sharp turns leads us to the patchwork of concrete and brick structures that make up his home. Sinewy mongrels lope about; Lazarus has recently slaughtered a donkey, and the meat lies drying on tree branches, all white ribs and red flesh, soon to be dog food.

He disappears into his house and returns with a plastic folder containing a single sheet of paper. Typed out, in Setswana, it is a circular from the 'Tshwaraganang Business Council'. Lazarus translates for us: 'This forum is created to protect small businesses in Ganyesa from people who come from outside.'

We ask Lazarus if he would mind reading it again, and the second time obviates the injustice – the brutal fact that the document should at least have pointed the Ganyesa police in the direction of its suspects.

Lazarus removes his reading glasses. 'You see,' he says, 'our side is weak in this village, because the so-called "concerned group" are using the tribal council. They have the real influence, and they have gotten rich from government tenders.'

A box of Peter Stuyvesants is passed round. 'You can interview everyone in Ganyesa,' says Lazarus, 'and they know very well. If it was an electrical fire, the Chinese would have made a plan. No, the young guys came and put some petrol, and that was that.'

Minutes later, rattling our way back to the strip mall, Lazarus forecasts the future of the village, and his place in it. He points out a small property that he hopes to develop, should his battles with the tribal council go his way.

Fifteen paces away from this property lies the circle of black earth that was once Ganyesa Fruit and Vegetable. While its circumference shrinks by the day, its mystery is unlocked – all that money lining all those pockets. The ground zero of Ganyesa's problems, and of its solutions too.

'Yes,' Lazarus says, tracing the outline of a shop with the smoke from his cigarette. 'I will take one Bangli from my brother, and I will put him there.'

The fire was set deliberately. Of this we are certain. In Lazarus's parting *words, we are reminded that in Ganyesa – and places like it across Africa – the stranger's body is a commodity. And when the value of that commodity is contested, when it does not serve as a source of capital to those who hold the most influence, violence is a likely recourse.*

Ganyesa is at war with itself over the strangers in its midst. The village represents at least one possible outcome to Chinese commerce on the continent: here, we have learnt that the action of spurring a local economy can sometimes be resented, reviled. Chen, and the three people who were murdered alongside him, were at the mercy of the powerful in their chosen African home. They existed in the gulf between official Africa and official China, and their only protection came from a friendship with 13 kindhearted Bangladeshis. It is clear to us now why the Ganyesa police did not want to assist us – because solving this crime is unnecessary. The reason the law can ignore the Chinese shopkeepers, the Bangladeshis, the Pakistanis, is that such people do not yet exist. They are people caught in the process of becoming, and as the South African writer Njabulo Ndebele once observed, for them there can be no peace.

Back on the road to Johannesburg, in the old man's Mercedes, the tang of his aftershave held in the leather, we still have not spoken. We are reminded, as much by the car as by anything, of the essential condition of the immigrant – in leaving Fuqing, in choosing to make a new life in Africa, Chen and Mi Zheng did what hundreds of millions have done since the dawn of time: they reached for something better.

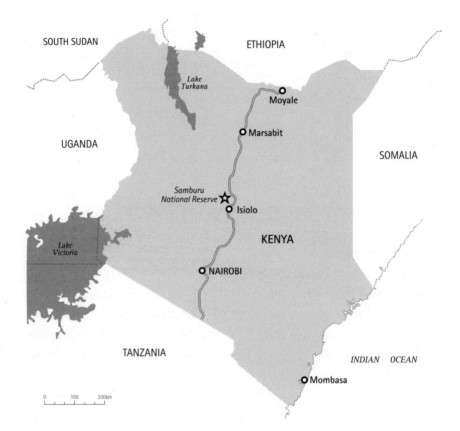

TEN

INSIDE, OUT

'Omnia mutantur, nihil interit.' – Ovid, *Metamorphoses*

A story from the road.

Or, again, from a road: 505 kilometres of first-rate tar that would connect Isiolo in central Kenya to Moyale in the north. The stretch, which cut through the acacias and doum palms of the lava plains, was a new link on the Trans-African Highway that would soon make good on the long-deferred dream of 'Cape Town to Cairo'. Beyond Moyale and the Ethiopian border, the stretch was destined to tack on to another critical link, the 197-kilometre run from Hawassa to Ageremariam, which would in turn complete the Addis Ababa-Nairobi-Mombasa corridor. We could see the road as we circled the airstrip of the Samburu National Reserve, the whine of the Bombardier's engines chasing off a herd of gerenuk. That the road was having a transformative impact on how those buck migrated was, in the context of this story, a detail both unimportant and supremely important. It's that sort of story, and that sort of road.

This road, unlike the Goma-Bukavu road that we tried to travel in the DRC, was not a riddle but a certainty. Indeed, it was the most certain thing in the region, so much so that it rendered everything else unreal by comparison. The road was the world coming at the ancient

351

lava plains at warp speed, bringing with it a future in which there was little room for negotiation.

The eleventh-hour negotiator, then, was a young man named David Daballen, a tall Samburu who worked as chief understudy to the self-styled saviour of the region's elephants, the famous British conservationist Iain Douglas-Hamilton. On our third day in the reserve, after we'd been shown as many dead elephants as live ones, we sat in the dust under an acacia tree talking to a Turkana tribesman wearing a lime-green sarong and a T-shirt that read 'Global Week of Action Against Gun Violence'. His name was Francis Lorot, and he was 32 – about the same age as David. 'These are criminals that the community doesn't want,' he said, when we asked him whether he could introduce us to a poacher. 'You cannot speak to them, they are all armed, wild and rough. They can easily kill you.'

In villages like this across the region, he went on, men with no experience in elephant killing could earn a $55 sign-up fee, the equivalent of a labourer's monthly salary. The fee was exclusive of meals and bullets, while the ivory split was dependent on the size of the tusks. 'The poachers are living out in the bush in gangs of between two and 10,' Lorot said. 'Elephants can take pain, sometimes up to 40 bullets before she dies. The killers are scared to death, because they are not experts. An expert can kill with one bullet.' When an elephant was killed, we were told, a call was put through via cellphone (not for nothing was Kenya's mobile penetration the pride of Africa) to a middleman in Archer's Post, Isiolo or Wamba. The middleman, always a local, would hire a taxi for the day and direct it to the point on the highway closest to the kill. Only the tusks would be packed into the taxi, 'no meat'. After enough tusks had been accumulated in his secret warehouse, the middleman would get ready to make his move. 'Then they're taken to the Chinese, or to Nairobi.'

The triangulation of climate change, ever-shrinking habitats and the increasing trade in wildlife has caught much of Africa's natural world in a death grip from which there is no clear escape. In our travels across the continent, we encountered landscapes so utterly degraded that they were as awe-inspiring as the mists of Kilimanjaro, or the saltpans of the Kalahari. We visited regions that were as remote as any on Earth, and yet nowhere struck us as untouched. Among even the most stirring grace notes of what we called 'nature', we detected the dissonance of the human hand. Sometimes, the hand came from afar – in the slow, steady push of greenbelts back into the dust of the desert on account of a world that had warmed one degree centigrade in the last century, and would perhaps warm as much as three in the next. And sometimes, the hand came from close by.

We left the Turkana village with David at the wheel of a 'Save the Elephants' Landcruiser. Within minutes, he'd pulled off the track to inspect trees that in his words had been 'burnt alive'. And it was true – the land was desiccated, the stumps black. The villagers, he told us, had forgotten their natural heritage, which meant they had forgotten how to fell trees in a sustainable way. Part of David's job was to show them the way home.

If these economies, which were only now powering up, were to follow a Western timeline of development, discussions about conserving energy and greening the environment would be about a century away. And while Africans were certainly playing a role in sharpening the debate about fairness and responsibility at international climate conferences (stand up and take a bow, Lumumba), at home there was little to be said.

Why, we were compelled to ask ourselves, should Africans give a damn whether outsiders grumbled every time an elephant was slaughtered to make an accent table for a Shanghai condo? After all, if Africa taught anything, it taught that the price of growth was death. If that meant better healthcare, higher pay, faster commutes, longer lives, and rump steak for dinner, was there even a moral case to be made for 'saving' the environment?

◆

For David Daballen, this wasn't a question – which is why we end the book with him. Of all the people we'd met, of the some 600 interviews we'd conducted across 18 countries, David *lived* Africa's twenty-first century binaries to an almost impossible extent. After leaving the Turkana village we sat with him at the nearby Samburu Lodge, drinking sundowners beside an enclosure where seven fat crocodiles were snapping goat femurs between their teeth. Behind us, a ring of sunburnt pilgrims listened to a bald American equate Jesus' agony on the cross with the plight of Samburu's elephants. The sermon reminded us that safaris were where outsiders came to look for something authentic, something that animated their faith in a fresh and visceral way.

David and his people were not, of course, on safari – they'd been tethered to this land for too many generations to count. He grew up, he told us, as a herder in a large family that roamed the plains near the town of Marsabit. In those days, the region's fauna was for David not an asset but a threat – lion would hunt his cattle, leopard would take his goats. Still, two of his brothers had become game rangers with local safari outfits, and they'd encouraged him to do the same. During his training with the Kenyan Wildlife Service, David saw a Landcruiser emblazoned with the 'Save the Elephants' logo. Pachyderms being something of a personal obsession, he won himself an internship with the company, which turned into a second internship, which turned into a fulltime position as camp manager. He would complete his education with a highly prized degree from a college in the United States, a qualification underwritten by the Wildlife Conservation Network.

At which point he sensed that he was witnessing a new alchemy, that global and local were binding into some preordained state.

'I would say that the most profound moment in my life, the one I remember most, was my circumcision ritual,' David told us. When he was 17, he sat in a chair in a circle of naked boys as an old man with a blade came around to sever all the foreskins. 'We could not blink or show pain,' said David, sipping his drink and shaking his head in wonder. 'We were taken to a hut to recover, no moving for eight days. After that, we emerged as men.' His wife had also been circumcised, he told us, adding that for the Samburu the endless speechifying from Western NGOs about 'female genital mutilation' was as much of a cultural insult as it was a nuisance. But then David *worked* for a Western NGO, and his hopes for Samburu were almost entirely in line with those of Iain

Douglas-Hamilton – which is to say that they did not square with his tribesmen in the bush who were aiming AK-47s at tuskers.

David's biography translated as epiphany, because in relating to us the complexities of his life, he had explained to us what we didn't know we'd been trying to do with our stacks of spiral-bound notebooks and our hundreds of thousands of words of transcribed text. We were doing what millions of Africans were trying to do: conjoining the strands of history with the present's crackling livewire, so that they could come to some understanding of the future.

'It's like with the road,' said David, as the last of the crocodiles slithered down the embankment and into the waters of the Ewaso Nyiro. 'People ask, is it good or is it bad? But it's not one thing. How can it be?'

◆

We never did find the word, the answer to the question of Africa's *what?* Instead, we found many words, and we strung them together to make this book. Somehow – and not for lack of trying – we came to the conclusion that you can't slap a bumper sticker on a billion-plus people. In Namibia, for instance, where the population was small enough and stable enough to serve as a test case for any number of ecstatic pronouncements, the middle class was a phenomenon that seemed to dissolve in the desert sands. In the DRC, where the endemic rent seeking and over a century's worth of selfish prospecting should have spelt more of the same, there was a massive gold mine in the northeast that appeared (really and truly) to be spreading the wealth. And in Ethiopia, where the world's most skilled agriculturalists were proposing an answer to the planet's looming food crisis, the global market system was as complicit as the quasi-socialist Ethiopian government in maintaining the status quo.

At a certain point, we had to admit to ourselves that the only honest way to digest what we'd seen and researched was to allow it to marinate in its complexities. Even South Sudan, where the oppositional forces seemed so stark, proved that the prevailing hue was grey. Nothing was one thing. How could it be?

The binaries and paradoxes that had at first nonplussed us were now the baseline hum of our everyday experience. Africa's greatest strengths – her ethnic diversity, growing population, vast landmass, boundless commodities – had also proved her greatest weaknesses. While the arbitrary borders of 1885 needed to vaporise in order for the continent to prosper, African countries needed to stay intact in order to develop.

Roads and borders, borders and roads. Sometimes the roads ferried people and goods, and sometimes they didn't. Sometimes the borders stopped people and goods from being ferried, and sometimes they didn't. In the South African village of Ganyesa, we bore witness to the rules of some future borderless world, where people marked their territory with fire. In CAR, we watched the Tenth Parallel become manifest *literally* before our eyes, as Christian was separated from Muslim in a balkanisation that echoed across the developing world.

The benefit of all this flux was a propulsive energy that allowed strivers like Boikanyo Mpho in Botswana to build a critical piece of his country's infrastructure strictly by the book; it provided a few video-tape merchants in Nollywood with the impetus to build a cultural juggernaut.

The flipside, of course, was a slow creeping chaos that permeated every facet of every life, a chaos that provided its own set of opportunities. This chaos was not new in Africa and it was not new globally, but what *did* seem new was how it limned the disparities between the outrageously rich and the pathetically poor, how it provided the conditions for a new gilded age in which the 80 richest people in Africa possessed the same wealth as the bottom 60 per cent.[1]

So no, we did not find the word.

But what we did find, amid the noise of all those binaries, was an Africa returning to herself. The successive horrors of slavery, colonial exploitation and war had wiped the lands of their people. Now, they were coming back. Two billion souls, maybe more, would by the middle of the century call the continent home. The sheer enormity of their requirements would force another series of wholesale realignments, of which those we had witnessed were the precursors, the dry runs.

356

Like the current of some vast unnamed ocean, we felt the pull of the coming two billion wherever we went. If there was a name for such a sensation, it was destiny.

◆

The elephant bull was enormous. 'This is the only place on the planet where you can get this close,' said David. 'Anywhere else, they will kill you. But don't worry, I know him.'

Mohembo, Botswana, February 2011

B1 south from Keetmanshoop, Namibia, December 2006

It was that hint of a smile at the edges of David's eyes that got us – we were going to sit back in the open Landie and pretend to be calm, pretend to be professional, pretend to be unimpressed. The thick secretion from the ducts on either side of the elephant's head, which he was now dipping and raising in preparation for a mock charge, was only one of the signs that he was in musth. The others were his engorged and dripping penis, his unmatchable scent of maleness. 'There are no bulls in the area to challenge him,' David added. 'So he is challenging us.' As we were noting this down, David revved the engine.

Two and a half years later, we would agree that that moment was the most frightened we had been on the book. It was a good frightened, a natural frightened. The road, David's road, was about seven kilometres to the west of us. We had, in our confrontation with the bull, forgotten that it existed.

NOTES

CHAPTER ONE: OUTSIDE, IN

1 According to *The Economist*, which had analysed and compared the global GDP data for the first decade of the twenty-first century, the Big Six in terms of growth, in order, were Angola (11.1 per cent), Nigeria (8.9 per cent), Ethiopia (8.4 per cent), Chad (7.9 per cent), Mozambique (7.9 per cent), and Rwanda (7.6 per cent). We'll interrogate African number crunching in more detail in Chapter 2, but suffice to say that no matter how one ran the numbers, sub-Saharan countries would make up not less than half of the world's top ten for the entire duration of our research. As for Africans comprising a fourth of the world's refugees, while the numbers fluctuated from conflict to conflict, 2011 'was a record year for forced displacement across borders' according to the United Nations Refugee Agency, with humanitarian crises flaring in Côte d'Ivoire, Libya, Somalia and Sudan. By mid-2014, global forced displacement would top 50 million for the first time since World War II, with the DRC, CAR and South Sudan serving as major contributors.

2 The rise in income per capita was a factor that was getting many Africa watchers excited, from global development institutions to fast food franchisees. But, as we would later discover, what very few Africa wonks were seriously acknowledging was that as per the World Food Programme, over a quarter of the continent's people were going to bed hungry every night – the highest prevalence anywhere in the world.

3 'The Middle of the Pyramid: Dynamics of the Middle Class in Africa', Mthuli Ncube, Charles Leyeka Lufumpa & Steve Kayizzi-Mugerwa (Africa Development Bank, 2011), p 4.

4 The United Nations, in the 2014 'special agricultural edition' of its online magazine *Africa Renewal*, presented the dilemma as a masterful piece of understatement: 'Africa could exploit several opportunities to overcome existing challenges facing agribusiness. First, despite possessing the world's largest reservoir of unused arable land, about 60%, Africa has the lowest agricultural productivity, amounting to approximately 10% of global agricultural output.' Full text available here: http://www.un.org/africarenewal/magazine/special-edition-agriculture-2014/we-need-more-agribusiness-africa

5 In a report entitled 'Land and Environmental Degradation and Desertification in Africa', the Food and Agriculture Organisation of the United Nations (FAO) claimed that '[over] 319 million hectares of Africa are vulnerable to desertification hazards due to sand movement. An FAO/UNEP assessment of land degradation in Africa suggests that large areas of countries north of the equator suffer from serious desertification problems. For example, the desert is said to be moving at an annual rate of 5 km in the semi-arid areas of West Africa.' The report is available at: http://www.fao.org/docrep/x5318e/x5318e00.htm#Contents

6 While elephant and rhinoceros poaching gets all the press, Africa's wildlife suffers from numerous threats, including habitat encroachment and the bushmeat trade. According to a BBC report by Mark Jones, programmes and fundraising director of Care for the Wild International, almost 2.5 million tons of bushmeat is annually hunted and consumed in CAR alone. The Bushmeat Crisis Task Force told the BBC that the hunting of and trade in bushmeat

represents 'the most significant immediate threat to the future of wildlife in Africa'.

7 Without getting into a lengthy Malthusian debate regarding the accuracy of population growth projections, the United Nations Department of Economic and Social Affairs Population Division's *World Population Prospects: The 2010 Revision CD-ROM Edition*, put the population of sub-Saharan Africa at 2 074 446 000 by 2050, and 3 815 646 000 by the end of the century. By then, the entire continent will apparently be home to 4 184 577 000 people.

8 This figure is emblazoned on the cover page of the *2013 Ibrahim Forum Facts & Figures* booklet, subtitled *Africa Ahead: The Next 50 Years*. Talk shops, think-tanks and policymakers love such papers, partly because they cough up some truly PowerPoint worthy stats. But Mo Ibrahim, a Sudanese/British cell phone billionaire, also started an initiative called the Mo Ibrahim Prize, which annually awards the worthiest African leader with $5 million dollars. More often than not the money goes unawarded, but in 2015, for the first time in five years, a winner *was* announced: the outgoing Namibian president Hifikepunye Pohamba.

9 All figures from *2013 Ibrahim Forum Facts & Figures – Africa Ahead: The Next 50 Years* (Addis Ababa, 2013).

10 We'll likely end up boring you with our circumspection, but Angola's GDP figures must be taken with a pinch of salt. Nonetheless, they come courtesy of the International Monetary Fund, and are therefore branded with official approval. It is also worth mentioning here that the IMF insisted Angola would generate $142 billion in 2015, representing the tail end of the world's oil boom.

11 Here's the odd thing about all the recent euphoria over Africa's growth figures: its proponents almost never take into account the fact that they represent the continent's *second* big boom. The first came during the 1960s, when the majority of countries on the continent were either winning, or had already won, independence. Throughout this book, reference will be made to the devastating impact of the 1970s – the oil crisis; the commodities price freefall; disastrous governance practices – on that original post-independence boom.

CHAPTER TWO: NAMIBIA

1 Properly called Tianshi Group, Tiens and its traditional Chinese medicine and health-care products are only one element in the conglomerate's business dealings, which include real estate development, education, logistics and 'cultural exchanges', amongst others. A perusal of its businesses suggests a company almost Enron-like in its interests. There is no word on its annual revenue or its valuation, nor is it listed on exchanges in China or elsewhere, although its founder, Li Jinyuan, was ranked in the 'Top 30' of the 2013 'CCTV China Economic Person of the Year' awards.

2 According to United States government statistics, the St Louis metropolitan area posted a GDP of $13.6 billion in 2012; according to the World Bank, Namibia's GDP was $13.07 billion in 2012.

3 The Gini coefficient is the measure by which wealth is distributed within a country (a score of zero represents even distribution, while a score of one, or 100 per cent, would mean that the rich hold all the wealth). As per World Bank figures, Namibia has been hovering for years around the 60 per cent mark, making it one of the most unequal countries on earth. As a means of balancing the narrative from GDP data, Gini coefficients are routinely cited when discussing emergent African economies.

4 During his 2013 State of the Union address, President Pohamba tub-thumped the need for decent statistical information, regardless of how gruesome the results. 'Last week,' he said, 'I launched the Basic Report of the 2011 Census, which contains statistics on fertility, mortality, housing, migration patterns, employment and industrial developments in the country. It will serve as a basis for all other major national surveys over the next ten years. According

to the Census results, [the] unemployment situation in the country now stands at 37 per cent.' Later in this chapter, we touch on a flap regarding African statistics that became very nasty indeed.

5 The Nigerian art critic and curator Okwui Enwezor, writing the introduction for architect Rem Koolhaas's *Under Siege: Four African Cities, Freetown, Johannesburg, Kinshasa, Lagos*, neatly summed up this world view when he wrote, '[N]ew types of relations and exchanges, development and subsistence, forms of solidarity and resistance are produced. On different levels, they reflect the expansion of the so-called informal economy, with its small traders, black markets, recycling, and all the numerous forms of urban survival which emerge as radical restructurings of the organisational forms of economic activity. With unemployment and underemployment rates of 70 per cent the norm for most African cities, the ways in which income is generated require constant provisionality and innovation. And it is in the polymorphous and apparently chaotic logic of the postcolonial city that we may find the signs and new codes of expression of new urban identities in formation.'

6 'Informal Employment in Namibia 2008' (International Labour Office, 2011), by Debbie Budlender, p 25. Available here: http://www.ilo.org/wcmsp5/groups/public/---dgreports/---stat/documents/publication/wcms_166605.pdf.

7 Simeon would no doubt have been alarmed at how tersely Tiens would ditch its business interests in the United States and Canada in December 2011. A note posted on the company website read (all English idiosyncrasies courtesy Tiens): 'Dear Value Customers: I regret to announce that Tianshi Head Office decided to close down the business in the United States and Canada. We will cease operation on January 31. Please bring any pending issue and unsolved problems you can clarify before this date. We will be no longer holding any responsibilities after the closure. Sorry for the inconveniences.' Source: 'Tiens Closing Down US and Canadian MLM Operations', 30 January 2012, businessforhome.org.

8 In the blurb for their article in the *Harvard Business Review* entitled 'A Note on Direct Selling in Developing Economies' (January 2010), Michael Chu and Joel Segre present the following: 'Informal and formal direct selling play a particularly important role in developing countries characterised by markets with limited retail sectors. This note explores the practice of direct selling for the company, the sales person and the consumer, as well as the potential of direct selling as a means of reaching the base of the pyramid for both commercial and social purposes.' Full text available for purchase here: http://hbr.org/product/A-Note-on-Direct-Selling-/an/310068-PDF-ENG.

9 According to a McKinsey Global Institute report that we carried with us on the trip, 40 per cent of Africans lived in cities by 2010, up from 28 per cent in 1980. 'And as more Africans move from farmwork to urban jobs,' noted the report, 'their incomes are rising.' Source: 'Lions on the Move: The Progress and Potential of African Economies' (McKinsey Global Institute, 2010), p 3.

10 If there is a classic example of the speech that bids farewell to the West and its newfound problems, while embracing China and its newfound global economic helmsmanship, it must be the one late Ethiopian president Meles Zenawi gave during the inauguration of the new African Union headquarters in Addis Ababa, in January 2012. Coded into the speech, which will be dealt with in more detail in the Ethiopia chapter, were numerous slights against the West, which had funded the old AU headquarters, as well as many hosannas to the Chinese, who had built the new.

11 As per a *Daily NK* report dated 21 June 2010, North Korea, in a bid to generate some foreign exchange earnings, had at the time built almost $160 million worth of projects in Africa through an outfit called the Mansudae Overseas Project Group of Companies. At $49 million, the Namibian presidential palace was by far the largest, and in all, Namibia had spent $66 million with Mansudae before the relationship soured. The figure of $70 million

probably refers to the overall amount that the Namibian government paid Mansudae over the course of their dealings.

12 By the time we found ourselves in Namibia, several major reports had appeared on Sam Pa and 88 Queensway in the international press; in 2011, when Chinese 'Yellow Peril' rhetoric was at its highest pitch, Pa seemed to exemplify for the West exactly how the Chinese operated in Africa. We'll encounter Pa again in the Zimbabwe chapter, but suffice to say for now that his real name is Xu Jinghua, that he flies around Africa in one of CIF's big commercial jets, and that he controls the group through a woman named Veronica Fung, who holds 70 per cent of a core company called Newbright. CIF's great asset is its value as a go-between from Angola's state-owned oil company Sonangol to the Chinese state-owned oil company Sinopec. Pa actually served as the main-ish character in Tom Burgis's superbly reported *The Looting Machine: Warlords, Tycoons, Smugglers and the Systematic Theft of Africa's Wealth* (William Collins, 2015), in which we learned that while Pa didn't have de facto links with Beijing power, his *guanxi* – his influence, his pull – was strong. But then in October 2015, Sam Pa was swept up in President Xi Jinping's anti-corruption dragnet, and placed under investigation for 'suspected serious disciplinary offenses'. Clearly Beijing had run out of patience with the notorious Pa, and as far as anyone knows he is currently languishing in detention courtesy of the ruling party.

13 *The Radical Middle Class: Populist Democracy and the Question of Capitalism in Progressive Era Portland, Oregon*, Robert D Johnston (Princeton University Press, 2003), p 1.

14 'Africa is becoming the new China and India', *Newsweek*, 18 February 2010.

15 'Africa Rising: The Hopeful Continent', *The Economist*, 3 December 2011.

16 'The Middle of the Pyramid: Dynamics of the Middle Class in Africa', Mthuli Ncube, Charles Leyeka Lufumpa and Steve Kayizzi-Mugerwa (Africa Development Bank, 2011), p 1.

17 In fact, there's evidence that the opposite might be true. According to an Afrobarometer survey, discussed at length later in this section, '[L]ived poverty does not appear to be a major hindrance to political participation. In fact, the continent's poorest citizens tend to be more active participants in political and civic affairs than their better off counterparts.' Source: 'After a Decade of Growth in Africa, Little Change in Poverty at the Grassroots', Boniface Dulani, Robert Mattes and Carolyn Logan (Afrobarometer, 2013), p 15.

18 Ibid, p 2.

19 Ibid, p 4.

20 Most notable among the detractors is the economist Duncan Clarke, CEO of the consultancy firm Global Pacific & Partners, and the author of the sobering *Africa's Future: Darkness to Destiny* (Profile Books, 2012). Clarke would perhaps be more widely read were his prose less baroque, but his point was chillingly succinct in a book extract that appeared in South Africa's *Business Day* on 8 August 2012: 'Images of the "rising middle class" mesmerise the corporate world and distort economic visions of the future. Some seek hope for growth in latecomer mobile telephony technology diffusion across Africa – an idea mooted for "transforming the continent" – which is akin to the "economics of wishful thinking" and a distraction from fundamental matters: unlocking natural capital and enhancing productive wealth accumulation. Such "analysts" place the commercial cart ahead of the economic horse.'

21 The briefs were titled 'After a Decade of Growth in Africa, Little Change in Poverty at the Grassroots' and 'Africa Rising? Popular Dissatisfaction with Economic Management Despite a Decade of Growth'.

22 'After a Decade of Growth in Africa, Little Change in Poverty at the Grassroots', Boniface Dulani, Robert Mattes and Carolyn Logan (Afrobarometer, 2013), p 1. Full text available here: http://www.afrobarometer.org/files/documents/policy_brief/ab_r5_policybriefno1.pdf.

23 In an article published in the South African press in September 2013 ('Stats SA chief denies lobbying against Canadian academic', *Business Day*), it was revealed

that South Africa's chief statistician, Pali Lehohla, appeared to take Morten Jerven's book personally, calling it 'a very sad piece of work'. While acknowledging that it was peer reviewed, Lehohla suggested that Jerven's peers weren't Africans, but outsiders with a similar agenda: to keep Africa down. Although conceding to 'problems with African statistics', he felt that Jerven's research was both second-hand and shoddy. Read from a distance, it seemed that Lehohla objected primarily to the tone of Jerven's work, and to the fact that he wasn't an African working in Africa. Lehohla decried those 'who wanted to create a pitiful image of Africa without conducting in-country research,' adding, 'Africa can do with help, but certainly only original research and not donated research.'

The countervailing view was provided in an article written by *The Globe and Mail's* Africa hand Geoffrey York, in our opinion the finest foreign correspondent working on the continent today, who noted that Jerven was 'manhandled' and thrown out of the statistics office of at least one East African country during the course of his research. Regardless of how controversial Jerven's work may have been, York stated that African statisticians were taking notice, and that reforms were in the offing. Wrote York: 'Even his sharpest critics may eventually be willing to back down. *The Globe and Mail* has learned that a group of leading African statisticians, including Mr Lehohla, has agreed to a private meeting with Prof Jerven early next year in Botswana – and both sides seem ready to resolve their battle.' ('BC professor ruffles feathers by spotlighting Africa's data problems', *The Globe and Mail*, 13 November 2013).

24 '2013 Ibrahim Forum Facts & Figures, Africa Ahead: The Next 50 Years' (Mo Ibrahim Foundation, 2013), p 44.

25 The Lived Poverty Index (LPI) is Afrobarometer's stated contribution to the ongoing debate regarding poverty in Africa. It is defined as: '[An] experiential measure that consists of a series of survey questions that measure how frequently people actually go without basic necessities during the course of a year. It measures a portion of the central core of the concept of poverty that is not well captured by existing measures, and thus offers an important complement to official statistics on poverty and development. Because people are the best judges of their own interests, respondents are best placed to tell us about their quality of life, though they might not be able to do it with a great deal of precision. If Amartya Sen is right and the value of one's standard of living lies in the living itself, an experiential measure of shortages of the basic necessities of life takes us directly to the central core of what the concept of poverty is all about.' Dulani, Mattes, Logan, 'After a Decade of Growth in Africa, Little Change in Poverty at the Grassroots', Boniface Dulani, Robert Mattes and Carolyn Logan, p 3.

26 Ibid, p 14.

27 *Africa's Future: Darkness to Destiny: How the Past is Shaping Africa's Economic Future*, Duncan Clarke (Profile Books, 2012).

28 At the time, much of the economic discussion in Namibia revolved around the so-called NDP 3 programme, the national development plan that set the economic agenda by instituting a series of goals. As we'll see in the Botswana chapter, national development plans, regardless of nomenclature, are standard all over Africa, and generally try to steer economies away from reliance on the extractive sector. In Namibia, NDP 3 saw the construction industry as a key means of diversifying the economy. MANWU unionised workers in the construction sector, and had therefore fully bought in to NDP 3.

29 There's something abjectly tragic about Namibia's WWI war memorials. Miserable chunks of granite mark the spots where once brotherly Afrikaners (fighting for the Queen) and Germans (on Team Kaiser) battled to the death over stretches of sand for purposes they could only dimly understand. It was, as Peter Orner put it in his peerless novel *The Second Coming of Mavala Shikongo*, a case of 'Shakespeare versus Goethe in the battle for the thorn

scrub'.

30 The Namibian economy would grow by only 3.8 per cent in 2011, down from a GDP growth rate of 6.6 per cent for 2010, a drop that *African Economic Outlook 2012* would attribute to a weaker demand for mineral resources off the back of the global recession, and severe flooding in the north of the country, which affected mining and agricultural activities. The construction sector, as the report noted, had doubled its contribution to Namibian GDP between 2000 and 2010. Source: http://www.afdb. org/fileadmin/uploads/afdb/Documents/ Publications/Namibia%20Full%20PDF%20 Country%20Note.pdf, pp 1 & 5.

31 As Salon.com noted in a post titled 'New Labour Movement Emerges in Scott Walker's Wisconsin': '[I]n one of the largest labour mobilisations in modern American history, as many as 100 000 Wisconsin residents surrounded and occupied the state capitol to protest Gov Scott Walker's effort to strip public sector workers of collective bargaining rights. The uprising reanimated the American labour movement and became the go-to image of domestic protest in the wake of the Great Recession – before Occupy Wall Street later that year.' Both movements tapered off, and it's difficult not to think of the Walker protests as one of international labour's last gasps. As of this writing, he is making a serious run for the Republican Party's 2016 presidential candidate.

32 'Africa Rising? Popular Dissatisfaction with Economic Management Despite a Decade of Growth', Jan Hofmeyr (Afrobarometer, 2013), p 3. Full text available here: http:// www.afrobarometer.org/files/documents/ policy_brief/ab_r5_policybriefno2.pdf.

33 Ibid, p 5.

34 Ibid, p 6.

35 At the time of our visit, Namibia's minimum hourly wage stood at N$9, or roughly $1.20 by January 2011 exchange rates.

36 It's impossible to separate the intent of current labour regulations from colonialism's legacy, a fact the 1992 Namibian Labour Act makes perfectly clear in its preamble: '[T]he Republic of Namibia has adopted in the labour field a policy aimed at enacting legislation, with due regard to the furtherance of labour relations conducive to economic growth, stability and productivity through the promotion of an orderly system of free collective bargaining, the improvement of wages and conditions of employment of employees *and the advancement of persons who have been disadvantaged by past discriminatory laws and practices* [...].' (Italics added).

37 *Chinese Investments in Namibia: A Labour Perspective*, Herbert Jauch and Lipumbu Sakaria (LaRRI, 2009), p 31.

38 In a *New York Times* article published 4 April 2010, titled '3 Plead Not Guilty to Corruption in Namibia', the brilliant Windhoek-based journalist John Grobler pointed out once again that Beijing's censors had blocked all references to Namibia on the Chinese Internet, an indication of the sensitivity of the matter in the upper echelons of the Chinese Communist Party: http://www.nytimes.com/2010/04/09/ world/africa/09namibia.html?_r=0.

39 Indongo's full statement, as reported in the *Namibian Sun* of 17 January 2011, read: 'They are the worst capitalists. They are into retailing, they don't bank here and don't pay tax, and they are always caught at the borders and airport trying to take their profits out of the country.'

40 *Chinese Investments in Africa: A Labour Perspective*, eds Anthony Yaw Baah and Herbert Jauch (ALRN, 2009), p 255.

41 Ibid, pp 256-57.

42 *The Telegraph* of the UK appeared quite fond of the irony that Hu Haifeng had been nicknamed the 'Teflon princeling' for his ability to keep his name out of the media: http://www.telegraph.co.uk/news/world-news/asia/china/5851056/Hu-Jintaos-son-linked-to-African-corruption-probe.html.

43 *Chinese Investments in Africa*, eds Yaw Baah and Jauch, p 258.

44 *The New Era*, last retrieved 27 August, 2013: http://allafrica.com/stories/201010041203. html.

45 *Chinese Investments in Africa*, eds Yaw Baah and Jauch, p 259.

46 Source: World Bank.

47 *Chinese Investments in Africa, eds* Yaw Baah and Jauch, p 275.

48 *Namibian Economist*, 21 June 2013, available here: http://allafrica.com/stories/201306211075.html.

49 *CIF and MANWU Agree on Minimum Employment Conditions*, Press Release, 30 May 2013.

50 Ibid.

51 The authors made a call to Mr Pupkewitz in January 2011, and were surprised to find that he answered his own phone (a landline number) on the second ring. 'Pupkewitz here!' the nonagenarian barked, with all the forcefulness of a man a third his age. He was equally forceful in telling us that he was not willing to discuss his business dealings with the Chinese, as he could not see how there was 'anything in it' for him.

When Mr Pupkewitz died in April 2012 at the age of 96, *Forbes* magazine gave him a fitting tribute, noting that he was 'widely believed' to be Namibia's richest man. 'Pupkewitz's exact net worth is unknown; he did not appear on *Forbes*' inaugural list of Africa's 40 Richest in late 2011,' the American publication stated – implying, perhaps, that had his net worth been known, he would have been right up near the top.

52 *Namibia Labour Act 1992*, available here: http://www.ilo.org/dyn/natlex/docs/WEBTEXT/29328/64850/E92NAM01.HTM#p11.

53 Gerrit Viljoen was in many respects the typical South West African Administrator-General. Born in 1924, he was a previous chair of the Broederbond, the influential Afrikaner society that advanced the interests of South Africa's Afrikaans Brahmins. He believed strongly in the tenets of apartheid, while maintaining a pragmatic streak that allowed for the occasional innovation, such as the creation of a narrow black elite.

54 By August 2013, the Namibian press was reporting that TIPEEG had failed. The *Informante*, for one, noted that only 18 per cent of the 74 052 jobs created were permanent: http://www.informante.web.na/index.php?option=com_content&view=article&id=12494:tipeeg-fails-to-create-permanent-jobs-&catid=19:inside-pages&Itemid=100.

55 All figures from World Bank.

CHAPTER THREE: BOTSWANA

1 The astonishing book from which we culled this material recreates the Three Kings' journey using press clippings from the day. The chiefs had termed journalists 'hunters of words', and a better definition of our vocation we have yet to hear. *King Khama, Emperor Joe and the Great White Queen: Victorian Britain through African Eyes*, Neil Parsons (University of Chicago Press, 1998), p 5.

2 Between 1887 and 1895, this sickly son of a Hertfordshire vicar would unite the disparate diamond concessions in Kimberley under his De Beers umbrella, emerge as a mining magnate in the Boer republic of the Transvaal, become prime minister of the Cape Colony, and name the territory north of the Limpopo for himself, calling it Rhodesia. Flash forward to 2015, and the Rhodes memorials that still peppered democratic South Africa were points of major contention, mostly at the country's universities. The movement coined the hashtag #RhodesMustFall.

3 These words were from a speech Rhodes made in 1883 before the parliament of the Cape Colony, which was then dominated by members who saw the future of South Africa as not British, but Dutch. At the time, President Paul Kruger of the Transvaal was considering annexing the Afrikaner-led Republic of Stellaland (part of modern-day Botswana), and he would act on these instincts the following year. In 1885, after a British force had been sent in to defeat the Boers, the Republic of Stellaland was abolished and incorporated into the British protectorate of Bechuanaland.

Chief Khama, a lifelong enemy of the Boers and a man who would have welcomed the British victory, would also no doubt have remembered the intentions of Rhodes when the latter had addressed the Cape parliament. 'I have learned how great are the prospects of the territory beyond the Transvaal,' the imperialist had said in 1883. Twelve years later, when the British South Africa Company was pushing to bring Bechuanaland under its administrative ambit, Khama, along with Chief

Bathoen and Chief Sebele, would angle for the more direct – and in their eyes more benign – stewardship of Queen Victoria.

4 As per the *African Statistical Yearbook 2010*, Libya and Equatorial Guinea were way ahead of Botswana, South Africa and Mauritius for much of the first decade of the millennium. Of course, what made the former two countries stand out on this GDP-per-capita chart, aside from their dictatorial regimes and comparatively abysmal governance records, was their reliance on that most destructive of African commodities: oil. (African Development Bank, 2010), p 48.

5 *Why Nations Fail: The Origins of Power, Prosperity and Poverty*, Daron Acemoglu and James A Robinson (Profile Books, 2012, Kindle edition).

6 *An African Success Story: Botswana*, Daron Acemoglu, Simon Johnson and James A Robinson (MIT, 2001), p 2. Available here: http://economics.mit.edu/files/284

7 As is dealt with in further detail in the chapters on Zimbabwe and the DRC, Acemoglu and Robinson (*Why Nations Fail*) argue that this vicious circle began with the slave trade, when the substantial profits to be made led to the loss of property rights for the people, and to the overall destruction of pre-existing political and economic institutions. 'Though the slave trade mostly ended after 1807,' they note, 'subsequent European colonialism not only threw into reverse nascent economic modernisation in parts of southern and western Africa but also cut off any possibility of indigenous institutional reform.'

8 In the period following the Jameson Raid, the British Colonial Office refused to allow the British South Africa Company to give priority to its commercial interests over its administrative duties in Rhodesia. Until 1924, when its administration of Northern Rhodesia was terminated, the company remained unprofitable.

9 The University of Botswana's Professor Neil Parsons, author of *King Khama*, provides the geopolitical background to these events, suggesting that Britain's Labour government had buckled to the apartheid regime's pressure because it needed South Africa's gold and uranium. By denying that his government was bowing to the precepts of institutionalised racism, writes Parsons, the Commonwealth relations minister lied to the House of Commons. What's more, when a judicial enquiry was set up to prove Khama's unfitness to rule, Justice Harrigan couldn't but conclude the exact opposite – and so the report was suppressed for 30 years. Ultimately, after an outcry from 'human rights activists, Scottish, West African, Indian and West Indian nationalists, British communists, and conservatives who supported the principle of aristocratic inheritance', a new Commonwealth relations minister allowed Seretse and Ruth Khama to return to Bechuanaland in 1956. Full text, courtesy of the University of Botswana History Department, available here: http://www.thuto.org/ubh/bw/skhama.htm.

10 On a relatively brief list that includes the names of Geoffrey Chaucer, Mohandas Gandhi, Jawaharlal Nehru and John Maynard Keynes, the Inner Temple of Court lists Sir Seretse Khama as a 'notable member'. Available here: http://www.innertemple.org.uk/downloads/prospective-members/Inner-Temple-Prospectus.pdf.

11 As we were writing these words and thinking, 'This would make a hell of a movie,' we learned that Pathé Pictures had secured financing to produce *A United Kingdom*, starring *Selma's* David Oyelewo as Seretse Khama, and Rosamund Pike as Ruth.

12 Although in *Why Nations Fail* Acemoglu and Robinson cite Botswana's language legislation as a key reason for its homogeneity, a factor that has minimised 'conflict between different tribes', other studies cite this as an example of the BDP's disregard for human rights, especially when it comes to non-Tswana groups. As one example, University of Botswana academic Lydia Nyati-Ramahobo ascribes the marginalisation of the country's numerous non-Tswana languages to the perpetuation of colonial-era laws. Source: http://kamanakao.org/wp-content/uploads/2010/07/Language-law-final1.pdf.

13 *Why Nations Fail: The Origins of Power,*

Prosperity and Poverty, Daron Acemoglu and James A Robinson.

14 Ibid.

15 The *New York Times*, relying on data from Edward Jay Epstein's classic *The Rise and Fall of Diamonds*, quoted these figures in an article published in August 2008. The journalist, Joe Nocera, did not however note what an IMF report published in March of that same year had stated: '[From 1998 to 2008], the mining sector has contributed an average of 38.5 per cent to GDP, with diamonds constituting nearly 94 per cent of the sector's total exports' (http://www.imf.org/external/pubs/ft/wp/2008/wp0880.pdf. Diamonds). Next to diamonds, according to such data, manganese and copper have always been tiny contributors to the Botswana economy.

Unfortunately, Nocera ignored something else in his article: the role of Seretse Khama and the BDP in initiating the joint venture with De Beers. The piece attributed the entire idea to 'De Beers's own sense of ... corporate social responsibility'. Unlike 'most Chinese companies operating in Africa today,' Nocera wrote, 'De Beers did not simply plunder Botswana'. Betraying a further disregard for the subtleties, the journalist cited the mining giant's donation of roads, hospitals, schools and 'a hundred other things that have helped make Botswana an African success story'.

For more on how even the most effective African political institutions are seldom given credit by mainstream Western media, the full article is available here: http://www.nytimes.com/2008/08/09/business/worldbusiness/09nocera.html?pagewanted=1&_r=1&ref=business.

16 *Africa Survey 2012* (South Africa Institute of Race Relations/Good Governance Africa, 2012), p 28.

17 As the *Africa Survey 2012* showed (p 26), Botswana's economy posted the steepest decline in 2009 of any country on the continent. At a negative 4.9 per cent, its GDP fall was 1.2 points steeper than Madagascar's (-3.7 per cent) and 3.2 points steeper than South Africa's (-1.7 per cent). Angola, the Central African Republic, Libya and Namibia were the only other African countries of those surveyed to post a negative growth rate on the back of the 2008 financial crisis.

18 'NDP 10 focuses on accelerated diversification', *Mmegi*, 10 July 2009. Available here: http://www.mmegi.bw/index.php?sid=4&aid=19&dir=2009/July/Friday10.

19 For a brief and lucid précis of this dilemma, few articles can match 'Africa's Economic Boom: Why the pessimists and the optimists are both right', published in the May/June 2013 issue of *Foreign Affairs*. Available to subscribers here: http://www.foreignaffairs.com/articles/139109/shantayanan-devarajan-and-wolfgang-fengler/africas-economic-boom.

20 Relying on data from Debswana itself, in March 2008 Olivier Basdevant published the IMF working paper 'Are Diamonds Forever? Using the Permanent Income Hypothesis to Analyse Botswana's Reliance on Diamond Revenue'. The paper, which argued that the downturn in production would begin in 2017, had at the time of this writing not been refuted by any governmental, NGO or private sector sources – 2029, it seemed, had been accepted as the year that diamonds would fade into Botswana's history. Available here: http://www.imf.org/external/pubs/ft/wp/2008/wp0880.pdf

21 On page 208 of the 357-page NDP 10 document, it states, 'Productivity in virtually every sector of the economy is affected by the quality and performance of the country's transportation, water, power supply and other types of infrastructure.' Right above this, NDP 10 notes the World Bank's estimate that 'a 1 percent increase in a country's infrastructure stock is associated with a 1 percent increase in the level of GDP'. Infrastructural development is thus a 'Key Result Area' for Botswana's sustainable economic growth, as presented in chapter 9 of the plan. Time and again, it is returned to as the factor that makes or breaks all others. Full text available here: http://www.finance.gov.bw/templates/mfdp/file/File/NDP%2010%20final%2016th%20Dec%202009%20edit%20in%2019%20Jan%202010.pdf.

22 In his foreword, President Ian Khama notes that NDP 10 represents the last stage in achieving this long-term vision. The creation of a diversified economy and enlarged middle class is implied in his acknowledgment of 'the need to change the mindset of Batswana through encouraging talents, creativity, hard work and discipline ...' Amongst the obstacles to realising *Vision 2016*, the president lists global competition, HIV/AIDS, and 'declining social values'. He further promises to 'provide the necessary infrastructure for private sector growth ...' Ibid, pp xxiii–xxiv.

23 The chapter on Namibia stresses the disregard of Chinese construction firms for local labour legislation, especially when it comes to issues such as minimum wage, work hours, and safety precautions, all of which incur obvious costs. What the chapter does not stress, however, is the ability of China's major financial institutions, such as Exim Bank and the China Development Bank, to facilitate the comparatively low tender bids. Exim Bank and the CDB have been able to do this through bond issues backed by the savings deposits of the Chinese people.

24 'Dam builder will launch deal next week to bankroll power projects', *China Daily*, 20 September 2011.

25 'Sinohydro corporation: Building a bridge of friendship between China and Africa', CRIEnglish.com, 14 October 2010. Available at: http://english.cri.cn/7146/2010/10/14/2041s599367.htm.

26 Sinohydro, as a state-owned Chinese conglomerate, had for years managed to keep most of its core financials a secret – until it was forced to confirm figures like these in its IPO prospectus. The company's initial public offering would raise $2.1 billion, the largest on the Shanghai stock exchange in 2011.

27 Although estimates vary depending on drought and disease, there have long been more cattle in Botswana than people. In 1966, the total livestock population (cattle, sheep and goats) was said to be 1.7 million, a figure that had grown to 5.5 million by 1991, with cattle accounting for 2.8 million of the total. At the same time, the human population, 574 000 in 1971, had grown to 1.5 million by 1995. Source: 'Desertification in Botswana', Michael BK Darkoh, available here: http://www.rala.is/rade/ralareport/darkoh.pdf.

But the drafters of NDP 10, perhaps appreciative of the minefield they'd be stepping into if they provided an updated breakdown, did not refer *directly* to the desertification problem posed by the predominance of cattle in rural Botswana. Cattle remain traditional units of wealth in the country, a core element of Tswana culture, and the BDP clearly knows better than to tell the electorate that its customs are environmentally and economically unsustainable. NDP 10 does, however, euphemistically state the following: 'The main policy concern ... is the limited availability of land ready for development, despite an apparently abundant land resource.' NDP 10, p 252.

28 In more prosaic terminology, NDP 10 echoes the sentiment when it refers to the water restrictions that had been imposed under previous development plans on the Gaborone and Lobatse areas. The restrictions, which led to a 10 per cent decrease in demand between 2002 and 2006, included a prohibition on watering golf courses and sports grounds with potable water, a prohibition on washing pavements with potable water, and a prohibition on watering gardens with hoses held by hand. Ibid, p 229.

29 In its review of NDP 9, after stressing that the water sector contributed 1 per cent of GDP, NDP 10 notes that only a single dam was built to completion during the period – the Ntimbale Dam, at 26.4 million cubic metres. Of the dams scheduled for completion during NDP 10, Dikgatlhong, at 400 million cubic metres, is by many multiples the largest. It is followed by the Thune Dam at 90 million cubic metres, the Lotsane Dam at 42.3 million, and the Mosetse Dam at 31.7 million. Combined, the expectation is that these four projects will raise the overall volume of Botswana's dams from 393 million cubic metres to 948 million. What such a marked increase implies in economic terms as a future contribution to Botswana's GDP, NDP 10 does not

venture to guess. Ibid, p 227.

30 The Merowe Dam on the Nile River, as journalists Juan Pablo Cardenal and Heriberto Araujo point out, is the project that President Omar al-Bashir thought would 'eliminate poverty in Sudan'. Inaugurated in 2009, its 10 turbines generate 1 250 megawatts of power, and through a mooted interlinking system of water canals the dam has reportedly revived the dream of making Sudan the 'breadbasket of Africa'. That said, its environmental and social consequences have also made it one of the most controversial dam projects in Africa, a scenario that the World Bank and other Western institutions apparently foresaw – in 1999, when a Sudanese delegation was sent by the president to look for funding, these institutions cited environmental and social concerns as the reason for their refusal to get involved. The Chinese model that funded the dam, in the typical form of a loan granted by China Exim Bank to Khartoum, was thought by some to be guaranteed by preferential access to China of Sudan's crude oil. Source: *China's Silent Army: The Pioneers, Traders, Fixers and Workers Who Are Remaking the World in Beijing's Image*, Juan Pablo Cardenal and Heriberto Araujo (Allen Lane, 2013), pp 136-42.

31 This was indeed the wrong word. According to the NGO International Rivers, in the mid-2000s the United Nations called upon Sinohydro to stop work on the Merowe Dam after reports that local villagers were being flooded out of their homes.

32 As per the statistics of the NGO Avert, 23.4 per cent of the adult population in Botswana (ages 15 to 49) was living with HIV/AIDS in 2011. The highest in Africa was Swaziland, at 26 per cent (source: http://www.avert.org/africa-hiv-aids-statistics.htm). NDP 10, on page 24, notes: 'The emergence of the HIV/AIDS pandemic has reversed some of the hard earned gains of past development plans. The disease affects mostly the productive segment of the population. The disease also diverts resources that could have otherwise been used for other development endeavours.'

33 The Selebi Phikwe Economic Diversification Unit is the latest in a long string of initiatives to stimulate non-mining growth in the district. From the very start, according to the SPEDU website, the Botswana government had been proactive about the town's development strategy, and had worked to attract investment from European donors. When these investments did not bring the required results, the Selebi Phikwe Regional Development Programme was set up in 1985, but despite input from Industrial Development Ireland and significant tax incentives for light industry, the SPRDP ultimately failed as well. In 2006, the government called on European donors once more, and the European Union funded a study that led to the creation of SPEDU.

34 From the BCL website, last accessed September 2013: http://www.bcl.bw/.

35 Indicative of the fact that BCL, despite the government's 94 per cent shareholding, has objectives somewhat different from the government itself, these figures are supplied courtesy of the SPEDU website.

36 'The voice of the jobseekers', *Mmegi*, 8 January 2010.

37 As stated elsewhere in this book, the expiry of the Multi-Fibre Arrangement in January 2005, whereby the export quotas that had previously governed the global textile trade were rendered null and void, was the chief cause behind the 100 per cent rise in garment exports from China to the West. Although the textile industries in many developing countries also suffered as a result, there were notable exceptions – Bangladesh, for instance, posted a $500 million increase in exports in 2006. The point, although debatable in view of Beijing's textile subsidies, is that Selebi Phikwe's textile companies were unable to compete in a globalised world (and this despite the business development assistance that many of them would have been entitled to under SPEDU).

38 The report, backing up the observations of our unnamed Zimbabwean engineer, notes that European and South African companies had long dominated the Botswana infrastructure space before the Chinese arrived. The competition from Beijing meant that the BDP government could gain

'substantial savings in its public infrastructure projects', which in turn brought benefits to the taxpayer. SAIIA estimates the savings in costs to be anything from 25 to 33 per cent. *China's Role in Infrastructure Development in Botswana*, Anna Ying Chen (SAIIA, 2009), pp 5 & 13.

39 'Botswana Unemployment Rate', Trading-Economics.com. Available at: http://www.tradingeconomics.com/botswana/unemployment-rate.

40 *China's Role in Infrastructure Development in Botswana*, Anna Ying Chen (SAIIA, 2009), pp 14-15.

41 Ibid, p 8. The rule of the Chinese Ministry of Commerce was that at least three companies must tender for a project before it is awarded.

42 Ibid, p 10.

43 Ibid, p 11. As the SAIIA report notes, CSCEC arrived in Botswana in 1988 to build the Chinese embassy, and moved from there to local government projects. Gaborone would eventually become the headquarters for projects throughout southern Africa, and in 2003 the company would properly globalise its brand when it won a $240 million tender to build a Marriott Hotel in New York.

44 Ramaduleka Seretse was acquitted of all charges in October 2011, and immediately reinstated as cabinet minister by President Khama. According to the independent newspaper *Mmegi*, this prompted the publicity secretary of the Botswana Congress Party, Taolo Lucas, to say that the president had been 'feeling vulnerable' without his cousin. Full article available here: https://www.mmegi.bw/index.php?sid=1&aid=1014&dir=2011/October/Thursday27.

45 In November 2012, journalist Yvonne Ditlhase would bundle all of these connections – plus a number of others – into an article for South Africa's *Mail & Guardian*. The official response of the Khama government to the piece would be that Botswana is a small country where 'everybody knows everybody'. Jeff Ramsay, the government spokesperson, would dismiss the allegations of cronyism and nepotism as 'baseless and senseless', and would further point

out that both South Africa's former president Nelson Mandela and sitting president Jacob Zuma had ex-wives serving in their cabinets. Full article available here: http://mg.co.za/article/2012-11-02-00-khama-inc-all-the-presidents-family-friends-and-close-colleagues.

46 The breakaway faction, which comprised around 20 MPs, listed among its grievances the alleged corruption of the BDP senior leadership, the preferential treatment given by this leadership to members of the so-called 'A-team', and the failure of Khama to follow the party's constitution. As *Mmegi* noted at the time, the main focus of the new party's wrath was the president himself; a wrath reflected in its anthem 'Saule We Saule O Mpogisetsang!' (Saul o Saul why do you persecute me!), and its talk of a 'Mogolo (elder) who refuses to listen'. Full article available here: http://www.mmegi.bw/index.php?sid=1&aid=1122&dir=2010/March/Monday22.

47 The report's exact wording is that water in Botswana is 'scarce enough to become a binding constraint on development given the rapid increase in consumer and industrial demand ...' A threefold challenge is listed: protecting surface and underground water from contamination; identifying more efficient technologies for household and industrial water use; raising general awareness about water conservation. *Botswana: Millennium Development Goals Status Report 2004* (Republic of Botswana/United Nations), p 63.

48 Employing understated euphemism once again, NDP 10 (pp 239-40) notes the 'supply difficulties in the region'. Famously, South Africa experienced a series of rolling blackouts in 2008, which plunged big industry in the country into turmoil, and seriously undermined the confidence of the international investment community in the continent's economic powerhouse. The Mmamabula project was partly conceived as an attempt to exploit the incompetencies of the South African power utility, Eskom. Situated 80 kilometres from the South African power grid at Matimba, Mmamabula aims to benefit from an inter-governmental 'memorandum of understanding'

between Gaborone and Pretoria. Ibid.

49 Further to this history, the NGO International Rivers notes in its factsheet on the Three Gorges Dam that by January 2012, with approximately 300 projects in 66 countries, the Chinese had come to dominate the global hydropower market. Full text available here: http://www.internationalrivers.org/files/attached-files/3gorgesfactsheet_feb2012_web.pdf.

50 'Sinohydro Corporation: The World's Biggest Hydropower Dam Company', InternationalRivers.org. Full text available at: http://www.internationalrivers.org/campaigns/sinohydro-corporation.

51 International Rivers notes in its factsheet that the Three Gorges Dam has completely altered the ecosystem of the Yangtze basin. It has interrupted fish migration, altered the river's chemical balance, probably driven the famous Chinese river dolphin to extinction, decimated the sturgeon and paddlefish populations, and seriously harmed commercial fishing in the East China Sea. The 500 million tons of silt that the river carries into the reservoir every year is being withheld from downstream areas, causing erosion in the coastal wetlands. 'The Three Gorges Project has also created serious seismic and safety risks,' states International Rivers. 'The reservoir sits on two major fault lines, and hundreds of small tremors have been recorded since the reservoir began filling in 2006.' (Three Gorges Dam, op cit.)

52 Peter Bosshard, in a report published by the South African Institute of International Affairs in November 2008, notes that the Bui Dam in Ghana, the Lower Kafue Gorge Dam in Zambia and the Merowe Dam in Sudan were all funded by China Exim Bank after delegations from each of these countries failed to secure financing from the West. In the case of the Bui Dam, the environmental concern was that the project would flood about a quarter of Ghana's Bui National Park, and so both the World Bank and the European Investment Bank (EIB) declined to finance the project. In Zambia's case, the concern was that the Lower Kafue Gorge Dam would place further pressure on the ecologically

important Kafue Flats, leading the World Bank and EIB, as well as private Western investors, to refuse the Zambian government. Sudan's Merowe Dam, as suggested in note 30 above, was by far the most controversial of these projects – aside from its impact on the ecology of the Nile River, it would result in the displacement of more than 70 000 people from the river's banks to arid locations, where poverty would be drastically increased. Consequently, the Sudanese government was refused by a range of investors that included the World Bank, IMF and COFACE (the official export credit agency of France), as well as other institutions in Canada, Europe and Malaysia. After Exim Bank approved the funding on the above three dams, Sinohydro was appointed the main contractor on each of them. *SAIIA China in Africa Policy Briefing: China's Environmental Footprint in Africa* (SAIIA, 2008), pp 3-4.

53 *White Writing*, JM Coetzee (Yale University Press, 1988), p 8.

54 'Little to fear but fear itself', *The Economist*, 21 September 2013.

55 In November 2012, confirming just how much heft *The Economist* still had when it came to shaping Western opinion on Africa, *Time* magazine published its very own cover story on the once-hopeless continent. *Time*'s strapline? 'Africa Rising', letter for purloined letter. Through 2013, the phrase would appear in countless columns, op-eds and blogs, some of them breathlessly optimistic, others more mindful of the fact that GDP growth charts meant little unless wealth was being transferred to the majority.

56 As Anna Ying Chen notes in the paper *China's Role in Infrastructure Development in Botswana* (SAIIA, 2009, p 5), Chinese government-funded aid projects are usually granted to the least-developed countries, a category that Botswana does not fall into. 'However,' she writes on page 5, 'the Chinese government does offer preferential loans to Botswana in the form of interest-free or low-interest concessional loans, but the percentage of such projects is very low compared to other local public tender projects run by Chinese construction firms in

Botswana.'

57 At the foot of the article headlined 'How Sinohydro lost P1.5 billion tender', dated 8 March 2012, *Mmegi* included a summary of the problems as outlined in the PPADB dossier. Amongst other items, the dossier noted that the new terminal at the Sir Seretse Khama Airport was 15 months behind schedule; that Sinohydro was 'illegally' mining a quarry in order to complete the Kang-Hukuntsi road; that the delay on the Francistown-Ramokgwebana road was due to poor planning by the contractor; and that the Dikgatlhong Dam had experienced 'communication' issues and labour strikes. Full text available here: http://www.mmegi.bw/index. php?sid=1&aid=291&dir=2012/March/ Thursday8.

58 'Sinohydro relocates from Botswana', *Mmegi*, 19 July 2013.

59 'Dikgatlhong Dam wall not cracking', *Botswana Guardian*, 1 February 2013.

60 'Khama wants fewer Chinese firms to receive state contracts', *Business Day*, 20 February 2013.

61 The Open Society Initiative for Southern Africa, in summarising the events in Botswana politics since the BDP split, ended off its report with the observation that it is 'always dangerous for a party to stay in power too long'. Noting the Khama government's so-called authoritarian tendencies, OSISA – in line with the general philosophy of its founder, the billionaire American philanthropist George Soros – expressed concern that the country's transparency record would be compromised. Nonetheless, the report did concede to Khama's popularity amongst all sectors of the population, noting that power would not change hands in the democratic elections of 2014. Full text available here: http://www.osisa.org/hrdb/blog/ scary-strength-botswanas-ruling-party.

62 *Policy Brief No 2: Africa Rising? Popular Dissatisfaction with Economic Management Despite a Decade of Growth*, Jan Hofmeyr (Afrobarometer, 2013), p 18.

63 Ibid, p xxiv.

64 'Botswana: Government fires Chinese firm Sinohydro over delays to Airport Expansion project', *The African Aviation Tribune*, 27 July 2012.

65 After its suspension of work on the Kang-Hukuntsi road, Sinohydro broke with tradition and gave a rare interview to the Botswana press. Project manager Yan Xing Hua told *Mmegi* that an Environmental Impact Assessment had been delivered late on the disputed quarry, and that the government hadn't paid the promised compensation settlement. 'Kang-Hukuntsi road halts as Sinohydro demands payment', *Mmegi*, 25 May 2012.

66 *The African Aviation Tribune*, 27 July 2012.

67 'Botswana Overview', JindalAfrica.com. Available at: http://www.jindalafrica.com/ botswana/botswana-overview.

68 As far back as May 2011, Bloomberg reported that a memorandum of understanding had been signed between the governments of Botswana, Zimbabwe and Mozambique. Construction on the $7 billion project, incorporating the 1 100-kilometre rail line and a new deepwater port in southern Mozambique, was supposed to have kicked off in 2012, with 2022 marked as the year of completion. As far as the authors could tell, the delay was a matter of funding, although the arrival on the scene of Jindal Africa in late 2012 seemed to reinvigorate the process. With the Delhi-based conglomerate seeking to partner with the Botswana government in exporting Mmamabula's coal to India and China (up until then, South Africa was the landlocked country's only export market), the project's commercial imperatives became more immediate. The quoted announcement by the Selebi Phikwe town councillor and the SPEDU marketing manager in February 2013 was, to our understanding, a direct result of this renewed urgency.

69 'Does Botswana deserve its reputation as a stable democracy?' *The Washington Post*, 20 October 2014.

CHAPTER FOUR: ZIMBABWE

1 In mid-2007, as Zimbabwe's fuel and food

shortages were becoming pandemic and inflation was edging past 4 000 per cent, the rush of refugees across the border was reaching epic proportions. There were frequent reports of people drowning or being eaten by crocodiles in the Limpopo River, and South African authorities were sending back an average of 4 000 'illegal' Zimbabwean immigrants every week – up 40 per cent on 2006. In 2008, unofficial estimates placed the number of Zimbabweans in South Africa at over 3 million, and it was this community that was a primary target of that year's xenophobic violence. In November 2013, attempting to get to the bottom of the wildly divergent estimates, now anywhere from 1.7 to 3 million, the respected organisation Africa Check published an investigative report under the title, 'How many Zimbabweans live in South Africa? The numbers are unreliable'.

2 As the biographical information on the website of the London School of Economics, where Dr Alden is at the time of this writing co-head of the Africa International Affairs programme, makes plain, the man is something of a savant when it comes to Sino-African studies. His interest in the subject can be traced back to the mid-2000s, before it was a blip on the radar of global media, and extends beyond the hype of 2010 and 2011, when he was a ranking international dial-a-quote. Interestingly, with reference to Fay Chung's mention of his name (and to the current chapter), Dr Alden was the author in 2010 of a paper entitled '"A pariah in our midst": regional organisations and the problematic of Western-designated pariah regimes – the cases of SADC/Zimbabwe and ASEAN/Myanmar'.

3 Fay Chung's use in her book title of the Shona term *chimurenga*, which translates roughly as 'revolutionary struggle', is as revealing of her life story as it is of her character. The First Chimurenga, a synonym for the Second Matabele War, refers to the Ndebele-Shona revolt against Cecil John Rhodes's British South Africa Company in 1896-97 (see the opening section of our Botswana chapter for why the timing of this revolt, soon after the

Jameson Raid, was so sublime). The Second Chimurenga refers to what was also known as the 'Rhodesian Bush War' or 'Zimbabwe Liberation War' of 1966-79, which is the central subject of this section of the current chapter. The Third Chimurenga, a lot more controversial as far as Western sensibilities go, refers to the process of Fast Track Land Reform, begun around the turn of the millennium.

4 Directly following this passage, Chung writes that the situation for blacks was 'slightly better' than it was for Asians and Coloureds, as in the 1950s there was already a secondary school set aside for black pupils – Goromonzi High School, which served the whole country. *Reliving the Second Chimurenga: Memories from the Liberation Struggle in Zimbabwe* (Nordic Africa Institute, 2006), p 33.

5 This 'work' was to clear the grounds of the rejected pupils and their parents. When Ascot Secondary in Gwelo (now Gweru) was opened in 1963, four classes of 30 pupils each were selected, while the rest were arbitrarily dismissed on the grounds of 'lack of some or other essential bureaucratic documentation'. Of her short time at the school, Chung writes that it was characterised by a 'military regime, racism, and sadism', factors she attributed to the fact that Gwelo was then the heart of the extreme rightwing Rhodesian Front, with the party's leader, Ian Smith, owning a farm not far from town. *Reliving the Second Chimurenga*, pp 47-51.

6 Ibid, p 67.

7 Ibid, pp 67-68.

8 The Unilateral Declaration of Independence, or UDI as it was known in the international press and on the placards of British protesters – 'UDI is Treason' – was declared during the two-minute silence for the fallen on Armistice Day, 11 November 1965. British PM Harold Wilson, instead of being swayed by this appeal to the sacrifices white Rhodesians had made during wartime, was 'deeply insulted' – as were 107 member states of the UN General Assembly. The only two nations that didn't oppose UDI in the condemnatory resolution were South Africa and Portugal, while

France abstained.

9 Chung, in outlining these three rules of discipline, notes that the freedom fighter song *Nzira ye MaSoja* (Soldiers' Guide), which was sung every day at rallies and based on a mixture of Maoist, Christian, and traditional values, encapsulated the ZANLA 'Code of Conduct'. The other rules of discipline were 'Obey orders in all your actions' and 'Turn in everything captured'. *Reliving the Second Chimurenga*, p 80.

10 Zambia's Kenneth Kaunda, who held presidential office from his nation's independence in 1964 until 1991, based the entirety of his foreign policy on extending support to southern Africa's various liberation movements, Namibia's SWAPO, Angola's UNITA, Mozambique's FRELIMO and Zimbabwe's ZANU foremost among them. As profound testament to the role Kaunda played in the region's struggle, Nelson Mandela's first international destination after his release from prison was Lusaka, where South Africa's African National Congress had been headquartered for well over a decade. The scenes on the streets of the Zambian capital on that February afternoon in 1990, when many ANC members saw their leader in the flesh for the first time, were some of the most moving in the continent's post-independence history.

11 *Reliving the Second Chimurenga*, p 84.

12 Ibid, pp 176-79. Chung attributes the various attempts to 'silence' her to ZANU's internal leadership battles and the counter-racism that emerged in the wake of the failed détente of 1974.

13 Ibid, pp 256-57. If only for its forced tone of restraint on Lancaster House and the land issue, it's worth quoting the following passage from Chung's memoir in full: 'An immediate problem was that the Lancaster House agreement was based on the preservation of all the settler-colonial institutions and systems. This would make it difficult, if not impossible to attain some of the most dearly held goals. For example, it had been agreed that the land resettlement programme would be based on the 'willing seller-willing buyer' system, which meant that perhaps not enough land would be made available to the land hungry peasants. Moreover, land resettlement might prove impossibly expensive, although both the British and the American governments had made vague promises to fund the purchase of white-owned farmland.'

14 Ibid, p 24. In his foreword to the book, Norwegian academic Preben Kaarsholm notes of these concluding chapters: 'In her memoirs, Fay Chung seems to support Robert Mugabe's and ZANU PF's attempt – through the "Third *Chimurenga*" – to monopolise the history of the liberation struggle, pose themselves as its only rightful heir, and dismiss the challenge of democratic opposition as something alien and hostile to this historical mission.'

15 Ibid, p 259. Chung used the same phrase in the interview that she used in the book.

16 Actually, the *Mail & Guardian* has a few major assets in Zimbabwe. Bulawayo-born Trevor Ncube is the paper's publisher, and splits his time between Harare and Johannesburg. Ncube is largely regarded as untouchable, but that doesn't mean that the *Mail & Guardian*, along with its Zimbabwean sister publications *The Independent, The Sunday Standard* and *NewsDay*, should be commended any less for their coverage. (Full disclosure: the authors of this book are occasional contributors to the *Mail & Guardian*.)

17 The number of dead following *Gukurahundi* is most often cited as 20 000 civilians; the authors of *Zimbabwe Takes Back its Land* (Kumarian Press, 2012), suggest a figure of 6 000 based on new scholarship – they have, however, a tendency to underplay Zimbabwe's recent atrocities. Still, most activists we've spoken with find it impossible to endorse the 20 000 figure.

For the Shona completest, *Gukurahundi* means 'the early rains that wash away the chaff before the spring rains'; the campaign was, for all intents and purposes, a final movement in the civil war between ZANU and ZAPU, which finally ended in 1987 with the signing of the Unity Accord, officially dissolving ZAPU into ZANU and creating the Zimbabwe African National Union – Patriotic Front, or ZANU-PF.

18 For many Zimbabwean intellectuals, the

sadness about 'what could have been' is linked inextricably to that speech. 'If ever we look to the past,' Mugabe had said, 'let us do so for the lesson the past has taught us, namely that oppression and racism are inequities that must never again find scope in our political and social system.'

19 What is there to say about the long-suffering Movement for Democratic Change, endorsed on 26 February 1999 by over 700 Zimbabweans, most of them drawn from the union movement? Morgan Tsvangirai became its president at the inaugural congress in January 2000, and has remained in that position ever since. Tsvangirai was sworn in as Zimbabwe's prime minister following the institution of the Government of National Unity (GNU) in 2008, but the MDC has hardly remained unified itself. At the time of this writing, slick-talking Arthur Mutambara runs MDC-M, while Tsvangirai heads up MDC-T. Although one must commend Morgan Tsvangirai on his bravery and stoicism – he has been consistently beaten by ZANU henchmen, and lost his wife in a suspicious car accident – he has been outwitted by Mugabe & Co at every turn.

20 'Diamonds: A good deal for Zimbabwe?' (Global Witness, February 2012), p 3.

21 'Soldiers tell of diamond field massacre', BBC Panorama, 8 August 2011.

22 For example, these two pieces: 'China wants Marange gems, Zimbabwe platinum, independent reports', *Bloomberg*, 4 February 2011, and 'Mugabe's darkest secret: An £800bn blood diamond mine he's running with China's Red Army', *Daily Mail*, 18 September 2010.

23 Ken Flower was another of those outsized Rhodesian characters regarding whom it is difficult to separate fact from fiction, although Fay Chung seems to do so with much certainty, stating on page 95 of her memoir: 'The killing of [former ZANU leader Herbert] Chitepo had all the marks of an assassination by the Rhodesian secret service, CIO, whose head, Ken Flower, later confessed to having ordered and implemented it.' And while that might have been so, Flower was said to have remained loyal to the British after the UDI, and to have spied on Ian Smith for Her Majesty. All of which suggests how *good* a spy he was, and why Mugabe kept him on following independence.

24 It's worth reading the blurb of the documentary as it appears on the Australian Broadcast Network website, because the film evinced a remarkably durable point of view of the land reform process, one that hasn't changed in the West in over 10 years: 'For the first 18 years of President Robert Mugabe's rule, Zimbabweans Iain and Kerry Kay lived a mostly peaceful life, building up the 5 000 hectare farm Iain's father had bought in 1948. With their five children, the Kays also built up a strong relationship with the 500 workers and their families who lived on the farm. But in the late 1990s with Mugabe's introduction of land reforms, black supporters were encouraged to invade and take over thousands of white-owned farms. The ensuing campaign of violence has resulted in the deaths of many white farmers and the severe beating of hundreds of others. Included in these was the outspoken opposition supporter Iain Kay. In this report, filmed by the Kays over a three-year period we witness the destruction of the farm and the devastation of the family, as Iain's initial acceptance of the settlers on his land changes to anger and a fierce determination to protect what was his. The family's refusal to leave the farm brought continued intimidation and violence. In April 2000 Iain Kay was brutally attacked on his property, and while he was still recovering twelve days later, a neighbouring farmer was murdered. Kerry Kay describes her anger the night they received word that the house was about to be petrol-bombed, and with little notice they fled under cover of darkness to South Africa, returning only a few months later to find their nightmare was not yet over. The Kays' story also describes the treatment suffered by the farm-workers who stood by their employers, and who came to be classed as the enemy by the very government who had pledged to help them. The emotional strength of Iain and Kerry Kay is clear throughout their ordeal and

now in 2003 they are optimistic about their country's future. Kerry Kay: *'We look forward to our new Zimbabwe and it's going to be the jewel of Africa without any shadow of doubt'.* (Italics theirs).

25 'Report of the Fact-Finding Mission to Zimbabwe to assess the Scope and Impact of Operation Murambatsvina' (UN Special Envoy on Human Settlements Issues in Zimbabwe, July 2005), by Anna Kajumulo Tibaijuka, pp 7/8. When it was released, the report technically represented an embarrassment for Mugabe, but by that point he was well beyond shame, once again proving that the international community had lost all ability to influence events in Zimbabwe. That said, the report did make an attempt to situate *Murambatsvina* within 'the broader context of the urbanisation crisis in Africa,' adding that if urban environmental stability was not promoted by the UN and its partners, 'other countries in Africa could well experience another "Operation Restore Order" sooner than later.' Ibid, p 10.

26 'State in Fear: Zimbabwe's Tragedy is Africa's Shame' (Africa Fighting Malaria, May 2005), R Bate, P Ncube & R Tren, p 10.

27 The *Daily Maverick's* wryly entertaining Africa correspondent Simon Allison, in an article entitled 'Zimbabwe goes after the little guys in latest indigenisation drive' (26 November 2013) noted: '[The law was] a canny political move. For a start, the targets of this particular indigenisation drive are in no position to fight back, possessing little financial or diplomatic clout (China, who has some weight to throw around, has not yet commented on the impending fate of its nationals). Then there's the facilitation of that all-important patronage network – the ruling party needs to keep finding favours to distribute among its support. Finally, targeting the low-hanging fruit covers up the failures of the government when it comes to nationalising the far more lucrative mining sector.'

28 Kwinjeh's testimony was chilling: 'I was given a public beating at the point of assembly at Construction House, one officer held me by the hand while another beat me up with a baton stick, mostly on my shoulder. I was then taken to an open truck in which they had already put our deputy secretary for health, Kerry Kay. The man who drove the truck went across to the Anglican Cathedral next to Parliament Buildings to talk to two Asian gentlemen whom I suspected to be Chinese, which was to be confirmed in a *Mail & Guardian* article days later of the deal between Zimbabwe and the Chinese aimed at capacity building the regime to quell any mass protests. The Chinese gentlemen wore smart suits and held long-lens cameras....'

29 'Zim gears up for mass action', *Mail & Guardian*, 15 September 2006.

30 'China wants Marange gems, Zimbabwe platinum, independent reports', *Bloomberg*, 4 February 2011.

31 'Chiadzwa diamond fields must be accorded the 8th wonder status – Marange CEO', Harare24.com, 16 March 2012.

32 'Blood and dirt', *The Economist*, 24 June 2010.

33 'Diamonds: A good deal for Zimbabwe?' (Global Witness, February 2012), p 5.

34 As Finance Minister Tendai Biti, an MDC man, noted regarding this deal: 'I want to make reference to the Chinese Agreement [sic] that was ratified by this Parliament. It is criminal Mr Speaker for a country like Zimbabwe to enter into an agreement with a rate of interest like 2%, 4% or 5%. I want to say that there are friends, let me put "friends" in inverted comas, "friends and countries", that have been prepared to give Zimbabwe money. Mr Speaker Sir, but when you look at the agreement, the agreements are levying interests in the name of concessions of 2% and above. A country like Zimbabwe does not have the capacity to repay this interest. It does not have the capacity of paying such amounts.' Ibid, p 4.

35 Ibid, p 5.

36 Ibid, pp 11-12.

37 The Kimberley Process grew out of the desire of southern African diamond producers to halt the trade of blood diamonds, a blight on the industry's otherwise unbesmirched reputation and, especially following the release of the Leonardo DiCaprio film *Blood Diamonds* in 2006,

a serious public relations disaster. The Process now represents 81 countries that function either as markets or producers (or both), and yet critics have long argued that the certification is either toothless or worse – a means of brushing under the carpet the genuine issues the industry faces with diamonds mined in conflict zones. For example, Zimbabwe is a participant nation, while Global Witness quit the Process in 2011. Where the industry once had a single master in De Beers, Russia is now the world's largest diamond producer, and this diffusion has led to fuzzier and fuzzier definitions of 'conflict zones', and the need to stabilise a global market that was rocked heavily by the global financial crash.

38 'Diamonds: A good deal for Zimbabwe', p 10.

39 Sam Pa once again rears his irrepressible head in a lengthy and well-researched piece by Khadija Sherife, for the *100 Reporters* journal. While principally a profile of 88 Queensway Group's busiest Airbus 319CJ – 'a flying hotel room' according to a wowed passenger – the piece touches in some detail on the Marange diamond fields, mostly because the plane is so busy ferrying product from Harare into South Africa's Lanseria airport. What is so terrifying about the piece is how it connects the aircraft to a web of international companies – some legitimate, many others not – that perfectly describes just how the malfeasance in Marange is obscured behind a paper curtain of contracts and connections, dodging customs and flying well above the law, at least as it is intended. 'Disappearing Diamonds', *100 Reporters*, 20 February 2013. Full text available at: http://100r.org/2013/02/disappearing-diamonds/

40 *Reliving the Second Chimurenga*, Fay Chung, p 177.

41 Ibid.

42 Like the top ten list of Africa's fastest growing countries per GDP, the continent also has a 'most corrupt' index on which all the usual suspects consistently appear. In 2013, Zimbabwe was third behind Nigeria and Egypt on one such list, and in a 2014 it came 163 out of 175 on the Global Corruption Perception Index, courtesy of Transparency International. Africans tend to roll their eyes at such lists, mostly because – as this chapter hopefully makes clear – corruption is baked into globalisation's mechanisms. Nonetheless, these lists are useful when encountering local politicians, because they invariably result in A-class sound bites.

43 There has of late been much new scholarship to dispute the fact that a) the white Rhodesian was an especially productive agriculturalist, and b) that the farm invasions, or Fast Track Land Reform in the official parlance, permanently destroyed food production in Zimbabwe. Ian Scoones et al's *Zimbabwe's Land Reform: Myths & Realities* (James Currey, 2010) revealed that, in Masvingo Province, small-scale farmers were proving to be remarkably successful in many cases. But the really controversial study was the abovementioned *Zimbabwe Takes Back its Land* (Kumarian Press, 2012), by Joseph Hanlon, Jeanette Manjengwa and Teresa Smart. As the authors note on page 209, 'In the biggest land reform in Africa, 6 000 white farmers have been replaced by 245 000 Zimbabwean farmers. These are primarily ordinary poor people who have become more productive farmers. The change was inevitably disruptive at first, but production is increasing rapidly. Agricultural production is now returning to the 1990s level, and resettled farmers already grow 40% of the country's tobacco and 49% of its maize.' While both Scoones and the authors of *Zimbabwe Takes Back its Land* have done much to balance what was for far too long a one-sided conversation, and have done even more to publicise the enormous amount of actual study on land reform that has been undertaken in Zimbabwe over the past decade, they conveniently ignore those most egregiously harmed in the whole process: black farm workers on large-scale farms. As Martin Plaut noted in a review of both works in *African Arguments*, 'The authors do acknowledge the suffering of the labourers, but appear to regard it as a residual problem that simply has to be tidied up.' (Source: AfricanArguments.org, 'Zimbabwe Takes Back its Land – A

377

Review', 21 March 2013). That said, the idea that Fast Track Land Reform was an unmitigated disaster is no longer viable, a fact that presents very real dilemmas on how policymakers in sub-Saharan Africa consider the issue of land transfers going forward.

44 'Selebi trial: State reaffirms the basics', *Daily Maverick*, 3 November 2009.

45 'Billy Rautenbach "scores" ethanol increase', *Mail & Guardian*, 4 October 2013.

46 One of the inevitabilities of the economic collapse following land reform was the endemic fuel shortages that periodically ground Zimbabwe to a halt from 2003 until shortly after dollarisation. This was the sort of thing that *Mad Max* movies were made of, and there were many prelapsarian articles written for the international press depicting a frozen, carless Harare. Here's one: 'Zimbabwe's bustle, business evaporate with fuel shortage', *Washington Post*, 25 July 2005.

47 'Ethanol project: A poisoned chalice', *Zimbabwe Independent*, 31 August 2012.

48 This, again, is one of southern Africa's great disputed numbers, but as far as we can tell, these bear the most scrutiny. *Zimbabwe's Land Reform: Myths & Realities*, Ian Scoones et al (James Currey, 2010), p 272.

49 Like hundreds of such cables, this one is worth reading in full for the eye-popping insight it offers into the sleaze of power. 'Viewing cable 09HARARE1012, OUTSID- ERS, VIEWS OF THE INSIDE OF ZANU-PF'. Full text available here: https://wikileaks. org/cable/2009/12/09HARARE1012.html.

50 Ibid.

51 'Big plans for ethanol ignore fears', *Mail & Guardian*, 10 January 2014.

52 Liu Guijin and various members of the Chi- nese Foreign Ministry would tell us other- wise – according to them, FOCAC was the idea of Madagascar's former minister of foreign affairs, Lila Ratsifandrihama.

53 Kangai, a veteran ZANU foot soldier, died in August 2013, but not before lifting the lid on details of ZANU's bad behaviour and shoddy preparation during several critical stages of the Bush War. One newspaper was prompted to ask whether Kangai was

Zimbabwe's Julian Assange. He was also the first cabinet minister to be arrested on corruption charges.

54 *Africa: Altered States, Ordinary Miracles*, Richard Dowden (Portobello, 2008, Kindle edition).

55 '19 horrifying facts about Robert Mugabe as world's oldest leader turns 91', Metro. co.uk, 21 February 2015.

56 'Tobacco provides road to agricultural recovery', *Business Day*, 16 April 2016.

57 'Zimbabwe turns up heat on diamond min- ers', EWN.co.za, 22 March 2015.

58 We come finally, as we must, to the legend- ary piece the Ugandan academic Mahmood Mamdani wrote for the *London Review of Books* in 2008, entitled 'Lessons of Zim- babwe'. The only other piece either of us can think of that so rattled the Africa Con- sensus cage was Binyavanga Wainaina's *Granta* classic 'How to write about Africa', but while the latter was satire, the former was hardcore analysis. Mamdani's conten- tion, which has been adopted by many a radical (and not so radical) southern Afri- can intellectual, is that land reform was a supreme act of de-colonisation, one that rendered Zimbabwe significantly more 'free' than any of its neo-liberal neigh- bours. Landing as it did in 2008, the argu- ment was deliciously provocative, and it shocks to this day: if farm invasions are not *the* way forward, they are at least *a* way forward.

CHAPTER FIVE: NIGERIA

1 According to a report prepared by the communications department of Nigeria's UNDP, the country has had a press cul- ture since the first missionary paper, *Iwe Iroyin*, was published in 1859. Nigeria's largest circulation newspaper, *The Sun*, is big on the country's music and film indus- try scuttlebutt, and it is one of 100 print media titles, and at least as many websites, that have a co-dependent relationship with Nollywood.

2 In a brilliant keynote address given by Nobel Laureate Wole Soyinka at a

FESPACO workshop in Ouagadougou, Burkina Faso, in February 2013, the term 'Nollywood' inspired him to new heights of enraged prolixity. 'Within the prolific field on which we are gathered here today – the cinema – there is a word that has become current, one that I still find difficult to utter,' he said. 'It sets my teeth on edge, this hideous child of lackluster imagination. And yet it appears to be a source of pride to the practitioners it implicates. What one would have regarded as a singular aberration, a regrettable moment of a verbal infelicity, has developed into a child of competitive adoption, sustained by a number of would-be surrogate parents. One shudders to imagine how many other variations can be squeezed out of the original banality, as each nation evolves a cinema industry and strains to force the original horror into the tube of its own nominal identity – again, with pride!' He went on to quote an opinion piece from the Nigerian journal *The Nation*, which stated that, 'Naming in Africa, especially in Yorubaland, is a special gift that the ancestors as progenitors of the nation bestowed on the elders. Names have meaning, and – as they would have us believe, names push their bearers to actualise their encoded meanings. (*Oruko a maa ro omo*) – literally – 'the name may mould the child'. So you don't find any Yoruba parent giving to their babies names that embed evil meanings.' In other words, Soyinka is not a fan of the 'Nollywood' tag. Full text of the speech available here: http://www.nigeriafilms.com/news/20655/20/everything-is-oversize-in-the-birthplace-of-nollyw.html.

3 Many visitors to southern Nigeria are struck by how prominent evangelical Christianity is in almost every sphere of daily life. As Eliza Griswold points out in her remarkable book *The Tenth Parallel: Dispatches From the Fault Line Between Christianity and Islam* (Farrar, Straus and Giroux, 2010), p 18: 'Being a citizen in Nigeria means next to nothing; in many regions, the state offers no electricity, water or education. Instead, for access to everything from schooling to power lines,

many Nigerians turn to religion. Being a Christian or a Muslim, belonging to the local church or mosque, and voting along religious lines become the way to safeguard seemingly secular rights.' Many southern Nigerian films have an obligatory church scene, and in September 2013, superstar Jim Iyke made an appearance at Prophet TB Joshua's Synagogue, Church of all Nations (SCOAN) mega-church, in order to have an evil spirit tamed. As the Gbooza.com website noted, 'The humility demonstrated by Jim Iyke in submitting himself to the power of God should prompt others in his industry to make the same life-saving choice.'

4 'Omotola Jalade-Ekeinde', *Time*, 18 April 2013.

5 Since Nollywood's inception in 1992, there have been numerous government initiatives to help support and grow the industry, most notably a promise made by then-president Olusegun Obasanjo in his 2004 budget speech. As we've already indicated, little has come of such efforts. Moreover, chunks of financing have languished in the coffers of French cultural bodies, with Nigerian producers tending to dismiss them as a means of asserting foreign control over the industry. (The French have anyway preferred to concentrate on 35mm feature-length productions made in the Francophonie, most of which debut at the bi-annual FESPACO festival in Ouagadougou, Burkina Faso.)

The state's two official regulatory organs, the Nigerian Film Corporation (NFC) and the National Film and Video Censors Board (NFVCB), have often fallen into pointless competition, and the latter is unsurprisingly viewed with deep circumspection. Instead, the filmmaking professionals have themselves set up a network of associations and guilds in order to provide a regulatory framework, including the Motion Pictures Practitioners' Association of Nigeria (MOPPAN), the Actor's Guild, and the Dancer's Guild. The filmmaker Mahmood Ali Balogun became the inaugural head of the Quality Control Committee, while fellow shooter Teco Benson headed the Committee for the Control of Film Releases, two organisations meant to inject a measure of standardisation into film releases.

6 'Goodluck Jonathan: Improbable rise to pinnacle of power', *Financial Times*, 29 September 2010.

7 The enduring punch of *Things Fall Apart* is to be found not only in the fact that it was one of the first books to properly humanise the African for Western audiences, but, equally, in the fact that it unforgettably demonstrated how the Western literary tradition had removed the African from his own narrative. Here, of course, we are referring to the famous closing line, which comes after the British district commissioner has encountered the dead body of the protagonist, Okonkwo, dangling from a tree (he has killed himself in despair at the unwillingness of his Igbo brothers to take on the white invaders). The district commissioner considers that the scene would make good material for his own book – a paragraph, at least, if not a chapter. Writes Achebe: 'He had already chosen the title of the book, after much thought: *The Pacification of the Primitive Tribes of the Lower Niger.' Things Fall Apart*, Chinua Achebe (Heinemann, 1990), p 148.

8 *There Was a Country: A Personal History of Biafra*, Chinua Achebe (Penguin, 2012), p 59.

9 *Nollywood: The Video Phenomenon in Nigeria*, ed Pierre Barrot (James Currey, 2009), p 3.

10 'Nollywood rivals Bollywood in film/video production', UNESCO Institute for Statistics, Media Services, September 2009. Available here: http://www.unesco.org/new/en/media-services/single-view/news/nollywood_rivals_bollywood_in_film-video_production/#.UkLxKRaTO8V.

11 *Nollywood: The Video Phenomenon in Nigeria*, ed Pierre Barrot, p 33.

12 'Lights, Camera, Action', *The Economist*, 16 December 2010.

13 'Hollywood, meet Nollywood', *Forbes*, 19 April 2011

14 'Nigeria's Jason Njoku is creating the next Netflix in Nigeria', *Fast Company*, April 2013.

15 *Nollywood: The Video Phenomenon in Nigeria*, ed Pierre Barrot, p 33.

16 'In Kinshasa,' the film scholar Matthias Krings has noted, 'Nollywood films have been employed as audiovisual likenesses during mass in Pentecostal churches, where Congolese bilingual pastors have translated and elaborated on them for the benefit of their congregations. In Kenya they have influenced local dress style to the extent that even politicians have been spotted wearing Nigerian gowns.' *Viewing African Film in the Twenty-First Century: Art Films and the Nollywood Video Revolution*, ed Mahir Saul and Ralph A Austen (Ohio University Press, 2010), p 89.

17 As Nathan Lee noted in a *New York Times* review of the film, dated 2 July 2009: 'The documentary concludes with a provocative, if shallow, examination of the impact of evangelical Christianity on Nigerian movies. The exploitation and wish-fulfillment ethos of Nollywood, Mr Addelman and Mr Mallal also imply, has a narcotic function on the culture, arresting its development from "tradition to modernity"' Full review available at: http://movies.nytimes.com/2009/07/03/movies/03noll.html?_r=0.

18 *Nollywood: The Video Phenomenon in Nigeria*, ed Pierre Barrot, p 53.

19 An observer wins no points in Nigerian intellectual circles for overstating Nollywood's anti-establishment credentials, especially considering the out-and-out stridency of Nigerian theatre's history, as practised by Wole Soyinka, Ola Rotimi, and the flamboyant impresario Hubert Ogunde, who considered the stage a 'political weapon'. (This is to say nothing of music or writing, which also have dissenting traditions.) Nonetheless, Nollywood films rarely offer the sort of anodyne depiction of government or the elite one finds in the Mexican telenova tradition. The leading Nollywood scholar Jonathan Haynes defines the political in Nollywood as 'the level of banal, everyday production of authority, the personal level of gender relationships, witchcraft discourses – all the myriad social tensions and controversies to which the video films have responded with literally thousands of stories whose

political valence deserves analysis'. *Nolly-wood: The Video Phenomenon in Nigeria*, ed Pierre Barrot, p 36.

20 In an article on its website somewhat paternalistically entitled 'Hooray for Nollywood?', the American production company Focus Features nevertheless nails the essence of the piracy issue: 'The NFVCB performs a more valuable service in attempting to counter piracy. But this is something of a losing battle, as there are 23,000 illegal video clubs in Nigeria and few of them purchase their V-CDs from approved suppliers. This means that marketers often make losses on even their bestselling films and they frequently withhold fees from their powerless casts and crews.' Full text available here: http://www.focusfeatures. com/article/hooray_for_nollywood_/print.

21 Soyinka in Burkina Faso again, regarding Nollywood films: '[W]e are speaking of an original work of art that is anything but original, filled with borrowings from so many genres. My complaint therefore is not against borrowings and adaptations as a principle, but against the lack of originality that translates as plain, unmediated imitation, or a tawdry, unenhanced borrowing that is conceived and delivered on the very edge of the pit of banality, and out of which it has no wish to clamber, once it has fallen in. It indicates a pre-set mind, a basically unadventurous mind dressed up in castoff clothing, of which nothing can be expected except as a breeding ground, a reproductive automatism of its own kind – especially in taste.'

22 'The Enemy Within: Oil in the Niger Delta', Fidelis Allen, *World Policy Institute*, Winter 2012. According to OPEC statistics in 2012, Nigeria had the tenth largest oil reserves in the world, with a further 5 110 billion cubic metres of natural gas, the ninth largest reserves in the world.

23 Ibid. Allen writes of a notorious Shell pipeline spill, which occurred in 2008: 'Large villages of hundreds of people are caked with oil. It has penetrated the earth and seeped into the groundwater. The family of Mene Eric Barizaa Doe in Goi village is one of thousands of victims, living in the vast oily quagmire that runs through the

streets, seeps up the side of buildings, and has left half his family victims of illnesses ranging from skin diseases to cancer. The 2008 spill destroyed his late father's fishing ponds, the only means of support for the family.'

24 Although our taxi driver was adamant that the situation was calmer than it had been in years, and while Bayelsa State governor Seriake Dickson would affirm as much in a speech we would hear that night, MEND was then still firmly on the offensive. In late March 2013, after the movement's leader Henry Okah had been sentenced to 24 years in prison by a South African court, a statement was released containing the words, 'The gates of hell have just been let loose.' In early April, less than two weeks before our arrival, 12 Nigerian policemen had been killed by MEND gunmen in Bayelsa State. The government's Joint Task Force managed to capture more than 100 MEND militants in April 2013 alone, but the kidnappings and bombings of oil pipelines would continue.

25 Ministry of Niger Delta Affairs Website, available here: http://mnda.gov.ng/mnda/trade-and-investments/. What makes the site worth a visit is the number of oil company logos that appear on the home page under the 'MNDA Partners' banner – a visual emphasis of just how integrated international oil corporations (IOCs) are in both the history and the governance of the Delta region.

26 'Nigeria: No. 1 in Africa by 2014?' FT.com, available here: http://blogs.ft.com/beyond-brics/2012/02/08/nigeria-no-1-in-africa-by-2014/#axzz2gZbd6nnG. In this construction, Nigeria would change the 'base year' for its economy from 1990 to 2008, in a move that would theoretically better reflect economic performance. When neighbouring Ghana rebased in 2010, its GDP was revised from $18bn to $31bn. Without rebasing, considering South Africa grows at roughly 2.5 per cent a year to Nigeria's 7.5 per cent, the D-day was around 2020. Again, we feel the need to emphasise the fact that this doesn't speak to the *quality* of the economies, but to their *size* measured by GDP.

27 *African Development Bank Group, Federal Republic of Nigeria, Country Strategy Paper 2013-2017* (ORWA, January 2013), p 2.

28 Dr Ngozi Okonjo-Iweala is an example of the dazzling talent in the diaspora who return home to 'give back', sometimes with ambiguous results. Before serving as foreign minister for the first time in 2003, during then-president Olusegun Obasanjo's second term in office, Okonjo-Iweala spent 21 years at the World Bank as a development economist, and ended her first tenure as the bank's vice president and corporate secretary. Armed with a degree from Harvard and a PhD from MIT, as finance minister she successfully negotiated with the Paris Club of Creditors a $30 billion write down of Nigeria's debt, 'including the outright cancellation of 60 per cent of Nigeria's external debt, equivalent to US$18 billion'. Despite these successes, Okonjo-Iweala's term was tumultuous, and she resigned in 2006 after Obasanjo removed her from Nigeria's Economic Team. She made a bid for the head of the World Bank, losing out to the American Jim Yong Kim, before returning as finance minister under President Goodluck Jonathan. She was left to dangle before the popular outrage surrounding the removal of the fuel subsidy at the beginning of 2012, which ushered in the precedent-setting Occupy Nigeria movement. More bumps in the road were guaranteed.

29 *Reforming the Unreformable: Lessons from Nigeria*, Ngozi Okonjo-Iweala (MIT Press, 2012), p 15.

30 '2013 World Population Data Sheet', Population Reference Bureau, September 2013. Available here: http://www.prb.org/pdf13/2013-population-data-sheet_eng.pdf.

31 'Can moguls untangle Nigeria's power lines?' *Wall Street Journal*, 23 April 2014.

32 *Chief Eddie Ugbomah: His Films @ 70*, self-published, 2011, p 17.

33 'When the police refused to assist me when I was shooting *Oyenusi*,' writes Chief Eddie, 'it was only General Danjuma who supported me by allowing us to shoot a real execution of armed robbers at the Bar Beach. I was allowed to meet and discuss with the Commander of the executors. On getting to the scene all the crew, sound man ... set up the equipment and ran away. We had to shoot both the real execution and false with the crew [sic]. I thank General Danjuma for his support. This is the only film in the world where real execution was shot in a film.' Ibid, p 9.

34 Ibid, p 3.

35 *The State of Africa: A History of the Continent Since Independence*, Martin Meredith (Jonathan Ball, 2011), p 76.

36 *The Tenth Parallel: Dispatches From the Fault Line Between Christianity and Islam* (Farrar, Straus and Giroux, 2010), p. 3: 'The tenth parallel is the horizontal band that rings the earth seven hundred miles north of the equator. If Africa is shaped like a rumpled sock, with South Africa at the toe and Somalia at the heel, then the tenth parallel runs across the ankle. Along the tenth parallel, in Sudan, and in most of inland Africa, two worlds collide: the mostly Muslim, Arab-influenced north meets a black African south inhabited by Christians and those who follow indigenous religions – which include those who venerate ancestors and the spirits of animals, land, and sky.'

37 'That night of January 15, 1966,' wrote Chinua Achebe, 'is something Nigeria has never really recovered from.' *There Was a Country: A Personal History of Biafra*, Chinua Achebe (Penguin, 2012), p. 70.

38 In a chapter in *There Was a Country* entitled 'The Question of Genocide', Achebe writes the following: 'Why were there one hundred thousand casualties on the much larger Nigerian side compared with more than two million – mainly children – Biafrans killed? The government of Harold Wilson proffered what it called a 'legitimate strategy' excuse in which it postulates that the indisputable excesses seen during the war were due to the Nigerian military's 'excellence' – clearly making it the strongest candidate for an all-time foot-in-mouth prize.' Ibid, p. 254.

39 'FESTAC for black people: oil capitalism and the spectacle of culture in Nigeria', Andrew Apter, Evanston, IL: Program of African Studies, Northwestern University

no. 6, pp. 1-3, 5, 1993. Available here: http://quod.lib.umich.edu/p/passages/4761 530.0006.002?rgn=main;view=fulltext.

40 *Lagos: A Cultural & Historical Companion*, Kaye Whiteman (Signal Books, 2012), p 130.

41 Martin Meredith, *The State of Africa*, p 220.

42 Ibid, p 221.

43 Pierre Barrot ed, *Nollywood: The Video Phenomenon in Nigeria*, p 64.

44 Ibid, p 74.

45 *Viewing African Cinema in the Twenty-First Century: Art Films and the Nollywood Video Revolution*, ed Mahir Saul and Ralph A Austen (Ohio University Press, 2010), 'What Is to Be Done: Film Studies and Nigerian and Ghanaian Videos', Jonathan Haynes, p 15.

46 'Movie studios are forcing Hollywood to abandon 35mm film. But the consequences of going digital are vast, and troubling', *LA Weekly*, 12 April 2012.

47 *Gorilla in the Room: Koos Bekker and the Rise and Rise of Naspers*, Anton Harber (MampoerShorts, 2012), p 8.

48 'Nigerians knock DStv services, bemoan exploitation', *Daily Independent*, 22 September 2013.

49 *Gorilla in the Room*, Anton Harber, p 31.

50 *AfricaMagic@10: Proudly and Passionately African!*, AfricaMagic 10th Birthday Press Release, November 2013.

51 In a 2011 article in *Forbes* magazine, Shoreline was named one of Nigeria's 'most storied' conglomerates. The piece looked at how Nigeria's millionaires were embracing polo, and included short items on Sayyu Dantata (half-brother to Aliko Dangote, Africa's richest man), oil trader Mustapha Fasinro, and the Makanjuola brothers, Bode and Rotimi. Karim was cited as 'one of the most popular polo players in Nigeria,' with an impressive handicap of -1. Full text available here: http://www.forbes. com/sites/mfonobongnsehe/2011/05/23/ nigerian-millionaires-embrace-polo/

52 *The Eagle and the Springbok: Strengthening the Nigeria/South Africa Relationship*, Policy Advisory Group Seminar Report (Centre for Conflict Resolution, 2012), p 23.

53 Black Economic Empowerment, or BEE, was the mandatory programme instituted in 2003 by South Africa's African National Congress government. BEE, later Broad-Based Black Economic Empowerment, was designed to address the abject lack of black representation among the country's business community. It formed an immensely complex piece of affirmative action legislation that would eventually be whittled down to the fact that it allowed a narrow band of politically connected black businessmen and women to successfully bid on government contracts, especially in critical sectors like energy. Although BEE has certainly uplifted many worthy businessmen and women, it has more often than not been seen as a replacement mechanism, one elite for another. Considered in this light, there was no way that Kola Karim, despite his skin colour, would have been deemed a successful BEE applicant.

54 As Kola Karim put it during our interview: 'There is this paint from the press on how bad we are as a people, as Africans. So that fear! There's 170 million Nigerians – I don't think there's even two-and-a-half per cent that are fraudulent or criminals. But there's a standard, a stigmatised standard, that Nigerians are criminals.'

55 *The Eagle and the Springbok: Strengthening the Nigeria/South Africa Relationship*, Policy Advisory Group Seminar Report, p 16.

56 As an example of this, it was reported in July 2013 that Aliko Dangote, Nigeria and Africa's richest man, had teamed up with the Nigerian central bank to establish a $25 million tomato paste factory. A study commissioned by the central bank had shown that it would be cheaper to process local tomatoes than import the product from China; what's more, the initiative would boost income for 8 000 farmers. Much more significant, however, was the announcement in September 2013 that Dangote had signed a multi-billion dollar deal with Nigerian and foreign banks to finance the construction of an oil refinery in the country – the $9 billion venture, to come on-stream in 2016, was seen as the ultimate in the local 'beneficiation' of not just Nigeria's natural resources, but of

Africa's as a whole.

57 *The Eagle and the Springbok: Strengthening the Nigeria/South Africa Relationship*, Policy Advisory Group Seminar Report, pp 4-5.

58 Full online video of the TED talk available here: http://www.ted.com/talks/chimamanda_adichie_the_danger_of_a_single_story.html.

59 'Nigeria's "Nollywood" seeks overseas acclaim', *Financial Times*, 10 October 2013.

60 The petition, amongst other things, noted the following: 'This petition is important, because we live in a world where mass media sells us the belief that white, and anything close to white is right, and black is not only wrong, it is unattractive, and undesirable. We are indoctrinated into these beliefs consciously and subconsciously through media images. Like many other countries in Africa, Nigeria suffers from the epidemic of skin bleaching. Many Nigerian women buy lotions, to lighten their once dark skin to become lighter. This practice has not only severe medical side effects, it is preaching an acceptance of self hate.' Full text available here: http://www.change.org/petitions/the-casting-of-thandie-newton-in-half-of-a-yellow-sun-reconsider-casting-of-half-of-a-yellow-sun.

61 'TIFF 2013 Review – Biyi Bandele's adaptation of "Half Of A Yellow Sun" misses the mark', *Indiewire*, 12 September 2013.

62 'Nigeria's "Nollywood" seeks overseas acclaim', *Financial Times*, 10 October 2013.

63 The piracy of intellectual property is an immensely complex issue, especially so in the African context. While the international film industry may indeed lose close to $20 billion a year (losses that hurt artists, are unfair and illegal, but were long ago accounted for in the system), it certainly does not represent, as so many anti-piracy advocates assert, a 'loss to the economy'. Far from it. As a 2010 US Accountability Office report pointed out, '[the] effects of piracy within the United States are mainly redistributions within the economy for other purposes and ... should not be considered as a loss to the overall economy'. In this case, what's true for the United States is true for Nigeria – the area boy selling a *Last Flight to Abuja* bootleg still, one assumes, belongs to the larger economy.

64 *A Survey of the Nigerian Middle Class*, Charles Robertson, Nothando Ndebele and Yvonne Mhango (Renaissance Capital, September 2011), p 3. Here we go again: the Renaissance Capital report is remarkably bullish on Nigeria, even by 'Africa Rising' standards. The report considers IMF estimations of $2 000 per-capita GDP by 2016 as 'pessimistic', and maintains that a figure of $2 500 is more accurate. However the survey group – 1 004 Nigerians, 70 per cent of whom were 40 years old or younger, and all of whom were located in Lagos, Abuja or Port Harcourt – strikes us as narrow. The report also makes little of the fact that its prognostications rely on oil prices remaining stable at over $100 a barrel.

65 Not that festivals should be the ultimate measure of literary trends, but at the 2013 *Etonnants Voyageurs* festival in St Malo, France – which the authors of this book attended – Sefı Atta, Teju Cole, Helon Habila and Noo Saro-Wiwa packed the halls as the touted representatives of Nigeria's emergent voice. One discussion was focused on Lagos as setting and as inspiration, and nobody in the audience seemed to doubt that the city's rampant fecundity bore a direct correlation to the strength of their prose. Where was Chimamanda Ngozi Adichie? According to sources, the festival, big as it was, could not afford her fee.

66 'A Scorsese in Lagos: The making of Nigeria's film industry', *New York Times Magazine*, 23 February 2012.

67 'The Megacity', *The New Yorker*, 13 November 2006.

68 'Jason Njoku writes: Iroko is dead, long live Irokotv', Ynaija.com, last accessed January 2014: http://www.ynaija.com/jason-njoku-writes-iroko-is-dead-long-live -irokotv/.

69 'Iroko's Jason Njoku is creating the next Netflix in Nigeria', *Fast Company*, April 2013.

70 'How Africa's new urban centers are shifting its old colonial boundaries', *The Atlantic*, 1 July 2013.

CHAPTER SIX: DEMOCRATIC REPUBLIC OF THE CONGO

1 David van Reybrouck, on page 95 of his remarkable *Congo: The Epic History of a People* (HarperCollins, 2014), points out that it is 'impossible to say how many people died as a direct or indirect result of Leopold's rubber policies'. Further, he rejects the use of the terms 'genocide' and 'Holocaust', preferring instead 'hecatomb', which denotes *unintentional* slaughter on a massive scale. The estimate of 10 million dead comes from what was perhaps the most influential mainstream text on Congolese history before Van Reybrouck's, Adam Hochschild's *King Leopold's Ghost: A Story of Greed, Terror and Heroism in Colonial Africa* (First Mariner Books, 1999), pp 225-34.

2 Ibid, p 279.

3 Ibid.

4 The story behind this is by now a famous one, easily *the* archetypal narrative of the Cold War in Africa – which is partly due to the fact that despite the intrigues and conspiracy theories, certain details remain true. As Van Reybrouck notes, both the United Nations *and* the United States had been keen to get rid of Patrice Lumumba, the Congo's first black head of state, after he had been in office for only a month (*Congo: The Epic History of a People*, p 309). Although the actual murder of Lumumba in January 1961 was 'the work of Katangan authorities', neither the UN nor the US's Central Intelligence Agency – which were both acutely aware of what was about to happen – did anything to stop it. Belgium's role in Lumumba's execution was less passive, as Belgian military men, who were in charge of the Katangan guardsmen, 'took part in the killing itself' (*Congo: The Epic History of a People*, p 310). For what reason, then, did the young prime minister die?

The ill-fated Katangan secession, which lasted from just a few months after independence to January 1963, certainly played a part in it: Lumumba had been a staunch unitarian, and thus an archenemy of the Katangan leader Moïse Tshombe.

But the real issue was a telegram Lumumba had sent to the Soviet Union in July 1960, asking Moscow for support in the event that Belgian troops did not immediately vacate sovereign Congolese soil. While Lumumba had always been more of a classic liberal than a socialist, the telegram had in a 'single swoop' brought Africa into the Cold War (*Congo: The Epic History of a People*, p 298). Joseph Mobutu, who on the day of independence had been Lumumba's 29-year-old private secretary, would prove to be the most skilful man in the country at negotiating this new reality. With the tacit backing of the CIA he would rise to commander-in-chief of the army, presiding over government troops during a battle with rebel forces in the east; on 24 November 1965, Mobutu himself would oust the government in a coup. For most of the rest of the century, the US would forgive Mobutu all of his transgressions – in return, the president would ensure that this giant chunk of the African continent never got painted Red.

5 Or this, at least, was Mobutu's own translation in the Ngbendu. As Martin Meredith drily notes, the Tshiluba translation is more succinct: 'Invincible warrior; cock who leaves no chick intact.' *The State of Africa: A History of the Continent Since Independence* (Jonathan Ball, 2011), p 296.

6 Ibid, p 297.

7 These landholdings were merged into an entity called Cultures et Elevages du Zaïre, or Celza. 'In one transaction alone in 1976,' notes Martin Meredith, 'one of the plantation companies [Mobutu] seized transferred $1 million to his Swiss bank account.' Ibid, pp 296-97.

8 By the close of the decade, Mobutu had become one of the world's wealthiest men, with a fortune that by the 1980s would grow to $5 billion. How did he spend this wealth? Much like Leopold II, he splashed out on property and palaces. In fact, as Adam Hochschild notes, Mobutu's Villa del Mare, a marble colonnaded chateau on the French Riviera replete with gold-fitted bathrooms and indoor and outdoor swimming pools, lay within sight of one of Leopold's former estates at Cap Ferrat. *King*

Leopold's Ghost: A Story of Greed, Terror and Heroism in Colonial Africa, p 304.

9 'Democratic Republic of the Congo: A Study of Binding Constraints', Alfie Ulloa, Felipe Katz & Nicole Kekeh (John F Kennedy School of Government, Harvard University, 2009), p 13. Full text available here: http://www.hks.harvard.edu/fs/drodrik/Growth%20diagnostics%20papers/DRC_Growth_Diagnostic.pdf

10 Ibid, pp 11-12.

11 Ibid, p 13.

12 'The more remote provinces of Katanga, Maniema, Orientale, the Kasaïs and the Kivus suffered a great deal from this forced economic isolation,' the authors of the Harvard paper write. 'The consequences are still visible today where large parts of the population are disconnected from trade routes and services, in particular in the rural areas.' Ibid, p 15.

13 Ibid.

14 Our flight onto the Kibali mine, DRC, in March 2012, was from Entebbe Airport in Uganda. As we were waiting in Uganda to catch it, the NGO Invisible Children's 'Kony 2012' video hit the net, and subsequently went massively viral. Has there ever been a weirder NGO campaign, with creepier results? The video, which as of this writing has 100 million views on YouTube, was meant to prompt the Obama administration into doing something about the LRA's use of child soldiers – which it did (he sent 100 training troops to the country). And while no one we met in Uganda or the DRC had seen or heard of the campaign, the fact that Invisible Children's Jason Russell subsequently underwent a very public meltdown served as further proof for Kony's backers of the rebel leader's incredible occult powers.

15 Che Guevara, who planned to use Laurent Kabila's 'liberated' mountain stronghold as a base for training revolutionary movements from across southern Africa, encountered only failure and fiasco on the 1965 expedition. After his brief meeting with Kabila in a jungle hideout above Lake Tanganyika, Guevara – as Martin Meredith notes – would write the following in his diary: 'He let the days pass without concerning himself with anything other than political squabbles, and all the signs are that he is too addicted to drink and women.' *The State of Africa: A History of the Continent Since Independence*, pp 149-50.

16 David van Reybrouck, in characterising the livelihood of the elder Kabila in these terms, goes on memorably to call it 'the mixed farming of African crime'. *Congo: The Epic History of a People* (HarperCollins, 2014), p 418.

17 The *génocidaires*, who had slipped into the eastern DRC along with the massive influx of Hutu civilian refugees, quickly gained control of the tented camps around Lake Kivu. It is to the development community's eternal shame that the vast bulk of international aid sent out to these camps was distributed – at a price – by the same men who'd been responsible for 800 000 deaths in a hundred days in early 1994.

18 Meredith, *The State of Africa*, p 531.

19 *Congo: The Epic History of a People*, David van Reybrouck (HarperCollins, 2014), pp 419-420

20 David Moore, in citing this figure from the *Journal of Modern African Studies* (June 2000, pp 163-202) writes: '[The invasion force] executed a quarter to a half the number that the *Interahamwe* slaughtered after [Juvenal] Habyarimana's jet was shot out of the sky on April 6 1994, and very few voices have uttered the word "genocide" about the massacres in the Congo.' *The War Economy in the Democratic Republic of the Congo*, Sagaren Naidoo, ed (Institute for Global Dialogue, 2003), p 23.

21 The sale of Okimo assets at the end of Mobutu's reign, a measure implemented in a desperate attempt to fill state coffers, was one of a number of public-private partnerships that sought to unlock the country's mineral wealth.

22 'The Political Economy of the DRC Conflict', David Moore, in Naidoo, *The War Economy in the Democratic Republic of the Congo*, p 23.

23 Ibid.

24 *Congo: The Epic History of a People*, David van Reybrouck (HarperCollins, 2014), p 438.

25 Ibid, p 439.

26 A reference to Ridley Scott's 2001 film, which was an adaptation of Mark Bowden's 1997 book of the same name, *Black Hawk Down* chronicles the events of the Battle of Mogadishu, in which US Army Rangers, Delta Force soldiers and aviators from the 160th SOAR attempted to capture or kill Somali warlord Mohamed Farrah Aidid. Although justifiably critiqued in the *New York Times* for being somewhat glib and racist, the film did highlight a seminal event in post-Cold War African history. The television news images of US soldiers being dragged through the streets of the Somali capital, and the failure of the mission itself, had resulted in a profound shift in US government policy in Africa. As Walter Clarke, the US's former deputy special envoy to Somalia, would later note: 'The ghosts of Somalia continue to haunt US policy. Our lack of response in Rwanda was a fear of getting involved in something like a Somalia all over again.'

27 Jason Stearns, in his authoritative *Dancing in the Glory of Monsters: The Collapse of the Congo and The Great War of Africa* (PublicAffairs, 2012), argues that it is for this reason that the theory of international mining capital *fuelling* the war does not hold water, pp 289-90.

28 'Africa burns, Canada fiddles: Empty words condemning genocide won't stop the bullets in the largest landmass war in history. Only forthright action stops wars', *Globe and Mail*, 20 March 1999.

29 *Congo: The Epic History of a People*, David van Reybrouck (HarperCollins, 2014), p 444.

30 *Congo: The Epic History of a People*, David van Reybrouck, p 445.

31 In the viper's nest of late Cold War African geopolitics, Kagame's Rwanda was, along with the Soviets and most notably the Cubans, backing Agostinho Neto's Movimento Popular de Libertação de Angola – Partido do Trabalho, or MPLA. Meanwhile, Mobutu, along with South Africa and the Americans, was behind the União Nacional para a Independência Total de Angola, or UNITA. Along the border between Angola and the DRC were diamonds in abundance, and being able to control the fields meant

access to significant war booty. The war tipped steadily in favour of the MPLA, and by the time the 1990s rolled around, UNITA was little more than a nuisance – albeit a deadly one – in the south. Nonetheless, Mobutu was punished for backing the wrong horse.

32 'The Curse of Gold', Human Rights Watch (2005), p 16.

33 The man's name, according to Human Rights Watch, was Samduo Tango, and he was serving at the time as the local Okimo director. A witness at the scene of the beating said: 'Samduo had to pay to be released and then he fled. Another person who was beaten was Aveto as he witnessed the Ugandans taking dynamite from the warehouse. He was arrested along with Samduo and also publicly beaten....' Ibid, p 17.

34 The Lusaka Ceasefire Agreement, heavily touted by the United Nations, was signed on 23 July 1999, between Angola, the DRC, Namibia, Rwanda, Uganda, Zambia and Zimbabwe. The full agreement is available at: http://www.ucdp.uu.se/gpdatabase/peace/DRC%2019990710.pdf

35 The first agreement didn't work, and so a second was signed at the South African golf and gambling mecca Sun City. It was an odd location to negotiate the putative end to one of the more deadly wars in living memory, but it further heralded then-South African president Thabo Mbeki's age of 'African Renaissance', a reference to a classic speech he delivered in slightly different iterations over the course of the late 1990s.

36 Known as the Porter Commission, the inquiry conducted interviews with a number of the same Ugandan officers mentioned in the Human Rights Watch report, all of whom denied involvement. The commission found that the officers were lying, and that there had been a cover up. 'The Curse of Gold', Human Rights Watch (2005), p 20.

37 Ibid.

38 This information on the background to the deal was provided courtesy of Louis Watum, who knew and had worked with the Damseaux family, and had been appointed an executive director at Moto Gold in 2006.

According to Watum, the total amount of the loans furnished by the family to Okimo through the 1980s and 1990s was $3 million, which had ballooned with interest to an overall debt of $30 million. Given that they would eventually sell their equity stake in the Moto Gold operation for $70 million, the family's return on investment would in the end (and by any measure) be substantial.

39 The World Bank 2012 figure placed US GDP at $15.68 trillion. For the same year, Eurostat placed the European Union's combined GDP at $16.57 trillion. The figure of $24 trillion worth of mineral resources is from a report of the United Nations Environment Programme, 'The Democratic Republic of the Congo: Post-Conflict Environmental Assessment' (2011), p 22.

40 The mission had for more than 10 years been known as MONUC, but its status had recently been upgraded by the Security Council, the conferred 'stability' now earning it the moniker MONUSCO. Resolution 1925 (2010), adopted by the Security Council at its 6 324th meeting, on 28 May 2010. Full text available here: http://www.un.org/en/ga/search/view_doc. asp?symbol=S/RES/1925(2010)

41 Albert Einstein, in a letter to United States President FD Roosevelt dated August 1939, wrote that the world's 'most important source of uranium is the Belgian Congo'. Three years later, in August 1942, the Manhattan Project director general, Leslie Groves, would purchase 1 250 tons of Belgian Congo uranium. 'Uranium in the Democratic Republic of Congo: Yesterday, Today and Tomorrow', François Kazadi Kabuya (Congo Atomic Energy Commission, 2010), p 9.

42 In November 2012, corroborating our source's version, the chair of the United Nations Security Council Committee on the DRC would send a detailed letter to the Security Council president, which would state on page 4 the following: 'The requirement of the Government of the Democratic Republic of the Congo for mineral exporters to exercise due diligence in accordance with United Nations and Organisation for Economic Cooperation and Development

guidelines has nearly halted all tin, tantalum and tungsten exports from the eastern Democratic Republic of the Congo, apart from north Katanga where mineral tagging was introduced in 2011. Smuggling into both Burundi and Rwanda is on the rise. The credibility of the mineral tagging system in place in Rwanda is jeopardised by the laundering of Congolese minerals because tags are routinely sold by mining cooperatives.' Full text available here: http://www.securitycouncilreport.org/ atf/cf/%7B65BFCF9B-6D27-4E9C-8CD3-CF6E4FF96FF9%7D/s_2012_843.pdf

43 Although the conspiracy theories surrounding Laurent Kabila's assassination are nowhere more alive today than they are in Kinshasa, the generally accepted version is that the president's cousin, Colonel Eddy Kapend, was the man behind the palace coup attempt on 16 January 2001. Kapend, who caught and killed the bodyguard that had actually shot Kabila, would himself be tried by a special military tribunal – he would be one of 25 defendants sentenced to death for the plot, but for some reason he would not be executed. Were Rwandan intelligence officers, working in conjunction with Lebanese diamond dealers, the real masterminds behind the scenes? It's not impossible: the documentary film *Murder in Kinshasa*, by Marlène Rabaud and Arnaud Zajtman, argues for the case. Whatever the truth, Joseph Kabila immediately assumed the presidency, as per his dead father's wish.

44 'Secrecy surrounding Glencore's business deals in the Democratic Republic of Congo risks exposing shareholders to corrupt practices', Global Witness, 9 May 2012, p 1. Full text available here: http:// www.globalwitness.org/sites/default/files/ library/Global%20Witness%20memo%20 on%20Glencore's%20secretive%20dealings%20in%20the%20Democratic%20 Republic%20of%20Congo_1.pdf

45 The Global Witness report would also note that since early 2010 the Congolese state had sold off stakes in six prize mining assets – including Kansuki, Mutanda and a third asset acquired by Glencore – and that, '[i]n all but one of these six projects,

the Congolese government [had] sold off the mines in their entirety, foregoing any future production revenues from the mines.' Ibid.

46 Ibid.

47 'Gertler earns billions as mine deals fail to enrich Congo', *Bloomberg*, 6 December 2012.

48 Ibid.

49 According to Norman Mailer, who was at the fight and would go on to write a boxing classic about it, 'the bet [Hunter] made was that the fight would be a bummer, and that he could still ace us even though he'd spent his time swimming...' Ralph Steadman, Hunter's long-time friend and creator of the distinctive illustrations that accompanied many of his pieces, said this: 'On the night of the fight, Hunter had a big bag of marijuana, and he took a bottle of Glenfiddich I had bought him down to the pool with a bucket of ice and the bag, threw the marijuana into the pool – everyone else was off watching the fight, you know – and dived into the middle of the marijuana and then just hung by the side of the pool, smoking and drinking and loving the whole meaningless nature of it.' *Gonzo: The Life of Hunter S Thompson*, Jann Wenner & Corey Seymour (Back Bay, 2008).

50 While there has been talk of it for years, and while it would be at most four kilometres in length, at the time of this writing there is still no road or rail bridge between Kinshasa and Brazzaville. There is a ferry link between the two cities, but the common understanding is that the government of the Republic of Congo does not want to 'overexpose' its calm and prosperous capital to the volatility and desperation of Kinshasa.

51 The figure of $100 billion was quoted by members of the Western donor community, who had an axe to grind with the Chinese. David van Reybrouck, in writing of the deal, correctly mentions the fluctuation in copper prices in recent years, and argues in this context that the monetary value of the reserve could be anything from $14 billion to $80 billion. *Congo: The Epic History of a People*, David van Reybrouck, p 530.

52 'The Sicomines Agreement: Change and Continuity in the Democratic Republic of Congo's International Relations', Johanna Jansson (SAIIA, 2009), p 5.

53 Ibid, pp 15-16.

54 As per the World Bank, the DRC's GDP for 2009 was $11.2 billion.

55 Jansson writes: 'The exact value of the concessions is not known, and Chinese stakeholders external to the Sicomines JV argued in interviews that CREC took a "wild card" when they agreed to the investment without having conducted in-depth feasibility studies.' 'The Sicomines Agreement', pp 16-17.

56 As a young man, Willem Jacobs played flank for the Orange Free State senior provincial team. 'Fuck, I had injuries,' he told us. 'Sport taught me you have to do the hard yards.'

57 'The Curse of Gold', Human Rights Watch (2005), p 2.

58 Ibid, p 67.

59 Ibid, pp 65-66.

60 'Anglogold Ashanti Regrets Paying Rebels', GhanaWeb.com, 4 June 2005. Available at: http://www.ghanaweb.com/GhanaHome-Page/NewsArchive/Anglogold-Ashanti-Regrets-Paying-Rebels-83108

61 'Letter dated 12 November 2012 from the Chair of the Security Council Committee established pursuant to resolution 1533 (2004) concerning the Democratic Republic of the Congo addressed to the President of the Security Council', (United Nations Security Council, 2012), pp 24-27. Full text available here: http://www.securitycouncilreport.org/atf/cf/%7B65BFCF9B-6D27-4E9C-8CD3-CF6E4FF96FF9%7D/s_2012_843.pdf

62 According to a survey of the International Rescue Committee published in January 2008, the Second Congo War and its aftermath had by that date resulted in 5.4 million deaths. The IRC claimed that 45 000 were then dying of '[m]alaria, diarrhea, pneumonia and malnutrition, aggravated by conflict', every month. Source: 'Congo war-driven crisis kills 45,000 a month: study', *Reuters*, 22 January 2008. Full text available here: http://www.reuters.com/article/2008/01/22/us-congo-democratic-death-idUSL2280201220080122

63 In terms of what this all meant for tax revenues out of Kilo-Moto, the UN Security Council report of November 2012 would note: 'Armed groups, criminal networks within the Congolese armed forces and miners easily shift to gold mines where due diligence requirements have not affected trade. Nearly all gold from the eastern Democratic Republic of the Congo is smuggled out of the country and channeled through a few major traders in Kampala and Bujumbura who ship out several tons per year, worth hundreds of millions of United States dollars.'

64 Randgold Resources Annual Report 2013, p 47.

65 'Randgold CEO says Congo mine-code may reduce investment', *Bloomberg*, 6 May 2014.

66 'Generating "ripple effects" in DR Congo', EITI News, 24 January 2014. Full text available here: http://eiti.org/news/generating -ripple-effects-dr-congo

67 'Review of the Mining Code in the DRC ... risks and advantages for private mining companies', Randgold Resources. Full presentation available here: http://www.randgoldresources.com/randgold/action/media/downloadFile?media_fileid=12076

68 'DR Congo's Lubumbashi hit by fighting', BBC.com, 7 January 2014.

69 United States freelance reporter Jacob Kushner, who in 2013 had published an outstanding multimedia e-book entitled *China's Congo Plan: What the Economic Superpower Sees in the World's Poorest Nation*, noted in March 2014 that although the Sicomines venture turned out to be Beijing's biggest lesson in the need for restraint on the continent, it was far from the only one. 'Risky business: Is China wavering in Africa?' *Think Africa Press*, 14 March 2014.

CHAPTER SEVEN: ETHIOPIA

1 As a night on the town in modern-day Addis Ababa will make abundantly clear, Ethiopians tend to trace their country's origin back to a legendary meeting between King Solomon and the Queen of Sheba, circa 1500 BCE.

2 A quick précis on Ethiopian naming is necessary in order to explain why we've used 'first' names instead of 'surnames' in this chapter. As we will hopefully demonstrate, Ethiopia is an enormously diverse and culturally rich country, and naming – like so many other traditions – is by no means consistent from region to region, from creed to creed, or from religion to religion. That said, as far as successive governments have succeeded in influencing the system, names follow a patriarchal line. An Ethiopian first name corresponds with the tradition of given names in other cultures, which is followed in turn by the father's given name, and then the grandfather's given name. (Women do not change their names when they marry.) In other words, referring to someone named Abebe Bikila Adessu as 'Adessu' would not properly identify that individual as an *individual*. Our interpretation is imperfect, of course, but it's fairly standard in the Ethiopian English language press, and seems to us *more*, rather than *less*, characteristically Ethiopian.

3 It's not too much of a stretch to think of 'Do They Know It's Christmas?' as the most troubling, precedent-setting encounter between Africa and the West of the postcolonial era. The single was the brainchild of Bob Geldof, who co-wrote it with Ultravox's Midge Ure, after watching a BBC special on the Ethiopian famine in October of 1984. Geldof assembled a super-group named Band Aid, and recorded the single in November 1984 with such luminaries as Bono, Sting, Paul McCartney, David Bowie and Phil Collins. It was an instant hit, and had sold about 11.8 million copies by mid-1989, when it was re-recorded by Band Aid II.

'Do They Know' would set the tone for much of what would eventually be termed the 'benevolence industry'. Nowadays, its pungent mix of celebrity and charity defines how the West 'sees' Africa – Darfur, for instance, cannot become an issue unless it has an endorsement from the likes of George Clooney. The track helped dumb down the political elements of the famine, conflated Ethiopia – or the parts of Ethiopia stricken by famine – with the whole of Africa, and drew an abject picture of the continent that has since been etched into the psyche of the MTV generation and their Kardashian-obsessed kids. What's more, the damage perpetrated by the song has extended deep into the geopolitical realm, and many of today's policymakers got their lasting impressions of this ghastly, simplified 'Africa' direct from Geldof's lyrics.

But don't take our word for it; take the word of The Smiths' acerbic former front man Morrissey, who in 1985 told *Time Out* magazine: 'I'm not afraid to say that I think Band Aid was diabolical. Or to say that I think Bob Geldof is a nauseating character. Many people find that very unsettling, but I'll say it as loud as anyone wants me to. In the first instance the record itself was absolutely tuneless. One can have great concern for the people of Ethiopia, but it's another thing to inflict daily torture on the people of Great Britain. It was an awful record considering the mass of talent involved. And it wasn't done shyly – it was the most self-righteous platform ever in the history of popular music.'

4 As anyone who has published anything about Ethiopia in a public forum is quickly reminded, there exist a number of Ethiopians with conflicting points of view, constituting the second most vicious trolling community in cyberspace. (They are narrowly beaten by neighbouring Eritreans). Eleni has had to defend her *Ethiopiawient* – her Ethiopian-ness – before a host of detractors, many of whom see her as either a collaborator or a charlatan. She published a heartfelt explication of her background on the popular Nazret blog, titled 'This is my Ethiopian Story', on 8 November 2009. The full text is available at: http://nazret.com/blog/index.php/2009/08/11/ethiopia_this_is_my_ethiopian_story_by_e

5 Regardless of what one makes of Paul Theroux's late-career crustiness, and reading him on Africa can be embarrassing, he is very good on Rimbaud in Harar. In his Africa travelogue *Dark Star Safari* (Houghton Mifflin, 2002), Theroux

reminds us that Rimbaud, during his years as an import-export merchant in Harar, supplied Menelik II's forces with 2 000 of the Remingtons they used to beat back the Italians. Harar is *khat* country, the growing region for the mildly narcotic *Catha edulis* that remains an evening ritual in many parts of Ethiopia and beyond. The writer, adventurer and inveterate bigot Richard Burton was, of course, the first Westerner to enter the forbidden city, which was itself inward-looking and xenophobic (and so in that case, city and man turned out to be the perfect match). But Rimbaud was its most famous *farenji*. 'No one knew what was in his heart,' Theroux wrote of the poet, 'nor heard his muttered ironies, nor understood his gift for concealment. He denied his wealth, complaining that he was cheated, while chinking tall stacks of thick silver Maria Theresa dollars and rustling banknotes from the king.'

6 In the early 1990s, the University of Pennsylvania's African Studies department translated and published a working draft of the Ethiopian constitution. This unauthorised version, which was tweaked ever so slightly over the course of the process, remains a fascinating insight into the framers' mindset. Available at: http://www.africa.upenn.edu/Hornet/Ethiopian_Constitution.html. The final version is available at: http://www.wipo.int/wipolex/en/text.jsp?file_id=234349

7 *A History of Ethiopia Updated Edition*, Harold G Marcus (University of California Press, 2002).

8 In 1997, while holding a discussion with Professor Donald Levine, an intellectual with five decades of Ethiopia experience, Prime Minister Meles Zenawi (who plays a starring role in this chapter) stated that Ethiopia had never been a country prior to Menelik II's conquest of the hinterlands. In emphasising his point, the prime minister stated that, 'The Tigrayans had Axum, but what could that mean to the Guragué? The Agew had Lalibela, but what could that mean to the Oromo? The Gonderes had castles, but what could that mean to the Wolaitai?' For Meles, Ethiopia as a *country* was a new conception, barely

a century in the making.

9 *A History of Ethiopia Updated Edition*, Harold G Marcus.

10 The Battle of Adwa, which followed almost a decade's worth of wrangling between Italy and Emperor Menelik's administration, is one of colonialism's stranger beasts. As Harold Marcus notes, 'Italy did much to assist its enemy, donating thousands of rifles and millions of dollars of bullets to soften Menilik's *[sic]* stance against Article 17'... which was the crux of the argument. The Treaty of Wuchale stipulated that Eritrean territory became an Italian protectorate in exchange for Italy acting as an intermediary for Menelik in Europe. The Italians interpreted Article 17 as Eritrea becoming an Italian colony, which the emperor understood as perfidy. War was the result of this disagreement, and in another of colonialism's ironies, Italians were shot at with their own guns, and felled by their own bullets.

11 Ryszard Kapuściński's *The Emperor: Downfall of an Autocrat* (Vintage International, 1978), nominally about the end of the Selassie regime, is now considered to be an allegory of Edward Gierek's Poland in the 1970s. The book, best read as a ruminative prose poem, renders a remarkably evocative portrait of what life must have been like on the cusp of the fall. We have come to mistrust the great Pole, but he can't be wrong about this: 'Two lusts breed in the soul of man: the lust for aggression, and the lust for telling lies. If one will not allow himself to wrong others, he will wrong himself. If he doesn't come across anyone to lie to, he will lie to himself in his own thoughts.'

12 'Derg' – sometimes 'Dergue' – is Amharic for 'committee'.

13 'Eleni Gabre-Madhin: A commodities exchange for Ethiopia', *Ted.com*, June 2007. Available at: http://www.ted.com/talks/elene_gabre_madhin_on_ethiopian_economics

14 The term 'green revolution', in its many versions and meanings, refers back to the enormous uptick in agricultural performance experienced by India during the 1960s. 'In 1966,' reported Michael Specter

in *The New Yorker*, 'India imported eleven million tons of grain. Today, it produces more than two hundred million tons, much of it for export.' But according to the subject of Specter's piece, the food activist Vandana Shiva, 'Until the 1960s, India was successfully pursuing an agricultural development policy based on strengthening the ecological base of agriculture and the self-reliance of peasants,' and 'by shifting the focus of farming from variety to productivity, the Green Revolution actually was responsible for killing Indian farmers.' While the aforementioned is not a widely accepted analysis, it nevertheless contributes to a growing number of revisionist opinions regarding the phenomenon, some of which creep into the overall circumspection of conservative economists like Eleni. Put another way, yields are not always the most important indicator of agricultural performance, and nor do high yields necessarily result in a well-fed population (see India). 'Seeds of Doubt', Michael Specter, *The New Yorker*, 25 August 2014.

15 'A Market for Abdu: Creating a Commodity Exchange in Ethiopia', Eleni Gabre-Madhin (International Food Policy Research Institute, 2012), p 2. Full text available at: http://www.ifpri.org/sites/default/files/publications/oc70.pdf

16 As Roger Thurow writes on his blog, '[C]ommon sense had long ago left the US food aid system. As the years went by, US business and political interests had come to wield ever more influence over food aid policy, keeping the focus on what was best for American agribusiness and for the politicians it supported rather than on what was best for the world's hungry. Even as American generosity grew – half of all international food aid has routinely been provided by the US – so did its self-interest.' Available at: http://thelasthungerseason.com/blog.html

17 *Enough: Why the World's Poorest Starve in an Age of Plenty*, Roger Thurow and Scott Kilman (PublicAffairs, 2010), p xi.

18 'One of the major lessons in agricultural development over the past decade is this: Markets Matter,' Thurow would write on his blog. 'The 2003 famine tragically, and

incomprehensibly, followed two years of bumper harvests in Ethiopia. The surplus production overwhelmed the country's weak and inefficient markets. There were no export channels; the domestic market's ability to absorb the harvests was crippled by woeful infrastructure. The food piled up on farms and prices collapsed, upwards of 80 per cent in some areas. Farmers lost incentive to plant the next year. Then the drought hit, and feast turned to famine. The markets had failed before the weather did.'

19 The reader is perhaps tiring of the *caveat emptor* stickers we've slapped on African GDP statistics, but please consider Ethiopia's warning stickers as printed in neon. There has been so much circumspection about Ethiopia's growth rates that no journalist in his or her right mind would stand by them. As the Ethiopian editor-in-chief of *Addis Fortune*, Tamrat Giorgis, put it to us in an interview in January 2012: 'The year 2003 was the turning point. Then, it was an economy of ten billion [dollars], now it is between thirty and forty billion. This isn't systemic, and I seriously question the growth. Much of it comes from fixed income driven by the government. This is still the most undeveloped country in the world.'

20 'African Development: Dead Ends and New Beginnings', Meles Zenawi (Unpublished Monograph, 2006). Most of Meles's thinking regarding African development was included in this monograph, which would almost certainly have comprised the basis for larger and longer works had the prime minister lived long enough to complete them. The disclaimer never fails to elicit a chuckle: 'The author is the Prime Minister of Ethiopia. The views expressed are personal and do not necessarily reflect the official position of the Government.' Available at: http://www.meleszenawi.org.uk/pdf/zenawi_dead_ends_and_new_beginnings.pdf

21 The Committee to Protect Journalists were not impressed by the statute, and nor should they have been. As they noted in a letter addressed to Meles, and faxed to the Ethiopian embassy in Washington DC

on 23 July 2009, the new law contained 'far-reaching statutes giving the executive branch sweeping powers to imprison for as long as 20 years' – and here they quoted directly from the proclamation – '"whosoever writes, edits, prints, publishes, publicizes, disseminates" statements deemed "encouraging, supporting, or advancing" terrorist acts'. The CPJ then explained that the statute 'effectively institutionalizes censorship of reporting the government deems favorable to groups and causes it labels as "terrorist." Worse, the law grants the federal police and national security agency exclusive discretion to carry out warrantless interception of communications, and search and seizure solely on the basis of "reasonable belief" that a terrorist act is in progress or "will be" committed.'

Which is all another way of saying that the proclamation was a declaration of war against Ethiopians' freedom of speech. This hasn't silenced the country's writers, editors, bloggers and Tweeters, but it has markedly influenced how they go about their day. Were one to pick up a copy of *Addis Fortune* at the airport, the spunky paper would lead the reader to assume that the press is free and fertile. But English and Amharic reporting are judged very differently. The former is allowed leeway, within reason. The latter is not.

22 'Ethiopia: Prominent Muslims Detained in Crackdown', Human Rights Watch, 15 August 2012. Available at: http://www.hrw.org/news/2012/08/15/ethiopia-prominent-muslims-detained-crackdown

23 GINBOT 7, or Movement for Justice, Freedom and Democracy, is a banned Ethiopian opposition organisation functioning as a lobby group in the United States and elsewhere. One of the group's leaders, Andargachew Tsige, was unlawfully deported to Ethiopia from Yemen, and the group constantly highlights the many human rights abuses perpetrated by the EPRDF government. Their mission statement is available on their website: http://www.ginbot7.org/mission-statement/

24 The $200 million figure was as impossible to confirm as one would expect, and was derived from the innumerable reports

flooding out of the new facility's media centre (ironically housed in the *old* building) during the inaugural celebrations. At the time of this writing, the biggest Chinese infrastructure operation in Africa remained the TAZARA Railway, linking Dar es Salaam in Tanzania and Kapiri Mposhi in Zambia, at a cost of about $400 million in 1970s dollars.

25 Much of Meles's AU inauguration speech riffed on his 'African Development: Dead Ends and New Beginnings' monograph, which contained a number of references to the African Renaissance. Here, Meles may have been grabbing the intellectual relay baton from South Africa's second democratically elected president, Thabo Mbeki, who tub-thumped similar themes in a series of famous speeches in 1997. Based on a departmental paper called 'African Renaissance: A Workable Dream', crafted by Mbeki and his inner circle, the most famous passage of the speech read as follows: 'A renaissance is an historical moment whose many elements will develop independently. It cannot simply be decreed or conjured up like a spell but will arise on the basis of certain minimum factors. However, without an integrated programme of action to *build* upon those minimum factors, the dream of the renaissance shall forever be deferred.'

26 'Cruel Ethiopia', Helen Epstein, *New York Review of Books*, 13 May 2010.

27 'Ethiopia's economy: miracle or mirage', *Good Governance Africa*, July 2012. Full text available at: http://gga.org/stories /editions/aif-2-african-growth-crunching-the-numbers/ethiopias-economy-miracle-or-mirage

28 Of the world's ten smallest stock exchanges, seven are in Africa: Mozambique, Cameroon, Cape Verde, Swaziland, Namibia, Libya and Tanzania. Combined, their market capitalisation is less than 1 per cent of the New York Stock Exchange. 'World's smallest stock exchanges can only go up', *Wall Street Journal*, 22 July 2012.

29 According to Eleni, 'Five initial donors – the US Agency for International Development, the Canadian International Development Agency, the World Bank, the International Fund for Agricultural Development, and the United Nations Development Programme – committed US$9.2 million in just two weeks. This figure grew over the years as commitments increased. The World Food Programme and the European Union joined the list, and donor funding eventually reached US$29 million.' 'A Market for Abdu: Creating a Commodity Exchange in Ethiopia' (International Food Policy Research Institute, 2012), p 8.

30 The US Department of State released a comprehensive human rights report on the post-election violence, which was published on their website on 8 March 2006. Well worth a read, the report is available at: http://www.state.gov/j/drl/rls/ hrrpt/2005/61569.htm

31 And so we arrive at the odd duck that is the World Bank's Protection of Basic Services Programme, which seeks to drive development funding directly into the sectors of the economy that require it, while lightly punishing the Ethiopian government for being taciturn grumps and bad democrats. According to the project's abstract, the objective 'is to contribute to expanding access and improving the quality of basic services in education, health, agriculture, water supply and sanitation, and rural roads delivered by subnational governments in Ethiopia, while continuing to deepen transparency and local accountability in service delivery'. Between 2009 and 2013, the programme committed $540 million. The full details are available here: http://www.worldbank.org/projects/ P103022/ethiopia-protection-basic-services-program-phase-ii-project?lang=en

32 Article 40 is worth including in full, because it allows the reader a complete portrait of the contradictions and potential pitfalls contained within the EPRDF's reasonably unique nationalisation policies, and offers a comparative framework against other African governments instituting land reform:

'Every Ethiopian citizen has the right to the ownership of private property. Unless prescribed otherwise by law on account of public interest, this right shall include the right to acquire, to use and, in a manner compatible with the rights of other citizens, to dispose of such property by sale or bequest or to transfer it otherwise.

1. "Private property", for the purpose of this Article, shall mean any tangible or intangible product which has value and is produced by the labour, creativity, enterprise or capital of an individual citizen, associations which enjoy juridical personality under the law, or in appropriate circumstances, by communities specifically empowered by law to own property in common.

2. The right to ownership of rural and urban land, as well as of all natural resources, is exclusively vested in the State and in the peoples of Ethiopia. Land is a common property of the Nations, Nationalities and Peoples of Ethiopia and shall not be subject to sale or to other means of exchange.

3. Ethiopian peasants have the right to obtain land without payment and the protection against eviction from their possession. The implementation of this provision shall be specified by law.

4. Ethiopian pastoralists have the right to free land for grazing and cultivation as well as the right not to be displaced from their own lands. The implementation shall be specified by law.

5. Without prejudice to the right of Ethiopian Nations, Nationalities, and Peoples to the ownership of land, government shall ensure the right of private investors to the use of land on the basis of payment arrangements established by law. Particulars shall be determined by law.

6. Every Ethiopian shall have the full right to the immovable property he builds and to the permanent improvements he brings about on the land by his labour or capital. This right shall include the right to alienate, to bequeath, and, where the right of use expires, to remove his property, transfer his title, or claim compensation for it. Particulars shall be determined by law.

7. Without prejudice to the right to private property, the government may expropriate private property for public purposes subject to payment in advance of compensation commensurate to the value of the property.'

33 'An Assessment of the Causes of Malnutrition in Ethiopia', Todd Benson (IFPRI, 2005).

34 After dropping out of his medical degree at the age of 19 to take on Mengistu as a guerrilla fighter, Meles would return to academia 17 years later and earn an MBA from the Open University. His second master's degree was earned through Erasmus University in Rotterdam, and his thesis, on the functioning of African economies, was explained to editor of *African Arguments* Peter Gill thus: '[It] was primarily intended for our own local consumption to see if our policies could stand up to the rigour of some academic scrutiny.'

As for the Stiglitz connection, it was well known that Meles's famous unpublished monograph (see note 20 above) was written partly as an extension of his ongoing conversation with the Nobel laureate. In a controversial op-ed published in the *New York Times* in 2007, Stiglitz revealed that he'd been visiting Ethiopia since 1971, and gave a summary of his views on the country's 'boom' under Meles. Available at: http://kristof.blogs.nytimes.com/2007/09/12/on-the-ground-joseph-stiglitz-in-ethiopia/?_php=true&_type=blogs&_r=0

35 Here, we refer the reader to Article 40(7) above.

36 The full gazette was published on 15 July 2005, and in the chaos of the election violence it must have seemed like a windfall to investors who were lobbying for such amendments. Federal Negaritgazeta, 11th Year No 44, 15 July 2005, Contents: Proclamation No 456/2005. Available at: http://faolex.fao.org/docs/pdf/eth95459.pdf

37 'Unheard Voices: The Human Rights Impact of Land Investments on Indigenous Communities in Gambella', (The Oakland Institute, 2013). Full text available at: http://www.oaklandinstitute.org/sites/oaklandinstitute.org/files/OI_Report_Unheard_Voices.pdf

38 Ibid.

39 'Ethiopian dam's ecological and human

fallout could echo Aral Sea disaster', *The Guardian*, 5 March 2014.

40 'Unheard Voices: The Human Rights Impact of Land Investments on Indigenous Communities in Gambella', p 6.

41 'What Will Happen if Hunger Comes? Abuses against the Indigenous Peoples of Ethiopia's Lower Omo Valley' (Human Rights Watch 2012), p 3.

42 'A Market for Abdu: Creating a Commodity Exchange in Ethiopia', Eleni Gabre-Madhin (International Food Policy Research Institute, 2012), p 15.

43 According to the Canadian Hunger Foundation's press material, '[The programme is] a large integrated initiative implemented by a six member consortium led by Save the Children Canada that includes CHF, Canadian Physicians for Aid and Relief, Food for the Hungry, OXFAM Canada, INBAR, World Vision Canada with technical support from the International Network for Bamboo and Rattan. The project is improving the livelihoods of over 25,000 households in seven *woredas* of Benishangul-Gumuz region in Ethiopia.

'CHF is taking the lead in market-led development in this project and oversees implementation in two *woredas*. CHF will also oversee capacity development to targeted communities, CSOs and local government on market-led approaches, including micro-enterprise and micro-credit.'

44 '4.5 million drought-stricken Ethiopians need food aid: govt', *Agence France Presse*, 3 June 2008.

45 'Speculation and World Food Markets', *IFPRI Forum*, July 2008, p 12. The concluding paragraph of the publication, due to the utter confusion it evinces, is worth citing in full: 'The complex problem of speculation needs a set of complex solutions. In the long run, investment in agricultural production is key for reducing the incentive for speculation. Another important route to reducing the influence of speculative behavior on food prices is international trade reform. Export restrictions and other forms of hoarding can affect food markets as much as any other speculative activity. Moreover, the current low levels of grain reserves need to be

addressed. A recent report by von Braun and Maximo Torero, director of IFPRI's Markets, Trade, and Institutions Division, proposes that a "virtual grain reserve" be established to help calm markets through the futures market. It is an innovative approach to creating a global reserve that would solve the problem countries face of insuring against abrupt price increases and supply disruptions without building up physical stocks of food – actions that can, by themselves, drive up prices.'

46 'Statement to the Press on Rising Prices and the Role of Commodity Exchanges', IFPRI.org, 17 April 2008, pp 2-3. Full text available at: http://www.ifpri.org/sites/default/files/20080417EleniPressStatement.pdf

47 Domesticated around the time of Ethiopia's founding, in 1500 BCE when King Solomon was supposed to have met the Queen of Sheba, it's hardly a stretch to point out the poetry in sesame's place as a 'saviour' crop.

48 'The Next Breadbasket: Why big corporations are grabbing up land on the planet's hungriest continent', *National Geographic*, July 2014. Full text available here: http://www.nationalgeographic.com/foodfeatures/land-grab/

49 Also known as the 'Great Guibi', Menelik Palace, built for Empress Taitu in the late nineteenth century by Menelik II, was the site around which the city of Addis Ababa sprang up. The official seat of the Ethiopian government ever since, it was where the Derg imprisoned, killed and buried Haile Selassie (apparently building a latrine above his grave), and would be the home from which Azeb Mesfin refused to move after the death, in 2012, of her husband Meles Zenawi.

50 'Open letter to the buyers of Ethiopian specialty coffee', Eleni Gabre-Madhin, 17 April 2009. Full text available at: http://www.coffeed.com/viewtopic.php?f=19&t=2796

51 A 2012 field report by the NGO International Rivers noted the damage the Derg had done through its villagisation campaigns, and the cascading problems that the Red Terror meant for the environment. 'The natural resource degradation in the

region,' noted the report, 'is the result of the state sponsored resettlement program that took place during the Derg regime, immigration into the region from people from the already-deforested highland regions, uncontrolled forest fires, and the absence of a well-defined land use policy.'

CHAPTER EIGHT: SOUTH SUDAN

1 Arabic for 'land of the black people', Sudan's etymological conception suggests a political conception. *Who* named it 'land of the black people'? Was the term 'black' a pejorative at the time of naming? What purpose did naming it thus serve the namers, and what became of the old names? What this name *does* suggest is a place in which the inhabitants did not have naming rights. And thus we arrive at the longest civil conflict in the history of the African continent.

2 The 'Lost Boys of Sudan', a name applied to these children in the late 1980s by the aid workers in the cross-border refugee camps, have since the signing of the CPA in 2005 generated more international interest in the plight of the southern Sudanese than any other local or foreign group – George Clooney's PR team included. The story of their initial journey through the virgin African bush (where older brothers would often save younger brothers from the jaws of lion or hyena), to their years of schooling in the camps, to their eventual arrival in the United States, appears to fit perfectly with a pair of essential narrative presuppositions: the West's idea of an Africa in need of saving; the West's idea of itself as the saviour. That said, of the dozens of books, films and plays that have appeared on or about the Lost Boys since 2005, the majority have been written or produced by former Lost Boys themselves. 'The world is what it is,' as the committed anti-colonialist VS Naipaul once wrote – and, in that sense, a world where these unique individuals are accorded a genre to tell their own story is far superior to one in which Bob Geldof and Bono do so for

them.

3 Racial identity is enormously complicated in Sudan, as it is throughout so much of the Sahel. The terms 'Arab' and 'African' are by no means immutable, and can refer to different aspects of identity – language, race, class status – that to outsiders may seem contradictory. As Mahmood Mamdani put it in his classic essay for the *London Review of Books*, entitled 'The Politics of Naming: Genocide, Civil War, Insurgency': '[B]oth "Arab" and "African" have several meanings in Sudan. There have been at least three meanings of "Arab". Locally, "Arab" was a pejorative reference to the lifestyle of the nomad as uncouth; regionally, it referred to someone whose primary language was Arabic. In this sense, a group could become "Arab" over time. This process, known as Arabisation, was not an anomaly in the region: there was Amharisation in Ethiopia and Swahilisation on the East African coast. The third meaning of "Arab" was "privileged and exclusive"; it was the claim of the riverine political aristocracy who had ruled Sudan since independence, and who equated Arabisation with the spread of civilisation and being Arab with descent.'

4 From the Arabic *sadd*, this 'barrier' has been preventing explorers from discovering the source of the Nile since at least the time of the Roman emperor Nero (as per Seneca's *Naturales Quaestiones*).

5 Stretching from Malakal in the north of modern-day South Sudan to Mangalla in the south, the Sudd covers an area of roughly 30 000 square kilometres in the dry season, and may extend to as much as 130 000 square kilometres in the wet season.

6 While the term means 'slave' in Arabic, in the region it was widely used to describe black southerners. Again, we have to be careful when we ascribe these tags as properly 'racist', because racial lines were slippery. That it was, and remains, an insult is, however, beyond disputation.

7 *Slaves into Workers: Emancipation and Labor in Colonial Sudan*, Ahmad Alawad Sikainga (University of Texas Press, 1996), p 11.

8 Ibid, p 12.

9 Why is the name Charles 'Chinese' Gordon still so prominent in the British imagination? Part of it has to do with the Victorians' world-beating talent for mythmaking. The iconic painting of Gordon, defiant and straight-backed as he's about to be impaled on a dozen rebel spears, has little to do with how he actually died – chopped up into pieces, his head paraded through Khartoum on a pike. But behind the lauded courage of the martyred general lies the deeper reason for his fame, the fact that he died in a battle that presaged a form of political revolt that would become one of the most dominant of the twentieth and twenty-first centuries (see note 10 below).

10 Popularised by Christopher Hitchens (who would quickly disclaim credit), the term 'Islamofascism', which controversially equates movements like al Qaeda, Hamas and Hizbollah with the European fascist organisations of the early twentieth century, seems applicable in hindsight to the *Mahdiyah* only if one takes into account the subtleties. As the Chadian academic Sharif Harir writes: 'The significance of the *Mahdi* for the formative stages of the Sudanese state lies, perhaps, not in his call for an Islamic state but rather in the ability of the charismatic leader to exploit the conditions of discontent precipitated by the colonial Turko-Egyptian rule and [to] unify the peripheral Sudanese to conquer the seat of central power in Khartoum.' *Short-cut to Decay: The Case of Sudan* (Nordiska Afrikainstitutet, 1994), p 31.

11 Published on the Library of Congress website above the caveat 'Data as of June 1991', the quote was last accessed on 14 May 2015 at the following URL: http://lcweb2.loc.gov/cgi-bin/query/r?frd/cstdy:@field(DOCID+sd0028).

12 'Sudan and South Sudan', US Energy Information Administration. Full text available here: http://www.eia.gov/beta/international/analysis.cfm?iso=SDN.

13 'Two Sudans' oil dispute deepens as South shuts down wells', *The Guardian*, 26 January 2012.

14 'Sudan and South Sudan', US Energy Information Administration.

15 Ibid.

16 'Sudan air force bombs two towns in South Sudan's Unity State', *Sudan Tribune*, 23 April 2012.

17 'Since 2006, 27 adults and three children have died because of contaminated water from the oil field.' So said Paul Bol Ruoth, county commissioner in Koch, a region about 70 kilometres from Bentiu, to Agence France-Presse in March 2008. The source of the contamination, according to him, was the Thar Jath oil refinery, built in 2006 by the White Nile Petroleum Company, a consortium led by Malaysia's Petronas. AFP claimed to have seen sample results from a Western NGO that indicated the water contained eight times the nitrate concentration recommended by the US Environmental Protection Agency. It was, incidentally, the new Thar Jath 'airport' at which we landed and departed in November 2012 – seen from the air, the refinery didn't look like it was doing much good for the environment; seen from the ground, the promised employment and development had simply not materialised.

The AFP article was published in South Africa's *Mail & Guardian* newspaper under the header 'Sudan villagers, environment suffer from oil boom', 4 March 2008. Full text available at: http://mg.co.za/article/2008-03-04-sudan-villagers-environment-suffer-from-oil-boom.

18 'Sudan, Oil, and Human Rights' (Human Rights Watch, 2003), p 38.

19 'Basic Services in South Sudan: An Uncertain Future', Kevin Watkins, in *South Sudan One Year After Independence: Opportunities and Obstacles in Africa's Newest Country* (Africa Growth Initiative at Brookings, 2012), p 3. As the paper notes, South Sudan had the world's highest maternal mortality rate and its lowest rate of basic education. It was a country in which 60 per cent of the population had no access to healthcare, where fewer than one in five births was attended by a medical professional, where half of the primary school age population (around a million children) never saw the inside of a classroom, and where there was one qualified teacher for every 117 students.

20 Ibid.

21 When accounting for conflict-related famine and disease, the two million number is accepted by the majority of sources as the official fatality figure for the second civil war (1983 to 2005), although some prominent South Sudanese citizens, such as the senior SPLM diplomat and politician Lumumba Stanislaus-Kaw Di-Aping, quote three million as the accepted death toll (see section II of this chapter). However the fatalities are counted, the scale renders the conflict one of the most deadly on earth since the end of World War II. Taken together with the Second Congo War, which happened in roughly the same geographic neighbourhood and had claimed an estimated death toll of 5.4 million by 2008, we begin to get an idea of just what humanity is ignoring as it continues to avert its gaze. At the time of this writing, the Second Sudanese Civil War has to all intents and purposes been back on again for 18 months. Meanwhile, the Second Congo War hasn't really ended.

22 'Future Engagement between South Sudan and the Republic of Sudan', Mwangi S Kimenyi, in *South Sudan One Year After Independence: Opportunities and Obstacles in Africa's Newest Country* (Africa Growth Initiative at Brookings, 2012), p 7.

23 In 2003, when the interview was conducted at his offices in Pretoria, Joel Netshitenzhe was in charge of South Africa's development vision – Lumumba's precise and technical questioning of the man, and his even more precise analysis of the answers, betrayed an interest that was more than just passing. Did he suspect at the time that he would one day serve the same function for South Sudan and the ruling SPLM as Netshitenzhe was then serving for South Africa and the ruling African National Congress? When asked this question in Juba in late 2012, Lumumba could only smile.

24 'Poor nations' fury over leaked climate text', CNN.com, 9 December 2009.

25 Cross-attribution for both the quotes and the series of events can be gleaned from a range of mainstream websites, including CNN as per note 24 above. Perhaps the most thorough and informative summary, however, was written by a South African delegate, Adam Welz, on his blog – available here: https://adamwelz.wordpress.com/2009/12/08/emotional-scenes-at-copenhagen-lumumba-di-aping-africa-civil-society-meeting-8-dec-2009/.

26 'Copenhagen: "Kyoto Killer" Rudd talks down hopes of strong outcome', Crikey.com.au, 16 December 2009. What's more, as Simon Butler pointed out on 16 January 2010 in Australia's *Green Left Weekly*, the Rudd delegation had been trying to coax a number of small-island nations into accepting the two degrees limit with offers of 'thirty pieces of silver'. Full text available at: https://www.greenleft.org.au/node/43033.

27 'Low targets, goals dropped: Copenhagen ends in failure', *The Guardian*, 19 December 2009.

28 Frantz Fanon's construction is a tragic indictment of the ultimate degradation of colonialism – the eventual befouling of the movement that arose to destroy it: 'The leader pacifies the people. For years on end after independence has been won, we see him, incapable of urging the people to a concrete task, unable to open the future to them or of flinging them into the path of national reconstruction, that is to say, of their own reconstruction; we see him reassessing the history of independence and recalling the sacred unity of the struggle for liberation... During the struggle for liberation the leader awakened the people and promised them a forward march, heroic and unmitigated. Today, he uses every means to put them to sleep.' *The Wretched of the Earth*, Frantz Fanon (Grove Press, 2007), p 169.

29 'Sudan, Oil, and Human Rights' (Human Rights Watch, 2003), p 119.

30 The SPLA in its early years owed much to the generosity of Ethiopia's Mengistu. In the usual regional quid pro quo, John Garang had offered the Ethiopian dictator a chance to hit back at Jafaar Nimeiri of Khartoum for the latter's support of the Eritrean rebels. As the Human Rights Watch report notes: 'The SPLM/A was sponsored, housed, supplied, and trained

by the repressive government of Pres
Mengistu Haile Miriam of Ethiopia. Ethiopia was reciprocating Sudan's own efforts.
Ethiopia had warned Sudan as early as
1976 that if Sudan did not stop supporting
Ethiopian and Eritrean dissidents, Ethiopia
would support Sudanese dissidents. With
the Cold War at its height, Ethiopia was
aligned with the Soviet Union and Cuba,
while Sudan was aligned with the United
States. President Nimeiri's dictatorship
received considerable aid from the US. The
SPLM/A received arms, training, and other
assistance from the Soviet bloc and sent
thousands of southern and Nuba boy soldiers and adult officers to Cuba for military
and academic education.' Ibid, p 99.

31 Ibid, p 15.

32 The images in the above two paragraphs
draw on Nick Turse's *Tomorrow's Battlefield: US Proxy Wars and Secret Ops in
Africa* (Haymarket Books, 2015). Turse has
done tireless work on the American military in Africa, but he is also remarkably
good on summarising American interest in
South Sudan. As a rule of thumb, anything
he writes on US-African relations is essential reading.

33 Anyanya is the namesake of the original
southern Sudanese guerrilla movement,
named for a local type of poison. Anyanya
II was formed in 1978, the same year oil
was discovered, by a group of Nuer dissidents. In 1983, when Garang was meant
to be pacifying Anyanya II in Bor at the
behest of the Sudanese military, he instead
rolled most of them into what would
become the SPLA.

34 The story of Chevron in South Sudan is not
dissimilar from the story of Barrick Gold
in the Democratic Republic of the Congo,
which features in chapter six of this book.
Despite having invested a billion dollars,
one of the company's advisors, the Sudan
scholar Robert O Collins wrote, '[T]hey
will not as a matter of principle, and their
employees will not as a matter of practice,
go to the South if they are going to get
their heads shot off.' *The New Kings of
Crude: China, India, and the Global Struggle for Oil in Sudan and South Sudan*, Luke
Patey (C Hurst & Company, 2014) p 3.

35 Ibid, p 43.

36 Ibid, p 44.

37 'Garang's speech at the signing ceremony
of S. Sudan peace deal', *Sudan Tribune*, 10 January 2005. Full text available
at: http://www.sudantribune.com/spip.
php?article7476.

38 For an insider's take on the characters in
these petroleum companies, the behind-
the-scenes wrangling, and the deal-making, there will perhaps never be a more
definitive record than Luke Patey's *The
New Kings of Crude: China, India, and the
Global Struggle for Oil in Sudan and South
Sudan*.

39 *The New Kings of Crude*, p 187.

40 Once again, we must refer to Mahmood
Mamdani's *LRB* piece, 'The Politics of
Naming: Genocide, Civil War, Insurgency'.
In the piece, Mamdani lays out the complex intricacies of the war – explaining to an audience conditioned by the
likes of Nicholas Kristof of the *New York
Times*, who portrayed the conflict as one
between 'good' Africans and 'bad' Arabs,
that things were somewhat more complicated than that. Mamdani puts it thusly:
'As the insurgency took root among the
prospering peasant tribes of Darfur, the
government trained and armed the poorer
nomads and formed a militia – the Janjawiid – that became the vanguard of the
unfolding counter-insurgency. The worst
violence came from the Janjawiid, but the
insurgent movements were also accused of
gross violations. Anyone wanting to end
the spiralling violence would have to bring
about power-sharing at the state level and
resource-sharing at the community level,
land being the key resource.'

41 This view is shared by most commentators on the region, who have noted that by
being so activist in south Sudanese secession, and in later sending 700 troops to the
newly independent country (see section V
of this essay), China could no longer claim
strict adherence to a non-interventionist
policy, if indeed it ever could. Unlike his
predecessors, Xi Jinping, who became
president in November 2012, did not wait
the customary full term to take firm rein of
the People's Liberation Army – he did so

almost immediately after assuming power. All of the above implied that China's stance was changing, and the most nervous of observers suggested that it would likely signal the beginning of a re-upped Cold War between China and America, fought by proxies on the African continent. Our book ends just as this historical crux comes into play – it is without doubt the end of one epoch, and the beginning of the next.

42 'S Sudan oil shutdown could fuel inflation, unrest', Reuters, 9 February 2012.

43 For a succinct and detached take on Taban Deng Gai's ability to consistently refashion himself in his own self-image (seems he was governor of Unity State before), it doesn't get any better than the Human Rights Watch Report: '[Deng] originally joined the SPLA in the 1980s and left to join his relative by marriage, Riek Machar, when he split from the SPLA in 1991. In 1996 he joined the government with Riek Machar and became a leader of the political party they formed, the UDSF. He won an election for governor of Unity State/ Western Upper Nile in December 1997 and was expelled from the governorship and the state in May 1999 by Maj Gen Paulino Matiep. He fled to Khartoum. He was appointed state minister for roads and communications in January 2000 by President Bashir and defected from the government in December 2000, and joined Machar's new faction, the SPDF, until he decided to rejoin the SPLA.' 'Sudan, Oil, and Human Rights' (Human Rights Watch, 2003), p 12.

44 'South Sudan: Compounding Instability in Unity State', Africa Report #179, (International Crisis Group, 17 October 2011). Full text available at: http://www.crisisgroup. org/en/regions/africa/horn-of-africa/ south-sudan/179-south-sudan-compounding-instability-in-unity-state.aspx.

45 'South Sudan army vows readiness to pull back from buffer zone', Sudan Tribune, 7 November 2012.

46 'Africa is the new land of opportunity, as they say,' Osman told us. 'I've been around, all over the Middle East, but everywhere else you're just a guinea pig – it's too perfect. Juba? That's as real as it gets.' For

more on our afternoon with Osman, see 'Africa 3.0: Making good food in a tough town', M&G Online, 8 November 2012. Available at http://mg.co.za/article/2012-11-08-good-food-in-a-tough-town.

47 'December 15 and the Nuer Self-Defence', South Sudan News Agency, 8 August 2014. Full text available at: http://www. southsudannewsagency.com/opinion/columnists/december-fifteen-and-the-nuer-self-defence.

48 'South Sudan: Ethnic Targeting, Widespread Killings', HRW.org, 16 January 2014. Full text available at: http://www. hrw.org/news/2014/01/16/south-sudan-ethnic-targeting-widespread-killings.

49 'New estimate sharply raises death toll in South Sudan', New York Times, 9 January 2014.

50 'Defectors warn S Sudan's Kiir risks deposition by inner circle', Sudan Tribune, 23 November 2014. Full text available at: http://www.sudantribune.com/spip. php?article53118.

51 Ibid.

52 'Attacks on Civilians in Malakal, Upper Nile State', HRW.org, 11 August 2014. Full text available here: http://www.hrw.org/ zh-hans/node/126087/section/10.

53 'Fallout from Leaked Minutes of August 31 Military/Security Meeting: Khartoum's Obligatory Lies', SudanReeves.org, 29 October 2014. Full text available at: http://sudanreeves. org/2014/10/29/fallout-from-leaked-minutes-of-august-31-militarysecurity-meeting-khartoums-obligatory-lies/.

54 'Complete text of Arabic original of minutes for 31 August 2014 high-level meeting in Khartoum of NCP/NIF regime security and military officials', SudanReeves.org, 20 September 2014. Full text available at: http://sudanreeves.org/2014/09/29/arabic-original-hand-written-english-translation-of-31-august-2014-meeting/.

55 Sudan People's Liberation Movement-North was founded by members of the SPLM/A who remained north of the border – ie, in the Republic of Sudan – after independence in 2011.

56 For many South Sudan observers, the carnage in Malakal was the most heartbreaking aspect of the renewed civil war. It had

changed hands numerous times since the fighting started and involved, according to Human Rights Watch, 'house-to-house searches, arbitrary arrests, and [the killing of] many civilians, often based on their ethnicity.' Malakal has always been a centre of Sudanese fighting, but this new war has brought a new viciousness. Between 17 and 23 February, whole neighbourhoods in the city were all but razed. Sudan, Oil, and Human Rights' (Human Rights Watch, 2003).

CHAPTER NINE: CENTRAL AFRICAN REPUBLIC

1 *Dark Age: The Political Odyssey of Emperor Bokassa*, Brian Titley (McGill-Queens University Press, 1997), p 6.

2 No CAR observer believes that Boganda's plane exploded without assistance, especially considering that traces of explosives were found in the wreckage. Was it expat businessmen from CAR's chamber of commerce, who did not want the apple cart overturned? Was it the French Secret Service, punishing the leader for establishing MESAN and being a regional rabble-rouser? Was it his estranged wife, a white French expatriate with ties to both institutions? The colonial business interests that still ran the show? The mystery will survive the country, it seems.

3 Is there any story more fascinating in the history of French Africa than the tale of Jacques Foccart? The jowly insider, in the words of the *London Review of Books*' RW Johnson, had 'an exclusive hold over France's African policy, the intelligence services and the whole shadowy world of covert action.' Johnson was writing a review of *Foccart Parle: Entretiens avec Philippe Gaillard*, a double-volume book of reminiscences that was published in 1995 and never got translated into English. '[While] a cabinet minister might see de Gaulle every few weeks and the Prime Minister once a week,' Johnson wrote for the LRB, 'Foccart had access to him every day and whenever he wanted.'

4 Sangaris butterflies have very short lifespans, so the reader probably appreciates where the French were going with this. And yet not everyone thought the Sangaris metaphor apposite: '[French President] Francois Hollande thought that the mission of the Sangaris troops would be over in a few months. A mistake,' the Bangui daily *Le Quotidien* stated on 28 February 2014.

5 According to the absolutely essential site TomDispatch.com, and its tireless pursuit of information regarding American military activity in Africa, Chad has become something of a 'pivot' state. The love triangle between the French, the Americans and N'Djamena hinges around the post 9/11, pan-Sahel initiative called the Trans-Sahara Counterterrorism Partnership (TSCTP), of which Chad is a 'founding' member. The country has always been a French base; it is increasingly becoming an American base. TomDispatch reported that in 2014, the American military command in Africa (AFRICOM) was building a 'mini-camp' in the country, from which Chadian troops, backed by the Americans (and the French) would continue to do their ambivalent work across the region. And as we'll learn, nowhere has their work been more ambivalent than in CAR.

6 According to the UNHCR, CAR's total number of internally displaced persons during the time of our visit was in excess of 894 000. There were another 252 865 persons living in refugee camps in neighbouring countries.

7 Of his 'Avenue Patrice Lumumba' series, in which he took pictures of modernist structures in six African cities all with their own Patrice Lumumba avenues, Tillim wrote, 'These photographs are not collapsed histories of post-colonial African states or a meditation on aspects of late-modernist-era colonial structures, but a walk through an avenue of dreams. Patrice Lumumba's dream, his nationalism, is discernible in these structures, if one reads certain clues, as is the death of his dream, in these de facto monuments. How strange that modernism, which eschewed monument and past for nature and future, should carry

such memory so well.'

8 The origins of the term are somewhat obscure, but it enters post-colonial discourse in a fascinating and completely surprising manner. In 1958, the French Canadian province of Quebec, governed by Maurice Duplessis and his Union Nationale regime, was in awful shape. Duplessis was your classic political thug, who ran a tight patronage network that enriched his cronies, and left the province embattled and riven with corruption. While the French-language press worked hard to expose his numerous wrongdoings, the province's English language dailies, owned by the local Anglophone oligarchs, were remarkably silent. To explain this phenomenon, a journalist for Le Devoir, named André Laurendeau, wrote the following (beware the acidic irony and bitterness):

'The British have political sense; they rarely destroy the political institutions of a conquered country. They dominate the Negro-king but they allow him fantasies. On occasion they permit him to cut off a few heads: these are the mores of the country. One thing never comes to their minds, and that is to demand that the Negro-king conform to the high moral and political standards of the British. The Negro-king must collaborate with and protect British interests. This collaboration assured, everything else goes by the boards. The kinglet violates democratic rules. Nothing else is expected from a primitive....' Duplessis, then, although a white Québécois, was the Negro King, and Laurendeau's vitriol became the 'Negro-king theory'. When Bokassa was nearing the end of his reign, and it was necessary for the French to build from his manifold mistakes and peccadilloes a monster, he became the King of Negro Kings, and the origins of Laurendeau's theory were forgotten.

9 These numbers were provided to us by the Sangaris's communications officer, Lt Colonel PY Sarzaud, during our interview which appears in section II of this essay.

10 'President Bozizé always felt that a strong army would be a direct threat to his government,' states a report by International Crisis Watch. 'According to a source close

to power, he refused to provide the Central African Armed Forces (FACA) with heavy military equipment for fear they would use it against him.' The French also did not want a strong local army, and so FACA is as neutered as they come. 'Central African Republic: Priorities of the Transition', Africa Report #203 (International Crisis Group, 11 June 2013), pp 5-6.

11 Ibid, p i.

12 Not unlike Sudan and South Sudan – indeed, inspired by the successful culmination of the talks there in 2005 – Bozizé's government signed a Comprehensive Peace Agreement with members of the more established northern rebel groups. This brought in a small contingent of South African trainers, along with a small French force at the airport, to maintain the peace. The Multinational Force of Central Africa (FOMAC), however, was hewed-together forces from the DRC, Chad, Gabon, Cameroon, Equatorial Guinea and Angola, all members of the Economic Community of Central African States, or ECCAS.

13 Chad helped install Bozizé in power in 2003, hosting the orchestration of the coup after the regional players had had enough of Ange-Félix Patassé's unpaid debts and misrule. But it appeared that Chad's President Idriss Déby was similarly fed up with Bozizé. Déby feared that the instability would flow back into Chad's southern oil-rich areas, where the government is widely loathed. Nor did he like it that Bozizé consistently reneged on his agreements with rebels. Each of CAR's leaders has lasted in power for around a decade – and it was, it seemed, time for Bozizé to go.

14 In South Africa, there was enormous controversy regarding the SANDF casualties in Bangui – few South Africans had been aware that there were any troops in the Central African capital in the first place. The figure of 13 dead came from Helmoed Römer Heitman, who wrote about the battle extensively and had worked as a paid consultant for the SANDF. Heitman was considered something of a Cassandra regarding these casualty figures, but there was no evidence to support criticisms of his death count – even if the

ruling African National Congress could not adequately explain the geopolitical reasons for the country's presence in CAR. It was rumoured that the ANC's business wing, Chancellor House, had an interest in CAR mining operations. This had yet to be proven. Heitman's account is certainly worth the read: 'How deadly CAR battle unfolded', *Sunday Independent*, 31 March 2013.

15 This is culled from a speech Bozizé made at the Place de la République, in the centre of Bangui, on 27 December 2012. The full text is available, in French, here: http://centrafrique-presse.over-blog.com/article-echos-et-images-du-meeting-de-bozize-du-pk-0-113855073.html.

16 *Central African Republic: A Failure in De-Colonisation*, Pierre Kalck trans Barbara Thomson (Pall Mall Press, 1971), p 1.

17 Ibid, p 17.

18 The Germans, at least officially, were reluctant colonialists, but a powerful colonial lobby called the *Kolonialverein* agitated for the acquisition of African protectorates in 1884. (In this, the second great age for lobby groups, it's worth remembering how much damage they did during colonial times.) Colonies were privatised – German South West Africa, for instance, was owned and operated by Alfred Lüderitz – with the exception of East Africa. But when Otto von Bismarck resigned in 1890, Wilhelm II, like most regents, enjoyed the idea of a single expansive empire. The idea of Mittelafrika was born.

19 *Central African Republic: A Failure in De-Colonisation*, Pierre Kalck, p. 11.

20 Remember Dar Al-Kouti, Michel Djotodia's neo-Islamic paradise? In the pre-colonial days it formed 'the military highway... to the heart of the Central African territory,' wrote Kalck. (Its name means 'Strong Land'.)

21 *Central African Republic: A Failure in De-Colonisation*, Pierre Kalck, p 27.

22 Ibid, p 46.

23 Here we arrive at a problem. French slavery had been declared 'over' in 1794, only to be revived by the Bourbon restitution, and then again in 1818. On neither occasion did the practice actually stop, largely because slavery was woven completely into the French economy. In 1830, the practice was officially outlawed under Louis-Philippe. Even so, as late as 1848, slaves were found in Martinique and elsewhere in French territory. There simply wasn't the outright revulsion for the practice that was found in Britain, despite the fact that France had its own vocal, well-represented anti-slavery lobbies.

24 *The Black Jacobins: Toussaint L'Ouverture and the San Domingo Revolution*, CLR James (Vintage Books Edition, 1989), p 5.

25 One of the world's first 'great' slaving companies was, of course, the largely state funded monopoly Compagnie des Indes Occidentales, organised in 1664.

26 *The Black Jacobins: Toussaint L'Ouverture and the San Domingo Revolution*, CLR James, p ix.

27 *Rulers of Empire: the French Colonial Service in Africa*, William B Cohen (Hoover Institution Press, 1971), p xiii.

28 *A Mission to Civilize: The Republican Idea of Empire in France and West Africa, 1895-1930*, Alice L Conklin (Stanford University Press, 1997), p 8.

29 Ibid, p 10.

30 Ibid, p 11.

31 The AOF, which existed from 1895 to 1960, encompassed Senegal, Mauritania, Mali (then French Sudan), French Guinea, Côte d' Ivoire, Burkina Faso (then Upper Volta), Benin (then Dahomey) and Niger. The governor general administered from Dakar.

32 The Afrique équatoriale française, or AEF, included Chad, Oubangui-Chari, the French Congo, and later French Cameroon. The capital was in Brazzaville.

33 *Central African Republic: A Failure in De-Colonisation*, Pierre Kalck, p 55.

34 Ibid, p 103.

35 *Central African Republic: A Failure in De-Colonisation*, Pierre Kalck, p 119.

36 We should note that in 1945 the French Empire became the French Union. The change in parlance brought several changes in policy, but not nearly enough to forestall independence movements in the Francophonie.

37 *A Mission to Civilize: The Republican Idea of Empire in France and West Africa,*

1895-1930, Alice L Conklin, p 80.

38 *Central African Republic: A Failure in De-Colinisation*, Pierre Kalck, p 150.

39 Ibid.

40 Ibid, p 151.

41 'Human Development Report 2013 – The Rise of the South: Human Development in a Diverse World', United Nations Development Programme. Available at: http://hdr.undp.org/sites/default/files/Country-Profiles/CAF.pdf.

42 What atrocities *hasn't* Ngaragba seen? It was, after all, the site of one of the country's great turning points. Emperor Bokassa's mistake, it transpired, was his over-reaction to the refusal of Bangui's students to procure school uniforms from a textile plant owned by the royal family. In April 1979, following yet another public protest against this imperial edict, around 100 schoolchildren were murdered on the streets of Bangui and in the cells of Ngaragba on Bokassa's express orders – an independent inquiry found that many of these students had been killed by the emperor's own hand, leading to the French media dubbing him the 'Butcher of Bangui'.

The government in Paris stalled and dissembled for another few months, but eventually sent in the troops in September 1979, while the wayward son was in Libya on state business. In the ensuing weeks, French forces discovered the following at Monsieur Bokassa's various residences: chests brimming with diamonds; hundreds of cameras alongside a vast pornography collection; two mutilated bodies in a refrigerator (including the headless and armless torso of a mathematics teacher); bone fragments in a drained pond from the remains of some 30 victims eaten by crocodiles.

43 *Dark Age: The Political Odyssey of Emperor Bokassa*, Brian Titley (McGill-Queens University Press, 1997), p 79.

44 There were three UN resolutions over the course of 2013 – numbered 2121, 2127 and 2134 – and three over the course of 2014, the most important of which – resolution 2149 – established the UN Multidimensional Integrated Stabilisation Mission in the Central African Republic (MINUSCA)

'with an initial deployment of up to 10 000 military and 1 800 police personnel'.

45 'The French Military in Africa', Andrew Hansen (Council on Foreign Relations, February 2008). Available at: http://www.cfr.org/france/french-military-africa/p12578.

46 This is the aforementioned Comprehensive Peace Agreement that brought the South Africans to CAR. 'Central Africa Republic, rebels sign peace deal', Associated Press, 13 April 2007.

47 *Tomorrow's Battlefield: US Proxy Wars and Secret Ops in Africa*, Nick Turse (Haymarket Books, 2015).

48 So seriously did the French leader take the situation in CAR that he visited *twice*, once in December 2013, and a second time in February 2014: the French did not, under any circumstances, want the optics to suggest that they had ignored the situation, a geopolitical syndrome we might refer to as 'Rwanda Hangover'. Then again, Hollande was fielding a major – and uncharacteristic, at least as far as the French go – scandal regarding a clandestine late night visit, on the back of a scooter, to the French actress Julie Gayet. His longtime companion, the journalist Valerie Trieweiler, was unimpressed, and promised a tell-all book (which she delivered, sordidly so). Cynics believed that CAR offered something of a decoy from all the personal scuttlebutt.

49 'Hollande justifie encore l'operation "Sangaris"', *Le Figaro*, 8 January 2014.

50 Catherine Samba-Panza, AKA 'Mother Courage', was sworn in on 23 January 2014, for one year – elections were set for February 2015, an utter absurdity given the situation in CAR. There was much fuss made about the country's first female president in the international press – as if a leader's gender could somehow magically transform a divided country into a united one, with no institutions or money to help her do so. Indeed, Samba-Panza's reign was compromised by more of the same, although she was streets ahead of either Djotodia or Bozizé.

51 'Muslims trapped in PK12 camp in Bangui, Central African Republic', *The Toronto Star*, 16 March 2014.

52 'For Bangui's last Muslims, to stray outside the safe haven is to court death', *GlobalPost*, 26 April 2014. Available at: http://www.globalpost.com/dispatch/news/regions/africa/140426/banguis-last-muslims-stray-outside-the-safe-haven-court-death.

53 'Hollande seeks Central African unity as France digs in', *Agence France-Presse*, 28 February 2014.

54 Detailed information about the Comboni Order can be found on its website, available at: http://www.combonisouthsudan.org/index.php/who-we-are/daniel-comboni.

55 '"Mad Dog" the cannibal pictured eating SECOND Muslim in as many weeks as Christians lynch and burn two men in Central African Republic', *Daily Mail*, 20 January 2014.

56 'Gold, diamonds fuelling conflict in Central African Republic: UN panel', Reuters, 5 November 2014.

CHAPTER TEN: INSIDE, OUT

1 That this should be the last note of the book is, we think, entirely appropriate. What is a work like this about if not the tendency of humanity, in its current evolutionary manifestation, to keep missing the narrative hints as to its fundamental either/or trajectory? The problem with a statistic like the 80 richest Africans having 60 per cent of the continent's wealth is that there aren't going to be many more opportunities to move onto the 'or' track.

ACKNOWLEDGEMENTS

The authors of this book are conceptually, financially and morally indebted to literally dozens of institutions and hundreds of individuals, not all of which would benefit from a show of appreciation. But as far as those we are able to thank are concerned, first among them must be Dr Martyn Davies, whom we met when he was the chief executive and founder of Frontier Advisory, and who now serves as the managing director of the emerging markets and Africa division at Deloitte. Davies shared with us his expertise, contact list and many hours of his time, all of which were essential in our developing an early understanding of the scale of the encounter we were adumbrating. Professor Tawana Kupe, then the dean of the humanities faculty at the University of the Witwatersrand, and now the institution's deputy vice-chancellor, was similarly generous with both email addresses and ideas. Branko Brkic and Styli Charalambous, the men behind South Africa's essential *Daily Maverick* news website, gave us a platform for the first stirrings of a thesis, to say nothing of the financial stability and the leeway to take off for far-flung places at a moment's notice. Indeed, Branko joined us for a portion of our first trip to Namibia in 2006, so it's fair to say he's been there from the beginning. He's never left.

The University of the Witwatersrand China-Africa Reporting Project, managed at the time by Brigitte Read, provided an essential component of the funding for our trips to South Sudan and Nigeria. Her colleagues Anton Harber, adjunct professor of journalism and media studies and director of the journalism programme, and Margaret Renn, then a visiting fellow in investigative journalism and joint administrator of the Taco Kuiper investigative journalism fund, awarded us a grant that assisted us in completing a first draft of the manuscript. The Rockefeller Foundation's Bellagio Institute housed Richard Poplak in their magnificent premises on Lake Como during the month of June

2013 – a period that serendipitously coincided with the stay of one of our principal subjects, the Ethiopian economist Eleni Gabre-Madhin. The International Writing Program at the University of Iowa hosted Kevin for a three-month fellowship in 2011, allowing for some of the earlier narratives and story arcs to be interrogated, tested, discarded and rewritten.

In terms of intellectual early adopters, former editors of South Africa's *Sunday Times,* Ray Hartley and Phylicia Oppelt, both commissioned numerous articles and essays. The same can be said of the former editors of the *Mail & Guardian,* Nic Dawes and Chris Roper. Former *Mail & Guardian* features editor Tanya Pampalone, along with current editor Verashni Pillay, were enormously encouraging of both our writing and our multimedia efforts. The editorial crew at Good Governance Africa, led at the time by Constanza Montana, were similarly supportive of our beta-testing ideas at their publication *Africa in Fact.* Jeffrey Sehume, Hester Du Plessis and Yacoob Abba Omar at the Mapingubwe Institute allowed us to cobble together a bespoke working model of the history of China in Africa.

Joshua Knelman, Rian Malan, Jens Pedersen, Simon Freemantle, Andrew Westoll, Laurence Hamburger, Tymon Smith, Lorna Poplak, Michael Bloom, Lebo Rasethaba, Professor Kupe and Achille Mbembe read early and, if they were more fortunate, later versions of this manuscript. The text would not have been possible without those who backed it in proposal form, including Shaun Bradley at the Transatlantic Literary Agency, and (most thankfully) Philip Gwyn Jones, late of Portobello Granta. Our current agent Oli Munson has been resolute over the long haul. Anne Meadows at Portobello provided a sensitive yet probing edit, while publisher Sigrid Rausing had the patience and faith to let us have another go. Jeremy Boraine at Jonathan Ball has lived with this book for a significant percentage of his working life; we hope it's been worth the wait.

In Namibia, we were assisted by Margie Orford, her sister Penelope, the brilliant local muckraker John Grobler, and Neil and Dieter Brandt. In Botswana, the late Felix Woods handed us our story on a platter. In Zimbabwe there are many we would like to thank, but can't – Sharon Hudson-Dean of the United States Embassy was, however, as forthright as she was open. In Zambia, Paul Cowie spoke to us of the past, and Shadrack Saili of the Zambia Development Agency spoke to us of the present and future. In Mozambique, the marine biologist Simon Pierce gave us the (unfailingly depressing) lay of the ocean, while Cian McClelland and Sean Lange served as guides to the maligned Tofu littoral. In Nigeria, we would not have found our story without Tiyan Alile, and we would not have been able to tell that story without the intellectual guidance of the writers Sefi Atta and Helon Habila. In the Democratic Republic of the Congo, Nicole Lauren Smith gave us the proverbial mining map, while Sedrick Filles de L'Homme helped us follow it in Kinshasa. In Kenya, the supremely talented novelist Dominique Botha opened the door to the story that closes this book. In Tanzania, Yuning Shen was profoundly hospitable and forthcoming—we regret that the remarkable story of his Mandarin-Swahili dictionary did not align with our narrative arc, and hope to write and publish the story as a standalone chapter at some point in the near future.

In Ethiopia, our old school chum Craig Kadish gave us the lowdown on Addis Ababa, while in South Sudan we relied on the experience of the enormously brave journalist Clement Lochio Lomornana. (As this book was going to press, we were shattered to learn that Clement had 'gone missing' after being detained by security forces in August 2015; we can only hope that his fate is imprisonment and not death, and that if indeed the former he will be mercifully released.) Also in South Sudan, our Afex Camp crew Chris Rollins and Megan Carroll provided invaluable information. In the Central African Republic, we benefited much from the magnanimously shared experiences of Stephan Hofstatter, Geoffrey York and David Smith. In China, Jeremy Goldkorn was our morning star, Noah Weinzweig our evening star, and Spartan Arinze our guide into the underworld of Guangzhou. Pierre Haski and Marie Furthner, whom we met at a literary festival in France, gave of their time and support in various ways. Our great friend Guy Lieberman wanted to provide us with an alternative, perhaps more spiritual perspective on our story, and along with the irrepressibly generous Colin

Kapeluschnik, he took us to India to meet the Dalai Lama, to whom we also owe a vast debt of gratitude.

In South Africa, Elizabeth Kennedy Trudeau at the United States Embassy, Chiefs Mangosuthu Buthelezi and Qhuzulini Sithole, Indira Gandhi, Hannah Edinger, Thandi Davids, Michele Magwood, Steve Barnett and Kathy Snyder were all immensely and munificently helpful. And no journalistic treatise written in Johannesburg is complete without thanking Manny Cabaleira, don of the Radium Beer Hall, patron saint of the ink stained and the travel weary.

Nobody, however, deserves greater thanks than our families. For five years they stood behind us, believed in the project, and believed in our ability to complete it. It would be wonderful to say that our toughest days were on the road. They weren't. Our toughest days were the ones battling the text at home. And so to Kevin's beloved, Kim Silberman, and Richard's wife, Medeine Tribinevicius, this is yours as much as it is ours. As a dose of eternal perspective, three newcomers came into the world while we were fooling ourselves about the divine right of books. Eve Silberman-Bloom, Alma and the late Manny Poplak — we hope we have done you proud.

INDEX

414